W9-DGL-092

PLATO AND ARISTOTLE ON CONSTITUTIONALISM

RAYMOND POLIN, 1918--

Executed from life by his father when he observed in the studio they shared
his son begin the writing of *Plato and Aristotle on Constitutionalism* on
1 January 1949. Israel Polin was born in Belarus in 1885, emigrated
to the United States of America after the turn of the century,
painted and drew in many media, and died in 1971.

Plato and Aristotle on Constitutionalism

An exposition and reference source

RAYMOND POLIN
Professor Emeritus of Government and Politics
St John's University, New York

Ashgate

Aldershot • Brookfield USA • Singapore • Sydney

Published by
Ashgate Publishing Ltd
Gower House
Croft Road
Aldershot
Hants GU11 3HR
England

Ashgate Publishing Company
Old Post Road
Brookfield
Vermont 05036
USA

British Library Cataloguing in Publication Data
Polin, Raymond
    Plato and Aristotle on constitutionalism : an exposition
    and reference source. - (Avebury series in philosophy)
    1. Plato 2. Aristotle, 384-322 B.C. 3. Constitution
    (Philosophy)
    I. Title
    321.8

Library of Congress Catalog Card Number: 98-71971

ISBN 1 84014 301 0

Printed in Great Britain by The Ipswich Book Company, Suffolk

Contents

Preface

Why another book on Plato and Aristotle?

My response is that it serves useful purposes to extract, explicate, and emphasize certain political ideas of Plato and Aristotle so that, among other reasons, we may consider whether they are relevant in this era of constitutional crisis, *dysnomia* (δυσνομία), *anomie* (ἀνομία), and *stasis* (στάσις). My finding is that, although current socio-politico-economic disorders are typical of conditions they aimed to prevent or remedy, their ideas in many areas are of limited relevance to the modern era of scientific-industrialism and the unfolding subatomic-space age that increasingly requires humanity-uniting global solutions to global problems. Nonetheless, it is well worthwhile, first of all, to present a concise exposition of the idea of constitutionalism and some of its basic principles that do have general relevance and applicability to the past, present, and future; and then to focus on the ideas of Plato and Aristotle that directly or indirectly deal with constitutionalism. Such a wide-ranging exposition of constitutionalism and examination of important roots of the Western political tradition can but increase the kind of *understanding* we should seek.

It should be convenient for instructor and student alike, therefore, to have a single work that explains basic concepts of constitutionalism, gives summary accounts of their lives and times, identifies many of their key political ideas, and provides verbatim some of the more significant passages in their major political writings: Plato's *Republic*, *Statesman*, and *Laws*; and Aristotle's *Athenian Constitution* and *Politics*. The utility of such a work, including its bibliography, should recommend its adoption as a textbook, despite presumed objections to views expressed and to included or excluded material and treatment of paradoxes.

However, although now eminently adaptable to use as a textbook, such was not my objective in pursuing this effort, nor is the resulting product, given the selection, organization, and treatment of its subject matter and themes, a typical textbook in structure or tone. Certainly its ultimately advocatory nature precludes such a rigidly narrow characterization of what was meant to be a didactic expression of personal views on a spectrum of matters related in varying degrees to the central topic of constitutionalism that would serve both an academic and a general readership. Yet it thus provides a book students and teachers lack.

My purpose, then, has been to produce a *teaching and learning tool* focused especially on their constitutional ideas, rather than an esoteric product or one equally given over to the more encompassing gamut of political theory. But more, rather than less, of selected kinds of information has therefore been included. For example, some terminology is given in both English print and Greek script and occasionally repeated, and dates of events and lifespans are frequently provided. Numerous and often lengthy notes are furnished that bring differing views to the attention of the uninitiated reader. Indeed this book was not written for the advanced scholar of Plato and Aristotle: especially in the text its *main track* is addressed primarily to the student of modern government and constitutionalism who lacks sufficient familiarity with some of its Greek origins and, unfortunately, all too often has not been properly grounded in political concepts and ideology. Thus, the reiteration is didactically purposeful.

The accompanying notes in particular provide a parallel *second track* meant to be a helpful guide to specialized studies on the point at issue as well as to serve as an immediate source of authoritative opinions and documentary information. Consequently, some matters that appear in Plato and Aristotle's writings that deserve to be considered at length have been merely touched upon or omitted so that other points could be more fully developed, and also to make room for selected provisions of recent constitutional documents and remarks about their operation. This treatment is intended to impart to the student a stronger grasp of both important early Greek concepts of constitutionalism and its practice and of the concepts and character of modern constitutionalism. In short, this work focuses attention on a long-past, critical era from which the student may gain greater understanding of the problems and politics of our own time and of the future. (For some relevant provisions of current constitutional documents and additional sources, see, e.g., ch. X, n. 1.) It is therefore devised to serve also as a *reference tool* for all who are interested in the political writings of Plato and Aristotle and in modern government and constitutionalism.

Accordingly, citation of sources is specific with respect to book and chapter as well as to manuscript portion, so that the reader may more easily find the cited passage in any edition of these works. The varied use of upper case and lower case lettering and of spacing generally corresponds to their variations in the Jowett editions. Early Jowett translations have been used because of their literary elegance, because they are often – although not invariably– more precise in terminology, and because they are in the public domain and have been little emended in later editions. For purposes of comparison of textual interpretation, some more recent translations have also been listed in the bibliography. The Loeb Library editions, which contain both the Greek text and opposite page English translations, are especially recommended when the reader may feel the need for clarification of Jowett's translations. The Loeb Library editions also present the descriptive subtitles appended by Diogenes Laertius as well as the main titles in Greek.

I accept responsibility for errors and controversial positions the reader may note. I regret the errors; but I hope the controversial positions, whether mine or those of others, lead to increased understanding, whether in agreement with the stand taken or not. My intention has been to avoid dogmatism and to preserve room for doubt; for doubt is the spark that sets aburning the fire of truth that frees us from received untruth.

The early roots of this project go back to undergraduate study more than half a century ago with late faculty of New York University: Marie Collins Swabey, Charles Coleman Thach, and James Burnham. Additional insights came during graduate study with Thach, the late Edward Conrad Smith, and Gisbert H. Flanz. I am indebted to Flanz especially for the terms 'curative constitutionalism' and 'inherent limitations'.

The resolve to write this book came out of a growing conviction that from my own concentration both on concepts of democratic limited government and constitutionalism and on Marxian concepts purposed to eliminate the state – as set forth in a pair of similarly apposing textbooks – I had gained certain understanding that could be applied to the political writings of Plato and Aristotle. The one who most encouraged me to act on this was the late Robert Morrison MacIver, who read the preliminary paper from which this extended effort has been developed. This book is therefore dedicated to the memory of MacIver, and this remembrance embraces as well his wife, Ethel. I have warm recollection of them both and much appreciation of his manliness and attainments. The late Eric Voegelin, who read a key portion of the preliminary manuscript, also encouraged publication.

David B. Evans and Bernard Cassidy provided expert help in checking use of Greek terminology and phrases in the draft typescript. The late John Edward Parsons Jr acted as devil's advocate in subjecting the draft to thoughtful testing and argumentation; and so objective was he in this task that when I look back I realize I came to know what he personally believed about the points of our discussion only that he was strongly persuaded the style and content of the Seventh Letter were such that Plato was indeed its author. In John H. Herz I had available within visiting-in-slippers distance a sounding board for legal, constitutional, and political concepts and history who is a multilingual treasury of Old World erudition with acumen, particularly *auf deutsch*. Francesco Cordasco gave incalculable support with his steadfast urging about the need for this book and his enthusiastic agreement with a number of its themes. In similar fashion, John B. Morrall read the typescript and then gave useful suggestions and heartening encouragement. My greatest indebtedness to a scholar with respect to this work, however, is to Edward Conrad Smith for cultivating in me the understanding that the very essence of genuine constitutionalism is the idea and practice of *limited government*. To represent the legion of former students who afforded myriad rich rewards and helped me sharpen my views and presentation of subject matter, I single out Frank Paul Le Veness, chairman, Department of Government and Politics, St John's University.

In the editorial department, I thank especially Pat FitzGerald for expertly making a long, complicated typescript into camera-ready copy and Sarah Markham, its publisher, for her supportive direction of this project and the evident goodwill from everyone at Ashgate that reached me through her. I have similar appreciation for Anne Keirby, editorial administrator, and Barbara J. Church, international marketing manager. Sonia Hubbard, managing editor, and her colleague, Rachel Hedges, are also thanked for their responsible role at the end of the editorial process.

My last and most profound expressions of gratitude, as always, are reserved for my beloved wife, Connie, and our children and their own spouses and offspring. My wife gave not only inspiration and faith but also frequent help with library research and preparation of the manuscript; our son Ted secured many a library book and article as needed, especially from law library holdings; our son Ken also gave legal counsel; and our son Larry guided me on mathematical and scientific matters.

Special Acknowledgments

During the long course of preparation of this work, it benefited from aid that deserves special acknowledgment. This came especially from librarians at the St John's University Library, New York Public Library at 42nd Street and Annex, Concordia College, Sarah Lawrence College, and branches of the Westchester Public Library System, particularly in Scarsdale, Mount Vernon, and Yonkers, New York. The British Library also earned my gratitude.

Additional holdings and services were made available by many college and university libraries that included the following: Binghamton University (SUNY), Brooklyn College (CUNY), University of Cincinnati, Cornell University, Duquesne University, Fordham University, Iona College, Marymount College, Mercy College, College of New Rochelle, New York University, Pace University, Princeton University, Purchase College (SUNY), and the University of Rochester.

The 'networking' of American college, university, and public libraries by interlibrary loans and photocopying is a major development in sharing resources that should be recognized; and it may be hoped that wider-spread use of the Internet and faxing may soon expedite many operations of the system. I must express, however, my stronger appreciation of the librarians, who are simply too numerous, and mostly anonymous, to thank here individually. Their dedication and professional skill in the Library Science of Information Storage and Retrieval provide an increasingly critical service in the use of a burgeoning system that is indispensable if we are to cope with the 'information explosion' and the devices that can deliver the relevant and specific information we need or want.

All of us therefore have a compelling obligation to follow Platonic-Aristotelian principles that would accord today's highly skilled librarians suitable recognition in every honorific and practical way.

To the memory of
Robert Morrison MacIver
1882–1970

If we are to develop an intelligent philosophy of the state, we must seek to do justice to both sides. We must accept the individuality of the unit, we must see the individual as the bearer and inheritor of human values, and on the other hand we must see the unity as that which sustains, incorporates, and promotes all human values. We must ask what this unity is, whether there is one unity that encompasses us, or more than one. These things are matters of social analysis and social perception. Our political philosophy should not dogmatically decide them, but should instead be built on the understanding of them. So let us look at them again.

Robert Morrison MacIver
The Web of Government, 1947

I   The Idea of Constitutionalism

Overview

The American system of government has been predicated upon separation of powers and mutual checks and balances. There has been such a continuing acceptance of the structure and principles of government set forth in the American federal and state constitutions, and the normative affirmation of them, that they represent almost articles of faith. To question them or consider other propositions represents something akin to political heresy. As a result, examination and appreciation of alternative approaches have been hampered in America by concentration on study of its existing political system and its rationale. Such restricted vision, however, is not limited to America but is, with allowance made for variations, usually the case in other countries as well.

What is needed, therefore, is to pay attention also to the contemporary constitutional systems of other nations and to a number of classical ideas and viewpoints that have become rather neglected. There should not be single-minded focus on the conventional approaches of one's own country and time to the fundamental problems of government and society. Thus, an introductory explanation and discussion at this point of both some familiar and unfamiliar concepts of constitutionalism is in order.

Confusion of Staticism with Stability

The need for such explanation becomes apparent when it is realized that the important principle of stability has been discussed extensively by American students of political science, but not always with precision. *Staticism* has been equated at times with stability, again largely crowding out of view other approaches that might shed considerable light on the nature and causes of popular disturbances and offer consequent suggestions as to how to deal with them.

It is therefore desirable to distinguish at the outset between the choice of a *static stability* or a *dynamic equilibrium*, two radically divergent alternatives

1

in attempting to bring peace and strength to a society. The need for this understanding becomes obvious when it is realized that stability and change are not antonymous terms.

On the one hand, an attempt may be made to create a condition of *static stability* wherein change and disorder are prevented by freezing the status quo. This is usually done within the form of an hierarchical structure which is justified by claims that society and the state are organic (i.e., literally living things), or at least organismic (i.e., figuratively comparable to living things), in their nature. A system predicated on an organological, hierarchical view of society and the state is intended to prevent general lawlessness (*anomie*: 'ανομία) or disorder (*dysnomia*: δυσνομία), and to cope with the condition of social and political restlessness the ancient Greeks called *stasis* (στάσις), literally a 'standing still'. In the final analysis, organological hierarchy maintains itself by a concentration of force that is sometimes used and sometimes held in reserve.[1]

On the other hand, an attempt may be made to produce a condition of *dynamic equilibrium* by meshing and harmonizing the various classes or interest groups by fitting them into a continuing process of orderly, balanced change. This is brought about by recognizing the motives that impel or restrain them individually and collectively, and by then establishing an equilibrium of power and rewards. This requires recognition of, and meaningful participation by, both the wealthy and groups who might otherwise be politically disenfranchised or economically underprivileged. Ideally, such a system functions through constantly adjusting the balance among various lawfully contending groups and individuals in a mobile society that is both free and peaceful, although not altogether quietly so. It rests less upon enforced obedience and more upon the voluntary support of those who believe they benefit in common from the established system.

Nomenclature

Need for Nomenclature

It is also desirable to provide nomenclature for, and explanation of, a number of less familiar constitutional principles that are employed by Plato and Aristotle or that are relevant to a study of their political thought. These include the following concepts which it will be useful to bear in mind while reading the later chapters that deal with a direct examination of their political writings:

constitutionalism, corrective constitutionalism, institutional arrangements, inherent limitations, and mixed, balanced government.[2]

Constitutionalism

Constitutionalism consists in the *practice* of faithful compliance with the formal provisions and spirit of a constitution that regularizes the structure, processes, powers, and limitations of a government, including the rights and duties of individuals and associations. Therefore, lip-service, mere observance of matters of form, and resort to escape clauses that avoid or pervert constitutional intent are all incompatible with genuine constitutionalism. (We may also note the following additional uses of the term constitutionalism: the *belief* that governments should operate according to constitutions, especially written constitutions; and the *movement* that advocates this.)

Corrective Constitutionalism

Corrective constitutionalism embraces the concepts of avoidance and redress of harm and injustice, and therefore deals with both preventive constitutionalism and curative constitutionalism.

Preventive Constitutionalism

Preventive constitutionalism holds that there are methods of conducting the basic operations of government and society that may anticipate, and also obviate or lessen, potential problems which would later on be difficult or impossible to correct. This includes injustices and errors which could not later be remedied, the most object example being capital punishment of an innocent person. Preventive constitutionalism recognizes that forces and individuals in society are bound to come into conflict or competition. Therefore, rather than waiting until dangerous precedents have been set, damage incurred, or animosities bred, it attempts to bring to bear pressures or machinery that can prevent the adoption or execution of unwise or unjust measures.

The principle of seniority, which helps determine the order of elevation to chairmanship of a legislative committee, is an example of preventive constitutionalism, because it tends to avoid or diminish personal and factional strife. Graduated income and inheritance taxes that militate against dangerous concentration of wealth and power are effective examples of preventive constitutionalism. Where governmental agencies act as collective bargaining and grievance machinery to prevent labour disputes, rather than waiting until a strike has occurred, we also have a present day exercise of preventive constitutionalism. As a judicial example, a court may issue a writ of injunction restraining a government official or agency, or a private party, from performing an illegal or possibly inequitable action, especially one where irreparable damage might be done. The United States Senate, however, has permitted its 'advise and consent' role with respect to foreign affairs to become a largely *ex post facto* formula of limited significance that does not correspond with its constitutionally intended purpose. Similarly, through the holding of lively question periods where ministers – including the prime minister – may be interrogated before the British House of Commons, the power is usually there for the Commons to require wanted hearings and to maintain *prior* accountability to the legislature before action is taken by 'the government'.

Curative Constitutionalism

Curative constitutionalism represents the view that there are practices, arrangements, and undertakings which may serve to eliminate, moderate, correct, or 'heal' improper, dangerous, or mischievous situations or abuses. Although one would expect a good constitutional system to be primarily self-corrective from within the government, at times the cure operates or may be applied from outside the government.

Examples of curative constitutionalism of a negative or purgative nature that operate from within government or according to constitutional provision, may include: impeachment (followed by trial and removal upon conviction); recall; forced resignation; dismissal; and forced exile because of ostracism. Examples of a negative nature that operate against the government from outside it – and are usually justified by an appeal to the right of resistance (*ius resistendi*) – may include: refusal to pay taxes or fines; conscientious objection to military service; passive resistance; boycotting; sit-down or sit-in strikes staged inside government offices; picketing; opposition by the communications media; a strike of capital or labour against government; sabotage; tyrannicide; rioting; and in its most extreme form, revolution.

Examples of curative constitutionalism of a more positive or constructive nature that operate from within government may include: firstly, and most importantly of all, the process of constitutional amendment which may cure even a defect within the constitution itself; the right of judicial appeal; judicial review of the constitutionality of legislation or official action; and administrative grievance machinery. Similar actions that operate from outside the government to bring corrective pressure to bear may include: freedom of speech, press, and pulpit, enhanced by the role of the communications media, the right of petition, lobbying, freedom marches, peace demonstrations, graffiti, code songs, the activities of civic improvement associations, and the manifold forms of legitimate party and pressure politics that have reform or justice as an objective or result.

Institutional Arrangements

Institutional arrangements consist in structural, procedural, and functional arrangements and habitual ways of doing things within a government and society that work to prevent too great a concentration of power, especially unchecked power, in the hands of any individual or group. They may, at the same time, promote accomplishment of the tasks of government and society. Many of these arrangements – commonly referred to as 'checks and balances' – have been formalized by their incorporation within the constitutional system. They are exemplified by the American and Canadian approach of attempting to divide functions among various branches, levels, agencies, and officials of government and then having them mutually (or in descending order) examine into the actions of one another and exercise checks against one another's power.[3] Responsibility to others is a basic principle of this approach to the dilemma of rendering government effective yet safe.

Under a unitary system, such as that of the United Kingdom, the Netherlands, or Sweden, the institutional checks are exercised by the central government over the territorial or administrative units on an hierarchical one-directional basis that may be called 'descending order'.[4] Examples of more collegial institutional arrangements that relate to a territorial division of functions, are to be found in federated and confederated systems of government, such as those of the United States of America, Canada, Australia, and the German *Staatenbund* (1815–66) that emerged from the Congress of Vienna.

There may also be a division of the population by property qualification, economic pursuit, religious affiliation, or inherited rank, with each segment accorded an allotted representation in the government; and in some cases, concurrence by some or all of these groups may be a constitutionally mandated condition for decision-making. The graduated income tax, which works to limit a concentration of economic power, and hence also limits a concentration of political power, is a most effective institutional check imposed by government (as well as a form of preventive constitutionalism). Ironically, because it was advocated by Karl Marx and Friedrich Engels in the *Communist Manifesto* and opposed by many of the wealthy, the graduated income tax may be an important reason why Marx's dire prediction of the demise of capitalism has not come to pass.

Inherent Limitations

Inherent limitations consist in an approach rooted primarily in the habits of thought and deed by which men live. Such an approach rests largely outside of government, for it is based on the belief that single-minded attention to the structure and functioning *per se* of government is inadequate. Therefore, it is held that it is necessary to limit and control the direction of government in advance of actual operations, and that it is humanity's nature – especially its conditioned nature – that sets these limits and potentialities. Humanity's nature, of course, is rather pliable, but its level of development and conditioned behavioural pattern at any time, limit or debar certain practices or policies a government might want to follow; and thus the pursuit of alternative courses is made easier or more likely. Expressed in the vernacular, a thing may be done because 'it is the right thing to do' or, often more importantly, it is not done because 'that just is not done'.

The force of education and tradition (i.e., the workings of political socialization), and the limits of human nature, it is felt, provide a climate of opinion and array of power to which government seldom can run directly counter. Government, in short, cannot ignore either the goodness in people or their self-serving motivations and still hope to be stable, efficient, and enduring.[5]

Mixed, Balanced Government

There is a traditional classification which holds that six basic forms of government may be categorized both quantitatively and qualitatively. *Quantitatively*, they are identified by whether the ruling power is in the hands of one (monarchy), a few (oligarchy), or many (democracy). *Qualitatively*, they are identified by whether it is an uncorrupted form, which is by definition one wherein the rule of law prevails; or whether it is a corrupted form, which is by definition one wherein the will or whim of the ruler prevails and the law may be set aside.

The *good* (i.e., uncorrupted) forms of the one, the few, and the many have commonly been referred to as, respectively: kingship or royalty (or constitutional monarchy); aristocracy (rule by the able); and democracy. The corresponding *bad* (i.e., corrupted) forms of the one, the few, and the many have commonly been referred to as, respectively: tyranny (or despotism), plutocracy (rule by the wealthy), and ochlocracy (or mob rule).

The concept of mixed or balanced government holds that various combinations of the basic six forms are theoretically and actually possible. In fact, proponents of mixed, balanced government usually regard a 'simple or unmixed' form as undesirable and may even argue that it is dangerous because it fails to include important structural factors and procedural practices that tend to produce harmony, stability, and practical results both in the functioning of government and 'out in the real world'.

Proponents of mixed constitutionalism also may relate the three basic processes of government – legislative, executive, and judicial – to each of the three quantitative categories. Thus, the chief executive role may be assigned to an individual; the judicial role to a numerical few; and the legislative role to numerically many. Ideally, these assignments would be representative, respectively, of characteristics of monarchy, aristocracy and democracy. Alternatively, the less-numerous upper house of a bicameral legislature may be viewed as representing the principle of aristocracy, while the more-numerous lower house may be viewed as representing the principle of democracy.

We may note, therefore, that it is possible for mixed, balanced government to combine the democratic practice of popular election with the aristocratic quality of ability in officeholders who are representative of the plutocratic element because they are wealthy.

Assessments

Orthodox American and Canadian approaches to constitutionalism have placed great reliance on such institutional arrangements as separation of powers, checks and balances, and territorial division, with Canada also opting for considerable fusion of legislative and executive powers.[6] There has also been a strong tendency by both to stick to the static formula of the familiar 'tried and true' as a provider of stability in government and society. In addition, there have been developed a variety of legal procedures and political processes that help to avoid or correct mistakes and injustices.

However, there are approaches to constitutionalism that are less familiar, especially to Americans, but worthy of objective examination in an age when it is desirable to reduce public tension, discord, and criminal behaviour and to increase public harmony, efficiency, and justice. Consequently, it is advisable to pay greater attention than we do now to such approaches to constitutionalism as inherent limitations, dynamic equilibrium, integration and fusion of powers, and preventive, rather than curative, modalities.

Modern constitutionalism is not patterned upon classical Greek political structure and practice. Much of the continuing value of Plato and Aristotle's political theory, then, lies in their recognition of the nature of constitutional problems and issues they set forth and discourse upon. For every age, they address continuing great problems of society and government. Some of their political propositions are still viable; some, happily, have been discarded; and others that have been neglected may deserve consideration for possible application; but all of them still merit our attention.[7] Thus, the principles of constitutionalism that were set forth in Plato and Aristotle and subsequent times, reached a fullness and clarity of expression in the contribution of Clinton Rossiter to *The Report of the President's Commission on National Goals* that also defines democracy (Rossiter, c. 1960, pp. 61 f):

> The essence of the democratic process has been respect for the rules; the guaranty of this respect in the public arena has been the spirit and practices of constitutionalism. Constitutionalism is the generic label for all those arrangements and techniques – separation of powers, checks and balances, due process, bills of rights, the rule of law – that force our governors to think, talk, bargain, and explain before they act, and that institutionalize the procedures through which public policy is made, administered, and enforced. Although the rule of the majority is, in Jefferson's words, the 'vital principle' of the American republic, constitutionalism seeks to assure us that the majority will be clear-cut and cool-headed on all occasions, and powerless on occasions when the consciences of men are at issue. Above all, it seeks to assure us that the consent of the governed will not be given lightly to decisions of great moment. This is why Americans have always believed stoutly that, while a government can be constitutional without being democratic, it cannot be democratic without being constitutional.[8]

Notes

1   The standard reference work for Classical Greek long used by British and American scholars is *A Greek-English Lexicon*, compiled by Liddell and Scott (1985). It presents compendious definitions and lists sources in which a word appears. See for meanings of *anomie, dysnomia, stasis,* and other Greek words used throughout the present work.

It may also be pointed out that the 'standing still' which *stasis* means, is a condition resulting from a containment of conflicting forces or of an infection, but not the resolution of the internal dissension; and therefore a 'rising up', a civil war, or the bursting of an infected spot is ultimately to be expected when the situation can no longer be controlled. In one way, Plato uses the word to mean faction in the soul, or a soul at war with itself: *Republic* (1978, tr. Shorey), Vol. I, Book IV, 440 E, pp. 402 f. In another way, Plato uses the word to mean a kind of civil war: *ibid.*, 444 B, pp. 416 f. *Astasiastos* (ἀστασίαστος), on the other hand, is used to describe a condition free from internal dissension or party strife: *ibid.*, (1979), Vol. II, Book VIII, 554 D, pp. 276 f. Shorey also suggests (footnote c, p. 276): 'For the idea 'at war with himself', cf. *supra* 440 B and E (*stasis*), *Phaedr*, 237 D–E and Arist. *Eth. Nic.* 1099 12 f'. *Stasis* is also explained by Mulgan (1977), pp. 118 f and 149, n. 4. Mulgan states (p. 118):

> Though most would have agreed that *stasis* involved taking the struggle for power beyond the limits of what was acceptable or lawful, there would often be disagreement about whether these limits had actually been crossed.

For a doctoral study devoted to *stasis* and related concepts, see in its entirety Mustacchio, 1972. See for definitions and descriptions of *stasis* especially pp. 2–31 and see for related concepts especially pp. 31–5. Plato's view of *stasis* is treated especially in ch. V, 'Plato: *Stasis* and Unity', pp. 129–62; and Aristotle's view in ch. VI, 'Aristotle: *Stasis* and *Politeia*', pp. 163–85. See also the insightful ch. VII, 'Conclusions', pp. 186–96, including the judgment (pp. 195 f) that: 'We may conclude that neither in the politics nor the political theory of the Greeks was the problem of *stasis* successfully resolved'.

For a reprinted paper that systematically poses and answers questions about the nature of *stasis* and historical developments and events that illustrate it, see Loenen, 1953. See for the meaning of the term and comparison of various definitions especially pp. 4–7. See also for additional references, sources, and discussion, the endnotes, pp. 39–48, including the inexact quotation from Lord Bolingbroke (dedication, *A Dissertation upon Parties* (1735)), p. 39, n. 3: 'National interests would be sometimes sacrificed and always made subordinate to personal interests, and that, I think, is the true characteristic of faction'.

For an historical account that provides detailed treatment of internal and external interrelationships that produced *stasis* in a number of Greek city-states, see Gehrke, 1985. For the political science view of *stasis*, Gehrke (p. 2, n. 9) notes Mustacchio.

For further discussion of Aristotle's use of *stasis*, see Burnet (ed.) (1900), pp. xlvi ff, n. 2, which refers to: *Phys.*, 192 B, 13; *Met.*, 1013 a, 29; and *Gen. An.*, 776 a, 35.

Note should also be taken of the use of *stasis* to refer to the factions or standings termed *Paraloi* (Παραλόι), *Pediakoi* (Πεδιακόι), and *Diakrioi* (Διάκριοι) – 'men from the coast, plain, and hills' – discussed in Manville (1990), pp. 159 ff. See also Manville's discussion of *eunomia* (εὐνομία) and *dysnomia* (δυσνομία), respectively 'lawfulness and good order' and 'the opposite condition', pp. 51 and 154. For additional aspects of *stasis*, see also in full ch. IX, note 24.

2   For additional discussion of such concepts as stability, equilibrium, change, a standing still, status quo, fusion of powers, and constitutionalism, see Polin, 1979, especially pp. 31–4, 61–71 and 237–62.

For an academic symposium on the subject, see Pennock and Chapman, 1977.

For clarification of the meaning of most philosophical terms and examples of their use in the classical period, see Peters, 1967.

For a general study of constitutionalism, see Friedrich, 1950. For a more specialized study with more specific applications, see Franklin, 1969.

3   For an authoritative exposition and perspicacious commentary on the role of the institutional

arrangements of separation of powers and representative government in promoting the values of 'justice, liberty, equality, and the sanctity of property', see in its entirety Vile, 1967. See statement of this theme, pp. 1 f, and further declaration (p. 7) that:

> ... in some form, a division of power, and a separation of function, lie at the very heart of our systems of government. An idea that finds its roots in ancient constitutionalism, and which in the seventeenth century became a central feature of a system of limited government, has obviously to be reformulated if it is to serve as an instrument of modern political thought, but it can only be rejected altogether if we are prepared to discard also the values that called it into being.

4   As used here, 'descending order' pertains to the *exercise* of superior authority over lower authority on a descending scale, and the word 'descending' has been taken from Walter Ullmann. However, this supervisory exercise is not to be confused with the rationale treated of by Ullmann that discusses the theoretical justification for what he terms the 'descending thesis' or 'descending theme' of government, as well as the 'ascending thesis' or 'ascending theme', that relate more to the *source* of governmental authority. See, e.g., Ullmann, 1965, pp. 12 f; 1967, pp. 9 and 58; and 1975, pp. 30 f.

5   A notable illustration of the essence of 'inherent limitations' is contained in the Roman concept of *fides*. For explanation of *fides* and more specialized sources on the subject, see Adcock, 1964, pp. 13 f and 106:

> A Roman entrusted with the care of the public interest was expected to pursue it conscientiously, single-mindedly, and honourably. The concept that embodied this expectation was *fides*. [23] (23. On *fides* see esp. E. Fraenkel, 'Zur Geschichte des Wortes *fides*', *Rhein. Mus.* 71 [1916], 187 ff; R. Heinze, '*Fides*', *Hermes*, LXIV [1929], 140 ff.) When the Senate suggested that a magistrate should act, it added the phrase that he should act as seemed good to him in accordance with the national interest and his own *fides*.[24] (24. 'Uti ei e re publica fidequa sua viderateur'; cf. Meyer, *op. cit.* [Ernst Meyer, *Römischer Staat und Staatsgedanke* (Zurich: Artemis-Verlag, 1948), pp. 109 ff.], p. 241.) It was the constant reminder of that sense of duty and scruple that the community expected to find in its leaders. The same idea, it may be added, governed the relation of a powerful Roman to clients who had placed themselves under his protection.[25] (25. This relation, with its reciprocal evocation of *fides*, means loyalty also in the sphere of politics. See below, p. 20.) The clients have no claim in law, but as they trust him, so he must deserve and earn their trust.

A striking example of the workings of 'inherent limitations' is contained in the restraints and legal devices self-imposed by government in Canada prior to passage of the Canadian Bill of Rights in 1960 and more especially by the Constitution Act, 1982, that included as Schedule B, the Canadian Charter of Rights and Freedoms. See in its entirety Blaustein and Flanz (eds), 1988, by Beckton, Ritter, Matkin, and Walsh, with explanatory essays by Beckton and Ritter and bibliography by Ritter. See especially pp. 17–25, including the following comments by Ritter (pp. 24 f) that describe how 'inherent limitations' operate, although necessitated in past Canadian practice that they do so through institutional arrangements:

> Until 1982, only politics and the British tradition of 'fair-mindedness' in a law prevented the federal Parliament and the provincial legislatures from substantially limiting basic freedoms and rights of Canadian citizens. While *political* conventions were not generally enforceable in a court of law however, *legal* delineations of government spheres of

authority were, and the courts, as evidenced in many landmark constitutional decisions, struggled to disallow unreasonable restrictions on fundamental rights based on the constitutional division of powers rather than on a codified and constitutionally-enshrined description of rights itself.

In contrast, we may note that the Commonwealth of Australia Constitution Act 1900 (which was amended by the Australia Act 1926, 'An Act to bring constitutional arrangements affecting the Commonwealth and the States into conformity with the status of the Commonwealth of Australia as a sovereign, independent and federal nation') contained in scattered clauses what in combination may be taken as an express 'bill of rights'. Indeed, the Australia Constitution Act is at times reminiscent of the Constitution of the United States. E.g., the U.S. Constitution, Amendment I, provides in part, 'Congress shall make no law respecting an establishment of religion, or prohibiting the free exercise thereof' and Article VI provides in part, 'no religious test shall ever be required as a qualification to any office or public trust under the United States'. The Australia Constitution Act, Chapter V, Clause 116, reads: 'The Commonwealth shall not make any law for establishing any religion, or for imposing any religious observance, or for prohibiting the free exercise of any religion, and no religious test shall be required as a qualification for any office or public trust under the Commonwealth.' See in its entirety Alex C. Castles and Kenneth R. Rush (1987), *Constitutions of the Countries of the World: Australia*, in Blaustein and Flanz, 1971–, especially p. 47, clauses 115–18.

Despite the absence of such express constitutional limitations, the principle of 'inherent limitations' was evidently applied to safeguard religious freedom in Canada before the Constitution Act, 1982 in the case of *Saumur v. Quebec and the Attorney General of Quebec* (1953) 2 SCR 299. Ritter, *loc. cit.*, p. 23, observes:

> The *de facto* result was that the right of religious expression was upheld, though it reserved to the federal government the right to legislate that right away. Political convention decreed that it would not, of course, but similarly, in cases where the federal authorities demonstrated excessive zeal in limiting fundamental rights in other areas, the courts have been just as likely to find that jurisdiction to enact such legislation rested with the provinces.

A similar set of circumstances in which an institutional arrangement (again, the process of judicial review of the constitutionality of legislative and executive action) has contributed to the wholesome influence of inherent limitations is to be found in recent judicial events in the Republic of Ireland. See Jay A. Sigler, *Constitutions of the Countries of the World: Ireland*, Constitutional Chronology to 1982 in Blaustein and Flanz, *op. cit.*; Constitutional Analysis and Bibliographia by Gerard Hogan, 1988, *ibid.* See especially pp. 18 f which report:

> The great achievement ... of the Constitution of 1937 was that it produced the environment in which a successful system of judicial review has flourished. The decision of the Supreme Court in *Buckley v. Attorney General* [1950] I.R. 67 was the landmark case which paved the way for the development of a sophisticated constitutional jurisprudence.

Also in contrast to past Canadian practice, detailed express provisions as to jurisdiction and procedure where matters of constitutionality and legality are involved are clearly set forth in the Basic Law of the Federal Republic of Germany, Chapter IX, THE

ADMINISTRATION OF JUSTICE, Articles 92–104, especially the role of the Federal Constitutional Court. See Flanz, 1985, *Constitutions of the Countries of the World: Federal Republic of Germany*, in Blaustein and Flanz, *op. cit.*, pp. 74–8; *cp.* 1994 ed.

6   Fusion of powers refers to the ministerial system that selects heads of executive departments and 'the government' from within the legislature and mingles especially legislative and executive powers within one body: e.g., the Parliament in the United Kingdom, Canada, and France. For the classic study on the development of Parliament's unchallenged supremacy in Great Britain, including relevant commentary on similar developments elsewhere, especially in the Commonwealth, and comparisons with the American constitutional system, see Dicey, 1982. Also recommended to the introductory student of constitutionalism for general background prior to World War II: McIlwain, 1939 and 1947; and Hawgood, 1939. More recently, see Bradshaw and Pring, 1981.

7   For thoughtful, probing treatment of modern constitutionalism and refutation of a number of commentators, especially on American politico-constitutional issues and events, see in its entirety Wolin, 1989. Wolin forthrightly reveals his viewpoint and purpose in observations on the socio-economic matrix of constitutionalism, global as well as American, pp. 6 f, where he states:

> These writings are intended as a contribution to a renewed democratic discourse, one that can be disentangled from the disillusions bred by recent neoconservative rhetoric and the cheap flattery of cynical demagogues of right-wing populism. That discourse must confront the meaning of the state and its cohabitation with corporate power.

Whether one be in agreement or disagreement with specific general points and analyses offered by Wolin, he provides especially for the graduate student an example of a wide-ranging frame of reference useful for consideration of issues basic to the theory, practice, and future of constitutionalism.

For consideration of aspects of the role played by inherent limitations in the emerging development of modern constitutionalism in an underdeveloped nation, see Vaughn, 1988, pp. 44–56.

8   Rossiter, ch. II.

Any system of government genuinely committed in theory and adhering in practice to constitutionalism of any form – and particularly to democracy – must invoke the principle of *responsibility* in all of its meanings, including especially: answerability; duty; obligation; oversight; accountability; trusteeship; and causality. A thinker who addressed this matter with profound perspicacity and historical knowledge was Hans Jonas (1903–93), a one-time student and later ardent opponent of Martin Heidegger (1889–1976) because of the latter's public support of Adolf Hitler and pronouncement of Nazi tenets. As Plato also seems to have done, Jonas saw his share of military combat at a comparatively advanced age: five years in the British 8th Army during World War II, thus fulfilling his own sense of responsibility. The advanced student of constitutionalism will want to read Jonas' major work on responsibility in either its English (1984) or German (1979 and 1981) versions.

I am indebted to John H. Herz for the opportunity to quote now from his typescript photocopy of the acceptance speech of Jonas in January 1993 of the Premio Nonino in Udine, Italy, in which he emphasized the common responsibility of all of humanity in the face of our endangered global environment that calls for 'moral education and unending political watchfulness': 'A new solidarity of the whole of humanity is beginning to dawn on us. A common guilt binds us, a common interest unites us, a common fate awaits us, a common responsibility calls us'.

II Athenian Constitutional Background

Overview

Plato and Aristotle were reared and lived the greater part of their lives in a period of Athenian *Sturm und Drang*, a time characterized by internal and external struggle, disorder, disunity, change, and the humiliation of conquest.

The constitutional system for the previous two centuries and during their lifetimes underwent the continuing stresses and strains imposed by a struggle between those who would widen popular participation in the government and those who would restrict the higher offices to elitist control. Thus, one may discern as the principal contenders those who inclined to a more democratic approach to the theory and practice of government and those who favoured an aristocratic-plutocratic-oligarchical approach.

The interaction and intermixing of these opposing ideas and forces produced the theoretical and actual synthesis called *politeia* (πολιτεία) or polity, whose objective was to be a constitutional, free *polis* (πόλις) or city-state that consisted mainly in a combination and balance of the principles of plutocracy and democracy. The principal plutocratic or oligarchical body was the administrative and probouleutic [pre-considering or substance-proposing] Council, the *boule* (βουλή); the principal democratic body was the popular assembly, the *ekklesia* (εκκλησία); and the Chief General or *strategos* (στρατηγός) by the time of Pericles was not only the presiding officer of the *strategia* (στρατηγία), a ten-member board of *strategoi* (στρατηγοί), but also *de facto* the chief magistrate and most important executive official of the Athenian state. The unity and loyal devotion to the state that it was anticipated would be prevalent under a *politeia*, would make this 'free, constitutional state' internally stable and externally strong, and promote the good life of justice, harmony, and accomplishment.[1]

The Passing of Athenian and Greek Supremacy

The Peloponnesian War

The Peloponnesian War (431–4 BC) destroyed the supremacy of Athens in the Aegean and ruined her as a first-rate military power. When Athens and Sparta were both powerful and allied against Persia, they bested that mighty empire. The weakening of Athens, therefore, did more than ruin Sparta's chief rival: it eliminated the power centre around which opposition to Macedonia could have been gathered and thereby assured Philip's conquest of Greece. Thus, the passing of Athenian supremacy also led to the passing of Greek supremacy; and so the years 427–322 BC, the period that covered the life-spans of Plato and Aristotle, were an unhappy century of political and military decline and humiliation for the once arrogantly proud and sometimes overly aggressive Athenians. Perhaps the personal fate of Pericles symbolizes what happened to his beloved Athens: unsuccessful in his prosecution of the war against Sparta in 430 BC, he was deposed from office, convicted on a biased charge of embezzlement, and fined, reinstated because of public revulsion over this treatment of such a heroic figure, and then himself fell victim in 429 BC to the plague that had ravaged Athens and killed a third of the population, including two of his sons.

With the death of Pericles, the leadership of the state fell to a mixed succession of demagogues, opportunitists, and statesmen, such as Cleon (d. 422 BC), the tanner; Nicias (d. 413 BC), the statesman-peacemaker and general; Alcibiades (c. 450–4 BC), the brilliant, ruthless, and controversial statesman, conqueror, and philanderer; Theramenes (d. 404 BC), the moderate, opportunistic oligarch; Critias (d. 403 BC), the Eupatrid orator, writer, and atheist; Thrasybulus (d. 388 BC), the democratic statesmen and general; Philocrates (fl. 4th cent. BC), the unfortunate peacemaker with Philip of Macedon; Demosthenes (385?–22 BC), the orator; and Lycurgus (390?–24 BC), the anti-Macedonian orator, financier, and administrator who guided the fortunes of Athens, 338–24 BC, following her crushing defeat by Philip at Chaeronea (338 BC).

Pericles had been virtually prime minister because he dominated the other generals and because he represented the general will. His successors tended to be demagogues or popular generals who held the position of *strategos* (στρατηγός) or strategus. The *demagogos* (δημαγωγός) or demagogue must be understood in terms of his contemporary meaning. He was, in effect, a popular spokesman or sponsor of the public will as he saw it and as he helped shape it.

> A demagogue was by no means what the term implies in modern times. He was what we should call a parliamentarian of experience and standing, who had gained the ear and confidence of the Assembly, and who advocated, and sought through his influence with the Assembly to carry into effect a line of policy. He held no office, and he ruled by influence (Barker, 1960, p. 41).[2]

During the fifth century BC, the demagogue was somewhat of a representative chief executive and when ostracism was in vogue, a demagogue could eliminate a rival bloodlessly yet effectively. However, ostracism was last used in 418 or 417 BC against Hyperbolus, who nevertheless was tracked down and assassinated by the oligarchy, on Samos in 411 BC. Thereafter, Athens was often left with contending or successive rival leaders, frequently with disastrous results because she no longer had an adequate remedy to deal with them. Chagrined that ostracism had been used by the combined forces of Nicias and Alcibiades – the intended candidates for the ostracism – against a man of such personal merit as Hyperbolus, the practice became discredited and fell into disuse.

The Peloponnesian War was also responsible for attempts to form larger political units than the individual *polis*. However, perhaps even more responsible for this growing tendency were the changes in the economy, which became less self-sufficient and more dependent on imports and exports. There were a number of attempts to bring this integration about by imposing hegemonies, but none of them were more than temporary arrangements held together by force rather than a sense of common interest. Attempts in the fourth century BC to bring this about on a more equal federal basis proved futile, also.[3]

Class War

The effects of the war with Sparta polarized the classes politically as well as economically. The wealthy, particularly landowners whose estates were ravaged repeatedly during the Spartan invasions, favoured appeasement. The wealthy bitterly attacked the constitution, which had given over control to the mass of less-well-to-do citizens who provided their manpower and lives, rather than property, to preserve Athenian independence and greatness. The sense of common participation, benefits, and unity that must be felt if a society is to be strong and prevail, steadily diminished:

The change is marked when we compare the assertion of the speakers in Herodotus and Thucydides, that democracy is government by the whole people not by any part, with the definition of democracy given a hundred years later by Aristotle, who describes it as the constitution in which the poor rule and use their power to oppress the rich. Instead of a constitution in which every one is on an equality and has an equal part in the government of the city, we find in practice that it tends more and more to a form in which the population falls into two social classes, and the larger class of the two (though it may not be necessarily very much the larger) uses its power in its own interests, and disregards the interests of the other as completely as if its members had been disfranchised. So that even in a democracy the State is no longer one in spirit. And if the democracy is overthrown and succeeded by an oligarchy of wealth, whose members in their turn consult only their own interests, the division of classes becomes more acute still. Enough has been said to show the significance of this in its effect on Plato's mind. In his boyhood and youth he saw the continued process of the break-up of an ideal unity of the State which must at one moment, shortly before his birth, have seemed almost established (Field, 1967, pp. 84 f).

As for the internal constitution of Athens in the fourth century BC, when Plato and Aristotle flourished, little need be added here. The changes that were introduced were routine adjustments of no great significance.[4]

Assessments

The internal history of Athens from the earliest days of its recorded history down to the fifth century BC was marked by the gradual assertion of the unity of the city-state and of its supreme claim as against the associations within it – 'the lesser loyalties' as they have been called – including such religious and kinship groups as the tribe, clan, phratry, and thiasus. The combination and balancing of the classes of citizens in a *politeia*, or free, constitutional state, were intended to produce a unity and loyalty to the state that, it was anticipated, would make it internally stable and externally strong, and promote the good life and justice. At this stage of the development of political theory, there was no substantial question of conflict between the rights of the individual and those of the state: the state was all-important and the individual insignificant.[5]

There developed, however, an increasing separation of the individual from the state by kinship bodies which represented themselves as more intimate and of greater influence in his life than the *polis* which embraced them all. The constant internecine conflicts which divided the whole state were an even more pressing detriment. There existed a deep cleavage between the limited number of the noble families on the one side, who had arrogated to themselves many rights and political privileges, and on the other side the great mass of underprivileged citizens. The situation was further aggravated by the privileged class's use of their political power for purposes of aggrandisement at the expense of the rest of the community and their establishment of a harsh economic tyranny. Thus, bitter class warfare was added to the struggle for political rights. Also, there were numerous outbreaks of strife among the various families of nobles, each of which was in all probability supported by the mass of dependents of the same clan or district.

These internal divisions so weakened Athens as against other *poleis* that they contributed to her defeat by Sparta in the Peloponnesian War; and her citizens had to suffer such wartime humiliations as looking on helplessly when the island of Salamis, adjacent to and dominating entrance to the Piraeus, the port of Athens, fell under Spartan control. The conquering Spartan leader, Lysander (d. 395 BC), thereupon imposed a crushing naval blockade, set a 700-man controlling force of Laconian soldiers atop the Acropolis, and interfered in support of the temporary government of the Thirty and their execution of opponents.

Subsequently, Athens was for a time under the supremacy of Thebes. Moreover, the failure of Athens, Sparta, Thebes, and the other highly separatist Greek city-states to integrate themselves into some kind of strong federation or union, led to the conquest of all of them by Macedonia.

Thus, Plato and Aristotle were to live in a period that saw the disruption and fall from pre-eminence of Athens – and the decline of all other Greek city-states. In any event, the Greek *city*-state, or *polis*, concerning whose government they wrote most of their political and constitutional theory, was already largely obsolete. Because it is obvious that the *nation*-state (or *multinational* state, in many cases) is today in grave difficulty and experiencing *dysnomia*, *anomie*, and *stasis* internally and externally, study of the political and constitutional ideas of Plato and Aristotle may be quite timely. We may thereby gain some insight into why, even under such trying circumstances, fourth century Athens developed internal basic stability and the flowering of philosophical achievement in what Eli Sagan (1991, p. 11) has termed 'The Golden Age of the Radical Democracy, 403–322':

> It was an amazingly stable time. Though intense competition for power and honor marked political life – as in all democracies – the Athenians had learned how to combat each other without violence. No class or social brutality, from

either oligarchs or lower-class economic radicals, broke the civil peace. Many modern historians, with Periclean stars in their eyes, have downgraded the fourth century as if it were a time of moral mediocrity compared to the glorious fifth century. Such superficial political analysis does not hold. It was a remarkably vibrant democratic era. It was also the greatest age of philosophy ever, giving us Plato and Aristotle, and, therefore, the basis of 2,500 years of Western thought.[6]

Notes

1   A useful discussion of the primary sources and scholarly works dealing with subject matter of this chapter is still to be found in Hignett, 1952, ch. 1. Discussion of the sources is continued by Hignett throughout this work, but especially useful are the Appendices, pp. 209–89 and the Supplementary Notes, pp. 390–7. Finally, Hignett's Bibliography, pp. 398–401, is to be recommended. Also still useful for the general historical background is Grote, 1971. For treatment of political personages, relationships, and terminology, see especially Connor, 1970. For a work that treats more of organs, processes, and character of government, as well as the nature of law, see Ehrenberg, 1969, pp. 42–67. For a selection of literary sources, see Rhodes, 1986, ch. 5. For an illuminating study of the judicial role of the Areopagus Council, which treats in detail of its historical development, membership, structure, jurisdiction, functioning, religio-ideological orientation, political involvements, and stablizing influence, see Wallace, 1989. For a general review of the subject matter of this chapter, see in its entirety Sinclair, 1988. For a profoundly thoughtful and scholarly collection of relevant essays and introduction to them, as well as an extensive bibliography, see Finley, 1982.

See also Raaflaub, 1983. This is an especially useful introduction to the political terminology, concepts, and ideological positions of the period in a concise but comprehensive essay that presents carefully considered positions on key points relating to democracy and oligarchy and also calls attention to a number of studies in German.

Especially relevant to this chapter are a pair of companion articles. Mion, 1986, concludes:

> In light of the evidence presented it seems clear that the Athenians not only invented democracy, but went further. Although they did not develop a formal division of powers checking and balancing each other, and although for a while they did practice ostracism, they did invent procedures by which the citizen could seek a 'redress of grievances.' The Athenians saw the unavoidable flaw in democracy, which is that it cannot protect itself from itself: it needs legal institutions to balance political institutions. The Athenians and constitutionalism emerged together, one the natural counterpart of the other.

Campbell, 1986, begins with a forthright statement of intent to redress a perceived imbalance in modern studies of constitutionalism and to develop a wider and more precise perspective for the generally accepted view of the subject:

> In claiming the principle of constitutional safeguards exclusively for the secular liberal state, modern scholarship betrays a parochialism that has resulted in a distorted perception of western constitutional history (as well, perhaps, as a certain blindness in

regard to contemporary legal institutions outside the liberal orbit).

The line of development and a number of viewpoints expressed in this section depend especially on: Field, 1967, ch. VI and ch. VII; Bonner, ch. I; Myres, 1927, in its entirety; and Botsford and Robinson, 1956, *passim*. Grant, 1989b, and Develin, 1989, appeared later. Develin presents a very useful compendious and documentary treatment of Athenian political offices and bodies, their functions, and their holders in the period considered.

Additional works consulted in the preparation of this chapter include: Barker, 1960; Bonner and Smith, 1930–38; Brumbaugh, 1962; Ferguson, 1963; Fustel de Coulanges, 1956; Glotz, 1929; Glover, 1966, Larsen, 1948; Moore, 1974; Sinclair, 1968; and Voegelin, 1957. Works on relevant topics that also merit close attention include: MacDowell, 1978; Traill, 1975; and especially Wood and Wood, 1978.

Various encyclopedias and lexicons provide basic information on the Athenian state, as do especially the now classical studies by German scholars. The standard reference work in English recommended here is *The Cambridge Ancient History*, 1923–39, Vols. I–IV, especially Vols IV, V, and VI, 1927. The *CAH* second edition has begun appearing; most relevant thus far is Vol. V, 1993. See also below, chs VII and IX.

For a more recent work in German on the origins and development of the social structure and political system of the Athenian *polis* in the sixth century BC, see Stahl, 1987. Among other subjects, Stahl treats of three important factions ('standings') and their leaders ('Lykurgos, Megakles und Peisistratos') and how their feuding contributed to the strengthening of social and political institutions that made possible the emergence of Athenian democracy: Section Two, 'Stasis und Tyrannei', pp. 56–136 and Section Three, 'Die Tyrannis und Die Entstehung des Staates in Athen', pp. 138–255. Stahl also provides a wider bibliography of sources in German than usually available in works printed in English.

For the student who does not read German and wishes to examine an English translation of German scholarship, a work more focused on the succeeding fifth century BC and the *Entstehung* (rise or origin) of the Athenian democratic political process and its increasing control over even socio-economic institutions may be recommended: Meier, 1990.

If available, for a concise yet substantial history and explication of its subject, see the still admirably useful survey by Greenidge, 1896.

Wood and Wood, which appeared after the first draft of this chapter had been completed, but is often in substantial agreement, calls important attention to economic origins of many socio-political viewpoints. Their work serves as a necessary corrective to past uncritical acceptance of the pronouncements of Socrates, Plato, and Aristotle on democracy and the labouring class of citizenry of Athens. Subsequently, the contributions of free and slave farmers, artisans, and labourers to the development and character of Athenian democracy are treated of, again in persuasive, revisionist fashion, in Wood, 1988. Wood relies to an important degree on Ostwald, 1986, as she acknowledges (p. x), 'to trace the institutional development of Athenian democracy', while it is her intention here 'to explore its social foundations'. Wood forthrightly states her revisionist purpose (p. 1): 'This book represents, among other things, an attack on conventional wisdom, but it is a conventional wisdom whose logic permeates scholarly studies'. Wood's contention is that posterity has uncritically accepted Plato, Xenophon, and Aristotle's negative misrepresentations of an Athenian democracy that, she maintains, was brilliantly creative, successful, and widely supported (p. 139).

Another revisionist work that should be carefully considered and is supportive of much of Wood and Wood is the ardently pro-democratic study by the political activist Cynthia

Farrar, 1988. Farrar finds democratic concepts – as well as democratic practices, successes, and failures in real-life classical Athens – in the available fragments and works of Protagoras, Democritus, and Thucydides. She makes skilful use of Thucydides' own work, his *History of the Peloponnesian War*, and of Plato's dialogue *Protagoras*, which presents Plato's account and rebuttal of Protagoras' views. (For an appreciative, judicious review of Farrar, see Wallach, 1989.) Farrar declares (p. 1): The purpose of this book is to retrieve a distinctive and neglected form of democratic thought from behind the shadows cast by Plato, by Aristotle, and by our own preconceptions'. Farrar comments on the manner in which Plato and Aristotle 'abandoned the aims of democratic politics and democratic thinkers' (pp. 265 f) and the resultant failure she perceives (pp. 272 f):

> In the search for stability, Plato and Aristotle both, from different directions, violated the fragile equilibrium of autonomy and order at the heart of a community that risks disintegration but is also, for that very reason, capable of achieving genuine reflective stability. At bottom, Plato and Aristotle base their conceptions of order on society and on man, respectively; they are unwilling to rely on the interaction of the two.

For a work on the development of the rule of law and the courts as safeguards and dispensers of justice, see Sealey, 1987. See, e.g., the comparison made between the supremacy of modern constitutions over 'the laws' [presumably statutes] and the supremacy of 'laws' (*nomoi*) over 'decrees' (*psēphismata)*, and reference to other senses of law (e.g., *ius*, *Recht*, and *droit*), pp. 32 f *et passim*.

A relevant study that includes a very lengthy, useful bibliography reached me during final stages of the present work: Manville, 1990. See in its entirety, especially pp. 53 f and Manville's appreciation of classical Athenian democracy in ch. 8, that finds (p. 218):

> With regard to a constitution, the rule of the people embodied in the fullest possible sense the unity of the state and its citizens; with regard to intangible civic spirit, the same, powerful themes seen in the Periklean funeral oration are visible (as generations of scholars have commented) throughout the drama, art and architecture, and political discourse of that 'golden age'.

See also Manville's definition of *polis*, pp. 53 f.

For a definitive study of the reputation – often quite inaccurate – of Athenian democracy, see Roberts, 1994.

For richly informative material and treatment in text, notes and bibliography, and for persuasive conclusions about the nature and functioning of the Athenian democratic system, including the disparate and common interests of the mass of citizenry and the elite and how they achieved an effective *modus operandi* and stable society, see in its entirety Ober, 1989. Ober concludes that the functioning hegemony of the Athenian mass was achieved along lines that refute (pp. 333 ff) the 'iron law of oligarchy' propounded by Robert Michels (1876–1936) and inverts (pp. 338 f) the [Marxian] principle of 'ideological hegemony' expounded by Antonio Gramsci (1891–1937). See further: Michels, 1958; and Gramsci, 1973.

For additional historical background and persuasive argumentation, buttressed by statistical analysis and functional description, that supports the viewpoint that the Athenian democracy was a successful and unifying system that was consciously formulated and effectively implemented, see also in its entirety Stockton, 1990. Stockton is challenging and illuminating throughout.

A recently published analytical survey that places the Athenian democracy in a context that provides broader geographical and historical perspective is O'Neil, 1995. See in its entirety, including appendices, with special attention (e.g., p. 37) to how *isonomia* (a term coined in the late sixth century BC that applied to 'government on the basis of equality') developed into *dêmokratia* (a term coined in the early fifth century BC that referred to 'power in the hands of the people').

For an historical account and bibliography of strife in classical Greece that pays important attention to Athens and *stasis*, see Lintott, 1981. For definition and concise analysis of *stasis*, see especially pp. 75 f, where Lintott places the blame for its appearance usually on 'aristocratic initiatives' where 'the societies in which they occurred did not have a high political culture or a securely established constitution'. Lintott finds:

> That every *stasis* leads to bloodshed is a typical orator's exaggeration and should be treated with caution where it appears in Herodotus. This is not necessarily the historian's view. On the other hand he does hold that the essence of *stasis* is conflict over power: the conflict over policy between Cleisthenes and Isagoras was merely a secondary development. This too was the view of Solon's enemies, who could not take his programme at its face value but only as the foundation of a tyranny.

For a landmark study (Froma I. Zeitlin in the Foreword) of myth (in particular, male autochthony) and politics in fifth century Athens, including congruent citizenship, interrelationships, exclusions, and division of functions of the sexes, that upgrades and dignifies the contribution of women, see Loraux, 1993. The central message of perceived injustice contained in this work is stated in the paragraph that begins (p. 10):

> There is no first Athenian woman; there is not, and never has been, a real female Athenian. The political process does not recognize a "citizeness," the language has no word for a woman from Athens, and there is even a myth to make the exclusion of women a corollary of the invention of the *name of Athens* – indeed, this name was invented by women [,] only for the city of men to deprive them of it forever. Can we say then that myth, in this case, does nothing more than account for reality? We can, in fact, but only if we read the myth as a political justification for the exclusion of women.

2 See also Bonner, 1967, p. 50; and Connor, 1970, pp. 108–11 and 143–7.
3 See for a history of attempts to integrate and unify Greece politically, a work that continues to be available in later editions and is followed here in part: Ferguson, 1913.
4 Note the revealing observation made in his discussion of the acquisition (or recognition) of citizenship by Todd, 1993, p. 181, n. 24:

> Nothing is asked here about wealth. Although constitutional historians tend to concentrate on the four property classes into which Solon in the 590s divided the citizen body, there is surprisingly little about these groups in the 4th-cent. legal sources (for rare exceptions see Dem. 43. 54, discussed at 11.d.iv below; Dem. 24. 144; and incomprehensibly IG [*Inscriptiones graecae* – RP] ii². 30. 12); *Ath. Pol.* 47. I may indeed indicate that by his [Demosthenes' – RP] time they were effectively obsolete.

Hignett, 1962, p. v, in the opening paragraph of his Preface, writes with some relevance to Todd's significant footnote:

> Some friendly critics have suggested that I ought to have carried the story down to the death of Demosthenes, but the year 401 BC, as the author of the *Athenian Politieia*

[Aristotle? – RP] realized, provides a more appropriate terminus for an historical treatment of the Athenian constitution. By then the radical democracy, assisted by the generosity of some of its Spartan conquerors, had finally triumphed, and nothing remained but to introduce minor modifications of detail and adjustments to changing conditions.

Forrest, 1966, seems in evident agreement.

5   This section of assessments, as well as much of the rest of this chapter, in good part follows Field, 1967, especially Part II, pp. 77–131. When one delves deeper into politico-socio-economic factors and developments, however, the present writer is inclined to accept the viewpoint of Wood and Wood, 1978 (ch. II, sec. 5, pp. 64–74) as against Ehrenberg and Polanyi on particular points as well as against the usually accepted unfavourable picturization of democratic forces in Athens. Wood and Wood rely more on evidence provided by Connor and Adkins. They cite, e.g.: Adkins, 1960, p. 231; Connor, 1970, pp. 11, 90, 105 f, *et passim*; Ehrenberg, 1969, pp. 11–21, 101 f; Ehrenberg, 1962, *passim*; and Polanyi, 1971, pp. 23, 41, 139–42, *et passim*. See also traditional sources cited in notes.

Perhaps Wood and Wood had in mind Napoleon Bonaparte's pithy observation, 'What is history but a fable agreed upon?', when they clarified the meaning of what may be regarded as a form of class struggle in producing a significantly democratic *polis* in Athens that has all too often been misrepresented. Although it seems to overlook Marxian doctrine that the working class can also be the ruling class (as in the case of a 'dictatorship of [i.e., by] the proletariat'), the following paragraph (pp. 68 f) calls for special consideration:

> The contention of this book, of course, has been that politics in the special Greek sense which Ehrenberg has in mind was *produced*, not destroyed, by the self-assertion of these classes against their aristocratic 'betters'. It can be argued that the very idea, as well as the reality, of civic-mindedness and public-spiritedness were creations of the demos in its struggle against its aristocratic rulers, while particularism and class-'egotism' were typical of the Athenian aristocracy. If, as Polanyi argues, an aristocracy uses political power 'to make human beings disposed to serve as an outcome of their status', if the state with its administrative apparatus and its institutionalized methods of coercion was created as a means of sustaining the power of an aristocratic ruling class over dependent labour, then the polis and politics in the specific Greek sense (especially as they developed in Athens) may be said to represent a new kind of political power, a countervailing power, the political response of the non-aristocratic classes to the 'politics' of the aristocracy. The assertion of the community principle against the particularism of tribe and class, and the concomitant rise in the status of the individual, both of which are inherent in the principle of citizenship, were essential weapons in the struggle of the demos against its hereditary rulers.

Traill, 1975, is a scrupulously careful and non-polemical account based largely on primary sources and archaeological evidence that may be read to give some support to Wood and Wood, especially his comments on the Council (p. xiii), on the deme (pp. 73 and 101 ff) and on the resurgence of the phratries and kinship groups (p. 96). Traill emphasizes both the representative nature of Athenian democracy and the central role of the Council in its endurance (p. xiii):

> These four elements, the Phylai, the Council, the Trittyes, and the Demes were combined by Kleisthenes to provide perhaps the most important, certainly the most enduring, feature of ancient Athenian democracy, representative government.

Representative government in ancient Athens, more precisely representation in the Athenian Council, is the subject of the present study.

Another spirited effort to lay low a myth about Athenian democracy is contained in Kagan, 1991. Indeed, the main message or thrust of this biography of the great Athenian general, orator, and demagogue, is that the Athenian system of democracy was not generally extremist or tyrannical, but generally just, under popular constitutional control, and remarkably effective and successful. Kagan goes so far as to express indignation over the misrepresentations of the character and achievements of the Athenian democracy presented by Plato, Alexander Hamilton in Federalist Number 6, and James Madison in Federalist Number 19 (pp. 269 f):

> The facts about Periclean Athens, as we have seen, were very different. Plato's assault on its character is a travesty. The Athenian people did not permit their leaders to usurp power. They were not slow to remove and punish even the most powerful men, as Pericles learned to his sorrow, and they withstood external as well as internal threats to their democracy. Through the horrors of almost three decades of the Peloponnesian War, military defeat, foreign occupation, and an oligarchic coup d'état, the people of Athens showed that combination of commitment and restraint that is necessary for the survival of popular government and life in a decent society.
> ... Disrespect for the law, they thought, was the way of tyranny. "In a democracy it is the laws that guard the person of the citizen and the constitution of the state, whereas the tyrant and oligarch find their protection in suspicion and armed guards." (Aeschines, *Against Timarchus*, 4–5)

Kagan also quotes here from Lysias, *Funeral Oration* 17–19, on 'the sovereignty of law and the instruction of reason'.

Additional sources consulted in preparation of this section and of this chapter in general include, e.g.: Berve, 1967, pp. 190–212, which presents an historical survey of Athenian tyrants in the fifth century BC; Ehrenberg, 1968, the second edition of which (1973) was cited by Wood and Wood, 1978; and Hammond, 1976, which provides a broader and more detailed background for the period.

A well-reasoned work based on a substantial amount of both factual and inferential evidence that supports a favourable view of Athenian democracy is Jones, 1957. Jones points out (p. 149, n. 138) that: 'Aristotle considered democracy "extreme" when working people are in a majority and can hold office, and the people is sovereign' and concludes the chapter on 'The Athenian Democracy and Its Critics' (p. 72) as follows:

> The opinions of Thucydides, Plato and Aristotle have naturally carried great weight, and so, curiously enough, have those of Isocrates. In the absence of any coherent statement of the democratic case, most modern historians have rather uncritically accepted the oligarchic view of Athens, and condemned what Aristotle calls the 'extreme democracy'.[138] ([138] The phrase is used in Pol. III. iv. 12 (1277b); IV. xii. 3 (1296b); IV. xiv. 7 (1298a); V. x. 30, 35 (1312b); VI. v. 5 (1320a).) In this article I have endeavoured to reconstruct the theory of government in which democrats believed and to assess the merits and defects of the Athenian democracy in the conduct of home affairs and of foreign and imperial policy. My readers can judge whether the 'extreme democracy', in which the people was sovereign, and vulgar persons who worked with their hands enjoyed full political rights, including access to all offices, and owing to their greater

numbers preponderated in the assembly, was indeed so pernicious a form of government as Athenian philosophers and historians represent.

6   See all of Sagan (1991) for important psychological insights into his subject, especially the paradoxes about the human condition it examines (e.g., as posed, pp. 2–6, and evaluated, pp. 362–75). An example of such apposite theoretical statements that illustrates why this entire work deserves the reader's close attention is Sagan's discussion of the psychological origins of political terror (pp. 150–8) that concludes with an apt phrase from an oration by Theseus in Shakespeare's *A Midsummer Night's Dream* (Act V, Scene 1):

> One thing seems clear. There is a pathological condition of the psyche that hates democracy, equality, and freedom with as much passion as human beings have ever felt about anything. Some people have it to a greater degree, some to a lesser. Some societies exhibit it in moderation, others run mad with it. Only by understanding it will we ever begin to know why oligarchic terror overwhelmed Athens twice within seven years. To call it 'paranoid' or 'paranoia' is, at the least, to give it a 'local habitation and a name'.

Of special importance is the problem posed (pp. 197 f) about 'the ultimate question of justice within society, especially within a democratic society', of its becoming more inclusive and 'whether it is possible to create a new *demos* capable of more mature and just action than in any polity yet seen'. This is to be accomplished by the kind of fundamental transformation within human nature postulated by the prophets of ancient Israel, Socrates, and Plato and was exemplified by Athenian democratic society.

Sagan's explanation (pp. 249–57) for the prevalent basic stability in fourth century Athens is the success in practice of the Solonian tacit agreement reached between the *oligoi* (few and largely rich) and the *demos* (many and largely poor but also cutting ideologically across economic lines to include most of the middle class and some of aristocratic background) that provided for a *balancing of classes* with respect to their rival claims and use of power. He finds (p. 253): 'The poor agreed not to use the political power of the radical democracy to dispossess the rich, not to confiscate and redistribute property. The rich agreed not to use their superior economic and social power to destroy the democracy'. He further finds (p. 279) that observance of this agreement was promoted by the value positions on which it was predicated.

In his concluding pages (pp. 374 f), Sagan relates that this period of greatness and stability was ushered in by an amnesty of extraordinary magnanimity that was extended after the oligarchic terror to its malefactors, allowing them to participate freely in political and military service to the Athenian *polis*. There then took place in Athens a fourth transformation, moral and psychological, that complemented: (1) establishment by Solon of social equity and compromise as the basis of politics; (2) the start under Cleisthenes of true democracy; and (3) the inclusion by Ephialtes and Pericles of the poor in a radical democracy.

For a monograph on the subject, see Strauss, 1987. Strauss cautions early on (pp. 1 f): 'Athenian political groups cannot have been parties in the modern sense. Most students of Athenian politics today refer instead to political groups or political friendships'. In a conclusion consistent with this reference, Strauss finds (p. 176):

> All things considered, slightly more of the political struggles of the period 403–386 were a matter of faction than of class. This state of affairs is less of a reflection of the inappropriateness of the class model to Athenian political history than of the peculiar

stalemate of classes in postwar Athens. ...

The specifics of the period 403–386 reveal a pattern to factional politics. A successful, popular general could dominate the political scene and unite conflicting factions, but only temporarily. Conon, victor of Cnidus [defeat of the Spartan fleet in 394 BC – RP], is the prime example: he dominated Athens in 393/92 in a manner reminiscent of Cimon or Pericles.

For a relevant multifaceted symposium, see Grofman et al., 1993. For evidential support of the view that the citizenry and dramatists of classical Athens widely supported their democratic system because of its values, stability, and effectiveness, see Roberts, 1994, pp. 33–47.

III Biographical Note on Plato

Early Years

Birth and Lineage

According to one account, the birth date of Plato, or Platon (Πλάτων), celebrated by the ancients was the seventh of Thargelion (May), and the year, calculated by Apollodorus, a chronologist of the second century BC, was 428–7 BC. However, neither the tradition as to the day nor Apollodorus' methods of calculation as to the year may be accepted with complete confidence as reliable; and there is general agreement, rather than certainty, that Plato died in 347 BC (Field, 1967, p. 3).[1]

According to another account (Taylor, 1960, p. 1):

> Plato, son of Ariston and Perictione, was born in the month Thargelion (May–June) of the first year of the eighty-eighth Olympiad by the reckoning of the scholars of Alexandra, 428–7 B.C. of our own era, and died at the age of eighty or eighty-one in 01.108.1 (348–7 B.C.). These dates rest apparently on the authority of the great Alexandrian chronologist Eratosthenes and may be accepted as certain.[2]

Thus, even the simple matters of when he was born and died are typical of the inexact knowledge we have of Plato. What is held to be correct about the events of Plato's life, the authenticity of his authorship of certain writings, and his meaning or intention, may therefore be only approximately accurate, probably or tentatively so, and often questionable.[3]

In any event, Plato was evidently born into a family of wealth and aristocratic lineage. His father, Ariston, claimed descent from Codrus, who, legend had it, was the last king of Athens (11th century BC, supposedly). His mother, Perictione, was probably descended from Dropides, a kinsman and friend of Solon, whose own father, also named Dropides, had been archon in the year 644 BC. Perictione was the sister of the male beauty Charmides (450?–04 BC) and the cousin of Critias (d. 403 BC), both of whom later were numbered among the Thirty Tyrants appointed by Sparta to rule Athens at the end of the Peloponnesian War in 404 BC. Both Charmides and Critias died in the struggle against the democratic Athenian statesman-general Thrasybulus (d. 388 BC) and both later became the subject of dialogues by Plato.

Plato was not the only child, there having been two brothers, Adeimantus and Glaucon, both of whom were principal speakers with Socrates in the *Republic*, and a sister, Potone, whose son, Speusippus (fl. 347–39 BC), became head of the Academy upon the death of Plato. The more authoritative evidence seems to indicate that Plato was the youngest child and that Ariston died while he was still quite young. Periction herself is known to have lived to a very advanced age (Taylor, 1960, pp. 1 f).[4]

Connections with the White Terror

Plato's writings seem to indicate that his uncle Charmides and cousin Critias had a greater influence on his life than did his parents or brothers. These two were among the nobles who became notorious as collaborators with Sparta and leaders of the oligarchic coup d'état and White Terror that followed the Peloponnesian War. There are those who believe, therefore, that Plato's upbringing and family connections inclined him from the first to the anti-democratic side. But John Burnet and Alfred E. Taylor report that the earlier affiliations of Plato's family were rather with the Periclean democracy, and seem to believe that Charmides and Critias became prominent members of the oligarchic party late in the war. This was a characteristic development of the time, when rich and noble families that had been proud to serve the Periclean democracy, were driven in increasing numbers into the ranks of the extreme opponents of the ensuing democracy by the oppressive financial burdens placed on them to pay for the war policy of the popularly controlled administration. 'At any rate', declares Field (1967, pp. 4 f), 'it is clear that during the susceptible years in which Plato was first coming to manhood those most near to him were becoming more and more hostile to the democracy and ready to go to any length to overthrow it'. The effects of such influences in his early, formative years on Plato's career and writings should not be glossed over. For Taylor (1960, pp. 7 f), they were very revealing and significant:

> Something of Plato's remarkable insight into the realities of political life must, no doubt, be set down to early upbringing in a household of "public men." So, too, it is important to remember, though it is too often forgotten, that the most receptive years of Plato's early life must have been spent in the household of his step-father, a prominent figure of the Periclean regime. Plato has often been

accused of a bias against "democracy." If he had such a bias, it is not to be accounted for by the influence of early surroundings. He must have been originally indoctrinated with "Periclean" politics; his dislike of them in later life, so far as it is real at all, is best intelligible as a consequence of having been "behind the scenes." If he really disliked democracy, it was not with the dislike of ignorance but with that of the man who has known too much.

There are no reminiscences in Plato's writings of his own childhood, although they do tell us something of what his youth in Athens must have been like. There are, however, accounts by others of an early interest by Plato in poetry and painting; and it is safe to speculate that from the age of 18 until the end of the Peloponnesian War in 404 BC, some five years later, Plato in all likelihood served in the cavalry, as would befit a young noble. There is also a garbled account that Plato took part in military expeditions in support of Thebes as late as 395 BC and that he was even decorated for valour (Field, 1967, pp. 5 f; Randall, 1970, pp. 10–4 and 17 ff).

Influence of Socrates and the Sophists

Two undoubted influences on the life and thought of Plato were Socrates and the Sophists. As is usual with Plato, however, we cannot always be sure of the degree and direction of these influences: i.e., how strong they were and when positive or negative. Although Plato himself is presumably called into evidence on these and other subjects through his Epistles, especially his Seventh Letter, there remains the problem of the authenticity of this and other letters ascribed to him.[5] Consequently, we must approach such matters as the influence exerted on Plato by Socrates and the Sophists with avowed uncertainty. However, because we can be somewhat surer about the methodology of Socrates and the Sophists than their points of advocacy, we can gain some fairly valid insights into the intellectual development of Plato by cautious attention to their known habits of reasoning, argumentation, and instruction. Thus, for example, the following statement by Paul Shorey (1933, pp. 12 f) helps in understanding Plato's intellectual development:

> The word Sophist in casual Athenian usage would have included Pythagoras, Socrates, Plato, and Aristotle. It meant learned man, professor, high-brow, "wise guy," and was complimentary or disparaging according to the taste and culture or purpose of the speaker. In Plato's *Meno*, Socrates in speaking to be understood by an uneducated slave calls geometers "Sophists." The youth Hippocrates, who in the *Protagoras* knocks Socrates up at early dawn to hear the great Sophist

Protagoras who has come to Athens, thinks that Sophist means, as its etymology implies, one who knows wise things. In the more technical meaning Sophist designates a group – they could hardly be called a school – of men who from the middle of the fifth century undertook to supply the need of a developing civilization for some form of higher education to supplement the traditional education of Athenian youth in gymnastics and music. ...

They are represented as humanizers of knowledge, itinerant university extension professors without a university base.[6]

Plato seems to have met Socrates at approximately the age of 20 and to have become his disciple, or at least his listener, for the remaining seven or eight years until his death in 399 BC. It is probable that during this period, Plato became one of the intimate circle of friends and philosophers that surrounded Socrates, and in the *Phaedo* (59B) he explains his absence at the time of Socrates' death as having been caused by illness.

It should also be pointed out that past scholarship has often placed Socrates and Plato in opposition to the Sophists. Therefore, the influence of the Sophists on Plato has been held as negative in character and to have called forth a rebuttal from Plato that followed the moralistic teachings of Socrates.[7]

Centrally important topics in Plato's political theory are his conceptions of law, justice, ethics, and God. William Archibald Dunning (1902, pp. 22 f; see Wild, 1953, esp. pp. 152 ff and 168 f) attributes to Socrates a contribution which may have profoundly influenced the development of Plato's ideas and attitudes on these related subjects:

> The ethical system of which Socrates laid the foundation is embodied for the most part in the doctrine that virtue is identical with knowledge, vice with ignorance ...
> ... Specifically, the knowledge which was identical with justice he laid down to be a knowledge of the laws. But laws he proceeded to define as including the two species – written, or the laws of the state, and unwritten, or the will of the gods. The former he held to be of limited and local obligation; the latter to be of universal binding force, and hence to take precedence of all others.

Ultimately, however, because Socrates left no written works and we know him mostly through Plato's dialogues, we cannot be sure of the extent of the influence of Socrates on Plato and we cannot be sure of how accurately Plato reports him. The Socrates who speaks in Plato's dialogues must inevitably be partly the authentic Socrates and partly the creation of Plato. Shorey opines that 'The Platonic Socrates is no less obviously the embodiment of Plato's ideal of the philosopher and the mouthpiece of Plato's ideas' and adds that:

In respect of method, Xenophon and Plato seem to confirm Aristotle's statement that there are two things that may be rightly attributed to Socrates, inductive argument and the quest for definitions. The only substantive philosophical dogmas that we can with any assurance attribute to Socrates are the principles that no man willingly does wrong, that virtue is knowledge, and that all wrongdoing and error are ignorance, to which we may possibly add that it is better to suffer injustice than to inflict it. These Socratic principles the piety of Plato always reaffirmed, but always as consciously edifying paradoxes subject to interpretation and explanation. How far such interpretations are covert criticisms of Socrates or mark the stages of Plato's gradual emancipation from Socratic limitations are questions which in the lack of evidence may be left to the speculations of over-ingenious philologists (Shorey, 1933, p. 21).[8]

After the death of Socrates, Plato went with other of his intimate friends for a stay at Megara, at the home of Terpsion and Euclides, two of the inner circle of Socrates' disciples. We have no way of knowing how long Plato stayed at Megara, consorting with the critical and ingenious luminaries of the Megarian school of philosophy. When he returned to Athens, he probably shunned political activism. Plato's hopes that Athens would reform politically to his liking were not realized, and his disillusionment grew, not only with the Athenian state, but also with all other *poleis* of which he had knowledge. 'And yet', remarks Field (1967, pp. 11 f), 'this still seemed to him the most important aim that a man could set before himself, and he never ceased studying and reflecting to see if a way out could be found from these evils'.

Middle Years

Plato in Sicily and Italy

Plato is reported to have travelled, during his *Wanderjahre*, to many points in the Middle East, including such places as Persia, Babylonia, Phoenicia, and Egypt. Of all these, a visit to Egypt is the most likely to have taken place. Sometime later, when he was about 40 (c. 387 BC), Plato went on his first visit to Italy and Sicily. From his suspect Seventh Letter we gather that his chief impression of Italy was of unrestrained and unashamed public and private luxury. For the rather ascetic Plato, nothing healthy in the way of personal character, institutions, or laws could result from such a hedonistic way of life. However, Plato also found scholars of merit in Italy. Thus, while at Tarentum he made the acquaintance of Archytas (fl. 400–365 BC), one of the chief representatives of the school of Pythagoreanism (ibid., pp. 14 ff).

After Italy, Plato proceeded to Sicily. At Syracuse, he found the reigning tyrant, Dionysius the Elder (c. 430–365 BC), in the process of establishing the most powerful dominion of the contemporary Greek world. Plato's writings, both his supposed letters and his dialogues, reveal the impressions he received there of the evils of absolute despotism and the notable achievements of Dionysius. His perception of public and private life in Sicily matched the unfavourable one he had developed in Italy.[9]

While in Syracuse, Plato made another friendship which was to exercise a profound influence on the remainder of his life – that with Dion (408?–353), then a young man of about 20, whose sister had just married the tyrant Dionysius. Dion proved susceptible to Plato's teachings and resolved himself to lead a very different life from that of the ordinary Italian or Sicilian and to love goodness more than pleasure or luxury, a mode of life that did not make him very popular at the tyrant's court.

There is a popular account about Plato's first visit to Sicily, to the effect that Plato infuriated Dionysius by his outspoken condemnation of tyranny and that the latter, in revenge, handed him over to a homeward-bound Spartan envoy to be sold into slavery. Another version has it that Plato was not openly seized by Dionysius, but that secret instructions were given by that worthy to Pollis, the Spartan envoy aboard whose ship Plato took passage, to sell him as a slave. In any event, the sale is said to have taken place at Aegina and Plato was saved by the timely arrival of a friend from Cyrene, one Anniceris, who ransomed Plato and sent him home in safety to Athens. Field is inclined to accept the view of Eduard Meyer that the complicity of Dionysius in the matter is an invention and that the Aeginetans had themselves seized Plato in one of their regular piratical raids on Athenian commerce between 389 and 387 BC. And so, in all probability, Plato returned to Athens toward the end of 387 BC and was once more settled there when the King's Peace had come into force (Field, 1967, pp. 21 f; Randall, 1979, pp. 21 f).

Plato and the Academy

It was about this time that Plato saw clearly what his remaining life's work was to be and set about organizing his Academy.[10] For the rest of his years, Plato was primarily a teacher and writer. However, this even course was twice interrupted by his ill-fated journeys to Syracuse (367 and 361 BC) when he vainly attempted to create something like his ideal state by trying to make a philosopher-ruler of Dion's nephew, the younger Dionysius (fl. 367–44 BC), who had succeeded to his tyrant father's throne (Field, 1967, pp. 18–26; Randall, 1970, pp. 23–26). Plato's personal life does not seem to have included a marriage.[11]

The organization of the Academy, about 386 BC, need not concern us greatly, but it is important to note its practical effects. Fuller (1923–30, Vol. II, pp. 170 f) provides an appreciation of the Academy's influence and the controversy over the harmful or beneficial nature of this influence:

> Though a number of his pupils took to an academic career, so many descended again to the lists of practical life and became law-givers, governors, military leaders, and even would-be despots, that later detractors accused him of having founded a school for making tyrants.
>
> The charge was perhaps not without its grain of truth. Plato's interest in politics tended to wax rather than to wane with the passing years, and the practical problem of establishing good government here and now had become, if anything, more absorbing than the vision of the abstract good or of the ideal state. This interest, to be sure, was suffused in his mind with a growing austerity in morals and by problems of religious reform that verged on theocracy. And these, in their turn, seem to have sprung from an ever intenser conviction that the world could be saved only through conversion to a rigidly ascetic discipline of life. Still, what drew and held a large proportion of his pupils was not so much his fame as a philosopher, or his program of moral reform, as the instruction he gave in constitutional law and the art of statesmanship, and the academy was winning its reputation in Greece as a school no less of the political sciences than of philosophy.

Final Years

Life's Work

Plato grew up in a period when the established order and accepted standards of the day appeared on the verge of dissolution under the pressure of events and theoretical criticism. At first, Plato attempted to grapple with the situation by himself engaging in politics. Disillusionment was not long in coming, brought on above all by the execution of Socrates, and in time he despaired of any good coming from any of the existing states of Hellas. He then turned to philosophical speculation as the only source from which improvement might come, although he continued to teach would-be politicians and occasionally advised practising statesmen (Field, 1967, p. 91).

Life's End

Plato's final years were relatively serene and happy. He had in his own lifetime already established for himself a reputation as a great philosopher and teacher to whom statesmen and rulers turned for advice; and the Academy was the foremost centre of learning of its day in Greece. Besides this reputation, Plato had in the course of many years of teaching, built up for himself the affection and warm regard of the successive classes of students who had attended the Academy. Physically and mentally, Plato was active and alert until the end, dying, according to Cicero's account, while writing, and according to another story, swiftly and easily at the marriage feast of a friend (Fuller, 1923–30, Vol. II, pp. 180 f).

Problem of Interpretation

One of the great problems Plato confronts us with, is how to interpret him.

Firstly, are we to interpret Plato overall as, roughly speaking, 'totalitarian or democrat' in message and purpose?[12] Those who represent Plato as some kind of liberal, progressive, or democrat certainly include, among modern writers, not only John H. Hallowell and John Wild, but also Paul Shorey, Ronald B. Levinson, Harold Cherniss, and John Herman Randall Jr.[13] Those who represent Plato as some kind of reactionary, authoritarian, or totalitarian certainly include, among modern writers, not only Richard H.S. Crossman and Karl R. Popper, but also Warner Fite, Eric A. Havelock, Alban Dewes Winspear, and Alvin W. Gouldner.[14]

Secondly, when are we to interpret Plato as writing his own opinions, when the opinions of Socrates, when candidly, and when ironically? There is much disagreement among Platonists as to which light he should be read in. Accordingly, all of Plato should be read with caution, and much of Plato should be read with uncertainty.[15]

Perhaps there are no clear-cut answers possible to the questions that have just been posed. However, perhaps some greater likelihoods or probabilities about a number of key points and purposes in Plato's political theory can emerge from an examination of his writings that identifies relevant concepts and principles, a number of which have been neglected or not fully appreciated. Perhaps some sort of coherent pattern of political and constitutional thought may be discerned that illustrates the grand ultimate purposes and consequent system of state and society he advocated.[16] And that is all we can ever realistically hope to attain; for Plato, as is true of everyone, must have remained ever changeable, tentative, or undecided in his own mind on quite a number of matters; although, unlike most of us, he was more aware of choices involved and his powerful mind ranged more widely and probed more profoundly even when going astray.[17]

Those who seek an enthusiastically laudatory appraisal of Plato and Platonism may turn to the work of Paul Elmer More, whose judgment of Plato's purposes and influence is stated in the superlative. For example, More (1926, pp. vii f) follows a reference to the origins of Christianity, the 17th century English revival of philosophic religion, and the 18th century rise of Romanticism with the declaration:

> My conviction is that behind all these movements the strongest single influence has been the perilous spirit of liberation brought into the world by the disciple of Socrates, and that our mental and moral atmosphere, so to speak, is still permeated with inveterate perversions of Plato's doctrine.

More (ibid., p. 280) also concludes that:

> In a manner not given to any other writer Plato must be regarded as the liberator of the spirit, who has set wings to the human soul and sent it voyaging through the empyrean.

Notes

1   Field also reports that another version put the date of Plato's birth as two or three years earlier.
2   Taylor also reports, whimsically, that Ariston's 'pedigree' was supposed to trace back to the god Poseidon.
3   The line of development and viewpoints reported in this biographical note are taken especially from: Field, 1967; Shorey, 1933; Levinson, 1970; Randall Jr, 1970; and Ryle, 1966.

Additional works consulted in the preparation of this chapter include: Barker, 1960; Burnet, 1964; Dunning, 1902; Friedländer, 1958; Fuller, Vol. II, 1930; Guthrie, Vol. IV, 1975; Ritter, Vol. I, 1910; Taylor, 1960a and b; Voegelin, Vol. III, 1957; and Wild, 1946.

A useful introduction to the primary and secondary sources on the life and writings of Plato, not restricted to publications in English, is contained in Taylor, 1960b, in footnotes, pp. 1–22; also helpful are the Chronological Table, pp. 519 f and the appendix, 'The Platonic Apocrypha', pp. 521–55. For similar purposes and occasional differences of viewpoint and additional material, see the influential work by Shorey, 1933, especially the section on 'Doubtful and Spurious Dialogues', pp. 415–44 and the section of Bibliography and Notes, pp. 445–670.

For various credible, apocryphal, and fictitious anecdotes, accounts, charts, and commentary about Plato's life and works, see in its entirety the carefully organized and thoughtful work by Alice Swift Riginos (Vol. III, 1976). Riginos presents many useful features, including a classification (pp. 202 f) of selected major classical and post-classical sources as Pro-Platonic, Anti-Platonic, and Neutral or Uncertain, in whole or in part, with corresponding pagination in her work also listed. Riginos cautions (p. 6):

> When one considers the question of the historicity of the 148 anecdotes discussed in the following chapters, it is clear that, while there may be some kernel of truth behind a number of the stories told about Plato, the truth is elusive and difficult to isolate from the fabricated details and embellishments, whether prejudicial or not, which are combined in a given anecdote.

This caveat is particularly apt with reference to anecdotes that centre around Aristotle, pp. 129–34.

4   Taylor gives a concise rendition of the family roots of Plato and includes references to the dialogues where some of these kin appear. Also see the family tree in Burnet, 1964, Part I, Appendix I, p. 357. Field, 1967, p. 4, challenges one of the more popular beliefs about the name Plato:

> We are safe in dismissing as fiction the story, which still finds its way into some modern writings, that his name was originally Aristocles and that Plato was given him as a nickname on account of some distinctive physical feature. The evidence for it is of the slightest, and Plato was a regular Athenian name.

Cf. Randall, 1970, pp. 18 f.

5   It should be borne in mind that not all Platonic scholars accept these Epistles as genuine – far from it. Some scholars believe the 13 letters attributed to Plato are all forgeries, and others believe them to be forgeries in part. For a brief discussion of this controversy, see Randall, 1970, pp. 8 ff, including his quotation in footnote 2 from Gilbert Ryle, 1967, Vol. VI, p. 314. For another discussion of the matter, see Ryle, 1966, especially pp. 68 f. *Cf.* Wild, 1946, p. 13, who wrote that 'Epistles VI, VII, and VII are now universally accepted as genuine', but this is a definite overstatement. For a careful and thoughtful study of the Seventh Letter, see Edelstein, 1966. Edelstein's basic conclusion (p. 166) is as follows:

> In my inquiry into the genuineness of the Seventh Letter, I proceeded on the assumption that the document is, as it claims to be, Plato's own work. The representation of his early life and of his attitude toward political action raised the first doubts concerning the authenticity of the letter. These doubts were confirmed by an analysis of the advice Plato is said to have given Dionysius. In part, the political counsel attributed to him presupposes a historical situation that existed only after Plato's death. A scrutiny of the philosophical digression also led to the result that Plato could not be the author of the letter. A doctrine such as that outlined in the apologia is not to be found in the Platonic dialogues. In fact, it appears to contradict the basic tenets of Platonism. Finally, when the epistle was considered as one of the many epistles which tradition has preserved under Plato's name, it again became evident that the autobiography could not be what it pretends to be – Plato's own account of his life and activities.

For an earlier study on the same subject, see Hackforth, 1913. See also the argumentation of Boas and Cherniss, 1948, to whom the Seventh Letter seems spurious; and the rebuttal by Bluck, 1949.

6   A somewhat similar view of the Sophists is presented by Field, 1967, pp. 31–4, who comments on Plato's attitude toward them, as follows (p. 32):

> Plato is sometimes described as treating the sophists with extreme hostility in his writings. Such a description, however, is not accurate. He could handle some of them severely enough. But his picture of the two best known figures, Protagoras and Gorgias, particularly the latter, is kindly and favourable. He was, however, undoubtedly fundamentally at variance with their ideals.

Cf. Randall, 1970, ch. VI; Rowe, 1983; and especially Wood and Wood, 1978, pp. 87–94, who conclude (p. 94), 'it was the Sophists to whom Socrates and Plato were responding …'. See especially the description of the Sophist in Benardete, 1984, particularly the Introduction, pp. xi f and II, pp. 99–106. Benardete is in substantial agreement with Shorey. See especially the discussion of the Sophists in Stone, 1989, pp. 40–50.

For a recent favourable evaluation of the character and role of the Sophists, see Demetriou, 1995. For an argumentation that Plato had an unfavourable view of the role and influence of the Sophists and that his Academy and *Republic* were meant to countervail them, see Mahoney, 1995, pp. 30–52.

7   For a presentation of this viewpoint, see Dunning, 1902–20, p. 21. *Cf.* Randall, 1970, ch. VI.

8   *Cf.* Dunning, 1902–20, pp. 25 ff. Field, 1967, pp. 8 f believes 'It is perhaps more than anything else as his ideal of the righteous man that Socrates impressed himself on Plato'.

9   As is true regarding many aspects of Plato's life and works, the sources, including Plato's Seventh Letter, that purport to provide information about his travels to and from Syracuse and his stays there, are suspect in whole or in part. See again the various judgments in n. 5 of this chapter, or see, e.g., Ryle, 1966, ch. III, especially pp. 68 f. If Ryle's conclusions are correct, this work may contain the most believable account of Plato's life and the chronology of his writings. According to Ryle, we cannot be sure about Plato's authorship of the *Letters*, including the Seventh. The reader who is interested in more than a background sketch of Plato's life would do well to study Ryle's work *in toto* in conjunction with other authorities who are more confident of the authenticity of the Platonic *Letters*: e.g., again, the statement that 'Epistles VI, VII, and VIII are now universally accepted as genuine', in Wild, 1946, p. 13. Field, 1967, pp. 12–25, who is being largely followed in this chapter section, places much reliance on Plato's Seventh Letter.

10   Ryle, 1966, pp. 222–5, puts in doubt the generally accepted view that Plato's Academy had been in existence for about 20 years before Aristotle joined it in 367 BC. Ryle believes that it was more likely founded in 370 or 369 BC. He questions throughout this work the commonly accepted chronology of Plato's writings and presents rather persuasive, albeit largely conjectural, arguments in support of his conclusions. Because the chronology of these writings may have a bearing on their motivation and messages, a more correct dating could lead to a more precise understanding of at least portions of them. *Cf.* Cherniss, 1962, *passim.*

11   On this point, Field, 1967, p. 28 comments: 'The fact that Plato never married tells us nothing. Marriage for most Greeks was thought of primarily as a way of founding a family rather than of satisfying sexual impulses'. The second sentence quoted here is probably closer to the truth; although *continuing* a family may be a more correct way of putting it and, according to treatment of such matters by Fustel de Coulanges, would set the first sentence at naught. *Cf.* Fustel de Coulanges, 1956, especially pp. 40–65. Fustel de Coulanges is more likely a better guide to whether Plato's failure to marry may be indicative of anything,

especially when viewed in the light of his treatment of religion, marriage, and the family in the classical period.

12 See the discussion of this issue as assembled in Thorson, 1963. For a weighty consideration, see Taylor, 1986, who concludes (p. 25) that Plato is not 'an extreme totalitarian' but: 'His theory is paternalist, as Vlastos shows ...'.

Information and observations relevant to this issue are scattered throughout the text and endnotes of the concluding chapter of Roberts, 1994, ch. 13. See especially pp. 294 ff and endnotes 15–24, including how (p. 295): 'Whereas many in Hitler's camp sought to identify Germany with Sparta, Germany's enemies, picking up on the analogy, tended to ally themselves with Athens instead'.

13 In addition to the excerpts from Hallowell and Wild contained in Thorson, 1963, see the entries for Hallowell, Wild, Shorey, Levinson, Cherniss, and Randall in the bibliography of this work.

14 In addition to the excerpts from Crossman and Popper contained in Thorson, 1963, see the entries for Crossman, Popper, Fite, Havelock, Winspear, and Gouldner contained in the bibliography of this work.

15 See Friedländer, 1958, ch. VII. Note also the following quotation from Goethe (p. 137) and comment thereafter by Friedländer in n. 1:

> "He who would explain to us when men like Plato spoke in earnest, when in jest or half-jest, what they wrote from conviction and what merely for the sake of argument, would certainly render us an extraordinary service."[1] ([1] Goethe, at the end of the essay, "Plato als Mitgenosse einer christlichen Offenbarung" [1796], *Werke*, [Stuttgart and Tübingen, 1827–34], XLVI, 28.) These words of Goethe do not seem to have been taken with sufficient seriousness even as an ideal postulate. It is quite certain, however, that one cannot approach Plato without taking into account what irony is and what it means in his work.

Note that Søren Kierkegaard takes this point quite seriously: see in Gross, 1968, ch. 15. Also relevant are parts of Seery, 1990, which includes criticism of many noted writers and scholars, especially, ch. 2. See also Cornford, 1968, ch. III, for insight into when Plato is probably reporting Socrates aright and when he is going beyond him and espousing Plato. With respect to Plato's early dialogues that include especially the *Apology*, *Crito*, *Euthyphro*, *Laches*, *Charmides*, *Lysis*, *Protagoras*, and *Gorgias*, Cornford states (p. 59): 'The Socrates of Plato is the real Socrates, a figure that inspired every noble character of Greek and Roman antiquity to the last hour of its decline'. Cornford is also of the opinion that in some of his later works, especially the *Phaedo*, 'Platonism goes beyond Socrates' (p. 78); and points out that Plato is attuned to obedience to local authority, whereas Socrates holds to the ideal of self-rule and 'cannot pay allegiance to the laws of any city narrower than the city of Zeus' (p. 84). *Cf.* Wood and Wood, 1978, pp. 101 ff, for a contrary view that emphasizes Socrates' 'firm belief in the strict observance of the law'.

There is important agreement, examined in his last major work by Vlastos, 1991, pp. 45–106, that there are two conflicting voices of Socrates in the Platonic dialogues, that he has labelled 'Socrates$_E$' and 'Socrates$_M$' (p. 46), for early and middle. Vlastos promises (p. 49): '... I shall call on evidence external to the Platonic corpus to support the claim that *in those essential respects in which S_E's philosophy differs from that of S_M it is that of the historical Socrates*, recreated by Plato in invented conversations which explore its content and exhibit its method'. Vlastos adds (p. 53) that when Plato 'finds compelling reason to strike out along new paths ... to new, unSocratic and antiSocratic conclusions, ... the dramatist's attachment to his protagonist ... survives the ideological separation'.

For support of Plato's account of Socrates in the *Apology*, see Allen, 1980, pp. 33–6. A generally relevant work on this topic is Brickhouse and Smith, 1994. See Brickhouse and Smith for analysis of Socrates' manner of inquisition and argumentation (viewed by himself as not having a specific method), teleology, values of life and death, epistemology, and thoughts on justice. A basic conclusion they reach (p. 212) is that: 'Socrates counts none of his beliefs about these matters as knowledge'. An accompanying guiding principle they discern is that: 'For Socrates, the greatest peril of all is to live a life that so corrupts one with evil that even one's afterlife is irredeemably spoiled. One's life, then, should be devoted to the care of that which continues after it – the soul. A life that follows this principle will not be lived in vain'.

While favourable to Plato in the extreme, the forthright work of More, 1926, pp. 1 f, reports:

> Of the two main witnesses on whom we must rely for our knowledge of his teaching, the one, our gossiping Xenophon, understood him too little, whereas the other understood him, in a manner, too well, developing his instruction into so rich and voluminous a body of thought that Socrates might have exclaimed with some apparent reason, as indeed he is said actually to have done on hearing one of the simpler of Plato's Dialogues: 'By Hercules, what lies the young man has told about me!'

16 *Cf.* Havelock, 1957, e.g., pp. 6 f, who argues that Plato and Aristotle were reactionaries who were out of step with liberal ideas and movements of their day. This may very well be so, but even then it could be rejoined that Plato and Aristotle were probably more in the mainstream of contemporary Greek thought and real-life events. However, this possible rejoinder is emphatically rejected by Wood and Wood, 1978, as no less than a distortion, a myth, a great historical untruth that, ironically, has been generally received as historical truth. See, e.g., Wood and Wood, 1978, pp. 119–25 and 262–5, for persuasive argumentation of their position.

17 For a work that presents a concise review of Plato's life and of origins, purposes, development, key points, and contribution of his thought, see in its entirety Hare, 1982. Hare does not really attempt to distinguish between Socrates and Plato in the latter's dialogues and concludes (p. 75): 'In the end he made many people see that personal or even national ambition and success are not the most important things in life and that the good of other people is a worthier aim. For this we can forgive him for being also the father of political paternalism and absolutism'.

For a challenging treatment of both Plato's political theory and of commentaries thereon by a variety of scholars that furnishes conceptual analysis, purposive speculation, and value judgments, see in its entirety Planinc, 1991. Planinc also gives a clear introductory statement of the rationale of his methodology (p. x): 'It is possible to study Plato and Aristotle directly, but not if one evades engagement with their writings in the name of scholarly distance. Proper scholarship requires both knowledge of the traditions of interpretation and direct engagement'.

A variety of well supported insights and speculations on Plato's purposes and how to interpret a number of his dialogues appears in Rosen, 1995. Rosen focuses on the *Statesman* but ranges more widely across Plato's political corpus; and in similar fashion, we may apply the following observation (p. 8):

> It may seem frivolous to suggest that the *Statesman* is an elaborate Platonic joke, but the suggestion is in no way intended to suppress the serious philosophical arguments

of the dialogue. The joke is on those, whether philologists or ontologists, who lack the wit to appreciate Plato's elegance or the playful seriousness that is required to penetrate the initially tedious details of the *Statesman* in order to enter the presence of its enigmatic author.

Commentary about Plato that was influential in America in the 19th century was contained in the lecture on 'Plato; or the Philosopher', by Ralph Waldo Emerson (1803–82), the popular Transcendentalist minister, reprinted in 1849 and now available in his *Essays and Lectures* (Porte, 1983), pp. 633–60. Himself a fierce egotist, Emerson recognized like qualities in Plato (p. 653):

> Plato would willingly have a Platonism, a known and accurate expression for the world, and it should be accurate. It should be the world passed through the mind of Plato, – nothing less. Every atom shall have the Platonic tinge; every atom, every relation or quality you knew before, you shall know again, and find here, but now ordered; not nature, but art.

Emerson concludes with the observation that (p. 660): 'Plato plays Providence a little with the baser sort, as people allow themselves with their dogs and cats.'

Apropos here also are the opening words by Angela Hobbs in the *Times Literary Supplement* of 9 February 1996 in her review of a book that subsequently reached the present writer (Rutherford, 1995):

> Plato's dialogues offer a formidable array of interpretative challenges. He never speaks in his own voice, preferring instead to present a main character (usually Socrates) in conversation with a varied cast: aristocrats, sophists, poets, soldiers – even a slave. It would be wrong to assume that Socrates is always, or indeed ever, simply Plato's mouthpiece; contrasting viewpoints, characters and ways of life are carefully juxtaposed to invite, rather than close, debate. Socrates' contributions are, furthermore, notoriously difficult to assess in their own right; irony, word-play and 'recantation' all make his position elusive; and further puzzles are provided by the use of imagery, fable and myth.

Rutherford's work, which focuses on literary rather than philosophical aspects, has many useful features that recommend it to the targeted readerships stated in its Preface: 'both academics and the general public'. And on its very first page of text it addresses the conundrum of what Plato really meant, beginning with his translation of 'one of the best-known, but also most puzzling, passages in the Platonic corpus', i.e.:

> I can say this much, at any rate, about all those who have written or intend to write, claiming knowledge of the subjects which are my concern, whether they maintain they have heard it from me or others, or that they have discovered it themselves: it is impossible, in my opinion at least, that these men know anything about the subject. No writing of mine exists on these subjects nor ever could exist; for this is not something that can be put into words like other teachings, but only when there has been long association and involvement with the subject, living together, then, as light is kindled from a fire as it blazes up, so it is born in the soul and at once nourishes itself there. Yet I know this much, that these matters, whether written down or spoken, would be best coming from me. I am injured not least because they are written down ill. But if I thought it was possible for them to be written down adequately for the multitude and voiced in words, what nobler task could I have spent my life upon than to write down

what would bring great benefit to mankind, and to bring to light the nature of the world for all to see? (*Letter vii*, 341b–d)

If one assume these words to be by Plato and candid, a plausible explanation, however, may easily suggest itself to anyone who has wooed and understood a woman – and more especially has been longtime happily married, seemingly forever – or to one who has taught students to puzzle out answers that must be learned by personal experiencing, not outside explanation. E.g., many a pathetic suitor has been mystified by feminine behaviour that the object of his affections or pursuit refuses to explain. She is wise enough to know that if he cannot, unaided by her save by subtle hints, with the passage of time come substantially to understand her – and that never means always and completely, for that would leave her more naked and defenceless than mere physical nakedness – he is not right for her. Thus Plato may mean here that no work of his, no matter how forthright or lengthy, could satisfactorily impart understanding of his purposes, meanings, nuances, and techniques. Only those who have the suitable talents and also apply enough attention and the ripening ingredient of time can hope to enjoy the prize gained in fathoming the mind of Plato. Plato is willing openly to flirt intellectually with many but believes much of the essence of his ideas may be perceived more fully only by those with the kind of required stronger and more active vision that comes from within. The teacher who tells the class one does not teach so much as one helps the student to learn – i.e., he really abets a self-learning process – is fully acquainted with this truism. To puzzle is to teach artfully.

Accordingly, if one ascribe to Plato touches of the mysterious, wily, and playful that are part of an intriguing woman's makeup and ways, we may perhaps make sense of the passage from the Seventh Letter and much else in Plato. And therefore, Plato may have chosen to write in a manner that only the truly wise, patient, and good or the boldly insightful – who are often scoundrels – can master. Thus, Rutherford is quite right to follow a literary trail in search of an increased dimension of understanding of Plato, and he regularly picks up the spoor of Plato's stratagems as, e.g., when he discerns (p. 92):

> Like his teacher, Plato does not see it as his task to do all the work for us. Often the dialogues suggest more than they assert, and leave it to the reader to develop some of these suggestions and explore the implications of what often seem perverse and paradoxical arguments.

Rutherford concludes (p. 312) with his perception of the central feature in the art of Plato:

> This tension between the ideal and the real, utopia and anarchy, philosophical revelation and worldly blindness, may well be what remains most vividly in the reader's memory after study of some of his greatest works. Fundamental to Plato's thought, this conflict is ceaselessly explored and illuminated by his art.

However, this final passage may be deemed more revelatory about Plato's *didactic purpose* rather than his *art*. And this didactic purpose is even more strikingly depicted (p. 196) by Rutherford when he explains the lovers' relationship in the *Symposium*: 'There Diotima describes the creative urge of mankind as compelling some to beget children, others to aim at a more permanent memorial – poetry, laws or other forms of wisdom. It is with the aim of creating something beautiful in mind that the man of virtue seeks a beautiful soul in another:

... Hence men like these have a much greater communion and a stronger bond of affection than the bond created by children, for they have shared in raising fairer and more eternal offspring (209bc).

But for the student, a necessary corollary explanation of the *art* of Plato may be found in the idea that it is the art, more heavy-handedly practised by Plato, of the eternally mischievously delightful, dramatic woman. By use of a myriad of coquettish or teasing suggestions, playful and serious remarks, and artful *questions*, we are lured to begin to follow her along a path where she keeps gracefully – and does Plato not usually write gracefully? – flitting ahead of us and unsnatchable until fairly earned. And in the case of Plato, this path – *Weg* or *tao*, as some modern students would put it – is a shining path of virtue, wisdom, understanding, and love that God sets before humanity as an in-guiding vision Plato feels he has glimpsed and wants others also to learn to see and follow.

Plato's enchantment is especially successful in his dialogues, because the dialogue is an inherently dramatic (even by definition) art form; and in all his writing he constantly spins out enticing embellishments that exhilarate us (which is why we attend the theatre) as we pursue his meaning – and even more so when we feel we have grasped and held it. These enticements are often quite simply the kind of flirtatious or courting fun and games that people have played with loved ones including spouses, offspring, and parents (and even strangers, too), and this helps to account for the continuing widespread attraction to Plato by posterity. Plato, as does woman often, woos and wins *us*, as we are sucked into trying to snare his slippery corpus. In short, Plato's *art* is in good part that of the eternal woman, practised a bit more clumsily by a man but still in all gracefully – as when a *danseur* leaps higher but not more artistically than the *danseuse* and never quite matches her floating effect. Appreciation of the art of Plato, therefore, may give some insight into Plato the person.

For treatment of Plato's cosmological views that parallels Rutherford's literary focus on his artistry, and occasionally presents similar conclusions and language, see Cropsey, 1995. Cropsey's work is an elaboration of themes he summarizes for our guidance at the outset. Thus, Cropsey's Introduction (pp. 1 f) sets forth that:

Through the medium of the Protagorean geometers, the persistent presence of the irrational or incommensurable in the natural world becomes conspicuous. Then in *Theaetetus* the young interlocutor's attempt to identify knowledge as perception will elicit from Socrates the revelation that that definition flows from Protagoras's doctrine of "man the measure," making Protagoras eventually responsible for the opinion that the corporeal is the true. As will be seen, Socrates will denounce that opinion in the last hour of his life in a tacit gesture toward his old adversary. When the revisionist Parmenidean Stranger enters as senior interlocutor in the subsequent dialogues, he will tell a tale of the cosmos according to which the whole must spin either under the hand of god or according to its natural impetus, the latter being both the reverse of the former and the actual condition of the world. Much then transpires to elaborate the predicament of humanity thrown so largely on its own resources within a nature that, like Janus, shows two faces, one that shines on the beautiful, noble, and wise and another that countenances cruelty, meanness, and stupidity. As natural as the excellence of Socrates is the hatred and the folly that destroyed him.

Cropsey continues (p. 3) by calling to our attention that:

It belongs to the genius of Plato that he constructed a universe out of elements that exist in a condition of mutual (dialectical) tension, in a tacit, however limited, concession to the cosmology of stress. ... Plato's sifting of Protagoras runs through *Protagoras* and *Theaetetus*, the former dialogue addressing the climactic question of the coming to be of good and evil among men, the latter the companion question, What is knowledge? If virtue is knowledge, as Socrates must forever insist, then why is virtue not transmissible just as knowledge is transmissible in the act of teaching? And if virtue cannot be somehow "taught," what becomes of the moral pedagogy by which the best political constitution stands or falls? *Protagoras*, on the bringing of good among men (if not by teaching, then how?), is a spacious portal into the Platonic edifice.

But one can never be fully sure of the way in all of the labyrinth within this artistic edifice. We are all forever aporetic seekers who can never fully comprehend the mind and meaning of Plato any more than a mere man can the mysteries of a woman. For when was *Plato* surely decided?

The serious student of Plato who cannot read German is also pointed to the English translation of Ritter, 1968. The detailed Table of Contents is a useful guide to the Platonic corpus and Ritter's Preface ends with opinionated remarks highly apposite to what has been discussed in this chapter section and this endnote:

In conclusion I should like to direct a critical remark against the recent attempts, oft repeated, to stamp Plato as a mystic. These are wholly based on forged passages of the *Epistles*, which I can only consider as inferior achievements of spiritual poverty which seeks to take refuge in occultism. I am astonished that anyone can hail them as enlightened wisdom, as the final result of Platonic philosophizing. With reference to this point I can confidently direct English readers to Richards' *Platonica*, pp. 271 ff.

The reference by Ritter is to a work which has not been available to consult: Richards (1848–1916) (1911), *Platonica*, G. Richards: London. Still widely available in German is the study of Plato's life and works by Ulrich von Moellendorff (1959).

IV Plato's Ideal Political Theory: *The Republic*

Overview

The *Republic* is a multifaceted work, probably written when Plato was about 40 years of age and at the height of his creative and intellectual powers. Not only is the *Republic* a treatise on political science, but it is also a fairly systematic examination of educational, historical, economic, social, metaphysical, moral, and psychological subjects. It is, in effect, an attempt to arrive at a comprehensive philosophy of humanity, with emphasis on how humanity should behave and can be brought so to behave.

Central to the ethical problem of justifying the existence and behaviour of the state, is the idea of justice. Therefore, it is quite appropriate that 'The *Republic* ... has come down to us with a double title – '*the State*' (πολιτεία, or in Latin, *respublica*; whence the name by which it generally goes), '*or concerning Justice*' (Barker, 1960, p. 168).[1] Thus, the title and classification often accorded this work when one follows Diogenes Laertius is, more fully: *Polity: or concerning Justice, Political (Politeia, e peri dikaion, politikos*: Πολιτεία, ἡ περὶ δικαιον, πολιτικός).

By attempting to formulate the conception of a just state, Plato hopes to discover the nature of justice in the individual; and by attempting to formulate the principles and practices that characterize the just man, Plato hopes to bring into being the just state.

To what end? Justice, for Plato, seems as much a means as an end. The end sought is obviously a strong state brought about by the efficiency, unity, and harmony that justice should promote. Thus, justice has a double value for Plato: it is both instrumentally utilitarian for the *polis* and spiritually rewarding for the individual.

But what is justice? For Plato, much of justice consists in each man doing what he is qualified to do and being given what is his due in terms of status, power, wealth, rewards, and punishments. For Plato, therefore, it is unjust for a man to be doing what he is not qualified to do – or overqualified to do – or to be given either more or less than his due in terms of status, power, wealth, rewards, and punishments. Plato concludes that the just state rests on an organological, hierarchical ordering of society and government that is consonant with this conception of justice. The three classes that Plato arranges in this hierarchical structure are, in descending order: the *Guardian* class of philosopher-ruler-educators (*phulakes*: φυλακες); the *Auxiliary* class of soldier-administrators (*epikouroi*: ε'πικουροι); and the *Producer* class of farmers (the generic term Plato used), artisans, and labourers (*gèorgoi*: γεωργοι) who composed the bulk of the citizenry.

Exposition

Imperfect Government by Fallible Men Requires Justice

In Book I of the *Republic*, Plato indicates that fallible men must frequently be responsible for the making of laws which cannot be all-wise, the implication being that one cannot trust to the law alone for good government or justice. Certainly, therefore, justice cannot be 'the interest of the stronger' as Thrasymachus declares, because even though the strong may pass laws which they believe to be in their own interest, they may err. Thrasymachus replies that in so far as he is a ruler, a ruler does not err but enacts what is best for himself, and the subject must obey. However, Socrates (the presumed voice of Plato in the *Republic*) leads Thrasymachus to accept the idea that the practitioner of any art practices it for the benefit of the weaker who are ruled by it. The political ruler must therefore likewise be guided by principles of *noblesse oblige* and rule for the benefit of the ruled. The passage concludes:

> Then, I continued, no physician, in so far as he is a physician, considers his own good in what he prescribes, but the good of his patient; for the true physician is also a ruler having the human body as a subject, and is not a mere money-maker; that has been admitted?
> Yes.
> And the pilot likewise, in the strict sense of the term, is a ruler of sailors and not a mere sailor?
> That has been admitted.
> And such a pilot and ruler will provide and prescribe for the interest of the sailor who is under him, and not for his own or the ruler's interest?
> He gave a reluctant 'Yes.'
> Then, I said, Thrasymachus, there is no one in any rule who, in so far as he is a ruler, considers or enjoins what is for his own interest, but always what is for

the interest of his subject or suitable to his art; to that he looks, and that alone he considers in everything which he says and does (Bk I, 338 C–342 E).[2]

Why, then, should one want to burden oneself with political participation and office? Socrates discourses with Thrasymachus along lines which show a strong dependence upon human nature and the incentives which motivate it, whether positively or negatively. At the proper time, he points out that the greatest inducement for the wise and able to participate in government lies in the possibility of avoiding misrule if they themselves control the government:

> Wherefore necessity must be laid upon them, and they must be induced to serve from the fear of punishment. And this, as I imagine, is the reason why the forwardness to take office, instead of waiting to be compelled, has been deemed dishonourable. Now the worst part of the punishment is that he who refuses to rule is liable to be ruled by one who is worse than himself. And the fear of this, as I consider, induces the good to take office, not because they would, but because they cannot help – not under the idea that they are going to have any benefit or enjoy themselves, but as a necessity, and because they are not able to commit the task of ruling to any one who is better than themselves, or indeed as good (346 A–347 D).

Plato posits that for government to exist, it must be based on principles of justice, for the purely unjust are destructive of one another and incapable of common action (353 B–C). 'And we have admitted that justice is the excellence of the soul, and injustice the defect of the soul?' and so, 'Then the just soul and the just man will live well, and the unjust man will live ill? … And he who lives well is blessed and happy, and he who lives ill the reverse of happy?' (353 E–354 A). Plato, of course, cannot and does not, prove this.[3]

In Book II, Plato continues to expatiate on the nature of justice; he sets forth the proposition that justice may be the virtue of a state as well as of an individual. He claims that the justice of a state is both larger and more discernible; and says that by our imagining the state in a process of creation, we may then see its justice and injustice. The state comes into being because individuals are not self-sufficient: they cannot satisfy alone their needs for food, shelter, and clothing, and they will also come to want relishes and pleasures. Thus, Plato's conception of justice begins to emerge here as one wherein each man does what he is best qualified to do in order to serve the needs of one another (Bk II, 368 E–374 E).[4]

Elitism, Asceticism, and Education

Consequently, what logically follows is the central political belief of Plato that it is just that those who are qualified to rule should participate in government and it is unjust for the unqualified to participate. The business of ruling a government should therefore be restricted to a ruling class of Guardians. But what are the qualities which make it just for an individual to be a member of such a ruling class? For Plato, they are those of the philosopher, who by his definition is a lover of learning and wisdom and therefore gentle to his friends and acquaintances. As one of his first safeguards of good government and justice – which Plato seems to regard as practically synonymous – we find Plato demanding in his Guardian class the love of wisdom, high spirit, quickness, and strength (376 B–C).[5]

In Book II, we further find Plato stressing the education of these heroes, as he calls them. The education is to include gymnastics for the body and music for the soul (376 C–377 A).[6] This education has added to it the reinforcing influences of a rigid censorship that starts even with the nursery tales that the very young are to be permitted to hear (377 B–E).[7]

Such an approach would, of course, be most difficult of accomplishment. Folk tales die hard, many of them surviving across millennia. Furthermore, the nursery tales told to children are sometimes the impromptu results of fanciful imaginations activated by importunate pleading. Evidently, Plato's experience with children, nurses, mothers, and women in general was all too limited. One suspects that a great deal of the asceticism that one finds in Plato may have been the result of a life of celibacy in which he missed much of the tender devotion, lust, anger, worry, heartache, laughter, and just plain silliness that go with marriage and parenthood. Indeed, in Book III, we find Plato unrealistically (or ironically?) inveighing against the enjoyment of excessive laughter by men or gods, or even representation of such indulgence by deities (Bk III, 388 E–389 A).

Having limited freedom and laughter and having eliminated the 'unworthy' from participation in government, Plato proposes also to limit lying and dishonesty in the state. The citizens are to be chastised for lying; and above all, they are not to lie to their rulers, for that would be against their own interests as well as those of the state. The analogy of maintaining the health of the body politic and of the body physical is employed to make his point in an interchange between Socrates and Adeimantus:

Again, truth should be highly valued; if, as we were saying, a lie is useless to the gods, and useful only as a medicine to men, then the use of such medicines should be restricted to physicians; private individuals have no business with them.

Clearly not, he said.

Then if any one at all is to have the privilege of lying, the rulers of the State should be the persons; and they, in their dealings either with enemies or with their own citizens, may be allowed to lie for the public good. But nobody else should meddle with anything of the kind; and although the rulers have this privilege, for a private man to lie to them in return is to be deemed a more heinous fault than for the patient or the pupil of a gymnasium not to speak the truth about his own bodily illnesses to the physician or to the trainer, or for a sailor not to tell the captain what is happening about the ship and the rest of the crew, and how things are going with himself or his fellow sailors (389 B–D).

Plato continues to discourse with reference to the Guardians by asking intemperate youth to be temperate, obedient, and self-controlled, especially regarding sensual pleasures (389 D–390 D). He opposes intemperate indulgence in food and drink, and calls for a Spartan diet:

That they must abstain from intoxication has been already remarked by us; for of all persons a guardian should be the last to get drunk and not know where in the world he is.

Yes, he said; that a guardian should require another guardian to take care of him is ridiculous indeed (403 D–404 E).

Plato decries intemperateness in sexual activity for the Guardians by deprecating the tempestuous affairs of Zeus with Hera and Ares with Aphrodite (390 C). He follows by pointing out the corrupting influence of money and gifts (390 D–E). More on the positive side, Plato asserts that conditioning and habits that include avoidance of bad example and emphasis on practice of what is good, can make the Guardians virtuous:

If then we adhere to our original notion and bear in mind that our guardians, setting aside every other business, are to dedicate themselves wholly to the maintenance of freedom in the State, making this their craft, and engaging in no work which does not bear on this end, they ought not to practise or imitate anything else; if they imitate at all, they should imitate from youth upward only those characters which are suitable to their profession – the courageous, temperate, holy, free, and the like; but they should not depict or be skilful at imitating any kind of illiberality or baseness, lest from imitation they should come to be what they imitate. Did you never observe how imitations, beginning in early youth and continuing far into life, at length grow into habits and become a second nature, affecting body, voice, and mind? (395 B–396 E).

Elimination of sensuous music and musical instruments is advocated, with only the lyre to be retained for use in the city and the pipe for shepherds in the country. In further discussion of the usefulness of a proper musical training, Plato declares it a more potent and ennobling influence than any other (398 E–403 C. After music, Plato favours gymnastics as an effective means of influencing character (403 C–404 E). In similar vein, Plato calls for the pursuit of such arts and crafts as painting, weaving, and architecture to develop appreciation of artistic beauty as a means of enhancing desirable personal qualities of grace, rhythm, and sobriety (401 A–C and 403 A).[8] Closely related to proper music and artistic grace and a guiding principle in all matters, is the central one of temperateness that promotes virtuous behaviour and the love of beauty while eschewing intemperance in physical love:

> But let me ask you another question: Has excess of pleasure any affinity to temperance?
> How can that be? he replied; pleasure deprives a man of the use of his faculties quite as much as pain.
> Or any affinity to virtue in general?
> None whatever.
> Any affinity to wantonness and intemperance?
> Yes, the greatest.
> And is there any greater or keener pleasure than that of sensual love?
> No, nor a madder.
> Whereas true love is a love of beauty and order – temperate and harmonious?
> Quite true, he said.
> Then no intemperance or madness should be allowed to approach true love?
> Certainly not.
> Then mad or intemperate pleasure must never be allowed to come near the lover and his beloved; neither of them can have any part in it if their love is of the right sort?
> No, indeed, Socrates, it must never come near them.
> Then I suppose that in the city which we are founding you would make a law to the effect that a friend should use no other familiarity to his love than a father would use to his son, and then only for a noble purpose, and he must first have the other's consent; and this rule is to limit him in all his intercourse, and he is never to be seen going further, or, if he exceeds, he is to be deemed guilty of coarseness and bad taste.
> I quite agree, he said.

Thus much of music, which makes a fair ending; for what should be the end of music if not the love of beauty? (402 E–403 C)[9]

Consequently, Plato would censor poetical rhyme and metrical forms in favour of simplicity and calls for grace and beauty in all forms of art, not ugliness (398 C–402 E).[10]

Indoctrination and Education for Justice and Security Based on Specialization and Hierarchy

The keystone of Plato's arch of justice is his rock-hard advocacy of the proposition that justice and resultant harmony and strength ensue when the shoemaker sticks to his last:

> And this is the reason why in our State, and in our state only, we shall find a shoemaker to be a shoemaker and not a pilot also, and a husbandman to be a husbandman and not a dicast also, and a soldier a soldier and not a trader also, and the same throughout?
> True, he said (397 E. See also 374 B–C).

Plato warns against what he considers to be the extremes of either the softness of a mere musician or the savagery of a mere athlete, and advocates instead the properly educated philosopher who is sober, brave, gentle, and orderly (410 B–411 A). The best of the elders should rule the younger; the houses of soldiers should be the houses of soldiers, not housekeepers; and the possession of private property by the Guardians should be limited to personal items only (412 C–417 B).

Perhaps the most significant concern of Plato in Book III is whether his educational programme actually can accomplish his aims. He therefore focuses his attention, for example, on the problem of protection of the community from the Auxiliaries or soldier class: i.e., that the protecting sheep dogs do not become wolves. 'The right education' is a *sine qua non* to accomplish this:

> And therefore every care must be taken that our auxiliaries, being stronger than our citizens, may not grow to be too much for them and become savage tyrants instead of friends and allies.
> Yes, great care should be taken.
> And would not a really good education furnish the best safeguard?
> But they are well-educated already, he replied.

I cannot be so confident, my dear Glaucon, I said; I am much more certain that they ought to be, and that true education, whatever that may be, will have the greatest tendency to civilize and humanize them in their relations to one another, and to those who are under their protection (416 A–C).[11]

Balancing and Unifying of Classes

Book IV includes discussion by Plato of class warfare and its deleterious effects. Indeed, Plato's projected scheme of government is predicated on the principle of balancing and unifying the various classes. Such an arrangement of the *polis*, Plato believes, would provide his city-state with the kind of tremendous strength that would enable it to rip enemy forces apart in the same manner as the Greeks had destroyed the Persian army at Marathon (490 BC):

> You ought to speak of other States in the plural number; not one of them is a city, but many cities, as they say in the game. For indeed any city, however small, is in fact divided into two, one the city of the poor, the other of the rich; these are at war with one another; and in either there are many smaller divisions, and you would be altogether beside the mark if you treated them all as a single State. But if you deal with them as many, and give the wealth or power or persons of the one to the others, you will always have a great many friends and not many enemies. And your State, will be the greatest of States, I do not mean to say in reputation or appearance, but in deed and truth, though she number not a thousand defenders. A single State which is her equal you will hardly find, either among Hellenes or barbarians, though many that appear to be as great and many times greater.
>
> That is most true, he said.
>
> And what, I said, will be the best limit for our rulers to fix when they are considering the size of the State and the amount of territory which they are to include, and beyond which they will not go?
>
> What limit would you propose?
>
> I would allow the State to increase so far as is consistent with unity; that, I think, is the proper limit (Bk IV, 422 E–423 B).

Plato does not have in mind for this united city a generally communistic, classless society. Only within certain groups – especially the Guardian class – is there to be a form of common ownership or utilization of facilities and sharing of functions. Ernest Barker (1960, pp. 198 f) lays bare the tripartite class structure of guardian-rulers, soldier-auxiliaries, and farmer-producers and consequent personality-limiting nature of Plato's *Republic*, in the following analysis:

The Platonic State as a whole, therefore, is a community marked by a division of labour between three specialized classes,[1] ([1] *I.e.* it is what Aristotle criticizes it for not being, a κοινωνία [*koinonia*: communion or association – RP] constituted of elements different in kind, each making a different contribution to a common good, and profiting by the contributions of the rest.) the rulers (or 'perfect guardians'), the soldiers (at first called 'guardians', and afterwards 'auxiliaries'), and the producing classes (whom Plato calls the 'farmers'). There is a *Lehrstand* [teaching class – RP], a *Wehrstand* [soldier class – RP], and *Nährstand* [servant class – RP]: there are, as in the medieval conception of 'the three estates', *oratores, bellatores,* and *laboratores.* The three several elements of mind which constitute the State are therefore not only to be logically distinguished as factors in its logical genesis (as has hitherto been done); they are actually distinct as classes in its external organization. This implies that each of the several elements (appetite, spirit, and reason) is particularly and essentially prominent in particular individuals or bodies of individuals. There is one small body in which reason is prominent: another, and larger, which is dominated by spirit: a third, by far the largest, in which appetite is paramount.[1] ([1] Plato seems to be adopting and amplifying the Pythagorean doctrine of the Three Classes – φιλοκερδεῖς, φιλότιμοι, and φιλόσοφοι. [Lovers of gain (*philokerdeis*), honour (*philotimoi*), and wisdom (*philosophoi*), respectively – RP.] This is quite another contention from the primary contention that each element of mind is a factor in constituting the full life of the State; and it is a contention which is far more dubious. The State may be and indeed is a product of mind; but it does not follow that the State is or should be divided into classes which correspond to the different elements of mind. In each individual mind all these elements are present; but if in the State each man is limited to an activity which corresponds to one element only, is he not forced to live as a citizen with a single part of his mind? The ruler must live by reason: therefore, Plato argues, he must abandon appetite; and he is accordingly brought under a communistic regime which prevents the play of appetite, and thus involves the paralysis of an integral element in human nature. Again the farmer must live for the satisfaction of appetite; he must be regulated in that life by the external reason of the perfect guardian; and thus he suffers an atrophy of his rational self.[12]

The main purpose of such class division and specialization, therefore, is the attainment of a self-sufficient unity. The ideal city, then, is to be of moderate size but surpassingly unified and complete unto itself.

Here then, I said, is another order which will have to be conveyed to our guardians: Let our city be accounted neither large nor small, but one and self-sufficing (423 C).

Environmentalism, Eugenics, and Religion

Plato returns again to his theme of the inherent justice to be found in specialization according to the talents of each individual. Such a basic premise logically requires a re-evaluation of each generation, and this Plato is prepared to do:

> And the other, said I, of which we were speaking before is lighter still, – I mean the duty of degrading the offspring of the guardians when inferior, and of elevating into the rank of guardians the offspring of the lower classes, when naturally superior. The intention was, that, in the case of the citizens generally, each individual should be put to the use for which nature intended him, one to one work, and then every man would do his own business, and be one and not many; and so the whole city would be one and not many (423 C–D).

More and more it appears that Plato may be anticipating the modern controversy over the relative importance of breeding versus environmental conditioning. Plato accepts the importance of both factors and seeks to improve each generation to the limit of its capacity and also to increase the potential of succeeding generations. At this point he touches but lightly on the subject of group marriage:

> The regulations which we are prescribing, my good Adeimantus, are not, as might be supposed, a number of great principles, but trifles all, if care be taken, as the saying is, of the one great thing, – a thing, however, which I would rather call, not, great, but sufficient for our purpose.
> What may that be? he asked.
> Education, I said, and nurture: If our citizens are well educated, and grow into sensible men, they will easily see their way through all these, as well as other matters which I omit; such, for example, as marriage, the possession of women and the procreation of children, which will all follow the general principle that friends have all things in common, as the proverb says.
> That will be the best way of settling them.
> Also, I said; the State, if once started well, moves with accumulating force like a wheel. For good nurture and education implant good constitutions, and these good constitutions taking root in a good education improve more and more, and this improvement affects the breed in man as in other animals (423 D–424 B).[13]

Plato also discusses the role of religion in achieving the unity and character of his model city-state. Although he seldom dwells upon religion in his political works, Plato treats it and 'the inhabitants of the world below' most deferentially and, in most matters, does not break with the core of theological orthodoxy of his time and place (427 B–C).[14] There is a modern ring to Plato's usual separation of the business of religion from the business of legislation. And because Plato is willing to employ myths that he recognizes to be untrue and that he may even tailor-make or alter to suit his purposes, one may suspect he is not altogether a sincere believer in the religious convictions and practices of his day.

Cardinal Virtues of the Ideal State

In Book IV, Plato also reviews the four cardinal virtues of the ideal state: wisdom, bravery, temperateness, and justice (427 E).

To wisdom, Plato assigns the position of being first among the virtues of the perfect state (428 B). The location of wisdom, as may be expected, is in the Guardian class (428 E–429 A).

Bravery, Plato ascribes chiefly to the Auxiliaries, the military class of his community: 'The rest of the citizens may be courageous or may be cowardly, but their courage or cowardice will not, as I conceive, have the effect of making the city either the one or the other' (429 A–B).

Here, again, Plato has permitted his use of logic to lead him astray, for the fighting force of any community must inevitably reflect to a great extent the general spiritual qualities of that community. No spiritual or intellectual quality may be exercised in any segment of the community without effect on, or from, other segments. Plato does, however, come close to this general proposition – although at the expense of some consistency – when he ascribes temperance to all classes. But there is something that does not ring true when Plato holds that it is only the wise few who can be relied upon to lead us into the paths of soberness or temperance. Even the act of following into such paths requires a bit of reasonableness and self-control (430 D–432 A).

Justice Based on Hierarchical Specialization

Plato now approaches the structural basis of his political theory, which is a pyramidal, hierarchical, organological arrangement of society – and this Plato represents as just. Small wonder that during the feudalistic Middle Ages both the clerical hierarchy and the politico-socio-economic hierarchy were to be typically neo-Platonic in outlook and to extol the virtues of Plato and Aristotle in their support of such a scheme. This description of Plato's view of justice is developed as follows:

Well then, tell me, I said, whether I am right or not: You remember the original principle which we were always laying down at the foundation of the State, that one man would practise one thing only, the thing to which his nature was best adapted; – now justice is this principle or a part of it.

Yes, we often said that one man should do one thing only.

Further, we affirmed that justice was doing one's own business, and not being a busybody; we said so again and again, and many others have said the same to us.

...

... Are not the rulers in a State those to whom you would entrust the office of determining suits at law?

Certainly.

And are suits decided on any other ground but that a man may neither take what is another's, nor be deprived of what is his own?

Yes; that is their principle.

Which is a just principle?

Yes.

Then on this view also justice will be admitted to be the having and doing of what is a man's own, and belongs to him?

Very true.

Think, now, and say whether you agree with me or not. Suppose a carpenter to be doing the business of a cobbler, or a cobbler of a carpenter; and suppose them to exchange their implements or their duties, or the same person to be doing the work of both, or whatever be the change; do you think that any great harm would result to the State?

Not much.

But when the cobbler or any other many whom nature designed to be a trader, having his heart lifted up by wealth or strength or the number of his followers, or any like advantage, attempts to force his way into the class of warriors, or a warrior into that of legislators and guardians, for which he is unfitted, and either to take the implements or the duties of the other; or when one man is trader, legislator, and warrior all in one, then I think you will agree with me in saying that this interchange and this meddling of one with another is the ruin of the State.

Most true.

Seeing then, I said, that there are three distinct classes, any meddling of one with another, or the change of one into another, is the greatest harm to the State, and may be most justly termed evil-doing?

Precisely.

And the greatest degree of evil-doing to one's own city would be termed by you injustice?

Certainly.

This then is injustice; and on the other hand when the trader, the auxiliary, and the guardian each do their own business, that is justice, and will make the city just (433 A–434 C).[15]

Women, Breeding, and Social Mobility

Book V is interesting for the ideas and practices Plato advocates concerning the rearing and role of women. Women are obviously different in some respects from men, and nature has assigned them fundamentally different roles when it comes to reproduction and nurturing of the young, but Plato would assign them similar training and duties because he finds that men and women are more alike than different. He argues, for example, that one does not differentiate between a male or female dog on the chase, and that both men and women are used for farm labour. Therefore, Plato urges similar nurture, education, activities, and – presumably – opportunities *for men and women of the Guardian class* (Bk V, 449 A–457 B, especially 451 C–452 A).[16] Accordingly, Plato proposes that the *Guardian class* have their women and children in common, and advocates a system of strict eugenic breeding. He considers such an arrangement as of the greatest good to the state (458 C–461 E).[17]

One cannot help wondering whether Plato was writing whimsically concerning group marriage for the Guardians. Although polyandry was at one time practised in Sparta as a means of keeping landed inheritances intact, there was at least a single family-hearth retained. Certainly what Plato proposes here was a revolutionary scheme that would have destroyed the family-hearth basis of Greek religion for at least the Guardians (464 A–D).[18]

Book V also repeats Plato's espousal of a certain degree of social mobility, especially where he advocates the downgrading of the cowards in battle to the rank of husbandman or artisan. On the positive side, he supports heaping rewards and honours upon the brave, some of which are decidedly not ascetic in character (468 A–E). In any event, what we have here again are proposals intended to promote a militarily strong state.

Doubt of Practicability

Book V is also important for Plato's admission of doubt concerning both the practicability and even the theoretical perfection of his model state. He acknowledges to Glaucon that it may be only a dream or wish-thought (450 C–D). However, Plato finds the task of the inquiry still worthwhile:

Would a painter be any the worse because, after having delineated with consummate art an ideal of a perfectly beautiful man, he was unable to show that any such man could ever have existed?

He would be none the worse.

Well, and were we not creating an ideal of a perfect State?

To be sure.

And is our theory a worse theory because we are unable to prove the possibility of a city being ordered in the manner described?

Surely not, he replied.

That is the truth, I said. But if, at your request, I am to try and show how and under what conditions the possibility is highest, I must ask you, having this in view, to repeat your former admissions.

What admissions?

I want to know whether ideals are ever fully realized in language? Does not the word express more than the fact, and must not the actual, whatever a man may think, always, in the nature of things, fall short of the truth? What do you say?

I agree.

Then you must not insist on my proving that the actual State will in every respect coincide with the ideal: if we are only able to discover how a city may be governed nearly as we proposed, you will admit that we have discovered the possibility which you demand; and will be contented. I am sure that I should be contented – will not you?

Yes, I will (472 D–473 B).

Scepticism, Philosophy, and Praxis

Book VI consists mainly of repetition and speculative philosophy, rather than political theory, and therefore calls for limited attention in this work (Bk VI, 484 A–511 E). In Book VII, however, careful note should be taken of the famous shadows-on-the-wall discussion of how appearances may be mistaken for reality. Indeed, there are in this discussion and in Plato's general philosophy the seeds of liberalism, especially scepticism, which must to some extent set at naught much of Plato's political theory that should simply be viewed as reactionary. For example, in addition to expressing some of his beliefs about mathematical education, astronomy, and dialectic (the 'coping-stone' of the sciences), Plato advocates that twice as much time be spent in the study of dialectic (or logic) as in bodily exercises (Bk VII, 514 A–541 B, especially 514 A–519 D, 524 E–531 C, 532 E–534 E, and 539 A–520 E). This study of dialectic (or logic) is embodied within the larger area of philosophy, Plato's greatest love (539 D–540 B).[19]

Cycle of Forms of Government

Books VIII and IX include a lengthy analysis of the cycle of different forms of government. It reveals Plato's fundamental beliefs about the causes of the decline and fall of various forms of government and also some of his ideas about what helps to stabilize and preserve a government. The forms of government discussed in these books are: *aristocracy* (government by the best, for which he expresses a preference); *timocracy* (the government of honour, exemplified by Crete and Sparta); *oligarchy* (defined by Plato as government by the rich, rather than by the few); *democracy* (government by the many); *tyranny* (government by one unrestrained by law, and the worst); and only in passing here, *monarchy* or *royalty* (government by one superior wise-man). It should be noted that Plato terms the hierarchical-organological *polis* he has been describing as, variously, aristocracy or royalty. He does not clearly indicate here, as he does in later works, that what he prefers above all – the rule of a philosopher-king (or philosopher-ruler) – is a form of monarchy (Bk VIII, 453 A–569 C).[20]

Aristocracy Yields to Timocracy

Plato starts his cycle of government in Book VIII by identifying four basic forms: timocracy, oligarchy, democracy, and tyranny. The transformation he first considers at any length is that from aristocracy to timocracy. Change from any form of government, he declares, originates in failure to keep its ruling class properly unified:

> First, then, I said, let us enquire how timocracy (the government of honour) arises out of aristocracy (the government of the best). Clearly, all political changes originate in divisions of the actual governing power; a government which is united, however small, cannot be moved (545 C–D).

But Plato relaxes this rigid assertion enough to permit even the best of governments to come to an end (546 A). Next, after describing what we may accept as a life-cycle or time clock that he ascribes to all forms of plant and animal life, Plato attempts to quantify and formularize them and to assert the existence of perfect numbers and mathematical controls that apply to human procreation and birth. Plato then declares as the reason for the decline and end of aristocracy the failure of his Guardian class to mate at proper times of the year (546 A–D).[21] Employing a literary device whereby the Muses explain this degeneration of the Guardian stock, Socrates (i.e., Plato) relates how there is a parallel degeneration of the form of government from aristocracy ('the perfect state') to timocracy, a mixture of good and evil that is 'intermediate between oligarchy and aristocracy':

> But in the fear of admitting philosophers to power, because they are no longer to be had simple and earnest, but are made up of mixed elements; and in turning from them to passionate and less complex characters, who are by nature fitted for war rather than peace; and in the value set by them upon military stratagems and contrivances, and in the waging of everlasting wars – this State will be for the most part peculiar.
>
> Yes.
>
> Yes, I said; and men of this stamp will be covetous of money, like those who live in oligarchies; they will have a fierce secret longing after gold and silver, which they will hoard in dark places, having magazines and treasuries of their own for the deposit and concealment of them; also castles which are just nests for their eggs, and in which they will spend large sums on their wives, or on any others whom they please (547 A–548 C).

Plato discourses at length on the nature of the timocratic young man and the circumstances and motivations that bring him to power. The timocratic youth may be motivated to rise to power because of the importuning of his mother and houseslaves to be 'more of a man than his father', who had exercised certain personal restraints and good taste. The father is nagged and shamed by the mother, who holds him up to ridicule by contrasting him with more aggressive men who have gained greater power and wealth. The young man becomes fired with ambition, haughty, self-willed, covetous, appetitive, and passionate; but he is submissive to higher authority in a manner that brings to mind Theodor Adorno and his associates' description of the authoritarian personality (see Adorno et al., 1950, pp. 599 f and 971). His contentious nature and that of the timocratic state are described as follows:

> He should have more of self-assertion and be less cultivated, and yet a friend of culture; and he should be a good listener, but no speaker. Such a person is apt to be rough with slaves, unlike the educated man, who is too proud for that; and he will also be courteous to freemen, and remarkably obedient to authority; he is a lover of power and a lover of honour; claiming to be a ruler, not because he is eloquent, or on any ground of that sort, but because he is a soldier and has performed feats of arms; he is also a lover of gymnastic exercises and of the chase.
>
> Yes, that is the type of character which answers to timocracy.
>
> Such a one will despise riches only when he is young; but as he gets older he will be more and more attracted to them, because he has a piece of the avaricious

nature in him, and is not single-minded towards virtue, having lost his best guardian.

Who was that? said Adeimantus.

Philosophy, I said, tempered with music, who comes and takes up her abode in a man, and is the only saviour of his virtue throughout life.

Good, he said.

Such, I said, is the timocratical youth, and he is like the timocratical State (548 E–550 B).

Timocracy Yields to Oligarchy

Oligarchy, the form of government that is supposed to succeed timocracy (or timarchy), is defined in Plato as a regime that today we should more properly term plutocracy (i.e., government by the wealthy): 'A government resting on a valuation of property, in which the rich have power and the poor man is deprived of it' (550 C–D).

The rise of oligarchy and Plato's aversion to it (i.e., really to plutocracy) are presented in a revealing exchange between Socrates and Adeimantus that shows Plato's firm belief in the corrupting influence of wealth and greed. The accumulation of private treasure is held to be the ruination of timocracy, along with the property qualifications they establish for citizenship and a share in the government. Both timocracy and democracy seem to pass over into plutocratic oligarchy by similar steps. But what would happen, Socrates asks, if pilots were chosen according to their wealth and a better pilot were not permitted to steer? The impractical results then are a bad voyage, a misruled city, and a divided city. The following relevant passages of dialogue conclude with the often-quoted, very significant observation about the disunited city of the rich and of the poor and the continuing class warfare between them:

And so they grow richer and richer, and the more they think of making a fortune the less they think of virtue; for when riches and virtue are placed together in the scales of balance, the one always rises as the other falls.

True.

And in proportion as riches and rich men are honoured in the State, virtue and the virtuous are dishonoured.

Clearly.

And what is honoured is cultivated, and that which has no honour is neglected.

That is obvious.

And so at last, instead of loving contention and glory, men become lovers of trade and money; they honour and look up to the rich man and make a ruler of him, and dishonour the poor man.

They do so.

They next proceed to make a law which fixes a sum of money as the qualification of citizenship; the sum is higher in one place and lower in another, as the oligarchy is more or less exclusive; and they allow no one whose property falls below the amount fixed to have any share in the government. These changes in the constitution they effect by force of arms, if intimidation has not already done their work.

...

First of all, I said, consider the nature of the qualification. Just think what would happen if pilots were chosen according to their property, and a poor man were refused permission to steer, even though he were a better pilot?

You mean they would shipwreck?

Yes; and is not this true of the government of anything?

I should imagine so.

Except a city? – or would you include a city?

Nay, he said, the case of a city is the strongest of all, inasmuch as the rule of a city is the greatest and most difficult of all.

This, then, will be the first great defect of oligarchy?

Clearly.

And here is another defect which is quite as bad.

What defect?

The inevitable division: such a State is not one, but two states, the one of poor, the other of rich men; and they are living on the same spot and always conspiring against one another (550 D–551 D).

The division and consequent weakness of oligarchy (plutocracy) are ascribed in the main to too much diversity of occupation by the same individual, to too much extremity of wealth and poverty, and to the opportunity to divest oneself of property, which may leave one dwelling in misery without occupation in the city (551 D–552 E).

Oligarchy Yields to Democracy

Under oligarchy (plutocracy), the wealthy become bloated and soft in property, body, and spirit. The poor come to see their greater strength of will and body, and despoil the wealthy of their lives, their property, and their control of government. The process whereby oligarchy yields to democracy is sketched in a passage which, again, indicates an organological aspect to Plato's political theory:

Such is the state of affairs which prevails among them. And often rulers and

their subjects may come in one another's way, whether on a journey or on some
other occasion of a meeting on a pilgrimage or a march, as fellow-soldiers or
fellow-sailors; aye and they may observe the behaviour of each other in the
very moment of danger – for where danger is, there is no fear that the poor will
be despised by the rich – and very likely the wiry sunburnt poor man may be
placed in battle at the side of a wealthy one who has never spoilt his complexion
and has plenty of superfluous flesh – when he sees such an one puffing and at
his wit's-end, how can he avoid drawing the conclusion that men like him are
only rich because no one has the courage to despoil them? And when they meet
in private will not people be saying to one another 'Our warriors are not good
for much'?

Yes, he said, I am quite aware that this is their way of talking.

And, as in a body which is diseased the addition of a touch from without may
bring on illness, and sometimes even when there is no external provocation a
commotion may arise within – in the same way wherever there is weakness in
the State there is also likely to be illness, of which the occasions may be very
slight, the one party introducing from without their oligarchical, the other their
democratical allies, and then the State falls sick, and is at war with herself; and
may be at times distracted, even when there is no external cause.

Yes, surely.

And then democracy comes into being after the poor have conquered their
opponents, slaughtering some and banishing some, while to the remainder they
give an equal share of freedom and power; and this is the form of government
in which the magistrates are commonly elected by lot (555 B–557 A).

Description of Democracy

Plato's description of democratic life has been quoted often, and its poetic,
flowing picturization has been used to unfair advantage by those who pose
this simplistic version of irresponsible and impolite people – and even animals!
– as representative of all democracy. Plato ascribes to democracy what is
more properly to be regarded as representative of dangers and undesirable
developments to be found in an exaggerated and spoiled form of democracy.
The jaundiced view of democracy that Plato offers for consideration is more
correctly to be perceived as that of a failed or very imperfect democracy. He
discourses upon democracy and the democratic man, for example, in the
following familiar passages:

> In the first place, are they not free; and is not the city full of freedom and
> frankness – a man may say and do what he likes?
>
> 'Tis said so, he replied.

And where freedom is, the individual is clearly able to order for himself his own life as he pleases?

Clearly.

Then in this kind of State will be the greatest variety of human natures?

There will.

This, then, seems likely to be the fairest of States, being like an embroidered robe which is spangled with every sort of flower. And just as women and children think a variety of colours to be of all things most charming, so there are many men to whom this State, which is spangled with the manners and characters of mankind, will appear to be the fairest of States.

Yes.

...

These and other kindred characteristics are proper to democracy, which is a charming form of government, full of variety and disorder, and dispensing a sort of equality to equals and unequals alike.

...

And when they have emptied and swept clean the soul of him who is now in their power and who is being initiated by them in great mysteries, the next thing is to bring back to their house insolence and anarchy and waste and impudence in bright array having garlands on their heads, and a great company with them, hymning their praises and calling them by sweet names; insolence they term breeding, and anarchy liberty, and waste magnificence, and impudence courage. And so the young man passes out of his original nature, which was trained in the school of necessity, into the freedom and libertinism of useless and unnecessary pleasures.

...

Yes, I said, he lives from day to day indulging the appetite of the hour; and sometimes he is lapped in drink and strains of the flute; then he becomes a water-drinker, and tries to get thin; then he takes a turn at gymnastics; sometimes idling and neglecting everything, then once more living the life of a philosopher; often he is busy with politics, and starts to his feet and says and does whatever comes into his head; and, if he is emulous of any one who is a warrior, off he is in that direction, or of men of business, once more in that. His life has neither law nor order; and this distracted existence he terms joy and bliss and freedom; and so he goes on.

Yes, he replied, he is all liberty and equality.

Yes, I said; his life is motley and manifold and an epitome of the lives of many; – he answers to the State which we described as fair and spangled. And many a man and many a woman will take him for their pattern, and many a constitution and many an example of manners is contained in him (557 A–562 A).

Democracy Breeds Tyranny

One of Plato's professed guiding principles is the traditional Greek habit in thought and deed of moderation, or the middle place or way (*meson*: μέσον). In the prevalent view of classical Greece, 'the golden mean between two extremes' produces *eudaimonia* (ἐυδαμονία), the practice of right, happy living (literally 'under a good demon') to which every true philosopher aspires for himself and others. Themistocles is reputed to have put the formula succinctly as 'nothing overmuch'. Plato anticipates Newton's third principle of motion that 'each action has an equal opposite reaction'. He does this in an extensive passage that again shows his organological assumptions and states his premise that an excess of liberty, in democracy as in oligarchy, brings about the destruction of liberty and leads to its opposite: slavery and tyranny. This commentary is so continuingly relevant that much of it reads like a description of our contemporary permissive society:

> And democracy has her own good, of which the insatiable desire brings her to dissolution?
>   What good?
>   Freedom, I replied; which, as they tell you in a democracy, is the glory of the State – and that therefore in a democracy alone will the freeman of nature deign to dwell.
>   Yes; the saying is in everybody's mouth.
>   I was going to observe, that the insatiable desire of this and the neglect of other things introduces the change in democracy, which occasions a demand for tyranny.
>   How so?
>   When a democracy which is thirsting for freedom has evil cupbearers presiding over the feast, and has drunk too deeply of the strong wine of freedom, then, unless her rulers are very amenable and give a plentiful draught, she calls them to account and punishes them, and says that they are cursed oligarchs.
>   Yes, he replied, a very common occurrence.
>   Yes, I said; and loyal citizens are insultingly termed by her slaves who hug their chains and men of naught; she would have subjects who are like rulers, and rulers who are like subjects: these are men after her own heart, whom she praises and honours both in private and public. Now, in such a State, can liberty have any limit?
>   Certainly not.
>   By degrees the anarchy finds a way into private houses, and ends by getting among the animals and infecting them.
>   How do you mean?

I mean that the father grows accustomed to descend to the level of his sons and to fear them, and the son is on a level with his father, he having no respect or reverence for either of his parents; and this is his freedom, and the metic is equal with the citizen and the citizen with the metic, and the stranger is quite as good as either.

Yes, he said, that is the way.

And these are not the only evils, I said – there are several lesser ones: In such a state of society the master fears and flatters his scholars, and the scholars despise their masters and tutors; young and old are alike; and the young man is on a level with the old, and is ready to compete with him in word or deed; and old men condescend to the young and are full of pleasantry and gaiety; they are loth to be thought morose and authoritative, and therefore adopt the manners of the young.

Quite true, he said.

The last extreme of popular liberty is when the slave bought with money, whether male or female, is just as free as his or her purchaser: nor must I forget to tell of the liberty and equality of the two sexes in relation to each other.

Why not, as Aeschylus says, utter the word which rises to our lips?

That is what I am doing, I replied; and I must add that no one who does not know would believe, how much greater is the liberty which the animals who are under the dominion of man have in a democracy than in any other State: for truly, the she-dogs, as the proverb says, are as good as their she-mistresses, and the horses and asses have a way of marching along with all the rights and dignities of freemen; and they will run at anybody who comes in their way if he does not leave the road clear for them: and all things are just ready to burst with liberty.

...

The ruin of oligarchy is the ruin of democracy; the same disease magnified and intensified by liberty overmasters democracy – the truth being that the excessive increase of anything often causes a reaction in the opposite direction; and this is the case not only in the seasons and in vegetable and animal life, but above all in forms of government (562 B–564 C).

Democracy is divided by Plato into three classes: those few who trade and become wealthy merchants; those who make their living by working with their hands and are the mass of the people; and an excess of drones who are largely nonproductive. The excess of liberty and drones in a democracy leads to its downfall and the emergence of tyranny. The tyrant appears first as a champion and protector of the people, and then becomes the enslaver and despoiler of all. The passage concludes with comparison of the tyrant to a voracious wolf (564 C–566A).

Tyranny Worst and Kingship Best

Book IX of the *Republic* begins with a discussion of the grossly self-indulgent nature of the tyrannical man. He is starkly painted as irrational, evil, and drunk with power, indulging – like Nietzsche's 'great blond beast' when abroad – in all kinds of actions that should be restrained by law, custom, or conscience. This is because the usually rational part of the psyche slumbers while the passionate part sallies forth to satisfy certain lustful appetites:

> I mean those which are awake when the reasoning and human and ruling power is asleep; then the wild beast within us, gorged with meat or drink, starts up and having shaken off sleep, goes forth to satisfy his desires; and there is no conceivable folly or crisis – not excepting incest or any other unnatural union, or parricide, or the eating of forbidden food – which at such time, when he has parted company with all shame and sense, a man may not be ready to commit (Bk IX, 571 B–D and 573 B–C).[22]

A theme that appears frequently in the Platonic dialogues is that the form of government and the nature of the individual and his degree of happiness correspond to one another. Thus, the tyrannical state produces a character in ruler and ruled that is in conformity with the nature of that state and the degree of happiness therein. Accordingly, kingship and tyranny are antithetical forms that are, respectively, the best and the worst forms of government:

> And must not the tyrannical man be like the tyrannical State, and the democratical man like the democratical State; and the same of the others?
> Certainly.
> And as the State is to State in virtue and happiness, so is man in relation to man?
> To be sure.
> Then comparing our original city, which was under a king, and the city which is under a tyrant, how do they stand as to virtue?
> They are the opposite extremes, he said, for one is the very best and the other is the very worst (576 C–D and 577 C–578 E).

How is this so? Under tyranny, all are enslaved in a sort of prison, with the tyrant more enslaved than anyone else. The tyrant cannot enjoy and partake of pleasures as he will, but becomes fearful, friendless, impious, and vicious; and makes others just as miserable (579 B–580 A).

The assessments of the degree of happiness under each form of government offered by Plato fit in so neatly with his opinion of the worth of each that they are apt to offend as too contrived. Plato indicates that the happiest man is the one who is in control of himself, and the unhappiest is the tyrannical man (the one who tries to exercise overmuch control over others) (580 A–C). In attempting to determine which type of man is happiest, and therefore which type of state is best, Plato ascribes three principles to the soul: the appetitive; the ambitious or contentious; and the wise or philosophical (i.e., those concerned with the love of knowledge and truth). These are set forth to correspond, respectively, with the lover of money or gain; the lover of honour and courage; and the lover of wisdom (580 D–582 E). In deciding whose judgment is best, Plato gives the nod to the philosopher, who by definition is the lover of wisdom (582 E–583 A).

The tendentious nature of what Plato has constructed is to be seen in the assessment which deprecates the tyrannical man and state as the most wicked and unhappiest and praises the rule of the (philosopher-)king as the best and happiest. Plato states that '... I see, as every one must, that a tyranny is the wretchedest form of government, and the rule of a king the happiest' (576 B–E).[23]

Divine Rule

Ultimately, there emerges as a basic theme in Plato's *Republic* the message that some form of divine purpose or method should prevail both in the workings of government and in the lives of families and individuals. It is better for the individual to govern himself, but the man whose 'better part' is naturally weak should follow the man whose 'better part' is strong and in whom the divine governing principle – also to be found in law – is therefore in control. Plato expresses this principle (which if not reason itself is, at the least, reasonable and just) as follows, placing the obligation to obey this divine rule first on the individual:

> And therefore, being desirous of placing him under a rule like that of the best, we say that he ought to be the servant of the best, in whom the Divine rules; not, as Thrasymachus supposed, to the injury of the servant, but because every one had better be ruled by divine wisdom dwelling within him; or, if this be impossible, then by an external authority, in order that we may be all, as far as possible, under the same government, friends and equals.
>
> True, he said.
>
> And this is clearly seen to be the intention of the law, which is the ally of the whole city; and is seen also in the authority which we exercise over children, and the refusal to let them to be free until we have established in them a principle

analogous to the constitution of a state, and by cultivation of this higher element have set up in their hearts a guardian and ruler like our own, and when this is done they may go their ways (590 C–591 A).[24]

Hence, primary reliance is placed by Plato on the constitutional concept of 'inherent limitations' to instill through education and socialization of the young, habits of self-control that should govern in both the individual and the state; and thereby Plato hopes to obviate need for excessive imposed control. This approach of emphasis on forms of moral suasion, rather than on force or the threat of force, which may be viewed as educative, inculcative, or a combination of both, has necessarily been resorted to by all regimes throughout history, and its eloquent expression in Plato should not be cause to view it as novel. It is important, however, to perceive the appreciation Plato has of the pervasive and lasting influence education and socialization may have and of the potential so to progamme them as to direct the individual and the state to follow paths of righteousness toward moral and useful objectives. This approach is consistent with Plato's view that the divine plan is a harmonious one and that it is both to our practical benefit and our highest duty to follow it individually and collectively. For, in effect, Plato asks 'what profiteth it a man' if we seek not the ways and goals of the divine plan of harmony. This harmony is to be achieved especially through the faithful practice of temperance and moderation. And whether an ideal form of city and individual way of life that are consonant with all he has set forth in the *Republic* be achievable or not, Plato concludes Book IX by stating that the wise man will live according to the precepts he has been presenting. Perhaps such a plan is laid up in heaven:

> I understand; you mean that he will be a ruler in the city of which we are the founders, and which exists in idea only; for I do not believe that there is such an one anywhere on earth?
> In heaven, I replied, there is laid up a pattern of it, methinks, which he who desires may behold, and beholding, may set his own house in order[1] ([1] Or, 'take up his abode there'.). But whether such an one exists, or ever will exist in fact, is no matter; for he will live after the manner of that city, having nothing to do with any other (591 A–592 B).[25]

Book X is repetitive of Plato's rejection of imitative poetry as a disorderly influence and of a number of other subjects we have considered. Its final words employ Greek mythology about the choice of individual human destiny to reinforce his message of adhering to divine purpose by seeking to be just, virtuous, and mindful of the immortality of the soul:

And thus, Glaucon, the tale has been saved and has not perished, and will save us if we are obedient to the word spoken; and we shall pass safely over the river of Forgetfulness and our soul will not be defiled. Wherefore my counsel is that we hold fast ever to the heavenly way and follow after justice and virtue always, considering that the soul is immortal and able to endure every sort of good and every sort of evil. Thus shall we live dear to one another and to the gods, both while remaining here and when, like conquerors in the games who go round to gather gifts, we receive our reward. And it shall be well with us both in this life and in the pilgrimage of a thousand years which we have been describing (Bk X, 621 B–D).

Assessments

Is Plato serious about the validity or attainability of the hierarchical, organological system in the *Republic* that in this century has drawn the critical judgment of some that it is tainted with ingredients of fascism and communism? Is he indulging in a playful intellectual exercise, with elements of wish-fulfilment mixed in with serious ideas, and all expressed with poetic effect? In any event, this plan is presented in the *Republic* even if only as an unattainable model; and the tone of the work usually suggests seriousness of purpose and advocacy rather than irony, although daydreaming whimsicality also is there at times. Perhaps, therefore, Plato's intent in his *Republic* has been grasped and encapsulated in the following observation by Adela Marion Adam (1913, p. 85):

> The name *Republic* is a translation into English of the Latin *respublica*, Cicero's equivalent for the Greek word πολιτέια [*politeia* – RP]. Plato meant by it 'a state,' 'a city,' or 'a commonwealth.' By a kind of metaphor, the word 'commonwealth' can be applied to the constitution of the individual soul in man. Plato's Republic seeks to depict the ideal State, and in the end he is driven to confess that such a State is nowhere to be found on earth, nor indeed is it ever likely to be. 'But perhaps,' he adds, 'it is laid up in heaven as an example for him who desires to behold it, and beholding, found a city in himself.' Though no society may represent the kingdom of heaven, yet a man whose soul is rightly attuned to virtue may have the kingdom of heaven within him.[26]

Indeed, Plato's theory of cosmic dualism (his 'theory of forms') holds that perfection is to be found only in the realm of ideas, whereas the actual – however excellent – is always imperfect.[27] And so, just as Plato asserts that the character of an individual corresponds with the character of a state, we may, in somewhat similar fashion, maintain that actual man – however good – is always imperfect and fits best into an imperfect form and operation of government that has built-in tolerances and safeguards that allow for human foibles and limitations.

Notes

1   Richard Lewis Nettleship (1963), in his Introduction to *Lectures on the Republic of Plato*, pp. 4 f, notes that while its title might suggest it is a book about political philosophy and that it starts from an inquiry into the nature of justice, 'It is a book about human life and the human soul or human nature, and the real question in it is, as Plato says, how to live best'. Like the Greeks of his day, Plato does not differentiate between the ethical and the political.

    Careful note should also be taken that *politeia* can mean 'citizenship' as well as the state, the form of constitution, or a particular form of constitution. See the discussion and sources for *politeia* that permit it to be translated also as 'citizenship', 'state', 'republican', or 'constitution', as stated in Manville, 1990. See especially pp. 5 f, including the observation that:

> Today, the state is often considered a formal, independent entity, in conflict with the individual and ultimately aloof from the citizens (and non-citizens) in its domain. For the Greeks, membership in the state and the state itself were closely related.

2   Unless otherwise noted, the translations of the Platonic dialogues presented throughout this work are from *The Dialogues of Plato*, translated into English with Analyses and Introduction by Benjamin Jowett, 1892. Translation and treatment of the *Republic* is contained in Vol. II.

    For the Greek text of the *Republic* and opposite-page translation into English, as well as extensive commentary, see *Plato's Republic*, translated and edited by Paul Shorey, 1978 and 1970. *Nota bene*: citations throughout this work are to entire passage under consideration, not simply to quoted portion. Accordingly, this entire passage is pertinent to Plato's conception of justice. This subject and related topics are treated of dialectically, diagrammatically, and philologically throughout Ophir, 1991, and especially in ch. 2, 'The Problem of Justice Restated'. Ophir offers the interpretation (p. 63) that: 'However, justice is different from all other things supposed to be good in some sense. It is not simply a state of mind (like thinking), it is not exercised through any particular faculty (like seeing) or skill. It will later turn out to be the proper constitution of the soul, hence analogous to health, the proper constitution of the body'.

    See also in its entirety Moors, 1984–85.

    For insightful speculation on Plato's purposes in Book I, particularly on his discussion of justice and its relationship to the entire rest of the *Republic*, see Lycos, 1987. Lycos posits that the *Republic* cannot be properly understood unless one perceives Plato's basic premise and purpose set forth through Socrates in Book I: to demonstrate the primacy of the internal justice of the individual, while external justice is dependent on internal justice and secondary in value. Lycos is concerned to call this to attention in his Introduction (p. 2), as follows:

The argument of this study is that the central theme of *Republic*, Book I is the relation of justice to human power. The underlying aim of much of Socrates' critical examination of his interlocutors is to 'convert' upholders of traditional ideas away from the notion that justice is 'external' to that which enables individuals and communities to achieve the best use of their capacities and talents. Socrates wants to urge that justice cannot be seen as an unqualified good unless its 'internal' links with human 'powers', with their best and fullest development, are understood.

See in its entirety Annas, 1981. For concurrence on the internal nature of justice, see pp. 34 f:

> We have been to some extent prepared for Plato's own definition of justice as a matter, not of the performance of certain defined actions, but of the state of a person's soul. Whatever it is, it will be internal, not external, and a matter of knowledge, not of blindly following convention.

For carefully crafted consideration of many facets of this subject, including the linguistic, see Vlastos, 1981, ch. 5, 'Justice and Happiness in the *Republic*'. Vlastos states his central argument (pp. 111 f) as follows:

> I shall use 'justice pays' as a handy capsule for what Socrates undertakes to prove in response to Glaucon's challenge (358B ff): justice is good in and of itself, not merely for its consequences; and it is so great a good that no good securable by injustice could be greater.

3   Thus, it may be that an important message to be perceived here is that the just individual enjoys as the greatest reward the benefits and enjoyment of that internal 'peace of mind' that comes from 'an easy conscience' that results from just and courageous living. For example, Lycos, 1987, p. 4, states:

> Not only may one's virtue prove powerless to avert misery; doing the 'right' thing may, in some contexts, prove harmful. It may be wrong to act 'rightly'. The 'internal' assessment of virtue cannot allow this. Though a measure of good fortune is necessary for the fully eudaimonic life, it can never be wrong to act virtuously, since the quality of mind that *is* the virtue is a good and enjoyable thing it itself.

4   See the discussion of the newly founded *polis* in Berry, 1989. This early city is characterized by the satisfaction of appetites (hence, a 'city of pigs'). Berry's theme is that justice pertains to the relationships that become operative between the classes that emerge as luxury develops within the city. See especially pp. 11 ff and 22 f.

For discussion of the proposition that it is in Book II that Plato sets forth his awareness of alternative basic approaches to the problems of justice and politics but pursues only one theoretical set of possible responses, see Hyland, 1988–89. For illuminating consideration of the topic, see in its entirety Moors, 1981, including his stress (p. 21) on: 'This overall demand that a consideration of nature comprise the basis of discussion ...'.

5   Sinclair, 1968, pp. 149 ff, identifies for us the three principal classes in the Republic:

> There will thus be three classes in the State: Rulers or Guardians [φύλακες: *phulakes* – RP], who are the supreme protectors, the Auxiliary protectors (ἐπίκουροι) [*epikouroi* – RP] organised as a military and police force and carrying out the rulers' orders in a variety of ways, and thirdly, as before, the general citizen-body, who carry on the

trade, profession or craft but do not participate in the government ....

From this point on (end of Book III) we hear virtually nothing about the mass of the citizens and very little about the Auxiliaries who are not always carefully distinguished from the senior protectors or Guardians .... The use of the word 'classes', though perhaps inevitable, is unfortunate in view of its modern associations. Plato's classification is based on function in society and on fitness for those functions. His third class embraces employers as well as workers; his Auxiliaries would include parts of a Civil Service as well as Army and Police. The Guardians proper are the supreme authority of government but educationists and judges (433 C) are included.

The reason for some of the confusion between the Guardians and Auxiliaries is explained by Barker, 1960, p. 198:

The Platonic State as a whole, therefore, is a community marked by a division of labour between three specialized classes,[1] ([1] *I.e.* it is what Aristotle criticizes it for not being, a κοινωνία [*koinonia*, an association of persons – RP] constituted of elements different in kind, each making a different contribution to a common good, and profiting by the contributions of the rest.) the rulers (or 'perfect guardians'), the soldiers (*at first called 'guardians', and afterwards 'auxiliaries'*), and the producing classes (whom Plato calls the 'farmers' [*georgoi*: γεωργοί –RP]) (italics added – RP).

6   *Nota bene* again, Fite, 1934, especially pp. 15–24, where he refutes the mistaken notion of those who interpret Plato to believe in a system of universal education. Plato's discourses on education relate largely to that of the Guardian class and their military Auxiliaries, who together compose only a small, elitest portion of the community.

7   Additional practices of censorship are also advocated in Bk III, 386 A–404 E.

8   See for relevant exposition, Pollit, 1974, especially pp. 31–52.

9   For extended treatment of the beautiful, including some of Plato's cosmological and theological views, see Benardete, 1984.

Because Plato's ideas on love and on the beautiful are often interrelated by his manifold 'love of the beautiful', close attention should be paid to Plato's views on erotic and non-erotic (so-called 'platonic' or non-sensual) love for fuller understanding of some of his religious, political, and educational propositions. For their multifaceted treatment of comparisons (commonly overdone) and contrasts between Plato and Sigmund Freud, see: Gould, 1963, especially ch. 9; Santas, 1988, especially pp. 176–88; and Singer, 1966, especially pp. 80–100 for 'Platonic Eros' and 'Friendship in Aristotle'. See also notes 22 and 24 below.

10   Plato seemingly fails to understand here that in art one may find expressions of the strongly ugly that also may be of service in giving us a better insight into life and nature and a better sense of relative values. For what is itself a beautiful expression on this point, see editorial comment by Jeffrey Kinkley in his study and translation (also by others) of Shen Congwen (1902–88), 1995, pp. 13 f: 'Shen Congwen said that Beauty was his God, a God that is not dead, and that Beauty exists in things apparently ugly, primitive, even abhorrent'.

11   Shorey at times refers to the *epikouroi* (ἐπίκουρι) as helpers (or aides to the Guardians), but they are more commonly known as Auxiliaries. For discussion of Plato's educational proposals, see Gadamer, 1980, ch. 4.

12   Perhaps the supreme irony in Plato's political theory – which Barker insightfully grasps – is that if carried into practice it would create a society of mostly specialized drones; yet Plato abhorred drones. Platonic aspects of medieval Christianity are made apparent in

Troeltsch, 1931. See, e.g., the section on 'A "Cosmos of Callings"', Vol. I, pp. 293–96. See also Fite, 1934, ch. II, especially pp. 37–40.

For seminal hierological and philological consideration by a modern scholar of tripartite division of society, see in its entirety Dumézil, 1988. Dumézil notes in the preface to this edition (pp. 13 f):

> ... I glimpsed the fact that dominates and structures a large part of the material: the existence – at the very foundation of the ideology of most of the Indo-European peoples – of a tripartite conception of the world and society; a conception that is expressed, among the Arya of India and Iran, by a division into three classes (priests, warriors and herdsmen-cultivators) and, in Rome, by the most ancient triad of gods (Jupiter, Mars, Quirinus). ... I used both my lecture courses [at the *Ecole des Hautes Etudes*, 1938–39 – RP] to begin an investigation of the fundamental myths of the first and second cosmic and social "functions," which is to say, the myths of magical and juridical sovereignty and the myths of warrior-power or, to put it in Vedic terms, the myths of Mitra-Varuna and those of Indra-Vrtrahan.

13 *Cf.* the ideas of Trofim Denisovich Lysenko (1898–1967) on the influence of environmental factors and conditioning and the purported transmission to progeny of acquired characteristics. See, e.g., Joravsky, 1970. For discussion of Plato's ideas on marriage, mating, and sex, see Fite, 1934, ch. III, especially pp. 52–60. There is little of romantic love in the modern sense in Plato, and his sexual morality may be better termed sexual amorality.

14 For a treatment of Greek religion in the time of Plato, still unsurpassed in some respects, see Fustel de Coulanges, 1864. A generally available edition is that translated by Small, 1956.

15 However, Aristotle's writings and ideas were, for the most part, earlier and better known and therefore more utilized in medieval Western Europe and especially during the Renaissance. See in its entirety Robb, 1935, and Lévêque, 1940, pp. 60 f and 133.

For a recent work that has become the definitive study of its subject in English and that also considers this point, see Hankins, 1990 (or the 1991 reprint with addenda and corrigenda), especially pp. 3–17. Also very relevant and informative in its entirety is Blythe, 1992, especially pp. 5–13, 243–6 and 300–7, including the finding on p. 300: 'Thus we see that even as Polybius becomes important in sixteenth-century Italian political discourse, it is Aristotle, directly through the *Politics* and as filtered through medieval Aristotelians and civic humanists, who remains the dominant force'.

For the contrasting Marxian view that holds man is alienated from his true multidimensional nature unless permitted to develop and practice a number of talents and a variety of occupations, *cf.*, e.g., Marx and Engels, 1947, pp. 21 ff. The *par excellence* follower of such multi-vocational habits was William Morris (1834–96), the multi-skilled English poet, essayist, novelist, historian, printer, publisher, designer, weaver, woodcarver, industrial executive, politician, preservationist, and activist for a variety of intellectual, humanitarian, and socio-economic causes. Morris' life and accomplishments are concisely treated in a Past Masters publication that, to say the least, undermines Plato's mono-vocational position: Stansky, 1983.

For a definitive treatment of the organological, hierarchical 'cosmos of callings' that clearly shows similarity to Platonism, see again Troeltsch, 1931, Vol. I, especially pp. 284–310. Pater, 1912, pp. 247 ff, supports the view that there is an organological approach in Plato's *Republic*. *Cf.* Fite, 1934, pp. 70 ff, who questions the organological element in Plato's theory of society and the state, ascribing it instead to Aristotle, but admits a single unmistakable appearance of the organic image or metaphor in the *Republic*, Bk V, 462 C–D, where the community is likened to the individual man. But see the curative *medical penology* emphasized throughout Saunders, 1991.

For a variation on this theme, which approaches the body-politic by focusing attention on the concepts of the 'physician-ruler' and the general practice of 'poliatrics', see Campbell, 1982.

In any event, the comparison seems to be repeated at 464 B by a direct reference back to it. See also the comparison between purging of the state and the body, Bk VIII, 567 C. *Cf.* Barker, 1960, pp. 202 and 270–5, who affirms the organological principle fits so neatly into Plato's entire pattern of social and political thought that it is probably correct to ascribe it to him as well as to Aristotle. See, e.g., *Statesman*, 293 A–C and 296 B–299 D. See also the characterization of the 'fevered' or 'inflamed' *polis*, as against 'the true and healthy city' in Berry, 1989, pp. 5 f, citing *Republic*, 372 E: 'This alternative description has obvious medical connotations'.

It should be recognized, then, that for Plato, accordance of justice to the individual is dependent on the higher principle of accordance of justice to the state in its collective and cooperative sense. See the comparable view offered in the Introduction by Thomas L. Pangle to Strauss, 1984, p. 6: 'What then is Plato's conception of the problem of justice, according to Strauss? Justice in the fullest sense comes to sight, in what men say about it, as an object of aspiration: as the common good which binds men together in mutual dedication in a political community.' See also the extensive treatment of the topic in Hall, 1981, ch. 5. See in addition: Dent, 1987; and Hall, 1987, pp. 116–26.

Dent speaks of a thesis 1 ('strong single function thesis') and a thesis 2 ('dominant function thesis') that he differentiates as follows (p. 92):

> In thesis 1 everything else derives its value and importance from further[ing] and fostering social service. In thesis 2 this is not so. Many things are of value in their own right, but social service has greater or dominant value so that its claims set limits to the claims of the other values on our endeavour.

Consequently (p. 110):

> Each citizen has a duty, in justice, to do that work for the *polis* for which they are by their nature best fitted, and should give to that duty such a limiting and bounding priority over their other concerns which ensures that they never fail to give enough in the course of undertaking that duty to enable their *polis* to survive and thrive as a forum in which they and others shall enjoy the possibility of living and opportunity to live a fully rewarding life.

Hall's perception of 'educated right opinion' obviously identifies another example of the important role of 'inherent limitations' (see p. 6, above) assigned by Plato for promotion of justice in both the individual and society (p. 124):

> The concept of educated right opinion, then, provides us with an answer to the objection that the ordinary individual can not acquire the necessary knowledge to be just. More than mere right opinion, less than knowledge of the forms, educated right opinion enables the ordinary individual of the ideal state to acquire Platonic justice and its concomitant virtues.

Wood, 1988, p. 148, perceives Plato's hierarchical scheme as a view of justice that produces a philosophical and political system based on a division between ruling and producing classes that results in an obviously exploitative situation that benefits an undeserving plutocratic class. It would seem fair to infer from her observations, then, that Plato's hierarchical plan is not a prescription for justice but – quite the contrary – for injustice.

For a paradoxical view of Plato's conception of justice – indeed, a study which concludes that the '*Republic*, was built around an attempt to conceptualize "justice"' – that considers both the political (outer and social) and personal (inner and psychological) aspects of justice presented by Plato, see Havelock, 1978, especially pp. 1, 14 and 322 f, where illustrative quotation is made from the *Republic*, 443C.

See also, again in its entirety, Moors, 1984–85, which examines justice therein from such standpoints as 'the just life', 'political justice', and 'soul justice'. Moors explains (pp. 208 f):

> The just individual, as we shall see, is just because of the internal order which structures his soul; he is not just by virtue of what he does. The actions, the outward appearances, of being just do not, themselves, make the individual just. Rather, the actions are as a result, not a cause, of justice. ... Justice becomes indistinguishable from the order which the city exhibits. ... The order is accomplished from the condition of the whole, not of its corresponding parts in isolation. Justice is regarded as in competition with wisdom, courage, and moderation because it is only in the presence of justice that the remaining virtues are allowed to continue governing their proper spheres of the city. Justice, therefore, is the constant mediating virtue which identifies the correct application of the soul.

Moors finds (p. 213), however, that: 'There emerges a fundamental incompatibility between justice in the city, a conventional enterprise, and justice in the soul, a philosophical concern, if one seeks the most essential and truthful understanding of justice'.

16 For discussion, sources, and bibliographical references concerning Plato's views on women, see Okin, 1979, especially pp. 15–70, 274–81, 303–8 and 347–51. For a compellingly persuasive argumentation that Plato advocated some women belonged in the Guardian class by virtue of merit and not simply to provide breeding mates for male Guardians, see Pierce, 1973. Also compellingly persuasive is the pro-feminist line or argumentation presented in the review of Bloom, 1987, by Martha Nussbaum, 1987. Nussbaum's negative judgment of Bloom's work is vigorously affirmed by Euben, 1990, pp. ix–xiv.

For a concise overview of the status and role of women in classical Greece, see Grant, 1989, Appendix II. See Grant also for general background, bibliographical sources, and numerous biographical sketches of leading personages of the period. For an essay that presents numerous examples and points for consideration based on both the contemporary literature and modern studies, see Gould, 1980. Gould cautions about the complexity, exceptions, and frequent obscurity he encountered and that he has not touched on many subjects.

For consideration of whether Plato proposed full sexual equality, anti-female bias in scholarship, and resurgence of interest in philosopher-queens, see in its entirety Bluestone, 1988.

17 Plato's advocacy of the communizing of the property of the Guardian class and of common meals also seems to foreshadow the practice of many religious orders of the medieval and modern periods. In fact, there is an ascetic quality to a great deal of what Plato presents in the *Republic*. Presumably it is also comparable to some contemporary and earlier monastic or other religious settlements in the ancient period.

18 See again Fustel de Coulanges, 1956, especially Book First.

But how serious was Plato about these communizing proposals, especially those that deal with women and children in such a manner that one could not be sure of one's parents or children and thus that incest was not being committed? Therefore, see again ch. III, n. 15 above, and also n. 25 of this chapter, below. The serious-minded Aristotle challenges their logic and practicability (see ch. IX, section B4–8, below). However, the most effective challenge of them, perhaps in advance of Plato's writing of the *Republic* and by the sharply cutting weapon of satirical, ironical comedy, was by Aristophanes in his *Ekklesiazusae* (393 BC, produced 392). See especially 590–643 and explicative discussion in Saxonhouse, 1992, ch. 1.

19 *Cf.* Fite, 1934, pp. 9 f, especially his conclusion that:

> In the *Republic* the state is described as the human soul "writ large." Really however the soul is only the state writ small. For it is the social classes that explain the different "parts" of the soul, *i.e.*, "reason," "courage," "appetite." Apart from the figure of the middle class 'courage' would be hardly intelligible. In the *Gorgias* he goes so far as to tell us that the science of the soul is politics! The universe on the other hand is simply the state writ large, the cosmic commonwealth. And thus when the philosopher is made statesman he is already a statesman: his universe is a polity. In the midst of what is probably the most inspired of Plato's compositions, the speech of Socrates in the *Symposium*, we find it revealed casually (209a) that for him the poet, the philosopher, and the *statesman* are one and the same.

20 The passing reference to monarchy in Bk VIII is at 543 A and in Bk IX at 576 D; and a brief characterization appears in Bk IV at 445 D.

21 See below, ch. VI, n. 11 in its entirety.

22 See the discussion by Shorey, *Plato, Republic*, Vol. II, pp. 334–7, footnote d, of the discovery by the Freudians of 'Plato's anticipation of their main theses'. See also remark by the present writer in n. 24 below.

23 See the relevant discussion in Nichols, 1984. Nichols distinguishes between the style of the philosopher Socrates and that of the more flexible philosopher-ruler depicted too sketchily in the *Republic*.

Attention is also called to a work that should be examined closely for the purposes and ideas of Socrates and Plato: Vlastos, 1991.

For a discussion of whether Plato viewed ruling as essentially a 'philosophical activity' or 'technical endeavour' of the Guardians, see Steinberger, 1989. See also the resulting inconclusive exchange in which Duncan and Steinberger (1990) address whether being a philosopher is incompatible with being a Guardian or Ruler.

For argumentation that Plato discerned strong parallels between the characteristic attitudes and aptitudes of the philosopher and of the warrior, see in its entirety Craig, 1994. For Craig's description of this thesis, supported by citation of relevant passages, see especially pp. 19 ff. After observing that, 'there is more to life than to a chess game', Craig opines:

> Still, the bare fact that there is a need for something – that, for example, it would be supremely *useful* were the qualities of hero and sage combined in one man – is no guarantee that it is a natural possibility.
>
> There are grounds for suspecting, however, that the relationship between the love of wisdom and a talent for war is more intimate than would be implied by this convenient marriage of the requirements of politics with those of philosophy. ... It is never suggested

that true philosophers would be any more common than the most pre-eminent of heroes (cf. 491ab, 503b, d).

24   Important principles of inherent limitations as well as institutional checks are contained in this key passage, with evident emphasis on inherent limitations. It is also interesting to note that in addition to Plato's anticipation of Freud on dreams, he seems here to anticipate Freud on the role of the superego as moral censor developed by parental training and social rules. Concerning religious implications of this passage, see ch. VI, n. 1 and n. 30 below.

25   *Cf.* Pater, 1912, p. 266, who regards Plato as somewhat playful and pensive and not always to be taken seriously:

> Like his master Socrates, as you know, he is something of a humorist; and if he sometimes surprises us with paradox or hazardous theory, will sometimes also give us to understand that he is after all not quite serious. So about this vision of the City of the Perfect. The Republic, Καλλίπολις [*Kallipolis*], *Uranapolis, Utopia, Civitas Dei, The Kingdom of Heaven –*
> Suffer me, he says, to entertain myself as men of listless minds are wont to do when they journey alone. *Republic*, 144.

For a discussion of the role of unity and harmony in Plato's philosophy and his debt to the mathematical and musical discoveries of Pythagoras, see, e.g., Cornford, 1932, pp. 68 f.

26   *Cf.* the observation on a purpose of the *Republic* by Benardete, 1989, p. 9: 'Regardless of whether it is of necessity imaginary or not, the one best regime comprehends the manifold of all inferior regimes. It guides one's understanding of political life even if it never shapes one's actions'.

Cf. Moors, 1982, *passim*, e.g., pp. 80 and 108. Note in particular the opinion on p. 80:

> Unlike the treatise, which can remain detached from the 'application' of its results to life, dialogue requires that conclusions or insights gained from the considerations of various themes and questions be directed to the very manner in which one practices one's existence. ... Unless one is obliged to combine thought and action, unless one is made to pursue the application of lessons learned from Platonic dialogue to the actual situations with which one is confronted, the dialogues' experiments have not proven successful.

Note also Moors' illuminating consideration throughout of Plato's complementary, carefully constructed use of myth within his dialogues, epitomized on pp. 112 f, where the conclusion reads: 'Plato did not write his dialogues merely so that he could use discussion as a backdrop, or as a vehicle for telling good stories. We are obliged not to approach his myths as if he had.' See also, *idem*, 1978–79 and multilingual sources offered.

For a challenging, unorthodox treatise on the role of females (both goddesses and earthly women), religion and mythology, and poetry and minstrelsy that makes occasional insightful references to Plato, see the revised 1997 edition redacted by Grevel Lindop of the speculative study *The White Goddess* (1948) by Robert Graves. The iconoclastic Graves makes interesting connections between Ancient Greece and the British Isles and advances important theses about fundamental changes from the matriarchal to the patriarchal in religious and secular spheres. Lindop's future publications on Thomas De Quincey (1785–1859) should also be looked for because of the latter's influential judgments on Plato and Aristotle in his popular writing.

Plato's 'ideal' political theory of the one best form of government – by a philosopher-ruler – may then have been part of a whimsical intellectual game of 'what if', daydreaming, fantasy, or wish-fulfilment. It may, however, simultaneously contain a common-sense message that is often, perhaps even usually, missed: e.g., that since no vastly superior and wiser philosopher-ruler is to be found among mortal men – barring the millennial visitation of God or a god in human form – primary reliance must therefore be placed on observance of the rule of law, especially by principal magistrates. Thus, as with many of his hasty or superficial readers, Thomas Jefferson and John Adams also may have failed to grasp important aspects of 'what Plato really meant'. (Note, e.g., Shorey's comment, *Republic*, Vol. I, p. 23, footnote d: 'Allegory and the allegorical interpretation are always conscious and often ironical in Plato'.) See, therefore, the condemnatory judgments of Jefferson in his letter of 5 July 1814, to Adams and the reply of 16 July 1814, that finds Adams in agreement. Reprinted in Cappon, 1959, , Vol. II, pp. 430–9.

27 In order to achieve even this excellence – or to seek to approach the ideal – it is stated by Browning, 1991, p. 29, that Plato required in 'the ideal community recommended in the *Republic*': 'Power is to be entrusted to philosophers, as they alone are considered capable of ordering the community along the rational lines conforming to the Forms as principles of rational order'.

For clarifying discussion of, and additional sources on, Plato's 'theory of forms', or his 'Theory of Ideas', as he prefers to call it, see Hare, 1982, especially pp. 19–38 and most especially pp. 31 f.

See also Ritter, 1933, trans. Alles, 1968, Introduction, pp. 21–34, as a helpful starting point for information and judgments on not only Plato's theory of forms (or ideas) but also on Plato's life and corpus (including findings about which dialogues were more faithfully the views of Socrates and which were somewhat more Platonic). Ritter argues (pp. 30 f) that Aristotle made some errors of interpretation of Platonism and Pythagoreanism, including what he and Alles refer to as Plato's 'doctrine of Ideas'.

For affirmation that Plato's Socrates believes the rule of philosophers could be introduced only by dreadful means and results, and that 'the city in the *Republic* is certainly a dream', see Rosen, 1995, p. 77.

V   Plato's More Realistic Political Theory: *The Statesman*

Overview

As is true of so many matters relating to Plato, the period when Plato wrote his *Statesman* (now descriptively entitled *The Statesman, or Concerning Kingship, Logical*) is conjectural. Although cognizant of the claim of others that the *Politikos, e peri basileias, logikos* (Πολιτικός, ἢ περὶ βασιλείας, λογικός) had been written earlier, Ernest Barker (1960, p. 314) opines: 'The *Politicus* (or 'Statesman') probably belongs to the last period of Plato's life; and its composition may be assigned either to the period of his connexion with Dionysius II (367–1) or to the years immediately following'.

More important from the standpoint of developmental perspective is that the *Statesman* is probably Plato's first serious attempt to replace the ideal political theory of the *Republic* with a more realistic approach that would be more applicable to his contemporary world of decidedly imperfect men. Thus, Plato's intent is perceived by William Archibald Dunning (1902, p. 34), the historian, as follows:

> In *The Statesman* Plato's chief purpose is to develop the "idea" of a ruler, and to set political science in its proper place in the broad scheme of knowledge. The result is embodied in an identification of the true statesman with the all-wise philosopher, and an identification of politics with education and character building .... The function of the true statesman is to make the citizens conform to the ideal standards of virtue; and true political science is that knowledge by which men are taken care of either with or without law, either with or without their consent.[1]

Thus, in the *Statesman*, as in the *Republic*, Plato is faced by the inescapable and obvious truth that the ideal philosopher-ruler is nowhere to be found. But where in the *Republic*, Plato sketches a theoretical outline of an ideal or model state and declares 'the rule of a king the happiest' (576 E), in the *Statesman*, although perhaps secondarily so, Plato is more concerned than previously with what is practicable for an imperfect system of government by imperfect governors over imperfect men. He is forced to conclude here that in practice it would usually be best to place main reliance on written law, national customs, and tradition, as more correct and trustworthy than the arbitrary judgment and actions of unrestrained men, however good and well-intentioned they might be. Yet even then, Plato cannot entirely give up his proposition that, in theory, rule by a wise Statesman possessed of superior knowledge would be the best form of government; and so he cannot resist ridiculing the idea of too much reliance on the rule of law if such a one were in power. (Perhaps he is obliquely arguing against too strict a reliance on the letter of the law in general?)

In the *Statesman*, Plato presents a six-fold cyclical theory of the usual forms of government that is more clearly defined than that discussed in the *Republic*. In many respects, it is similar to that previously offered by Herodotus in his historical works. We find a qualitative classification of forms of government on the basis of whether they are subject to law (good) or unrestrained by law (bad). The quantitative classification is on the basis of whether they are ruled by one, the few, or the many. Government by one is monarchy; good government by one according to law is royalty or kingship; and bad government by one is tyranny. Good government by the few is aristocracy; and bad government by the few is oligarchy (although we would today regard Plato's description of oligarchy as plutocracy, or rule by the wealthy). Good government by the many is democracy; and bad government by the many is another form of democracy.

Plato's ideal preference would be a seventh form, 'really scientific monarchy' or rule by a Statesman who would employ his superior knowledge and wisdom to improve upon law and custom: i.e., still the ideal of the philosopher-ruler of the *Republic*. His reason is that real knowledge of the art of government cannot be acquired by a large portion of the community and certainly not by the citizenry at large. However, Plato reluctantly states that in the absence of such a wise king in the flesh, the proposition of rule by a superior statesman is apt to remain merely an ideal.

We see, therefore, that Plato's practical choice for a *Politicus*, acceptable because the ideal philosopher-ruler is not available, seems to represent the concept of limited monarchy: the rule of a superior − yet fallible − man, restrained by law, who practices the art of government by weaving different but complementary elements of a *polis* into a strong social fabric. Thus, Plato has moved essentially from advocacy in the *Republic* of the rule of one superior man unrestrained by law, to advocacy in the *Statesman* of the rule of one man restrained by law, as the most practicable and practical. However, to the very end of the *Statesman*, Plato holds up the ideal of a superior *Politicus*, who rules primarily by science but with reliance also on law, as the criterion by which all governments are to be rated in terms of the extent to which they 'imitate' the rule he would provide. In short, all other forms of government are to some extent imitations of the one true form and rule that the *Politicus* would in theory have provided.

Exposition

Scientific and Imitative Forms of Government

As in the *Republic*, so in the *Statesman*, Plato classifies government quantitatively as government by one, the few, or the many, and qualitatively as according to law or with the absence of law (291 D–292 A). Speaking through the person of the Eleatic Stranger as his protagonist, Plato has him explain all of this to the Younger Socrates and that best of all would be the rule of a wise king unrestrained by imperfect or incomplete law. It is significant that in distinguishing among forms of government, Plato is concerned first with the principle of rule according to science rather than according to law or whether by voluntary compliance or by enforced obedience:

> *Str.* There is a criterion of voluntary and involuntary, poverty and riches, law and the absence of law, which men now-a-days apply to them; the two first they subdivide accordingly, and ascribe to monarchy two forms and two corresponding names, royalty and tyranny.
> *Y. Soc.* Very true.
> *Str.* And the government of the few they distinguish by the names of aristocracy and oligarchy.
> *Y. Soc.* Certainly.
> *Str.* Democracy alone, whether rigidly observing the laws or not, and whether the multitude rule over the men of property with their consent or against their consent, always in ordinary language has the same name.
> *Y. Soc.* True.
> *Str.* But do you suppose that any form of government which is defined by these characteristics of the one, the few, or the many, of poverty or wealth, of voluntary or compulsory submission of written law or the absence of law, can be a right one?
> *Y. Soc.* Why not?

...

Str. If I am not mistaken, we said that royal power was a science?

Y. Soc. Yes.

Str. And a science of a peculiar kind, which was selected out of the rest as having a character which is at once judicial and authoritative?

Y. Soc. Yes.

...

Str. Hence we are led to observe that the distinguishing principle of the State cannot be the few or many, the voluntary or involuntary, poverty or riches; but some notion of science must enter into it, if we are to be consistent with what has preceded.

Y. Soc. And we must be consistent.

Str. Well, then, in which of these various forms of States may the science of government, which is among the greatest of all sciences and most difficult, be supposed to reside? That we must discover, and then we shall see who are the false politicians who pretend to be politicians but are not, although they persuade many, and shall separate them from the wise king.

...

There can be no doubt that legislation is in a manner the business of a king, and yet the best thing of all is not that the law should rule, but that a man should rule supposing him to have wisdom and royal power. Do you see why this is?

Y. Soc. Why?

Str. Because the law does not perfectly comprehend what is noblest and most just for all and therefore cannot enforce what is best. The differences of men and actions and the endless irregular movements of human things, do not admit of any universal and simple rule. And no art whatsoever can lay down a rule which will last for all time.

Y. Soc. Of course not.

Str. But the law is always striving to make one: – like an obstinate and ignorant tyrant, who will not allow anything to be done contrary to his appointment or any question to be asked – not even in sudden changes of circumstances, when something happens to be better than what he commanded for some one.

Y. Soc. Certainly; the law treats us all precisely in the manner which you describe.

Str. A perfectly simple principle can never be applied to a state of things which is the reverse of simple.

Y. Soc. True.

Str. Then if the law is not the perfection of right, why are we compelled to make laws at all? The reason of this has next to be investigated (291 D–294 D).[2]

Inherent Human Capabilities

The previous selection is also of great significance for the manner in which Plato seemingly abandons the whole concept of institutional or constitutional checks in favour of an approach based on the inherent *capabilities*, not limitations, of true statesmen in whom a greater degree of immediately applicable wisdom and justice may be found than in the laws of a people. Plato stresses at this point the impossibility of setting forth universal codes of law which could render a greater degree of justice and practical solutions in all matters. He does not, therefore, at first acknowledge that because of the frailty of judgment of the all-too-human judges and officials who are the only kind we have available, there is the necessity of adopting laws with flexible provisions that will allow for the constant changes in human affairs he mentions, individual differences, and the input of the limited wisdom of imperfect judges and officials. At this point, instead, he emphasizes an ineluctable inability of written or traditional law to provide exact justice for each individual:

> *Str.* And now observe that the legislator who has to preside over the herd, and to enforce justice in their dealings with one another, will not be able, in enacting for the general good, to provide exactly what is suitable for each particular case.
> *Y. Soc.* He cannot be expected to do so.
> *Str.* He will lay down laws in a general form for the majority, roughly meeting the cases of individuals; and some of them he will deliver in writing, and others will be unwritten; and these last will be traditional customs of the country (294 D–296 D, especially 294 E–295 A).

In the ensuing dialogue, Plato maintains that there are times when the physician, the statesman, and the ship's captain who have correct knowledge of their profession may properly use force to achieve justice and nobler results. In addition to justifying his use of force under appropriate circumstances, Plato would exempt the true statesman, were he available, from the rule of punishment by death that Plato would apply under other forms of government for violating the law. However, if there truly be a 'kingly art', then the other forms must never contravene law if it be their aspiration to imitate as far as possible that true form of government. But to make the rules of law or fill offices of government by vote, expression of the inexpert, or by lot, is as absurd as to practice medicine or navigation in similar fashion; and it would be similarly absurd to have government by the unskilled according to inflexible written laws instead of by the wise according to knowledge. Portions of this exchange between the Eleatic Stranger and the Younger Socrates read as follows:

> *Str.* ... The idea which has to be grasped by us is not easy or familiar; but we may attempt to express it thus: – Supposing the government of which I have been speaking to be the only true model, then, the others must use the written laws of this – in no other way can they be saved; they will have to do what is now generally approved, although not the best thing in the world.
>
> *Y. Soc.* What is this?
>
> *Str.* No citizen should do anything contrary to the laws, and any infringement of them should be punished with death and the most extreme penalties; and this is very right and good when regarded as the second best thing, if you set aside the first, of which I was just now speaking. ...
>
> ...
>
> To go against the laws, which are based upon long experience, and the wisdom of counsellors who have graciously recommended them and persuaded the multitude to pass them, would be a far greater and more ruinous error than any adherence to written law?
>
> *Y. Soc.* Certainly.
>
> ...
>
> *Str.* And, as we were saying, he who has knowledge and is a true Statesman, will do many things within his own sphere of action by his art without regard to the laws, when he is of opinion that something other than that which he has written down and enjoined to be observed during his absence would be better.
>
> *Y. Soc.* Yes, we said so.
>
> *Str.* And any individual or any number of men, having fixed laws, in acting contrary to them with a view to something better, would only be acting, as far as they are able, like the true Statesman?
>
> *Y. Soc.* Certainly.
>
> *Str.* If they had no knowledge of what they were doing, they would imitate the truth, and they would always imitate ill; but if they had knowledge, the imitation would be the perfect truth, and an imitation no longer.
>
> *Y. Soc.* Quite true.
>
> *Str.* And the principle that no great number of men are able to acquire a knowledge of any art has been already admitted by us.
>
> *Y. Soc.* Yes, it has.
>
> *Str.* Then the royal or political art, if there be such an art, will never be attained either by the wealthy or by the other mob.
>
> *Y. Soc.* Impossible.
>
> *Str.* Then the nearest approach which these lower forms of government can ever make to the true government of the one scientific ruler, is to do nothing contrary to their own written laws and national customs (296 B–301 A).[3]

Thus, we see Plato posing the fundamental problem he must confront: there is greater safety in general for ordinary men in the rule of law, but the rule of an extraordinary man who can rise above the restrictions and rigidity of law is to be preferred; however, only ordinary men are available. Nonetheless, Plato seems dissatisfied with the idea of being limited to far-less-than-ideal solutions and wants to achieve the optimum attainable out of the situation. What seems to emerge is a working compromise that would adhere to the basic law, but would improve it by the application of later knowledge and the wisdom of statesmen whenever they could be found. What comes to mind is that Plato may have a vision of principles of Talmud, of Equity, of Montesquieu's *Spirit of the Laws,* and the United States Supreme Court's 'rule of reason'. All of these may afford relief from deficiencies of the strict letter of the law by promoting its objectives.

The commentaries and decisions to be found in Talmud do not set aside the guiding pre-eminence of Torah, but apply Torah with merciful kindness and in the light of knowledge acquired by reason and experience. Equity does not set aside the common law of the kingdom ('Equity follows the law'), but attempts to fulfil its purpose by 'filling up the interstices' that leave room for more equitable interpretation and application. Montesquieu's understanding of law is not merely one of 'necessary relationships', but also includes a spirit of justice and fair play. The 'rule of reason' invoked by the United States Supreme Court examines the intent and effects of application of a law as well as its strict letter.

Good Laws and Wise Rulers

In seeking both good laws and wise rulers of men,[4] Plato must examine imperfect forms of government to try to determine which are better and which are worse; but he still cannot help longing for 'one best or ideal' form, however impossible of realization. Accordingly, Plato will ultimately place but a limited reliance on the efficacy of, and adherence to, the law. Plato will espouse a philosophy of human capabilities, of freedom to rule in conformity with principles of justice and reason that should be the underlying purposes and guiding-principles-in-application of all law. Thus, Plato apparently does not place his primary reliance on constitutional forms and institutional limitations in the system of government he would most prefer, but rather on strength of human character, improvability of human knowledge and understanding, and freedom for wise rulers to innovate. (Was this in some respects an optimistic philosophy of possible progress, however limited?) His preference, therefore, is for a government of enlightened men rather than of law, but of men paying respectful attention to what is contained in law. However, Plato does not announce himself as most in favour simply of 'royalty' or 'kingship' (rule by a king according to law), but as most in favour of a seventh form of government: that of a truly superior statesman who could rise by means of his greater wisdom and science above restrictions of law to dispense greater justice and to govern more effectively. Dialogue relevant to these points is to be found especially in the exchange, beginning as follows, which epitomizes much of the *Statesman*:

> *Str.* Or, again, when an individual rules according to law in imitation of him who knows, we call him a king; and if he rules according to law, we give him the same name, whether he rules with opinion or with knowledge.
>
> *Y. Soc.* To be sure.
>
> *Str.* And when an individual truly possessing knowledge rules, his name will surely be the same – he will be called a king; and thus the five names of governments, as they are now reckoned, become one.
>
> *Y. Soc.* That is true.
>
> *Str.* And when an individual ruler governs neither by law nor by custom, but following in the steps of the true man of science pretends that he can only act for the best by violating the laws, while in reality appetite and ignorance are the motives of the imitation, may not such an one be called a tyrant?
>
> *Y. Soc.* Certainly.
>
> *Str.* And this we believe to be the origin of the tyrant and the king, of oligarchies, and aristocracies, and democracies, – because men are offended at the one monarch, and can never be made to believe that any one can be worthy of such authority, or is able and willing in the spirit of virtue and knowledge to act justly and holily to all; they fancy that he will be a despot who will wrong and harm and slay whom he pleases of us; for if there could be such a despot as we describe, they would acknowledge that we ought to be too glad to have him, and that he alone would be the happy ruler of a true and perfect State.
>
> *Y. Soc.* To be sure.
>
> *Str.* But then, as the State is not like a beehive, and has no natural head who is at once recognized to be the superior both in body and in mind, mankind are obliged to meet and make laws, and endeavour to approach as nearly as they can to the true form of government.
>
> *Y. Soc.* True.
>
> *Str.* And when the foundation of politics is in the letter only and in custom, and knowledge is divorced from action, can we wonder, Socrates, at the miseries which there are, and always will be, in States? Any other art, built on such a foundation and thus conducted, would ruin all that it touched. Ought we not rather to wonder at the natural strength of the political bond? For States have

endured all this, time out of mind, and yet some of them still remain and are not overthrown, though many of them, like ships at sea, founder from time to time, and perish and have perished and will hereafter perish, through the badness of their pilots and crews, who have the worst sort of ignorance of the highest truths – I mean to say, that they are wholly unacquainted with politics, of which, above all other sciences, they believe themselves to have acquired the most perfect knowledge.

Y. Soc. Very true.

Str. Then the question arises: – which of these untrue forms of government is the least oppressive to their subjects, though they are all oppressive; and which is the worst of them? Here is a consideration which is beside our present purpose, and yet having regard to the whole it seems to influence all our actions: we must examine it (301 A–302 B).

The Eleatic Stranger continues by indicating that monarchy can be either the best or the most oppressive of the six usual forms of government, depending on its qualitative distinction: i.e., according to law or contrary to law. Government by one, the few, or the many are all to be adjudged according to this standard, and thus six forms of the practicable state are to be discerned. However, Plato's seventh form – that of the 'truly scientific ruler' – which is ideally the best, must be conceived of as apart from all the available rest:

Str. The division made no difference when we were looking for the perfect State, as we showed before. But now that this has been separated off, and, as we said, the others alone are left for us, the principle of law and the absence of law will bisect them all.

Y. Soc. That would seem to follow, from what has been said.

Str. Then monarchy, when bound by good prescriptions or laws, is the best of all the six, and when lawless is the most bitter and oppressive to the subject.

Y. Soc. True.

Str. The government of the few, which is intermediate between that of the one and many, is also intermediate in good and evil; but the government of the many is in every respect weak and unable to do either any great good or any great evil, when compared with the others, because the offices are too minutely subdivided and too many hold them. And this therefore is the worst of all lawful governments, and the best of all lawless ones. If they are all without the restraints of law, democracy is the form in which to live is best; if they are well ordered, then this is the last which you should choose, as royalty, the first form, is the best, with the exception of the seventh, for that excells them all, and is among States what God is among men (302 C–303 B).

Next, Plato characterizes as political processes the choice of persuasion or force to bring about compliance, of whether or not to engage in war, and of what the law shall provide (304 B–305 C). However, he declares that execution of these governmental decisions is not truly 'political or royal' in nature, but ministers to the royal power, which is used most importantly to exercise leadership to weave various discordant or discrete elements of the society by the 'science' of statecraft into a harmonious, unified state:

> *Str.* The review of all these sciences shows that none of them is political or royal. For the truly royal ought not itself to act, but to rule over those who are able to act; the king ought to know what is and what is not a fitting opportunity for taking the initiative in matters of the greatest importance, whilst others should execute his orders.
>
> *Y. Soc.* True.
>
> *Str.* And, therefore, the arts which we have described, as they have no authority over themselves or one another, but are each of them concerned with some special action of their own, have, as they ought to have, special names corresponding to their several actions.
>
> *Y. Soc.* I agree.
>
> *Str.* And the science which is over them all, and has charge of the laws, and of all matters affecting the State, and truly weaves them all into one, if we would describe under a name characteristic of their common nature, most truly we may call politics (305 C–E).[5]

Plato evidently believes that it is not possible or desirable to produce the monistic kind of harmony that conceivably might result from the elimination of a competing or opposite factor. For example, Plato writes that it is commonly said that all the parts of virtue are friendly to one another; but he also points out that temperance and courage both are part of virtue, despite, 'That they are two principles which thoroughly hate one another and are antagonistic throughout a great part of nature'. Therefore, the Eleatic Stranger says, 'We must extend our enquiry to all those things which we consider beautiful and at the same time place in two opposite classes' (305 B–306 C). Plato has the Eleatic Stranger admonish the Younger Socrates that it is not easy to explain this thought about what we would today view as a Hegelian-like 'union of opposites', and then neatly accomplishes the feat. He points out that in some cases energetic action represents courage and in others violence or madness; in some cases gentler action represents decorum and restraint, and in others cowardice or sluggishness. Those who represent these different natures in their extremes are bound to come into conflict with one another and can produce disease and paralysis in the state. Thus, a virtue may contain two apparently contradictory tendencies or qualities that are in proper balance (306 E–308 B).

A Heaven-born Race and System

We see more and more that Plato builds his political theory on what we may call 'inherent capabilities or potentialities', as well as 'inherent limitations' of humankind. Because Plato is not satisfied with humanity as they are or what happens to humanity if they follow their own uncontrolled inclinations, Plato believes it essential to improve the human stock by breeding as well as by training. Thus, humanity, as individuals and as collective animals, is the most important prop, the keystone, in Plato's political system. As for the detailed structure of branches and offices, there is comparatively little in Plato because it is secondary in importance. And so we find the Eleatic Stranger discoursing further upon the use of eugenics and education, combining their practice with a mystical religious doctrine. He attempts to include the good and exclude the bad, while also weaving into a Hegelian fabric of unity the warp and woof of the divergent parts of virtue. In the final analysis, it is law – acting upon noble, intelligent natures – that is the unifying bond that can hold humanity together in a rational, just society governed according to principles of virtue and therefore able to conform more nearly to what is divine. We see here Plato's belief that true political science follows the concept theologians terms natual law that God has more widely implanted in rational humanity's nature, and that there is also a law of retribution:

> *Str.* In like manner, the royal science appears to me to be the mistress of all lawful educators and instructors, and having this queenly power, will not permit them to train men in what will produce characters unsuited to the political constitution which she desires to create, but only in what will produce such as are suitable. Those which have no share of manliness and temperance, or any other virtuous inclination, and, from the necessity of an evil nature, are violently carried away to godlessness and insolence and injustice, she gets rid of by death and exile, and punishes them with the greatest of disgraces.
>
> *Y. Soc.* That is commonly said.
>
> *Str.* But those who are wallowing in ignorance and baseness she bows under the yoke of slavery.
>
> *Y. Soc.* Quite right.
>
> *Str.* The rest of the citizens, out of whom, if they have education, something noble may be made, and who are capable of being united by the statesman, the kingly art blends and weaves together; taking on the one hand those whose

natures tend rather to courage, which is the stronger element and may be regarded as the warp, and on the other hand those which incline to order and gentleness, and which are represented in the figure as spun thick and soft, after the manner of the woof – these, which are naturally opposed, she seeks to bind and weave together in the following manner:

Y. Soc. In what manner?

Str. First of all, she takes the eternal element of the soul and binds it with a divine cord, to which it is akin, and then the animal nature, and binds that with human cords.

Y. Soc. I do not understand what you mean.

Str. The meaning is, that the opinion about the honourable and the just and good and their opposites, which is true and confirmed by reason, is a divine principle, and when implanted in the soul, is implanted, as I maintain, in a nature of heavenly birth (308 C–310 A).[6]

Plato then continues by discussing the role of eugenics in bringing about a state composed of citizens of such combined, variant virtues. It becomes apparent that he is clinging as much as possible to ideas of improvement, if not perfectibility, in hope of achieving the Guardian-class principle of the *Republic*. However, establishment of a Guardian class is not discussed here. The more limited hope is that perhaps the desired qualities may be found mingled in at least a ruler, presumably his Statesman. His plan is to breed out extremes of temperament by having the decorous marry the courageous, instead of having arranged marriages that amalgamate wealth or power. This would prevent the development of strains of madness or torpor. In addition to the original 'divine' bond which 'unites dissimilar and contrary parts of virtue', the additional 'human' bonds, properly developed, could help unite the state. The president of a board, therefore, should be both brave and decorous, while the board should include men of each sort. The Eleatic Stranger explains to the Younger Socrates:

Str. Where one officer only is needed, you must choose a ruler who has both these qualities – when many, you must mingle some of each, for the temperate ruler is very careful and just and safe, but is wanting in thoroughness and go.

Y. Soc. Certainly that is very true.

Str. The character of the courageous, on the other hand, falls short of the former in justice and caution, but has the power of action in a remarkable degree, and where either of these two qualities is wanting, there cities cannot altogether prosper either in their public or private life (310 A–311 B).[7]

Assessments

It is, of course, just as well that Plato does not elaborate on how such a system as that described in the *Statesman* would be put into operation and who would be the judges of it and the judges of those judges. But however achievable or not some of Plato's fundamental objectives may have been, in the *Statesman* he presents us with a vision of an ennobled and unified citizenry and state under a law-abiding ruler. Thus, the final words of the *Statesman* provide an appropriate peroration:

> *Str*. This then we declare to be the completion of the web of political action, which is created by a direct intertexture of brave and temperate natures, whenever the royal science has drawn the two minds into communion with one another by unanimity and friendship, and having perfected the noblest and best of all the webs which political life admits, and enfolding therein all other inhabitants of cities, whether slaves or freemen, binds them in one fabric and governs and presides over them, and, in so far as to be happy is vouchsafed to a city, in no particular fails to secure their happiness.
> *Y. Soc*. Your picture, Stranger, of the king and statesman, no less than of the Sophist, is quite perfect (311 B–C).

We may therefore note that the admirable concluding statement that Plato has given us in the *Statesman* is one of its central themes: a reconciliation of complementary differences to bring about unity, harmony, and strength.

Further reflection on what Plato unfolds in the *Statesman* leads to the conclusion that ineluctably he must move from something ideal but unattainable to something imperfect but practicable – yet he still wishes to embody within his system a fail-safe formula, or one with a high degree of probability of success in promoting not only unity, harmony, and strength but also justice, happiness, and efficient achievement.

As in the case of the *Republic*, where the unavailability of the philosopher-ruler makes Plato turn to a greater reliance on the rule of law, Plato's model *Politicus* also proves unavailable, and Plato must again fall back on essentially the same alternatives: the rule of law, education and training, and eugenics. The *Politicus*, however, seems less awesome and more human than the philosopher-ruler of the *Republic*; and no complicated, quixotic scheme such as that of the Guardians, Auxiliaries, and Workers of the *Republic* is outlined in the *Statesman*. Thus, in the important respects of being more faithful to the real world and real people and less complicated and doctrinaire, the *Statesman* is a more realistic work than the *Republic*. Therefore, when viewed in the context of the *Laws* as well, Benjamin Jowett has caught sight of a very significant feature of the *Statesman* in his Introduction thereto (*The Dialogues of Plato*, 1892, Vol. IV, p. 440):

> Thus in the Statesman as in the Laws, we have three forms of government, which we may venture to term, (1) the ideal, (2) the practical, (3) the sophistical – what ought to be, what might be, what is. And thus Plato seems to stumble, almost by accident, on the notion of a constitutional monarchy, or of a monarchy ruling by laws.[8]

In short, we may view the *Statesman* as a transitional work between the more fanciful *Republic* and the more sophisticated *Laws*.

Notes

1   Fowler (1925, 301 B, n. 1, p. 158) terms this 'really scientific monarchy' in a footnote to his translation and editing of *The Statesman*. For the Greek text of the *Statesman* and opposite-page translation into English, as well as extensive commentary, see this volume.

Unless otherwise noted, all translations from the *Statesman* in this chapter are from *The Dialogues of Plato*, translated into English with analyses and introduction by Jowett, 1892, contained in Vol. IV. *Cf.* the more recent translation and commentary in Benardete, 1984, pp. III. 3–156, and observations in the Introduction, pp. xi–xx. Benardete's multidimensional treatment includes useful discussion of philological, epistemological, and purposive aspects of the *Statesman* that recommends itself especially to the advanced scholar. Benardete touches on problems of accurate translation of the term *Politikos*, p. xii, and does settle for 'statesman'.

A relevant selection of assorted papers on the *Statesman* is available in Nicholson and Rowe, 1993. The more inclusive version has not yet reached this writer: Rowe, 1994.

For a philosophically oriented examination of such topics in the *Statesman* as mythological symbolism and its cosmological bases, see Rosen, 1995. Rosen employs a great deal of the methodological approach – diaeresis – he finds in the *Statesman* to present his own unravelled and rewoven tapestry – his 'Web of Politics' – that portrays his version of Plato's exposition of the ruling art of the *Politicus*. See, e.g., ch. 6, pp. 98–118, and his criticisms of diaeresis, which Rosen defines (p. 2) as 'the art of division and collection in accordance with kinds ...'. Also, *nota bene* his finding (p. 46) of the implicit thesis that:

> Although there is an inseparability of theory from practico-production in human life and, in particular, in the art of politics, this weaving together of theory and practico-production must be distinguished from the pure theory of the philosophical contemplation and analysis of intelligible order.
>
> There can thus be no identity between the statesman and the philosopher but at most only a partial overlapping.

2   There is something refreshingly modern in the latter portion of this excerpt where Plato is geared to constant change and decries arbitrariness in any science. There is also something

that may not be forthright in this passage, however, for Plato's reluctance here – as elsewhere – to rely without reservation on the rule of law (even when absent an heroic, superior philosopher-ruler) may result from the democratic source and character of the statutory law (*nomos*: νόμος) that in the time of Kleisthenes had replaced the older statutory law (*thesmos*: θεσμός) handed down by a superior legislator or legislature. Wood and Wood, 1978, pp. 178 ff, follow Ostwald, 1969, p. 55, in descrying an anti-democratic motive when Plato hesitates to rely on the rule of law.

We may also note here the observation by Todd and Cartridge, 1990, ch. 1, p. 5: '... a general textbook on Athenian law should give priority to a legal procedure rather than to substantive law'.

Cf. the somewhat differing discussion of *nomoi* in the Introduction by Ernest Barker to *The Politics of Aristotle* (1975, pp. lxix–xii).

Ostwald expands on his treatment of the subject of the 'replacement of *thesmos* by *nomos*' and argues convincingly in support of his viewpoints in his subsequent work whose title reveals its major theme: *From Popular Sovereignty to the Sovereignty of Law: Law, Society, and Politics in Fifth-Century Athens*, 1986, *passim*, especially pp. 85–93, 112 f, 134 f, and 509–24. Ostwald concludes (p. 524): 'Thus the democracy achieved stability, consistency, and continuity when the higher sovereignty of *nomos* limited the sovereignty of the people'.

3   *Cf.* Friedländer, *Plato, Vol. 1: An Introduction*, translated from the German by Hans Meyerhoff, 1958, pp. 288 f:

> Was Plato hostile to law? That is a necessary question in any account of Plato's jurisprudence. There is no doubt that as a seeker after an ideal, the Plato of the *Republic* preferred the adaptable intelligence of the all-wise autocrat to the impersonality of the rule of law.
>
> ... Against this, Plato of the *Laws* and *Statesman* had come to realize that on this earth benevolent dictatorship was a counsel of perfection and that he would better propose a solution which had a possibility of realization. In the arts we trust the experts absolutely; but in the realm of government the expert is rarer than in any other art. Plato therefore believed that society should fall back upon law as a second best (875 D; *Statesman* 300 C), perhaps even as something in the nature of a *pis aller* – the supremacy of the rigid rule being adapted to the 'average' man and the general situation and incapable of dispensing equity in the particular case.[7] ([7] *Statesman* 295 AB. Plato again brings in the idea of equity in *Laws* 875 D.)
>
> Plato thus came to his final view on the necessity of law. He insisted that it was indispensable; without it we were indistinguishable from animals.

4   *Cf.* Friedländer, 1958, pp. 289 f:

> Anticipating subsequent analysis, Plato considered the suggestions that law is of divine origin and that man's function is to discover its true rules (624 A, 835 C);[9] ([9] Plato believed that law was unknown in primitive society [680 A].) that it is a product of impersonal social and natural forces – economic, geographical, and sociological or, as he expressed it, the result of chance and occasions (709 A); and that it is an invention of man to meet the needs of society, Art co-operating with Occasion.

One may add that Thrasymachus' purpose in the *Republic* is confined mostly to defining justice as the interest of the stronger, rather than unity as Friedländer indicates. In any event, we are still left with the basic problem under any constitution or system of law of determining the intent of a particular provision of law and how properly to apply it to particular cases. See, e.g., the tripartite symposium on 'Interpreting the Constitution', contributed to by Attorney General Edwin Meese III, Associate Justice William J. Brennan Jr, and Professor Raymond Polin, 1986.

5 The 'truly royal science', 'kingly art' or role described here is, of course, the executive function, in the main.

6 In fact, the contentious may vie more with one another than with the peaceable. For a modern work on the subject of improving the human stock, see Karp, 1976. For an introduction to the 'nature versus nurture controversy', see Bowler, 1989, especially pp. 152–7.

7 We may note here that Robert M. MacIver (1947) entitled one of his principal works *The Web of Government*. The foreword to that work is a passage from Plato's *Protagoras*, 322, on reverence and justice.

8 For discussion of the dual nature and role of any individual within any political community, see Rosen, 1995, p. 68:

> Perhaps the simplest formulation of the main point is that political existence is mutual caring by humans for one another; this is so regardless of the form of the regime. In other words, the statesman, whether one or many, exemplifies the duality of human nature; we are all of us both masters and servants, and in a multiplicity of senses.

In another example of pairing (p. 78), Rosen states that Plato uses Socrates as the protagonist of the philosopher for whom there is no defence except in philosophy and the Eleatic Stranger as the proponent of the view that the only defence for the philosopher is as a citizen who can practice the science of the free person. A more challenging subsequent conclusion (p. 100) is that:

> The fundamental question raised by the *Statesman* is then not at all that of the nature of the royal art, but rather the nature of the dialectic. But this amounts to the assertion that the fundamental theme of the *Statesman* is the question of the nature of philosophy and so, by extension, of the philosopher.

The fundamental answer that appears in Rosen (p. 127) is for the Statesman to employ *phronesis* (φρόνησις: good, prudent judgment) to produce *to metrion* (μέτριον: the noble, moderate balance) between excess and deficiency that combines technical efficiency and moral virtue and thus to practice political *technē* (τέχνη: 'science', skill, or art). The basic reason for this is because Socrates associates political knowledge with philosophy and uses *technē* in his own philosophical investigations.

However, Rosen concludes (p. 106) that: 'The crucial point here is that there is not and cannot be any example of the statesman that serves as a model of statesmanship because of the comprehensive nature of the royal art'. He states further (p. 118) that the picture of Plato to be discerned from detailed study of not only the *Statesman* but also of Plato's other works is not the conventional portrayal; and so he accepts that: 'It may appear anachronistic to some readers when I say that the one thinker in the entire tradition of Western philosophy who is closest to what is today regarded as the rejection of Platonism is Plato himself'. Accordingly, Rosen (pp. 135 f) rejects the notion that Plato regarded the art of weaving as a paradigm, whether as model or example, or the *technē* of politics and argues that, instead, Plato viewed both weaving and politics, as well as spelling, as examples of concatenative arts. Politics is first emphasized as a defender of the body (its primary concern) and finally of the soul (the primary concern, one could say, of philosophy, poetry, the fine arts, mathematical science, and religion).

VI Plato's More Sophisticated Political Theory: *The Laws*

Overview

The Laws (*Nomoi*: Νόμοι) of Plato is descriptively entitled *Twelve Books of Laws, or Concerning Legislation* (*Nomon e peri nomothesias biblia ib*: Νόμοι ἢ περί νομοθεσίας βιβλί α ιβ). It is a rambling, at times disjointed, work that contains gaps, repetitions, and inconsistencies. All of these faults lend credence to the tradition of antiquity that it was an unfinished, unpolished work that its reputed posthumous editor, Philip of Opus, Plato's pupil and amanuensis, did not tamper with overly. Not only the longest of his works, the *Laws* is also considered by many to present the ripest of Plato's thoughts on ethics, education, and jurisprudence. It was believed that its plan was drafted as early as 361 BC and that it was published within a year after Plato's death in 347 BC. Because of differences of vocabulary, style, and viewpoint, there are those who have adjudged the *Laws* to be spurious. However, this last political testament of Plato is generally accepted as a work that has come down to us with the essential Plato intact (Barker, 1960, pp. 338 f; Shorey, 1933, p. 58; Sinclair, 1968, p. 186; Taylor, 1960b, p. 462).[1]

In the *Laws*, Plato is again reluctant to depart from the ideal, in theory at least, or even from the best practicable; but he is inexorably forced to make one concession after the other to arrive at a system that is more in accordance with the real world, more acceptable to the citizenry, and more likely in *some* respects to be practical or workable than his earlier proposals. Thus, Plato is driven in the *Laws* to make at least three major concessions to reality or the sophisticated life: namely, a government of laws (although here, again, he would prefer an ideal code); individual marriage and family life for the governing class as well as for the other classes; and private property, likewise, for the governing class, although on a limited scale and restricted by a fundamental equality that avoids extremes of wealth and poverty. The *Laws* also sets forth plans for a balancing of the classes, the principle of moderation, the spirit of friendship, the importance of discipline and education, and a small size for the state.

94

In the *Laws*, as previously, Plato still strives to come up with a 'fail-safe' formula. If an all-wise philosopher-ruler be not available, then a combination of laws (each of which is prefaced by explanations that seek to persuade as well as coerce) and despotic rulers, resting on claimed divine authority, is advocated:

> The authority thus claimed for the State is justified by means of the deification of Law. The supreme Divinity is Reason (νοῦς) [*nous* – RP], the Ruler of the heavens, and Law (νόμος) [*nomos* – RP] is nothing else than the dispensation of Reason (νοῦ διανομή) [*noi dianomē* – RP]. Hence our State is, in fact, a Theocracy; and all the sanctions of religion can be invoked in support of its constitution and its laws. He that offendeth against the law, or its officers, offendeth against God (Bury, ed., *Plato, The Laws*, Vol. I, p. xiv).

This combination of authority is used to maintain both the status quo and the subordination of the individual to the state; and this domination – by the elderly – from birth to death is justified as in accord with the universal principle that no part is ever independent or exists for itself, but exists for the sake of its whole. Unlike his other political works, the *Laws* details a structure of government, including especially an ultimately ruling Nocturnal Synod that caps a theocratic gerontocracy. However, like his other political and ethical works, Plato's *Laws* emphasizes the importance of education and the cultivation of desirable personal qualities and the use of reason, all directed toward realization of the good (ibid., pp. xiv f).

Thus, in the *Laws*, as always, Plato falls back upon a system of education, indoctrination, and inculcation as his most important source of stability and constitutional safeguard. In short, Plato believes that humanity can be conditioned to acquire the habit of being good and just. This is not an altogether pessimistic view of humankind, even though it does imply at the same time inherent capacities for bad and injustice that need to be controlled both by the individual himself and those placed in control over him as a reinforcing influence. On balance, however, Plato does not trust much in the good judgment, good will, good behaviour, or ability of the general citizenry if left to their own choice and devices without effective early conditioning and continuing constraints. Plato stresses moderation but also advocates authoritarian measures in economic and other areas. Indeed, Plato remains inherently paternalistic and haughty to the last in this delineation of a desirable form and practice of government – a constitutional model – for the imaginary projected settlement of Magnesia.

Exposition

Peace and Happiness Preferable to War

There can be little doubt that the constant primary objective of Plato in his political writings is the strength of the *polis*, to be achieved through its unity and harmony. This strength includes military strength to protect against external danger as well as to maintain internal order. However, Plato realizes that a greater strength than that of the armed forces is the overall kind of apparent and actual strength that makes use of the military unnecessary; and that the maintenance of external and internal peace under such circumstances is a greater victory than success in war, armed combat, or strife. But to be real, such external and internal peace requires victory and control by the better part in all cases, including within oneself.

The dialogue of the *Laws* begins with Cleinias responding to an inquiry from the Athenian Stranger, Plato's protagonist in this work, whether a god, reputedly Zeus, and not some man, made the Cretan laws (Bk I, 624 A). Cleinias describes the training and preparation for war that are always going on in Crete, his homeland, and pronounces it – in Hobbesian manner – as the price that must be paid lest everything of value be lost to conquerors:

> *Cle.* I think, Stranger, that the aim of our institutions is easily intelligible to any one. Look at the character of our country: Crete is not like Thessaly, a large plain; and for this reason they have horsemen in Thessaly, and we have runners – the inequality of the ground in our country is more adapted to locomotion on foot; but then, if you have runners you must have light arms, – no one can carry a heavy weight when running, and bows and arrows are convenient because they are light. Now all these regulations have been made with a view to war, and the legislator appears to me to have looked to this in all his arrangements: – the common meals, if I am not mistaken, were instituted by him for a similar reason, because he saw that while they are in the field the citizens are by the nature of the case compelled to take their meals together for the sake of mutual protection. He seems to me to have thought the world foolish in not understanding that all men are always at war with one another; and if in war there ought to be common meals and certain persons regularly appointed under others to protect an army, they should be continued in peace. For what men in general term peace would be said by him to be only a name: in reality every city is in a natural state of war with every other, not indeed proclaimed by heralds, but everlasting. And if you look closely, you will find that this was the intention of the Cretan legislator; all institutions, private as well as public, were arranged by him with a view to war; in giving them he was under the impression that no

possessions or institutions are of any value to him who is defeated in battle; for all the good things of the conquered pass into the hands of the conquerors (625 C–626 C).

The first response of the Athenian Stranger to this rather Hobbesian statement of Cleinias, is to inquire of him whether the primary principle of the government he would lay down, then, is victory in war. Replies Cleinias, 'Certainly; and our Lacedaemonian friend, if I am not mistaken, will agree with me' (626 B–C). Cleinias then goes on to address the Athenian Stranger with an extension of his previous declaration by making all men as individuals enemies to all other men and also to themselves. For, Cleinias states, 'all men are publicly one another's enemies, and each man privately his own' (626 D–E).

The Athenian Stranger and Cleinias agree that the same principle of war is carried on within each individual, house, village, and state. For each, it is a struggle between better and worse parts of self. At each level there is an internal or 'civil war', and the greatest victory or defeat, therefore, will be a victory over self or a defeat by self:

> *Cle.* ... Moreover, there is a victory and defeat,– the first and best of victories, the lowest and worst of defeats, – which each man gains or sustains at the hands, not of another, but of himself; this shows that there is a war, against ourselves going on within every one of us.
>
> *Ath.* Let us now reverse the order of the argument: Seeing that every individual is either his own superior or his own inferior, may we say that there is the same principle in the house, the village, and the state?
>
> *Cle.* You mean that in each of them there is a principle of superiority or inferiority to self?
>
> *Ath.* Yes.
>
> *Cle.* You are quite right in asking the question, for there certainly is such a principle, and above all in the states; and the state in which the better citizens win a victory over the mob and over the inferior classes may be truly said to be better than itself, and may be justly praised, where such a victory is gained, or censured in the opposite case.
>
> *Ath.* Whether the better is ever really conquered by the worse, is a question which requires more discussion, and may be therefore left for the present. But I now quite understand your meaning where you say that citizens may unjustly conspire, and having the superiority in numbers may overcome and enslave the few just; and when they prevail, the state may be truly called its own inferior and therefore bad; and when they are defeated, its own superior and therefore good (626 E–627 C).

What emerges next from the dialogue is that Plato does not seek to destroy or eliminate the internal rival, but to control it. His main concern, instead, is with principles of *right* and *wrong* that have a natural-law ring to them and with the higher peace of reconciliation without destruction. It is not that peace is to be used to prepare for war, but that the purpose of even war itself is peace:

> *Ath*. And would not everyone always make laws for the sake of the best?
> *Cle*. To be sure.
> *Ath*. But war, whether external or civil, is not the best, and the need of either is to be deprecated; but peace with one another, and good will, are best. Nor is the victory of the state over itself to be regarded as a really good thing, but as a necessity; a man might as well say that the body was in the best state when sick and purged by medicine, forgetting that there is also a state of the body which needs no purge. And in like manner no one can be a true statesman, whether he aims at the happiness of the individual or state, who looks only, or first of all, to external warfare; nor will he ever be a sound legislator who orders peace for the sake of war, and not war for the sake of peace (627 C–628 D).

Thus, we see Plato preferring peace, internally and externally, to war and a harmonious balancing of the classes, not a destruction or brutal suppression of a class. This, of course, does not alter his fundamental objective of a militarily strong state; but it recognizes that military strength is a means rather than an ultimate end, and that the virtuous and happy life is the superior ultimate end. We find, in fact, and pleasantly so, an increasing emphasis on reason and that the proper aim of laws is to make people happy. The heart of Plato's more mature political philosophy, including his conception of the aims and nature of both divine and human goods, is to be found in the passage which lists the elements of justice (wisdom, temperance, and courage):

> *Ath*. Stranger, you ought to have said, the Cretan laws are with reason famous among the Hellenes; for they fulfil the object of laws, which is to make those who use them happy; and they confer every sort of good. Now goods are of two kinds: there are human and there are divine goods, and the human hang upon the divine; and the state which attains the greater, at the same time acquires the less, or, not having the greater, has neither. Of the lesser goods the first is health, the second beauty, the third strength, including swiftness in running and bodily agility generally, and the fourth is wealth, not the blind god [Pluto], but one who is keen of sight, if only he has wisdom for his companion. For wisdom is chief and leader of the divine class of goods, and next follows temperance; and from the union of these two with courage springs justice, and fourth in the scale

of virtue is courage. All these naturally take precedence of the other goods, and this is the order in which the legislator must place them, and after them he will enjoin the rest of his ordinances on the citizens with a view to these, the human looking to the divine, and the divine looking to their leader mind (631 B–632 D; *cf.* Bury translation).

The Golden Cord between God and Humanity and among Humanity: Reason and Law Intertwined

In Book I, Plato, as usual, invokes – or asserts – divine sanction for the laws and conditioned obedience from the young. Only elders may discuss and criticize the laws (634 D–E). And, again, in the *Laws* we see Plato placing great emphasis on the role of education from an early age onward. But, Plato carefully points out, vocational education or training is education in the narrower sense and not to be confused with the education in virtue that is the proper preparation for citizenship. The contrast between training to become a perfect technician and education to become a perfect citizen is expressed as training in understanding, as against training in goodness:

> *Ath.* ... The most important part of education is right training in the nursery. The soul of the child in his play should be guided to the love of that sort of excellence in which when he grows up to manhood he will have to be perfected.
> ...
> ... At present when we speak in terms of praise or blame about the bringing up of each person, we call one man educated and another uneducated, although the uneducated man may be sometimes very well educated for the calling of a retail trader, or of a captain of a ship, and the like. For we are not speaking of education in this narrower sense, but of that other education in virtue from youth upwards, which makes a man eagerly pursue the ideal perfection of citizenship, and teaches him how rightly to rule and how to obey. This is the only education which, upon our view, deserves the name; that other sort of training, which aims at the acquisition of wealth or bodily strength, or mere cleverness apart from intelligence and justice, is mean and illiberal, and is not worthy to be called education at all (643 B–644 A).

Although in the *Laws*, Plato never lets up in his search for a 'fail-safe' formula to use in building and maintaining his state, we see again and again more sophisticated, dualistic, and pluralistic approaches and explanations. Life and politics are portrayed as both simple and complicated, and the way to understand and traverse them properly is to seize hold, and never let go, of a golden cord (which Plato finds present in the common law of the state) that is mixed in with other cords and strings that would pull us, puppetlike, in wrong directions. Plato unravels this scheme of things, with a revealing touch of cynicism:

> *Ath.* Let us look at the matter thus: May we not conceive each of us living beings to be a puppet of the Gods, either their plaything only, or created with a purpose – which of the two we cannot certainly know? But we do know, that these affections in us are like cords and strings, which pull us different and opposite ways, and to opposite actions; and herein lies the difference between virtue and vice. According to the argument there is one among these cords which every man ought to grasp and never let go, but to pull with it against all the rest; and this is the sacred and golden cord of reason, called by us the common law of the State; there are others which are hard and of iron, but this one is soft because golden; and there are several other kinds. Now we ought always to co-operate with the lead of the best, which is law. For inasmuch as reason is beautiful and gentle, and not violent, her rule must needs have ministers in order to help the golden principle in vanquishing the other principles (644 C–645 C).[2]

A Multiple Governmental Contract

Of interest in Book III especially to the political theorist is Plato's favourable discussion of an agreement that fulfils the requirements of a *governmental contract* and its external extension along lines of the Holy Alliance of the early 19th century, whether the people will it or no:

> *Ath.* ... Three royal heroes made oath to three cities which were under a kingly government, and the cities to the kings, that both rulers and subjects govern and be governed according to the laws which were common to all of them: the rulers promised that as time and the race went forward they would not make their rule more arbitrary; and the subjects said that, if the rulers observed these conditions, they would never subvert or permit others to subvert those kingdoms; the kings were to assist kings and peoples when injured, and the peoples were to assist peoples and kings in like manner. Is not this the fact?
> *Meg.* Yes.
> *Ath.* And the three states to whom these laws were given, whether their kings or any others were the authors of them, had therefore the greatest security for the maintenance of their constitutions?
> *Meg.* What security?
> *Ath.* That the other two states were always to come to the rescue against a rebellious third.
> *Meg.* True.
> *Ath.* Many persons say that legislators ought to impose such laws as the mass

of the people will be ready to receive; but this is just as if one were to command gymnastic masters or physicians to treat or cure their pupils or patients in an agreeable manner (683 E–684 C).[3]

Ignorance a Cause of Ruin

Speaking in the positive sense, Francis Bacon writes in his *Religious Meditations* (1597) that 'Knowledge itself is power'. Speaking in the negative sense, Plato declares in the *Laws* that ignorance is ruination and the greatest ignorance is to hate what a man knows to be good and noble and to love what he knows to be unrighteous and evil. For Plato, this is the greatest of defeats, when the senses and desires triumph over reason, whether in the state or in the individual (687 E–689 C).

Natural Right to Rule

We see next a repetition of Plato's principles of authority that illustrate his concept of a natural right to rule: parents over children, noble over ignoble, older over younger, master over slave, stronger over weaker, wise over non-understanding, and the winner of the lot. (Omitted from listing here by Plato is husband over wife.) Basically, the supremacy of authority predicated on wisdom, and preferably without force, is asserted, but with the will of the gods expressed through the chance of the lot, and lastly the rule of law over willing subjects:

> *Ath.* And what are the principles on which men rule and obey in cities, whether great or small; and similarly in families? What are they, and how many in number? Is there not one claim of authority which is always just, – that of fathers and mothers and in general of progenitors to rule over their offspring?
> *Cle.* There is.
> *Ath.* Next follows the principle that the noble should rule over the ignoble; and, thirdly, that the elder should rule and the younger obey?
> *Cle.* To be sure.
> *Ath.* And, fourthly, that slaves should be ruled, and their masters rule.
> *Cle.* Of course.
> *Ath.* Fifthly, if I am not mistaken, comes the principle that the stronger shall rule, and the weaker be ruled?
> *Cle.* That is a rule not to be disobeyed.
> *Ath.* Yes, and a rule which prevails very widely among all creatures, and is according to nature, as the Theban poet Pindar once said; and the sixth principle, and the greatest of all, is, that the wise should lead and command, and the

ignorant follow and obey; and yet, O thou most wise Pindar, as I should reply to him, this surely is not contrary to nature, but according to nature, being the rule of law over willing subjects, and not a rule of compulsion.

Cle. Most true.

Ath. There is a seventh kind of rule which is awarded by lot, and is dear to the Gods and a token of good fortune: he on whom the lot falls is a ruler, and he who fails in obtaining the lot goes away and is the subject; and this we affirm to be quite just (690 A–C).

Division of Powers with Checks and Balances

An important addition to Plato's political theory appears next: some rudiments of a constitutional division of powers, including the concept of mutual checks, is presented. It follows the principle that too great an amount of power should not be given to any individual or group. The corrupting nature of power is treated in a manner reminiscent of Lord Acton's dictum about the corrupting nature of power, as the Athenian Stranger addresses Megillus of Lacedaemon about the founding of the Spartan dual kingship and the need for proportionality. He states what to him is a clear proposition:

> *Ath*. That if any one gives too great a power to anything, too large a sail to a vessel, too much food to the body, too much authority to the mind, and does not observe the mean, everything is overthrown, and, in the wantonness of excess, runs in the one case to disorders, and in the other to injustice, which is the child of excess. I mean to say, my dear friends, that there is no soul of man, young and irresponsible, who will be able to sustain the temptation of arbitrary power – no one who will not, under such circumstances, become filled with folly, that worst of diseases, and be hated by his nearest and dearest friends: when this happens his kingdom is undermined, and all his power vanishes from him. And great legislators who know the mean should take heed of the danger. As far as we can guess at this distance of time, what happened was as follows:–
>
> *Meg*. What?
>
> *Ath*. A God, who watched over Sparta, seeing into the future, gave you two families of kings instead of one; and this brought you more within the limits of moderation. In the next place, some human wisdom mingled with divine power, observing that the constitution of your government was still feverish and excited, tempered your inborn strength and pride of birth with the moderation which comes of age, making the power of your twenty-eight elders equal with that of the kings in the most important matters. But your third saviour, perceiving that your government was still swelling and foaming, and desirous to impose a curb upon it, instituted the Ephors, whose power he made to resemble that of magistrates elected by lot; and by this arrangement the kingly office, being

compounded of the right elements and duly moderated, was preserved, and was the means of preserving all the rest (691 B–692 A).[4]

Constitutional Monarchy Advocated

We find next the fundamental nature of constitutional monarchy being advocated by Plato. For Plato, this consists of a combination of monarchy, whose chief virtue is wisdom, with democracy, whose chief virtue is freedom. By blending these two constitutional 'mother-forms', the consequent characteristics of the state would be moderation and friendship:

> *Ath.* Hear me, then: there are two mother forms of states from which the rest may be truly said to be derived; and one of them may be called monarchy and the other democracy: the Persians have the highest form of one, and we of the other; almost all the rest, as I was saying, are variations of these. Now, if you are to have liberty and the combination of friendship with wisdom, you must have both these forms of government in a measure; the argument emphatically declares that no city can be well governed which is not made up of both.[1] ([1] Cp. *infra*, vi. 756 E; Arist. Pol. ii. 6 § 18.)
>
> *Cle.* Impossible.
>
> *Ath.* Neither the one, if it be exclusively and excessively attached to monarchy, nor the other, if it be similarly attached to freedom, observes moderation; but your states, the Laconian and Cretan, have more of it; and the same was the case with the Athenians and Persians of old time, but now they have less. Shall I tell you why?
>
> *Cle.* By all means, if it will tend to elucidate our subject.
>
> *Ath.* Hear, then:– There was a time when the Persians had more of the state which is a mean between slavery and freedom. In the reign of Cyrus they were freemen and also lords of many others: the rulers gave a share of freedom to the subjects, and being treated as equals, the soldiers were on better terms with their generals, and showed themselves more ready in the hour of danger. And if there was any wise man among them, who was able to give good counsel, he imparted his wisdom to the public; for the king was not jealous, but allowed him full liberty of speech, and gave honour to those who could advise him in any matter. And the nation waxed in all respects, because there was freedom and friendship and communion of mind among them (693 D–694 B).

Rugged, Masculine Education to Produce Strong Character

But what of the continuity of strong, yet temperate, government from one generation to the next? Again, education is centrally important, but a masculine education that strengthens and disciplines by exposure to conditioning through hardships, rather than a feminine education that pampers and weakens mind, character, and body. The children of rulers and the wealthy, therefore, should receive the same kind of education as all other men, lest the unfortunate stories of the indulgent, luxurious rearing of Cambyses and Xerxes be repeated (694 C–696 B).

Not only should there not be a pampering, soft upbringing of the wealthy young, but also the wealthy adults should not be given undue honours. The safety and happiness of the state require observance of a proper scale of values: goods of the soul (i.e., character) first; goods of the body second; and monetary goods and property third. The Athenian Stranger and Megillus voice the following agreement:

> *Ath.* We maintain, then, that a State which would be safe and happy, as far as the nature of man allows, must and ought to distribute honour and dishonour in the right way. And the right way is to place the goods of the soul first and highest in the scale, always assuming temperance to be the condition of them; and to assign the second place to the goods of the body; and the third place to money and property. And if any legislator or state departs from this rule by giving money the place of honour, or in any way preferring that which is really last, may we not say, that he or the state is doing an unholy and unpatriotic thing (697 B–C)?

Rule of Law by Elected Magistrates Conducive to Patriotism and Unity

Plato leaves off his discussion of the strengths and weaknesses of the Persians and turns to a consideration of the Athenians and their government. He lauds the moderate, elected government of the latter at the time of Marathon (490 BC), attributing to it virtues of patriotism and friendliness which he ascribes to satisfaction with their rulers and the rule of law and to reverence for them:

> *Ath.* Next we must pass in review the government of Attica in like manner, and from this show that entire freedom and the absence of all superior authority is not by any means so good as government by others when properly limited, which was our ancient Athenian constitution at the time when the Persians made their attack on Hellas, or, speaking more correctly, on the whole continent of Europe. There were four classes, arranged according to a property census, and reverence was our queen and mistress, and made us willing to live in obedience to the laws which then prevailed. Also the vastness of the Persian armament, both by sea and on land, caused a helpless terror, which made us more and more the servants of our rulers and of the laws; and for all these reasons an exceeding harmony prevailed among us (698 A–B).[5]

Plato continues by discussing the strong sense of unity and self-reliance – plus the desperation of the moment – which led to victory at Marathon and a strong spirit of friendship among the Athenian warriors. The Athenian Stranger adds the following comment: 'Under the ancient laws, my friends, the people was not as now the master, but rather the willing servant of the laws' (698 B– 700 A).

Danger of Too Much Freedom for the Multitude

What led to the breakdown of such an exemplary balance within society and government and of the spiritual values of the people? Plato ascribes it to: too much freedom for the multitude; too much power for the uninstructed many to make decisions in poetry contests and concerning music; the corrupting influences of the innovators and contemporary modernists among the poets; and the general corruption, lawlessness, breakdown of manners, and conceit of the unqualified that spread like a contagion from music audiences into other areas. The necessary correctives, Plato believes, are to have three proper objectives (freedom, unity, and sense) and to achieve a proper mean between the most despotic and the most free kinds of government. Therefore, too much freedom to perform or to criticize should not be given, because licentious works and the habit of careless criticism will carry over to become licentious behaviour in general, with widespread deleterious consequences. Again, Plato seeks a golden mean between extremes to correct a situation of disorder; it is to be found in moderate types of even the worst forms of government:

> *Ath.* We were maintaining that the lawgiver ought to have three things in view: first, that the city for which he legislates should be free; and secondly, be at unity with herself; and thirdly, should have understanding; – these were our principles, were they not?
> *Meg.* Certainly.
> *Ath.* With a view to this we selected two kinds of government, the one the most despotic, and the other the most free; and now we are considering which of them is the right form: we took a mean in both cases, of despotism in the one, and of liberty in the other, and we saw that in a mean they attained their perfection; but that when they were carried to the extreme of either, slavery or licence, neither party were the gainers (700 A–701 E).

Location and Composition of Colonies

Book IV begins with a discussion of the location of the proposed colony of

Magnesia: at some distance from the sea, with a fair proportion of hill, plain and wood – with more rock than plain – to provide for the needs and defence and to promote virtue rather than moneymaking among the people. Also, Plato places his main reliance on land forces who must be brave and stand and fight; and in the true fashion of many a soldier, Plato downgrades by comparison the navy and its ships that may invite men to escape from combat and become cowards. The demographic composition of the proposed new colony elicits the further observation that there are advantages and disadvantages when its population is homogeneous. The conclusion reached seems to be in favour of the benefits that may be gained from some new legislation and some mixture of other peoples in addition to the best of the old legislation and a majority of population from the mother city. Most important of all for our purposes in this portion of dialogue, is Plato's reiteration of the principal objective of every work he ever wrote. It may be stated as the attainment of whatever is best or most good:

> *Ath.* ... And in estimating the goodness of a state, we regard both the situation of the country and the order of the laws, considering that the mere preservation and continuance of life is not the most honourable thing for men, as the vulgar think, but the continuance of the best life, while we live; and that again, if I am not mistaken, is a remark which has been made already[1]. ([1] Cp. ii, 661.) (Bk. IV, 704 A–708 D, especially 707 D).

God and the Tyrant Legislate Together

There are those who believe that war, pestilence, accidents, and the unforeseen, because they result in instability, change, and revolution, are the most powerful agents of legislation and that they are beyond mortal control: 'human affairs are nearly all matters of pure chance'. Secondly, there are those who believe that God governs all things, using all of these circumstances as means to work His will, and this is equally true. Thirdly, there is the less extreme view that makes room for a wise legislator (fashioned in the image of Plato?) to practice his art in combination with God and through the instrumentality of a vigorous, but temperate, young tyrant or absolute monarch. These passages in Book IV conclude with the thought that the easiest way to found an improved state is by using such a handy tyrant:

> *Ath.* Then our tyrant must have this [temperance – RP] as well as the other qualities, if the state is to acquire in the best manner and in the shortest time the form of government which is most conducive to happiness; for there neither is

nor ever will be a better or speedier way of establishing a polity than by a tyranny (709 A–710 B).[6]

According to Plato, improvement of the form of government of a state takes place most easily out of tyranny; secondly, out of constitutional monarchy; thirdly, out of democracy; and fourthly, out of oligarchy (plutocracy). However, the great difficulty is to find the divine love of temperate and just institutions existing under any powerful form of government, yet this is precisely what needs to be done to bring about the best laws and constitution: i.e., to unite supreme political power with the greatest of wisdom and temperance:

> *Ath.* ... I mean rather to say that the change is best made out of a tyranny; and secondly, out of a monarchy; and thirdly, out of some sort of democracy: fourth, in the capacity for improvement, comes oligarchy, which has the greatest difficulty in admitting of such a change, because the government is in the hands of a number of potentates. I am supposing that the legislator is by nature of the true sort, and that his strength is united with that of the chief men of the state; and when the ruling element is numerically small, and at the same time very strong, as in a tyranny, there the change is likely to be easiest and most rapid.
>
> ...
>
> Let no one, my friends, persuade us that there is any quicker and easier way in which states change their laws than when the rulers lead: such changes never have, nor ever will, come to pass in any other way. The real impossibility or difficulty is of another sort, and is rarely surmounted in the course of ages; but when once it is surmounted, ten thousand or rather all blessings follows.
>
> *Cle.* Of what are you speaking?
>
> *Ath.* The difficulty is to find the divine love of temperate and just institutions existing in any powerful forms of government, whether in a monarchy or oligarchy of wealth or birth. You might as well hope to reproduce the character of Nestor, who is said to have excelled all men in the power of speech, and yet more in his temperance. ... And this may be said of power in general: When the supreme power in man coincides with greatest wisdom and temperance, then the best laws and the best constitution come into being; but in no other way (710 D–712 A).[7]

Hierarchical Polity and the Rule of Law

The Athenian Stranger inquires as to the form of polity or government their proposed new city should take. Cleinias asks whether it would be some form of democracy, oligarchy, aristocracy, or monarchy. Megillus then describes the Spartan state, which seems to be a combination of all these, plus the tyranny that Cleinias has rejected out of hand; he wonders, therefore, which of these it is. Similarly, Cleinias does not feel that Knossus is any of these forms. The Athenian Stranger says that the forms of government named are not polities, but arrangements of states named for their rulers who make laws in their own interest. At first glance, it may seem that Plato is aware of and is advocating a mixed, balanced government, such as a John Adams or Alexander Hamilton at various times supported. However, we should not be too quick to read such an interpretation into it. Mixture, yes. Balance, only possibly; but more definite is a *pluralistic participation on an hierarchical basis* which follows what for Plato is a principle of reason and divine law that was commonly received in his day: namely, that the superior should rule over the inferior in a chain of command. Also, unquestionably so at this point, is that the law should be superior to the rulers; and thus may the state call forth upon itself every blessing of the gods. The topic concludes with a modern ring, especially because it shows that Plato had a conception of rulers as servants of the law, if not of the people. Our quotation from this portion of the dialogue begins with the Athenian Stranger holding forth about a tradition of how Cronos, by using daemons to rule over men, established a most prosperous government and settlement on which the best of states continue to be modelled:

> *Ath.* ... There is a tradition of the happy life of mankind in days when all things were spontaneous and abundant. And of this the reason is said to have been as follows:– Cronos knew what we ourselves were declaring[1], ([1] *supra*, iii, 691.) that no human nature invested with supreme power is able to order human affairs and not overflow with insolence and wrong. Which reflection led him to appoint not man but demigods, who are of a higher and more divine race, to be the kings and rulers of our cities; he did as we do with flocks of sheep and other tame animals. For we do not appoint oxen to be the lords of oxen, or goats of goats; but we ourselves are a superior race, and rule over them. In like manner God, in his love of mankind, placed over us the demons, who are a superior race, and they with great ease and pleasure to themselves, and no less to us, taking care of us and giving us peace and reverence and order and justice never failing, made the tribes of men happy and united. And this tradition which is true, declares that cities of which some mortal man and not God is the ruler, have no escape from evils and toils. Still we must do all that we can to imitate the life which is said to have existed in the days of Cronos, and, as far as the principle of immortality dwells in us, to that we must hearken, both in private and public life, and regulate our cities and houses according to law, meaning by the very term 'law,' the distribution of mind. ...
>
> ... [W]hen there has been a contest for power, those who gain the upper hand so entirely monopolize the government, as to refuse all share to the defeated

party and their descendants – they live watching one another, the ruling class being in perpetual fear that some one who has a recollection of former wrongs will come into power and rise up against them. Now, according to our view, such governments are not polities at all, nor are laws right which are passed for the good of particular classes and not for the good of the whole state. States which have such laws are not polities but parties, and their notions of justice are simply unmeaning. I say this, because I am going to assert that we must not entrust the government in your state to any one because he is rich, or because he possesses any other advantage, such as strength, or stature, or again birth: but he who is most obedient to the laws of the state, he shall win the palm; and to him who is victorious in the first degree shall be given the highest office and chief ministry of the gods; and the second to him who bears the second palm; and on a similar principle shall all the other offices be assigned to those who come next in order. And when I call the rulers servants or ministers of the law, I give them this name not for the sake of novelty, but because I certainly believe that upon such service or ministry depends the well- or ill-being of the state. For that state in which the law is subject and has no authority, I perceive to be on the highway to ruin; but I see that the state in which the law is above the rulers, and the rulers are the inferiors of the law, has salvation, and every blessing which the Gods can confer (712 D–715 D).[8]

God's Will is Justice

For Plato, justice always accords with God's purposes and will. Therefore, Protagoras was wrong, says Plato, in declaring that man is the measure of all things, for these words are far more true of God. Therefore, it behooves us to follow the divine law that has placed a hierarchy of God, gods, daemons or spirits, heroes, and parents above us, and to do legal homage to them and follow their laws and commandments. To do so will invite blessings and prosperity; not to do so will invite ruin. The way to do so is to labour, to sweat, and to follow the difficult path of virtue, rather than the more easily travelled road to wickedness:

> *Cle*. Every man ought to make up his mind that he will be one of the followers of God; there can be no doubt of that.
> *Ath*. Then what life is agreeable to God, and becoming in His followers? One only, expressed once for all in the old saying that 'like agrees with like, with measure measure,' but things which have no measure agree neither with themselves nor with the things which have. Now God ought to be to us the measure of all things, and not man[1] ([1] Cp. Crat. 386 A foll.; Theaet. 152 A.), as men commonly say (Protagoras): the words are far more true of Him. And he who would be dear to God must, as far as is possible, be like Him and such as

He is. Wherefore the temperate man is the friend of God, for he is like Him; and the intemperate man is unlike Him, and different from Him, and unjust. And the same applies to other things; and this is the conclusion, which is also the noblest and truest of all sayings,– that for the good man to offer sacrifice to the Gods, and hold converse with them by means of prayers and offerings and every kind of service, is the noblest and best of all things, and also the most conducive to a happy life, and very fit and meet (715 E–719 A, especially 716 A–E).[9]

There is also a somewhat softer Plato revealed in Book IV of the *Laws* than in previous works, for Plato now more strongly counsels a government that persuades – even the laws contain exhortations and explanations – as well as commands. This important idea is dwelt upon at length (719 E–723 D). As an example, Plato first presents a 'simple law' of marriage in terms of command; and then in terms of command, explanation, and persuasion. A significant indication of how Plato would approach the content and operation of legislation is given when he states that he is not really presenting a double law but one law in two parts: the command of the law and its explanation, prelude, or preamble (725 A–723 B).

Example and Admonition to Train the Young

Book V begins by stressing again the idea of self-control. Next to the gods and secondary divinities, his soul is a man's most divine possession; but there is a dualism in man's nature, and his soul is properly honoured only when he is not conceited about it or self-exculpating about his misdeeds and when the better and superior part in him rules and the worse and inferior part serves (Bk V, 726 A–728 C).

Plato continues by warning parents against piling up riches for their children. Instead, parents should seek to develop their characters, their bodies, and their minds; and this is best done by example and admonition, but not by admonition alone, and by seeking the mean rather than the extreme. The scale of honour they should accordingly pay, is to the gods first, their souls second, and their bodies third (728 D–729 C).

Some of the desirable habits that parents should practice for their children to see, include reverence, self-control, and just treatment of others, especially of strangers and most especially of suppliants (729 B–E). All of these things are good in themselves and as means also. They are especially important as a means of developing the habit of obedience to the laws; and for Plato, the law-abiding man is best:

Ath. ... And surely in his relations to the state and his fellow-citizens, he is by far the best, who rather than the Olympic or any other victory of peace or war, desires to win the palm of obedience to the laws of his country, and who, of all mankind, is the person reputed to have obeyed them best through life (729 D–E).

In addition, Plato considers other habits, practices, and principles that are not commanded by law, but are matters of praise and blame that make the individual more tractable and amenable to the laws. Among these, truth leads all the rest, with temperance and wisdom of similar worth:

Ath. ... Truth is the beginning of every good thing, both to Gods and men; and he who would be blessed and happy, should be from the first a partaker of the truth, that he may live a true man as long as possible, for then he can be trusted; but he is not to be trusted who loves voluntary falsehood, and he who loves involuntary falsehood is a fool. Neither condition is enviable, for the untrustworthy and ignorant has no friend, and as time advances he becomes known, and lays up in store for himself isolation in crabbed age when life is on the wane: so that, whether his children or friends are alive or not, he is equally solitary. – Worthy of honour is he who does no injustice, and of more than twofold honour, if he not only does no injustice himself, but hinders others from doing any; the first may count as one man, the second is worth many men, because he informs the rulers of the injustice of others. And yet more highly to be esteemed is he who co-operates with the rulers in correcting the citizens as far as he can – he shall be proclaimed the great and perfect citizen, and bear away the palm of virtue. The same praise may be given about temperance and wisdom, and all other goods which may be imparted to others, as well as acquired by a man for himself ... (730 C–E).

But just as the pursuit and practice of truth is the greatest good for men and gods, there is a greatest evil that is to be avoided. For Plato, excessive concern with self-interest, rather than with impartial justice, is this chief source of error. In rather naïve-sounding fashion, reminiscent of Socrates, Plato states that every wrongdoer is so involuntarily because he is so because of ignorance! For the man who can remedy his evils, Plato recommends gentle treatment; for the totally wicked man who cannot see the error of his ways and will not correct them, Plato recommends 'passionate', wrathful punishment. Thus, the good man should try to be 'both gentle and passionate' and must not insist too much on his own correctness or self-righteousness and must 'follow a better man than himself':

Ath. ... Now every man would be valiant, but he should also be gentle. From the cruel, or hardly curable, or altogether curable acts of injustice done to him by others, a man can only escape by fighting and defending himself and conquering, and by never ceasing to punish them; and no man who is not of a noble spirit is able to accomplish this. As to the actions of those who do evil, but whose evil is curable, in the first place, let us remember that the unjust man is not unjust of his own free will. For no man of his own free will would choose to possess the greatest of evils, and least of all in the most honourable part of himself. And the soul, as we said, is of a truth deemed by all men the most honourable. In the soul, then, which is the most honourable part of him, no one, if he could help, would admit, or allow to continue the greatest of evils[1] ([1] Cp. Rep. ii, 382.). The unrighteous and vicious are always to be pitied in any case; and one can afford to forgive as well as pity him who is curable, and refrain and calm one's anger, not getting into a passion, like a woman, and nursing ill-feeling. But upon him who is incapable of reformation and wholly evil, the vials of our wrath should be poured out; wherefore I say that good men ought, when occasion demands, to be both gentle and passionate (731 D–732 B).

Purification or Purging of the State

In the *Laws*, as in the *Republic* and the *Statesman*, Plato addresses himself to the imperfect world of imperfect men who seek pleasure rather than pain. But even the noblest – in a manner reminiscent of modern utilitarian philosophy – seek to avoid pain and enjoy the pleasant. But what is the 'right' way of life that gives these rewards? It is the temperate, wise, brave, and healthy life, in contradistinction to the foolish, cowardly, licentious, and diseased one. Thus does Plato encapsulate the way of life he rather consistently advocates for mundane man in all of his writings:

Ath. ... Enough has been said of divine matters, both as touching the practices which men ought to follow, and as to the sort of persons who they ought severally to be. But of human things we have not as yet spoken, and we must; for to men we are discoursing and not to Gods. Pleasures and pains and desires are a part of human nature, and on them every mortal being must of necessity hang and depend with the most eager interest. And therefore we must praise the noblest life, not only as the fairest in appearance, but as being one which, if a man will only taste, and not, while still in his youth, desert for another, he will find to surpass also in the very thing which we all of us desire. – I mean in having a greater amount of pleasure and less of pain during the whole of life (732 E–733 A).

And so in the *Laws*, as somewhat in the *Republic* and more so in the

Statesman, Plato is concerned with an approach to constitutionalism that relates in his mind to 'the real world', and is therefore both preventive and curative, and comparable to the practice of medicine by the familiar physician.[10] He discusses both more painful kinds of purification available to the despotic legislator and milder kinds to which the non-despotic legislator may be limited. He follows with the fundamental proposal that the economic infrastructure of landed property-holding and other wealth be widespread and limited to moderate size. For Plato, there can be no real goodwill and harmony in a society, and consequently no safe, stable, and strong state, unless extremes of wealth and poverty be actively prevented (734 A–736 E).

Three Best Forms of the State

Plato states that there are three forms of the state that are respectively first, second, and third in excellence, but describes here only the first and second forms. In the first and highest form, there will be a communion of women, children, and property; but this is not practicable because the citizens will not accept it. In the second highest form, the land will be divided into 5,040 houses or lots, each to be regarded as in trust from the city. The number 5,040 is to remain always the basis of division, although there may be some changes in amounts that will be limited to such proportions that the richest citizen shall not have more than four times the wealth of the poorest; and the estates shall be entailed, descending intact to a single, favoured child. Colonization is a device that can remove any excess population or children from the city, so the number of 5,040 households can be maintained; and although not desirable, citizens of spurious birth and origin might have to be introduced if the population be lowered by war or plague. The question to be borne in mind when reading the obvious nonsense of especially the mathematical proposals in this passage, however, is whether – or when – Plato is spoofing, ironical, serious, or engaging in an evidently make-believe exercise he uses to further the desideratum of stability (737 C–741 E). Was he perhaps groping for some kind of general mathematical form of measurement or modality akin to what provides the notes of a musical scale, the Pythagorean theorem of the hypotenuse, or an algebraic formula that could be used in constructing his model state?[11]

Limitation of Riches and Occupation

A man who is very rich, in the opinion of Plato, cannot be very good; but it is goodness, not riches, that brings about the best and happiest state. Therefore, no marriage dowries should be given or taken. There should be a system of strict internal regulation and supervision and restriction of travel and contacts abroad. The law is to forbid any private person to have gold and silver; there is to be a legal tender of coins good only within the state; and the state is to provide and control external coinage that is needed for its diplomatic missions and foreign state business. The state is also to provide any currency needed by private persons who get its permission to go abroad; and they must turn over to the state any foreign coins they come home with, receiving in exchange an equivalent amount of internal money. Such practices and restrictions, Plato believes, should help make the citizens both good and happy rather than wicked and rich (741 E–743 C).

The rationale of Plato's opposition to excessive wealth also includes an order of values and corresponding priorities. Of the three things in which all persons have an interest, Plato repeats that money is the lowest, the body midway, and the soul highest. The legislator should legislate according to this scale of values: by limiting profits to those gained in agriculture; by use of gymnastics to develop the body; and by education to elevate the soul (743 C–744 A).

As well as rejecting the practicability of having all things in common, Plato rejects as also impracticable his second-best hope: that there might be an equality of property. Again in parallel fashion, Plato would therefore have offices, contributions, and distributions of honour made in proportion to one's wealth. This would be accomplished in great part by a fourfold classification of the population based on amount of property, with ability to pass from one class to another as one's amount of wealth changed. Thus, all possessions would have to be registered before the magistrates (744 B–745 B).

Location and Division of the City

Plato would locate the city as centrally as possible within the country; allot territory for temples; divide the rest into 12 radiating districts and 5,040 lots; and make each lot consist of one section near the city and a second away from it, with the sections of inferior quality made larger in size. Similarly, the citizens would be divided into 12 equal parts (745 B–E).

Book V of the *Laws* concludes with the Athenian Stranger rejoicing in the mathematical beauties and other advantages of the number 5,040 and how it could lend itself to such varied matters as political and military units, a coinage system, weights and measures, and development of the mind and character of the young. Climatic and nutritional influences on bodies and souls must also be taken into account in selecting a proper location for a city. Lastly, there would be included the requirement that the location bear a divine inspiration because inhabited by friendly demigods who also have their appointed lots (746 C–747 E).[12]

Need to Select Qualified Officeholders

Plato discerns for us, concerning officeholders, two important areas of what today is called *public law*: laws governing the manner of selection of officeholders and laws governing the conduct of their office. Two other areas of public law regulate the manner of enacting legislation and the dealings of government with the public. That Plato is cognizant of these four subjects of modern public law and their importance is shown at the beginning of Book VI. He points here to the need for both fit officers and well-framed laws (Bk VI, 751 A–D).

But how to choose the right officeholders? Institutional arrangements in the form of the procedure whereby an officeholder qualifies and is selected is only a final step for Plato. Stability and continuity of a state require first and foremost a long process of creating inherent limitations among the public (752 B–C). An important qualification for electors of magistrates is therefore to be military service. The election itself is to be sanctified by being held in the most sacred shrine within the state, and safeguards are to be provided in the form of public protesting of improprieties, publicizing of results, and elimination-stages that finally produce the Council of Thirty-Seven (753 B–D).

The Council of Thirty-Seven

The most important body in the state proposed in the *Laws* is the Council of Thirty-Seven. Some of their duties, qualifications, and liabilities are stipulated in 'the three first ordinances about the guardians of the law', especially the requirement that they be between 50 and 70 years of age (754 D–755 B).

One of the functions of the wardens, or guardians, of the law, by which term is presumably meant the Council of Thirty-Seven, is to be the nomination of generals. Interestingly enough, however, the citizen-soldiers have the power of election and may also propose additional candidates (755 B–756 E).

The Council of 360

An object example of Plato's preoccupation with fail-safe mathematical formulas, or applied quantification, is presented in his description of the manner in which the Council of 360 (the *boulé*: βουλή) is to be selected. It is based on the division of the citizenry into four classes according to amount of wealth. Although every citizen, no matter his class, is to be permitted to vote for the 90 representatives from each of the four classes, a system of fines for not voting is to be applied that bears more heavily on the two wealthier classes and most heavily on the first class. Plato himself denotes this mode of election (presumably speaking of the Council of Thirty-Seven, the generals, other officers, and the Council of 360) as a mean between monarchy and democracy. Inasmuch as it is neither monarchical nor fully democratic, there is a plausibility to Plato's judgment of this arrangement. However, if we wish to be more detailed and more precise, we may add that a balancing and integration of the classes in some form of mixed government takes place and that we have here some important elements of both democracy and plutocracy – and this had been the character of the Athenian *politeia* since Solon. We should also note carefully how Plato tries to make this selection formula conform to: first, his ideas of justice that accord equality of treatment to equals and inequality of treatment to unequals; second, the divine scheme of things which dictates such an approach to justice; and third, the practical consideration of avoiding popular discontent. The Athenian Stranger concludes this passage as follows:

> *Ath.* ... The mode of election which has been described is in a mean between monarchy and democracy, and such a mean the state ought always to observe, for servants and masters never can be friends, nor good and bad, merely because they are declared to have equal privileges. For to unequals equals become unequal, if they are not harmonized by measure; and both by reason of equality, and by reason of inequality, cities are filled with seditions. The old saying, that 'equality makes friendship,' is happy and also true; but there is obscurity and confusion as to what sort of equality is meant. For there are two equalities which are called by the same name, but are in reality in many ways almost the opposite of one another; one of them may be introduced without difficulty, by any state or any legislator in the distribution of honours: this is the rule of measure, weight, and number, which regulates and apportions them. But there is another equality, of a better and higher kind, which is not so easily recognized. This is the judgment of Zeus; among men it avails but little; that little, however, is the source of the greatest good to individuals and states. For it gives to the greater more, and to the inferior less and in proportion to the nature of each; and, above all, greater honour always to the greater virtue, and to the less less;

and to either in proportion to their respective measure of virtue and education. And this is justice, and is ever the true principle of states, at which we ought to aim, and according to this rule order the new city which is now being founded, and any other city which may be hereafter founded. To this the legislator should look,– not to the interests of tyrants one or more, or to the power of the people, but to justice always: which, as I was saying, is the distribution of natural equality among unequals in each case. But there are times at which every state is compelled to use the words, 'just,' 'equal,' in a secondary sense, in the hope of escaping in some degree from factions. For equity and indulgence are infractions of the perfect and strict rule of justice. And this is the reason why we are obliged to use the equality of the lot, in order to avoid the discontent of the people; and so we invoke God and fortune in our prayers, and beg that they themselves will direct the lot with a view to supreme justice. And therefore, although we are compelled to use both equalities, we should use that into which the element of chance enters as seldom as possible (756 A–758 A).[13]

We should recognize, moreover, that it is not only in the manner of selection of councils, magistrates, and military officers that Plato advocates what had for a long time been more or less practised in Athens, but also in their duties and manner of functioning. Some very apt comparisons may be made, for example, with the organization, tasks, and procedures of the Council of the Areopagus, *boulé*, *ekklesia*, *strategoi*, prytanies (rotating council executive committees composed of representatives of the tribes), and the four military classes of *pentakosiomedimnai*, *hippeis*, *zeugites*, and *thetes*. In addition to what has been quoted above, we may also remark upon the similarities to the Athenian system of government that appear in this portion of the dialogue, as well as elsewhere in the *Laws*. The Athenian Stranger explains some of the purpose and manner of operation of his proposed system in his description of a controlling council of elder guardians he would set up to exercise executive, or 'presidential', control of the state. To meet both the personal need of the councillors to attend to their domestic affairs and the civic need of continuity of their services, one-twelfth of their number would in rotation be on full-time service to the state:

> *Ath.* ... Their business is to be at hand and receive any foreigner or citizen who comes to them, whether to give information, or to put one of those questions, to which, when asked by other cities, a city should given an answer, and to which, if she ask them herself, she should receive an answer; or again, when there is a likelihood of internal commotions, which are always liable to happen in some form or other, they will, if they can, prevent their occurring; or if they have already occurred, will lose no time in making them known to the city and healing

the evil. Wherefore, also, this which is the presiding body of the state ought always to have the control of their assemblies, and of the dissolution of them, ordinary as well as extra-ordinary. All this is to be ordered by the twelfth part of the council, which is always to keep watch together with the other officers of the state during one portion of the year, and to rest during the remaining eleven portions (758 A–D).

Organization and Administration of the City

Plato treats here of people and conditions too much as though they were factors or constants in mathematical formulae. Whether he believes his proposals to be feasible or not, he constantly indulges himself in playing with numbers as though he believes the problems of government might somehow be 'solved' – or at least its practice greatly improved – by utilizing certain divisions or proportions. And so, Plato moves on from the higher legislative and policy-making bodies to a consideration of the routine administration of the state (758 E–760 A).[14]

Military strength, efficiency, and beauty are evident desiderata for Plato as he draws up plans to safeguard and beautify his city-state. Little will be left to chance, whether it regard person, beast, building, or public work. He tries in authoritarian, if not totalitarian, fashion, to think of everything of consequence that has to be done and to assign to it a guardian or attendant (760 A–761 D).[15]

But who is to guard the many lesser guardians and make sure that what has to be done is done and done in proper fashion: i.e., providing utility, beauty, security, and just, harmonious relationships? This requires a combination of oversight and accountability:

Ath. ... Every judge and magistrate shall be liable to give an account of his conduct in office, except those who, like kings, have the final decision. Moreover, as regards the aforesaid wardens of the country, if they do any wrong to those of whom they have the care, whether by imposing upon them unequal tasks, or by taking the produce of the soil or implements of husbandry without their consent; also if they receive anything in the way of a bribe, or decide suits unjustly, or if they yield to influence of flattery, let them be publicly dishonoured; and in regard to any other wrong which they do to the inhabitants of the country, if the question be of a mina, let them submit to the decision of the villagers in the neighbourhood; but in suits of greater amount, or in the case of lesser if they refuse to submit, trusting that their monthly removal into another part of the country will enable them to escape – in such cases the injured party may bring his suit in the common court, and if he obtain a verdict he may exact from the defendant, who refused to submit, a double penalty (761 D–762 B).

The pervasive nature of Plato's scheme may be grasped from his account of how the countryside is to be patrolled by ascetic, honourable young men who have been carefully inspected by the wardens or guardians of the law. These land-stewards or overseers of the country are to serve a two-year tour of duty, living under military conditions and at times performing the functions of secret police in rural areas (762 B–763 C). As a counterpart to the stewards and overseers of the country, Plato would have stewards of the agora and of the city. The duties of the stewards of the city, men of influence, leisure, and wealth, and their manner of selection, are also specified with unrealistic exactness (763 C–E). The stewards of the agora, or market, are to be selected, examined, and confirmed in somewhat similar fashion, and their duties and powers are to extend to the agora, the temples, and fountains (763 E–764 C).

Education and the Courts

In all of his political works Plato makes provision for music and gymnastics. He takes pains to detail how the city is to direct and conduct musical and gymnastic activities (764 C–765 D). And also in all of his political works, it is the minister of education of the youth who is regarded by Plato as having the greatest office in the state. Therefore, he wants the best possible man among the Law-wardens selected for this office, and then he wants him rotated out of office after five years of tenure. Seemingly as an afterthought, Plato also prescribes how vacancies caused by death among officeholders and trustees of orphans should be filled:

> *Ath.* … There remains the minister of the education of youth, male and female; he too will rule according to law; one such minister will be sufficient, and he must be fifty years old, and have children lawfully begotten, both boys and girls by preference, at any rate, one or the other. He who is elected, and he who is the elector, should consider that of all the great offices of state this is the greatest; for the first shoot of any plant, if it makes a good start towards the attainment of its natural excellence, has the greatest effect on its maturity; and this is not only true of plants, but of animals wild and tame, and also of men. Man, as we say, is a tame or civilized animal; nevertheless, he requires proper instruction and a fortunate nature, and then of all animals he becomes the most divine and most civilized[1] ([1] Arist. Pol. i. 2 §§ 15, 16.); but if he be insufficiently or ill educated he is the most savage of earthly creatures. Wherefore the legislator ought not to allow the education of children to become a secondary or accidental matter. In the first place, he who would be rightly provident about them, should

begin by taking care that he is elected, who of all the citizens is in every way best; him the legislator should do his utmost to appoint guardian and super-intendent. To this end all the magistrates, with the exception of the council and prytanes, shall go to the temple of Apollo, and elect by ballot him of the guardians of the law whom they severally think will be the best superintendent of education. And he who has the greatest number of votes, after he has undergone a scrutiny at the hands of all the magistrates who have been his electors, with the exception of the guardians of the law,– shall hold office for five years; and in the sixth year let another be chosen in like manner to fill his office (765 D–766 D).

Plato also looks upon courts of law as of fundamental importance to a state. Perhaps this is because of his constant concern with the nature and dispensation of justice. This does not mean, however, that Plato wishes to encourage litigiousness. Far from it, for he wishes first to try to have disputes amicably settled by neighbours, friends, or arbitrators, and then to have further recourse to as many as three courts if need be. In addition to such matters as how the courts are to be erected, Plato makes provision for one form of trial or court to hear cases which deal with an accusation of wrongdoing by a citizen against another citizen, and for a second form of trial or court to hear cases which deal with an accusation of wrongdoing against the public interest. Anyone may bring an accusation before the Law-wardens when he believes a judge has deliberately made an unjust judgment, and a judge convicted on such a charge is subject to heavy penalties to be paid to his victim and sometimes also to the state. In cases of offence against the state, Plato believes that all are wronged and that therefore the people should be involved in originating the charges and in the final disposition of them. But the need to involve the populace applies also to private suits (766 D–768 E).

Legislation, Marriage, and Mathematics Directed to Virtue

Plato is now ready to address himself to the Guardians and their role as legislators. Their guiding principle, the Athenian Stranger advises Megillus and Cleinias, will, in effect, be the promotion of virtue. The Athenian Stranger points out that the lawgiver attempts to write down the laws as fully and precisely as he can; but no lawgiver is foolish enough to believe that his constitution and laws will not be in future need of revision to keep the system of the state improving instead of worsening. Thus, the three of them should say to the guardians of the law:

Ath. ... There was one main point about which we were agreed – that a man's whole energies throughout life should be devoted to the acquisition of the virtue proper to a man, whether this was to be gained by study, or habit, or some mode of acquisition, or desire, or opinion, or knowledge – and this applies equally to men and women, old and young – the aim of all should always be such as I have described; anything which may be an impediment, the good man ought to show that he utterly disregards. And if at last necessity plainly compels him to be an outlaw from his native land, rather than bow his neck to the yoke of slavery and be ruled by inferiors, and he has to fly, an exile he must be and endure all such trials, rather than accept another form of government, which is likely to make men worse (769 B–771 A).

And again, Plato returns to mathematics and the number 5,040 and to religion as a means of promoting his immediate purpose: in this case it deals with marriage. He hopes to provide the opportunity for suitable marriage at a suitable age between mutually agreeable partners who have had a good look at one another's bodily appearance. Plato describes for us a religio-mathematical, prenuptial game-plan that is so contrived and restrictive that it raises anew the question of how serious he is being, as well as other doubts:

Ath. ...Now every portion should be regarded by us as a sacred gift of Heaven, corresponding to the months and to the revolution of the universe[1] ([1] Cp. Tim. 39, 47 A.). Every city has a guiding and sacred principle given by nature, but in some the division or distribution has been more right than in others, and has been more sacred and fortunate. In our opinion, nothing can be more right than the selection of the number 5040, which may be divided by all numbers from one to twelve with the single exception of eleven, and that admits of a very easy correction; for if, turning to the dividend (5040), we deduct two families, the defect in the division is cured. And the truth of this may be easily proved when we have leisure. But for the present, trusting to the mere assertion of this principle, let us divide the state; and assigning to each portion some God or son of a God, let us give them altars and sacred rites, and at the altars let us hold assemblies for sacrifice twice in the month – twelve assemblies for the tribes, and twelve for the city, according to their divisions; the first in honour of the Gods and divine things, and the second to promote friendship and 'better acquaintance,' as the phrase is, and every sort of good fellowship with one another. For people must be acquainted with those into whose families and whom they marry and with those to whom they give in marriage; in such matters, as far as possible, a man should deem it all important to avoid a mistake, and with this serious purpose let games be instituted[1] ([1] Cp. Rep. v. 459 E.) in which youths and maidens shall dance together, seeing one another and being seen naked, at a proper age, and on a suitable occasion, not transgressing the rules of modesty (771 A–777E).[16]

Following this, Plato tells how he would address the young man who is contemplating marriage. And again, we cannot be sure how serious Plato is regarding his proposals, made in seeming earnest, that amalgamation of wealth or power should not be an objective in marriage and that a young man should not seek a marriage that is pleasing to himself. He should instead, says the Athenian Stranger, prefer an alliance with a family of modest means and seek a marriage beneficial to the state in that it would mix two different temperaments and conditions, in hope of producing temperate, better-balanced offspring. The thought that love for one another and happiness of the parents might be more apt to produce such children, does not seem to be considered by the bachelor Plato. He adds that these requirements cannot be compelled by written law but should be urged by reproaches of the contrary (773 A–E).

Plato also exhorts a young man to marry as a means of participating in immortality through his offspring, and also to avoid the financial and social penalties he would impose on bachelors; but Plato would discourage dowries and lavish wedding garments, as tending by their absence, among other benefits, to make wives less insolent and husbands less subservient (773 E– 774 E). What makes a betrothal valid? Plato also makes it his business to make pronouncements on this subject, the marriage festival, begetting of children, relations with parents and parents-in-law, and the need to maintain sobriety and good health (774 E–776 B).

Next, Plato intermixes some remarks on firm, just, and serious treatment of slaves. He recognizes that slaves are a source of trouble and revolt, and even considers the possibility of not having slaves; but settles for trying to have aliens as slaves and having them kept under proper control (777 B–778 A). Also included here are observations on defence of the city. He prefers no walls, so that the young men will be prepared to fight like the Spartans, in the open. However, placement of homes and public buildings to enhance defence of the city is to be utilized to advantage if there must be walls (778 C–779 D).

Regulation of Individuals for Public Good

Plato returns to his proposals for the regulation of the individual in his model state by pointing out that to be consistent and effective, private as well as public behaviour needs to be controlled. For the same reasons, Plato advocates that the neglect of regulation of the private lives of women be corrected, although he states he does not believe this can be done in most states. Those who are under the mistaken judgment that Plato views women as the equals of men or with proper appreciation, may be disabused of these erroneous impressions by reading Plato's pronouncement that 'females are inferior in goodness to males'. Indeed, Plato feels that women therefore require more regulation than men and that their regulation should not be neglected, as is usually the case. Had Plato had a more sympathetic, affectionate feeling for, and more correct view of, women and therefore understood that, in general, women have a capacity for greater virtue, greater vice, greater love, and greater hatred than men (that they are like men, only more so), he probably would have modified the following inexact, unfair, and incomplete remarks:

> *Ath.* He who imagines that he can give laws for the public conduct of states, while he leaves the private life of citizens wholly to take care of itself; who thinks that individuals may pass the day as they please, and that there is no necessity of order in all things; he, I say, who gives up the control of their private lives, and supposes that they will conform to law in their common and public life, is making a great mistake. ...
>
> ... For with you, Cleinias and Megillus, the common tables of men are, as I said, a heaven-born and admirable institution, but you are mistaken in leaving the women unregulated by law. They have no similar institution of public tables in the light of day, and just that part of the human race which is by nature prone to secrecy and stealth on account of their weakness – I mean the female sex – has been left without regulation by the legislator, which is a great mistake. And, in consequence of this neglect, many things have grown lax among you, which might have been far better, if they had been only regulated by law; for the neglect of regulations about women may not only be regarded as a neglect of half the entire matter[1] ([1] Arist. Pol. i. 13, §§ 15, 16.), but in proportion as a woman's nature is inferior to that of men in capacity for virtue, in that degree the consequence of such neglect is more than twice as important. The careful consideration of this matter, and the arranging and ordering on a common principle of all our institutions relating both to men and women, greatly conduces to the happiness of the state. But at present, such is the unfortunate condition of mankind, that no man of sense will even venture to speak of common tables in places and cities in which they have never been established at all; and how can any one avoid being utterly ridiculous, who attempts to compel women to show in public how much they eat and drink? There is nothing at which the sex is more likely to take offence. For women are accustomed to creep into dark places, and when dragged out into the light they will exert their utmost powers of resistance, and be far too much for the legislator. And therefore, as I said before, in most places they will not endure to have the truth spoken without raising a tremendous outcry, but in this state perhaps they may (780 A–781 D).[17]

Plato is more correct, or at least more modern in viewpoint, when he speaks of three basic appetites of man – for food, drink, and sex – as not corrupting in themselves but only so if misused. Rightly used and constructively controlled, as is true of many of humanity's other drives, they are conducive, instead, to great good. Plato, however, characterizes these natural desires or drives as disorders and proposes to deal with them by a combination of fear, law, and reason, reinforced by the influence of religion:

> *Ath.* I see that among men all things depend upon three wants and desires, of which the end is virtue, if they are rightly led by them, or the opposite if wrongly. Now these are eating and drinking, which begin at birth – every animal has a natural desire for them and is violently excited, and rebels against him who says that he must not satisfy all his pleasures and appetites, and get rid of all the corresponding pains – and the third and greatest and sharpest want and desire breaks out last, and is the fire of sexual lust, which kindles in men every species of wantonness and madness. And these three disorders we must endeavour to master by the three great principles of fear and law and right reason; turning them away from that which is called pleasantest to the best, using the Muses and the Gods who preside over contests to extinguish their increase and influx (782 D–783 A).

Book VI concludes with by-now-familiar themes. Among them are that the bride and groom are 'to produce for the state the best and fairest specimens of children', that the begetting of children and the performance of their parents be supervised by women-inspectors, and that divorce of barren mates after ten years be encouraged. Numerous other forms of conscription, coercion, coaxing, and invasion of privacy are also advocated. The passage concludes with suggested ages for marriage, office-holding, and military service:

> *Ath.* ... The limit of marriageable ages for a woman shall be from sixteen to twenty years at the longest,– for a man, from thirty to thirty-five years; and let a woman hold office at forty, and a man at thirty years. Let a man go to war from twenty to sixty years, and for a woman, if there appear any need to make use of her in military service, let the time of service be after she shall have brought forth children up to fifty years of age; and let regard be had to what is possible and suitable to each (783 D–785 B).

Education and the Role of Inherent Limitations

Book VII of the *Laws* is largely concerned with *paideia* (παιδεία), the rearing and education of the young directed to realize their purpose of 'spiritual perfection'. It reveals that Plato does not trust to his detailed structure and processes of government to bring forth, unaided, the virtuous inhabitants and good society he wants his strong, united state to work towards. Indeed, he organizes his state to be efficient and pervasive so that it will effectively aid in the developmental and educational process, especially in activities to further what we now call political socialization. Accordingly, Plato does not place single-minded reliance on statutes and the letter of the law, but seeks to employ the inherent limitations of custom and tradition as well to help bond his state together by filling up the interstices of the law. He presses the point:

> *Ath.* That all the matters which we are now describing are commonly called by the general name of unwritten customs, and what are termed the laws of our ancestors are all of similar nature. And the reflection which lately arose in our minds[1] ([1] Cp. *supra,* 788 A.), that we can neither call these things laws, nor yet leave them unmentioned, is justified; for they are the bonds of the whole state, and come in between the written laws which are or are hereafter to be laid down; they are just ancestral customs of great antiquity, which, if they are rightly ordered and made habitual, shield and preserve the previously existing written law; but if they depart from right and fall into disorder, then they are like the props of builders which slip away out of their place and cause a universal ruin – one part drags another down, and the fair superstructure falls because the old foundations are undermined. Reflecting upon this, Cleinias, you ought to bind together the new state in every possible way, omitting nothing, whether great or small, of what are called laws or manners or pursuits, for by these means a city is bound together, and all these things are only lasting when they depend upon one another; and, therefore, we must not wonder if we find that many apparently trifling customs or usages come pouring in and lengthening out our laws (793 A–D).[18]

The object of all this is consistent with what Plato has preached and repeated again and again: that we seek the path of temperance and that careful attention, therefore, must be given to the formative periods of pregnancy and infancy (792 C–794 A). Thus, the great emphasis in Plato is on what he calls education. Today, we would be inclined to say that Plato's theory of education contains too much tendentious indoctrination and not enough opportunity for individual self-development and freedom of choice and expression; and therefore it embodies too much indoctrination and inculcation, which straitens, and not enough genuine or liberal education, which broadens and frees. Book VII contains an object example of this. In it, the bachelor Plato explains how the child learns and should be taught, from suckling babe to young manhood. The studies and pursuits include mathematics, music, dancing, serious and comic theatre, military tactics and strategy, astronomy, and hunting; but there is little or nothing in the way of vocational, agricultural, or commercial education (790 C–824 A).[19] The ultimate objective, however, is not merely to control a young man's actions by making him fear to do wrong, but also to promote the positive virtue of wanting to do what is right and honourable. Thus, in his discussion of what is to be learned from hunting and fishing in the proper manner, Plato turns again to the socially controlling principle of inherent limitations when the Athenian Stranger declares in his final statement in Book VII:

> *Ath.* Enough of laws relating to education and learning. But hunting and similar pursuits in like manner claim our attention. For the legislator appears to have a duty imposed upon him which goes beyond mere legislation. There is something over and above law which lies in a region between admonition and law, and has several times occurred to us in the course of discussion; for example, in the education of very young children there were things, as we maintain, which are not to be defined, and to regard them as matters of positive law is a great absurdity. Now, our laws and the whole constitution of our state having been thus delineated, the praise of the virtuous citizen is not complete when he is described as the person who serves the laws best and obeys them most, but the higher form of praise is that which describes him as the good citizen who passes through life undefiled and is obedient to the words of the legislator, both when he is giving laws and when he assigns praise and blame. This is the truest word that can be spoken in praise of a citizen; and the true legislator ought not only to write his laws, but also to interweave with them all such things as seem to him honourable and dishonourable. And the perfect citizen ought to seek to strengthen these no less than the principles of law which are sanctioned by punishments (822 D–824C).[20]

On Sexual Morality, Crafts and Trade, and Residence

In Book VIII of the *Laws*, Plato inveighs against the insatiable love of wealth and private possessions and the beastlike satisfaction of appetites and lusts. He calls for a code of sexual morality limited to intercourse between husband and wife, and proscribes with sanctions of dishonour the barren, unnatural, or disgraceful activities involved in homosexuality, harlotry, adultery, incest, and premarital sex. A course of physical education, contests in the use of arms rather than wrestling, and equestrian competition are also prescribed and emphasized. The importance of husbandry is so highly regarded and so carefully to be regulated that Plato says, 'Let us first of all, then, have a class of laws which shall be called the laws of husbandmen' (842 E).

With respect to economic activities, Plato's disdain for handicraft and other forms of manual labour is clearly expressed. He repeats his strong commitment to the practice of one calling only and wants strict economic controls that would limit imports to non-luxury items needed at home (especially for military purposes), limit exports to what is not needed at home, eliminate import and export tariffs, and – as a guiding principle – militate against the profit-making motive. Two important prohibitions pronounced in this passage should be noted, the first one foreshadowing a similar position of Aristotle in the *Politics* (Bk VII, 1328 b–1329 a):

> *Ath.* ... In the first place, let no citizen or servant of a citizen be occupied in handicraft arts; for he who is to secure and preserve the public order of the state, has an art which requires much study and many kinds of knowledge, and does not admit of being made a secondary occupation; and hardly any human being is capable of pursuing two professions or two arts rightly, or of practising one art himself, and superintending some one else who is practising another. ...
> ... But let there be no retail trade[1] ([1] Cp. Arist. Pol. vii. 9, § 7.) for the sake of moneymaking, either in these or any other articles, in the city or country at all (Bk VIII, 846 B–847 E).

The system of division and distribution of food and produce that Plato outlines is so artificial, so impossible of achievement in his time and place, and so contrary to contemporary practice and Greek temperament and tradition that, again, one wonders whether Plato is writing ironically with tongue-in-cheek, seriously but irrationally, or with simple indulgence in daydreaming mathematical games:

> *Ath.* With respect to food and the distribution of the produce of the country, the right and proper way seems to be nearly that which is the custom of Crete;[2] ([2] Cp. *ibid.* ii. 10 § 8.) for all should be required to distribute the fruits of the soil into twelve parts, and in this way consume them. Let the twelfth portion of each (as for instance of wheat and barley, to which the rest of the fruits of the earth shall be added, as well as the animals which are for sale in each of the twelve divisions) be divided in due proportion into three parts; one part for freemen, another for their servants, and a third for craftsmen and in general for strangers, whether sojourners who may be dwelling in the city, and like other men must live, or those who come on some business which they have with the state, or with some individual. Let only this third part of all necessaries be required to be sold; out of the other two-thirds no one shall be compelled to sell. And how will they be best distributed? In the first place, we see clearly that the distribution will be of equals in one point of view, and in another point of view unequals.
> *Cle.* What do you mean?
> *Ath.* I mean that the earth of necessity produces and nourishes the various articles of food, sometimes better and sometimes worse.

> *Cle*. Of course.
>
> *Ath*. Such being the case, let no one of the three portions be greater than either of the other two;– neither that which is assigned to masters or to slaves, nor again that of the stranger; but let the distribution to all be equal and alike, and let every citizen take his two portions and distribute them among slaves and freemen, he having power to determine the quantity and quality. And what remains he shall distribute by measure and number among the animals who have to be maintained from the earth, taking the whole number of them (847 E– 848 C).[21]

We may wonder in the same manner about Plato's purpose and mood when he advocates an artificially contrived arrangement of residences, evidently influenced by his experience with military life and organization, to accompany the scheme of land and food distribution he would impose:

> *Ath*. ... In the second place, our citizens should have separate houses duly ordered; and this will be the order proper for men like them. There shall be twelve hamlets, one in the middle of each twelfth portion, and in each hamlet they shall first set apart a market-place, and the temples of the Gods, and of their attendant demi-gods; and if there be any local deities of the Magnetes, or holy seats of other ancient deities, whose memory has been preserved, to these let them pay their ancient honours[1] ([1] Cp. *supra*, v. 738 C.). But Hestia, and Zeus, and Athene will have temples everywhere together with the God who presides in each of the twelve districts[2] ([2] Cp. *ibid*. 745.). And the first erection of houses shall be around those temples, where the ground is highest, in order to provide the safest and most defensible place of retreat for the guards. All the rest of the country they shall settle in the following manner:– They shall make thirteen divisions of the craftsmen; one of them they shall establish in the city, and this, again, they shall subdivide into twelve lesser divisions, among the twelve districts of the city, and the remainder shall be distributed in the country round about; and in each village they shall settle various classes of craftsmen, with a view to the convenience of the husbandmen. And the chief officers of the wardens of the country shall superintend all these matters, and see how many of them, and which class of them, each place requires; and fix them where they are likely to be least troublesome, and most useful to the husbandman. And the wardens of the city shall see to similar matters in the city (848 C–849 A).[22]

Book VIII closes with a similar, even more detailed, catalogue of proposed regulations for trading in the agora, the purpose of which is seemingly laudable; but on the face of them, his proposals here are often so unwieldy, impractical, and unenforceable, that the absurdity of what Plato is advocating is patent. As one example, barter and cash sales are to be encouraged to the extent that credit sales will not be enforceable at law (849 A–850 D). What is not clear, however, is what real use there may be to confining the sale of certain items to certain days, regardless of the need for them, and whether Plato is fully aware of their ludicrous nature; and, if so, what is his purpose? Is it to say that attempts to regulate the dealings in the agora are all doomed to failure and that therefore the flow of the marketplace should simply be allowed to follow its natural course? This last would largely preclude attempts to regulate in the interests of justice, fair-dealing, and rational use, and is therefore out of character with Plato. Perhaps what he may have in mind is to show what a properly, mathematically organized and operated market would be like in theory and principle and to loft it as a flight of the imagination from which a few features might be chosen to be put into practice.

On Crime and Punishment

Book IX of the *Laws* advocates strict laws dealing with sacrilege, slaves, children, and habitual criminals, with death prescribed for many offences. The discussion touches on various kinds of crime and their causes, including those brought on by lust fed by great wealth. Interestingly enough, there is again an assumption by Plato that humanity is not inherently bad, but rather that their misdeeds are due to lack of enlightenment and that being bad is therefore against the will of even the unjust person. Perhaps surprisingly, what emerges is that Plato holds to a basically optimistic view both of humanity's nature and of the correctibility for most individuals through law and education of their acquired faults. So much so is this the case, that one may justifiably say that an important key to at least a partial understanding of Plato may be that he, in some respects, may be a naïve romantic. He probably could have adjusted to many of the ideas, causes, and movements of modern romanticism, a message of which is a passionate call to action, to do something constructive, rather than to accept as inevitable the shortcomings, incongruities, and injustices of any socio-politico-economic system that happens to be extant. Plato is conservative and traditionalist only in some respects, and he is not a simplistic law-and-order reactionary. The dialogue also reveals that Plato makes a careful distinction between injustice and injury and between premeditated and unpremeditated actions (Bk IX, 860 C–861 C).[23]

Thus, although difficult to prove, intent is important to Plato, and he draws a distinction between an injury which is in violation of law and a hurt which may not be so. Some hurts are justly caused and some are unjustly caused. Whatever the case, however, there emerges here, again, a positive attitude on the part of Plato – indeed, a magnanimity – that looks to soothe enemies and win them over to friendship. But this view is carried only so far. There is a point reached by repeated crimes beyond which Plato is not willing to go; and then he would resort to capital punishment as a permanent cure of the incurable, habitual offender, no matter whether the repeated offences be great or small (861 D–863 A).

There follows another interchange between Cleinias and the Athenian Stranger wherein Plato identifies three irrational causes of being bad: passion, pleasure, and ignorance. The ignorance may be the kind of simple ignorance that causes lighter offences; or it may be the kind of double ignorance that is accompanied by a conceit of wisdom and may be the source of great and monstrous crimes. Plato also distinguishes between injustice which is voluntarily committed, yet irrationally caused by emotions that tyrannize over the soul, and hurts which are committed because of honest mistakes. In addition, Plato distinguishes between crimes committed by violence in the light of day and those committed in darkness and by deceit, and would punish most severely those involving both violence and deceit (863 A–864 C).

One of the more important passages on crimes and their punishment identifies three major causes of crime: lust for wealth as the greatest; overpowering ambition; and cowardly, unjust fear. Intertwined with liability to mundane legal punishment for those who commit murder are the prospects of punishment in the world below. Also, the same kind of ending at the hand of another awaits in this life, as well as deprivation of legal and religious privileges. Relatives of the victim are expected to initiate prosecution of the perpetrator and his branding as outlaw, or themselves suffer the wrath of the gods and liability to their own persecution for neglect of duty (869 E–874 B).

Book IX also contains what is probably the most significant admission of all by Plato concerning the unattainability of rule by all-wise philosophers because none such can exist among men. And because men are all somewhat selfish, it is therefore necessary to rely on the superior wisdom and protection of law and custom. This may well be the single most important passage in the Platonic dialogues in revealing Plato's fundamental political conclusion and resultant objectives:

> *Ath.* ... Mankind must have laws, and conform to them, or their life would be as bad as that of the most savage beast[1] ([1] Cp. Arist. Pol. i. 2, § 15.). And the reason of this is that no man's nature is able to know what is best for human society; or knowing, always able and willing to do what is best. In the first place, there is a difficulty in apprehending that the true art of politics is concerned, not with private but with public good (for public good binds together states, but

private only distracts them); and that both the public and private good as well of individuals as of states is greater when the state and not the individual is first considered. In the second place, although a person knows in the abstract that this is true, yet if he be possessed of absolute and irresponsible power, he will never remain firm in his principles or persist in regarding the public good as primary in the state, and the private good as secondary. Human nature will be always drawing him into avarice and selfishness, avoiding pain and pursuing pleasure without any reason, and will bring these to the front, obscuring the juster and better; and so working darkness in his soul will at last fill with evils both him and the whole city[1] ([1] Cp. *supra*, iii, 691; iv. 711 E, 713 C, 716 A.). For if a man were born so divinely gifted that he could naturally apprehend the truth, he would have no need of laws to rule over him[2] ([2] Cp. Statesman, 297 A.); for there is no law or order which is above knowledge, nor can mind, without impiety, be deemed the subject or slave of any man, but rather the lord of all. I speak of mind, true and free, and in harmony with nature. But then there is no such mind anywhere, or at least not much; and therefore we must choose law and order, which are second best. These look at things as they exist for the most part only, and are unable to survey the whole of them. And therefore I have spoken as I have (874 E–875 D).[24]

However, despite concessions to hard reality and consequent adjustments, Plato never completely departs from certain of his basic premises, objectives, and methods. Although now expressing a willingness to place primary reliance on the rule of law instead of the rule of a superior yet fallible mind, Plato still leaves room for some flexibility by judges and some opportunity for them to correct deficiencies and omissions in the law. But the guidelines and room for judicial freedom of decision and punishment are tightened and reduced by the legislator in the interest of safer, surer justice, while leaving determination of fact to the court. The Athenian Stranger continues his dialogue with Cleinias:

Ath. I may reply, that in a state in which the courts are bad and mute, because the judges conceal their opinions and decide causes clandestinely; or what is worse, when they are disorderly and noisy, as in a theatre, clapping or hooting in turn this or that orator – I say that then there is a very serious evil, which affects the whole state. Unfortunate is the necessity of having to legislate for such courts, but where the necessity exists, the legislator should only allow them to ordain the penalties for the smallest offences; if the state for which he is legislating be of this character, he must take most matters into his own hands and speak distinctly. But when a state has good courts, and the judges are well trained and scrupulously tested, the determination of the penalties or punishments which shall be inflicted on the guilty may fairly and with advantage be left to them. And we are not to be blamed for not legislating concerning all that large class of matters which judges far worse educated than ours would be able to determine, assigning to each offence what is due both to the perpetrator and to the sufferer. We believe those for whom we are legislating to be best able to judge, and therefore to them the greater part may be left (875 D–876 E).[25]

A Hierarchical Cosmos of Callings

Book X of the *Laws* discusses religion, the nature of God and the universe, and the priority of soul over body. What is shown here is a philosophy of idealism and an architectonic plan. It is a system of hierarchy, complete with the concept of suitable callings for the individual, who is to fulfil his own smaller purpose and function through his contribution to the greater purposes of the state and God (i.e., what constitutes justice of the individual), something done by proper exercise of individual free will. The exhortation that Plato would therefore direct to a youth who would accuse the gods of neglecting him, is developed in the following address by the Athenian Stranger to Cleinias:

> *Ath.* Let us say to the youth:– The ruler of the universe has ordered all things with a view to the excellence and preservation of the whole, and each part, as far as may be, has an action and passion appropriate to it. Over these, down to the least fraction of them, ministers have been appointed to preside, who have wrought out their perfection with infinitesimal exactness. And one of these portions of the universe is thine own, unhappy man, which, however little, contributes to the whole; and you do not seem to be aware that this and every other creation is for the sake of the whole, and in order that the life of the whole may be blessed; and that you are created for the sake of the whole, and not the whole for the sake of you. For every physician and every skilled artist does all things for the sake of the whole, directing his effort towards the common good, executing the part for the sake of the whole, and not the whole for the sake of the part. And you are annoyed because you are ignorant how what is best for you happens to you and to the universe, as far as the laws of the common creation admit. Now, as the soul combining first with one body and then with another undergoes all sorts of changes, either of herself, or through the influence of another soul, all that remains to the player of the game is that he should shift the pieces; sending the better nature to the better place, and the worse, to the worse, and so assigning to them their proper portion. ...
>
> ... And he contrived a general plan by which a thing of a certain nature found a certain seat and room. But the formation of qualities he left to the wills of individuals. For every one of us is made pretty much what he is by the bent of his desires and the nature of his soul (Bk X, 904 C).

So seriously does Plato view the association of religious observance with propitious influence of the gods, that the Athenian Stranger would punish practitioners of illegal religious rites with death and he would require all sacred rites and sacrifices to be public, in temples, and not in private houses (909 D–910 D).[26]

Ethical Economic and Legal Principles

As we have seen repeatedly, Plato's guiding principle is the pursuit of virtue. At the very start of Book XI (continuing from Book X), Plato states a precept by which one may keep virtuous. This simple guide to righteous behaviour turns out to be the familiar Golden Rule of how we should 'do unto others' expressed mostly in negative terms:

> *Ath.* In the next place, dealings between man and man require to be suitably regulated. The principle of them is very simple:– Thou shalt not, if thou canst help it, touch that which is mine, or remove the least thing which belongs to me without my consent; and may I be of a sound mind, and do to others as I would that they should do to me. First, let us speak of treasure trove:– May I never pray the Gods to find the hidden treasure, which another has laid up for himself and his family, he not being one of my ancestors, nor lift, if I should find, such a treasure. And may I never have any dealings with those who are called diviners, and who in any way or manner counsel me to take up the deposit entrusted to the earth, for I should not gain so much in the increase of my possessions, if I take up the prize, as I should grow in justice and virtue of soul, if I abstain; and this will be a better possession to me than the other in a better part of myself; for the possession of justice in the soul is preferable to the possession of wealth (Bk XI, 913 A–B).

Before he is done with this lengthy passage, the Athenian Stranger offers his rules for what he regards as just and proper treatment of slaves and freedmen. It seemingly never occurs to him that a strictly logical application of his 'comprehensive rule' would rule out slavery altogether unless he were willing himself to be the slave of another. Thus, viewed in the light of present-day ethical standards which unequivocally proscribe slavery completely and reserve capital punishment for only the most heinous of crimes, if at all, Plato does not seem as magnanimous or consistent with his guiding general principle as he felt he was because of accepted belief and practice in his time:

> *Ath.* ... Any one who is of sound mind may arrest his own slave, and do with him whatever he will of such things as are lawful; and he may arrest the runaway

slave of any of his friends or kindred with a view to his safe-keeping. And if any one takes him who is being carried off as a slave, intending to liberate him, he who is carrying him off shall let him go; but he who takes him away shall give three sufficient sureties; and if he give them, and not without giving them, he may take him away, but if he take him away after any other manner, he shall be deemed guilty of violence, and being convicted shall pay as a penalty double the amount of the damages claimed to him who has been deprived of the slave. Any man may also carry off a freedman, if he do not pay respect or sufficient respect to him who freed him. Now the respect shall be, that the freedman go three times in the month to the hearth of the person who freed him, and offer to do whatever he ought, so far as he can; and he shall agree to make such a marriage as his former master approves. He shall not be permitted to have more property than he who gave him liberty, and what more he has shall belong to his master. The freedman shall not remain in the state more than twenty years, but like other foreigners[1] ([1] Cp. *supra*. viii, 850.) shall go away, taking his entire property with him, unless he has the consent of the magistrates and of his former master to remain. If a freedman or any other stranger has a property greater than the census of the third class, at the expiration of thirty days from the day on which this comes to pass, he shall take that which is his and go his way, and in this case he shall not be allowed to remain any longer by the magistrates. And if anyone disobeys this regulation, and is brought into court and convicted, he shall be punished with death, and his property shall be confiscated (914 E–915 C).[27]

Plato is also much exercised about adulteration of goods sold in the agora, and he repeats the astonishing recommendation that rules of trading in the agora should be limited to one asked-price – or no sale. He also equates deceit and falsehood in the agora with lack of reverence for God and respect for humanity; but for some reason or other, the punishment for these offences would be mild in comparison with those Plato would customarily require. Because trading in the agora was such an important part of Athenian economic life, the following quotation bears close scrutiny for the insight it may give into the mind and character of Plato, especially if he be altogether serious here:

> *Ath.* ... Certainly it is an excellent rule not lightly to defile the names of the Gods, after the fashion of men in general, who care little about piety and purity in their religious actions. But if a man will not conform to this rule, let the law be as follows:– He who sells anything in the agora shall not ask two prices for that which he sells, but he shall ask one price, and if he does not obtain this, he shall take away his goods; and on that day he shall not value them either at more or less; and there shall be no praising of any goods, or oath taken about

them. If a person disobeys this command, any citizen who is present, not being less than thirty years of age, may with impunity chastise and beat the swearer, but if instead of obeying the laws he takes no heed, he shall be liable to the charge of having betrayed them. If a man sells any adulterated goods and will not obey these regulations, he who knows and can prove the fact, and does prove it in the presence of the magistrates, if he be a slave or a metic, shall have the adulterated goods, but if he be a citizen, and do not pursue the charge, he shall be called a rogue, and deemed to have robbed the Gods of the agora; or if he proves the charge he shall dedicate the goods to the Gods of the agora (916 D–918 A).[28]

The *naïveté*, pretended or real, of Plato with respect to trade, however, shows itself even more clearly and in greater detail when he returns to another notion of his on how to keep the citizenry virtuous. Plato regards the retail trade as inherently corrupting of those engaged in it. But since we must have retail trade and also merchants who deal with one another, almost strictly from the standpoint of a consumer who has probably been much put upon in the past, Plato tries to formulate rules of trade to make it of benefit to everyone and of the least possible injury to those engaged in it. Among other ideas, he suggests three regulations: first, that none of the 5,040 landowning families engage in retail trade; second, that retail trade be limited, therefore, to resident aliens or foreigners; and third, that there be strict, written rules and enforcement of limitation of profit-making to a fair percentage (918 A–920 C).

Almost as an afterthought, Plato slips in a good word for the military and how they should be honoured for executing their work and craft well. Appreciation of the service provided by the military is a virtue of good citizenship and should be promoted by law:

> *Ath.* … Let this then be the law, having an ingredient of praise, not compelling but advising the great body of the citizens to honour the brave men who are the saviours of the whole state, whether by their courage or by their military skill;– they should honour them, I say, in the second place; for the first and highest tribute of respect is to be given to those who are able above other men to honour the words of good legislators (912 D–922 A).

Again, the bachelor Plato pays close attention to marital and family relations. When reconciliation of disputing marriage partners cannot be effected by a committee of law-wardens and women assigned to regulate marriages, then they are to be divorced and, if possible, reassigned to other marriage partners, with a blend of different temperaments intended to produce a temperate balance in offspring. Care and disposition of orphans, the children of widowed parents, and illegitimate children all come within the scope of Plato's attention here, which ranges from kindness and considerateness to cruelty and callousness, with exile to be the fate especially when a slave and a free man or woman produce offspring. The passage includes an admonition to give true service and reverence to parents and grandparents that is reminiscent of the biblical injunction to 'Honour thy father and thy mother, that thy days may be long upon the land which the Lord thy God giveth thee'. The conclusion of this passage is as follows:

> *Ath.* ... Neither God, nor a man who has understanding, will ever advise any one to neglect his parents. To a discourse concerning the honour and dishonour of parents, a prelude such as the following, about the service of the gods, will be a suitable introduction:– There are ancient customs about the Gods which are universal, and they are of two kinds: some of the Gods we see with our eyes and we honour them, of others we honour the images, raising statues of them which we adore; and though they are lifeless, yet we imagine that the living Gods have a good will and gratitude to us on this account. Now, if a man has a father or mother, or their fathers or mothers treasured up in his house stricken in years, let him consider that no statue can be more potent to gain his requests than they are, who are sitting at his hearth, if only he knows how to show true service to them (929 E–931 A).[29]

Book XI of the *Laws* concludes with a mixture of understanding, magnanimity, fair-mindedness, inflexibility, and, sad to say, meanness that are all characteristic of Plato. He understands the noble and civilizing role of systems of justice and also how they may be misused and corrupted. He is magnanimous and fair-minded in willingness to forgive penitent and desisting offenders and in seeking the truth of a matter. But there is a point of rigidity and an overreacting ruthlessness that comes to the fore when he ends his declamation with a call for death to those who would, according to the Athenian Stranger's lights, pervert the purposes of justice. Whether stated seriously or ironically with a negative intent, Plato, as he does other times, lessens himself and what he has to say by the manner in which he concludes Book XI with a demand for the death penalty for the unjustly litigious – especially if he was speaking in earnest:

> *Ath.* ... If any one thinks that he will pervert the power of justice in the minds of the judges, and unseasonably litigate or advocate, let any one who likes indict him for malpractices of law and dishonest advocacy, and let him be judged in the court of select judges; and if he be convicted, let the court determine whether he may be supposed to act from a love of money or from contentiousness. And

if he is supposed to act from contentiousness, the court shall fix a time during which he shall not be allowed to institute or plead a cause; and if he is supposed to act as he does from love of money, in case he be a stranger, he shall leave the country, and never return under penalty of death; but if he be a citizen, he shall die, because he is a lover of money, in whatever manner gained; and equally, if he be judged to have acted more than once from contentiousness, he shall die (937 D–938 C).

Public Theft and Checking on Public Officials

In Book XII of the *Laws*, there is discussion of: punishment for theft and public misbehaviour; the proper training and behaviour of soldiers; and the mode of selection, duties, and honours of the examiners who check upon the magistrates. We find that the examiners are themselves subject to a counter-check (Bk XII, 941 A–948 B and 953 E–960 B). The book begins with strictures against, and recommended punishment for, the carrying of false messages between cities by heralds or ambassadors; and then passes on to inveigh against theft and robbery, especially of anything belonging to the public. The penalty for the latter type of crime is to be death, whether for large or small amounts:

> *Ath.* ... If a man steal anything belonging to the public, whether that which he steals be much or little, he shall have the same punishment. For he who steals a little steals with the same wish as he who steals much, but with less power, and he who takes up a greater amount, not having deposited it, is wholly unjust. Wherefore the law is not disposed to inflict a less penalty on the one than on the other because his theft is less, but on the ground that the thief may possibly be in one case still curable, and may in another case be incurable. If any one convict in a court of law a stranger or a slave of a theft of public property, let the court determine what punishment he shall suffer, or what he shall pay, bearing in mind that he is probably not incurable. But the citizen who has been brought up as our citizens will have been, if he be found guilty of robbing his country by fraud or violence, whether he be caught in the act or not, shall be punished with death; for he is incurable[2] ([2] This passage is not consistent with ix, 857 A, where theft of public property is punished by imprisonment.) (941 B–D).

Military matters require a great deal of attention and legislation. Spartan living and training conditions are advocated, as well as iron discipline, unquestioning obedience, unremitting command over every individual, and suitable rewards or punishment for bravery or dereliction of duty (942 A–943 D).

The manner in which public officials are to be checked upon is essentially a proposal for an institutional check rather than for inherent limitations. What is interesting and should not be lost sight of concerning this plan of remedy is that: it is to have a great deal of popular input in the selection of the two or three examiners chosen at a time; this is to be an annual affair; it is consistent with his usual division of the city into 12 parts; it will tend toward a gerontocracy because of the requirement that the three principal selectors be a minimum of 50 years of age and the eligibility of the examiners themselves to continue to serve after completion of their seventy-fifth year; and a reference indicates the organological principle is implicit in Plato's political theory. The passage concludes with stipulations how the elected three citizens of the state shall appoint examiners and with proposed penalties for erring magistrates:

> *Ath.* ... And these shall appoint in their first year twelve examiners, to continue until each has completed seventy-five years, to whom three shall afterwards be added yearly; and let these divide all the magistracies into twelve parts, and prove the holders of them by every sort of test to which a freeman may be subjected; and let them live while they hold office in the precinct of Helios and Apollo, in which they were chosen, and let each one form a judgment of some things individually, and of others in company with his colleagues; and let him place a writing in the agora about each magistracy, and what the magistrate ought to suffer or pay, according to the decision of the examiners. And if a magistrate does not admit that he has been justly judged, let him bring the examiners before the select judges, and if he be acquitted by their decision, let him, if he will, accuse the examiners themselves; if, however, he be convicted, and have been condemned to death by the examiners, let him die (and of course he can only die once):– but any other penalties, which admit of being doubled let him suffer twice over (945 B–946 E).[30]

The Cosmic Connection

A paragraph devoted to Rhadamanthus, the supposed son of Zeus and Europa, should not be glossed over. It follows from contemporary prevailing Greek beliefs about the cosmos and the origin and place of the Greek people in it that had profound influence on their politico-legal system – indeed, on almost all aspects of their society – and their history. Simply put, the Greeks believed themselves, or represented themselves as, sons of gods, not mere mortals; and this placed on them an extra inclination to take oaths and religious practices seriously (*cp*. Genesis 6:1–4). This belief also contributed to the extraordinary pride and confidence that led to many of their remarkable accomplishments and victories. However, if written in earnest, the following paragraph which speaks of a bygone day when oaths were taken more seriously, is perhaps another indication of a probable streak of *naïveté* on the part of Plato. Alternatively, it may be another example of playful, ironical musing:

> *Ath.* ... The so-called decision of Rhadamanthus is worthy of all admiration. He knew that the men of his own time believed and had no doubt that there were Gods, which was a reasonable belief in those days, because most men were the sons of Gods[1] ([1] Cp. Tim. 40 D.), and according to tradition he was one himself. He appears to have thought that he ought to commit judgement to no man, but to the Gods only, and in this way suits were simply and speedily decided by him. For he made the two parties take an oath respecting the points in dispute, and so got rid of the matter speedily and safely. But now that a certain portion of mankind do not believe at all in the existence of the Gods, and others imagine that they have no care of us, and the opinion of most men, and of the worst men, is that in return for a small sacrifice and a few flattering words they will be their accomplices in purloining large sums and save them from many terrible punishments, the way of Rhadamanthus is no longer suited to the needs of justice; for as the opinions of men about the Gods are changed, the laws should also be changed;– in the granting of suits a rational legislation ought to do away with the oaths of the parties on either side – he who obtains leave to bring an action should write down the charges, but should not add an oath; and the defendant in like manner should give his denial to the magistrates in writing, and not swear; for it is a dreadful thing to know, when many lawsuits are going on in a state, that almost half the people who meet one another quite unconcernedly at the public meals and in other companies and relations of private life are perjured (948 B–949 C).[31]

Plato also presents a plan restricting – not completely prohibiting – travel abroad and sojourn within the state by outsiders. No one under 40 years of age is to be permitted to travel abroad or in a private capacity; although 'spectators' or inspectors of at least 50 years of age may be sent abroad to seek out wise men whose fame has spread and to report their findings to the assembly. And so we find Plato advocating his own form of Iron Curtain with special two-way sieves built in; and we may note also in the same passage his remarks about the importance of being virtuous and having a reputation to match (494 E–953 E).[32]

Hierarchy of Courts, Cases, and Burials

In somewhat repetitive fashion, and almost as an interjection here, Plato returns to a consideration of the courts. He offers some precise details and some generalities on how they should be constituted, try cases, and dispose of suits, with his usual mixture of magnanimity and harshness. The magnanimity is apparent in his attempts to resort first to arbitration; and the harshness is in the usually severe penalties he would impose, including death in certain circumstances. The latter part of this statement emphasizes the need for: notions of what is good, just, and honourable within one's state; means of discouraging and settling suits; and strict enforcement of the courts' judgments. The passage concludes:

> *Ath.* ... In the first place, the judge shall assign to the party who wins the suit the whole property of him who loses, with the exception of mere necessaries[1] ([1] Cp. *supra*, ix. 855 B.), and the assignment shall be made through the herald immediately after each decision in the hearing of the judges; and when the month arrives following the month in which the courts are sitting (unless the gainer of the suit has been previously satisfied), the court shall follow up the case, and hand over to the winner the goods of the lower; but if they find that he has not met the means of paying, and the sum deficient is not less than a drachma, the insolvent person shall not have any right of going to law with any other man until he have satisfied the debt of the winning party; but other persons shall still have the right of bringing suits against him. And if any one after he is condemned refuses to acknowledge the authority which condemned him, let the magistrates who are thus deprived of their authority bring him before the court of the guardians of the law, and if he be cast, let him be punished with death, as a subverter of the whole state and of the laws (956 B–958 C).

In speaking of funerals and burials, Plato signals that he is near the end of this work. Although it would appear from his description of the curbs he would impose that Plato would still permit some rather lavish funerals, the principles of limitation of cost and display are urged, lest they eat up the sustenance of the living. This practical approach, however, seems in some of his restrictions on cries of lamentation to be mixed with callous insensitivity to the emotions of the mourners (958 C–960 C).

The Nocturnal Council: Guardians, Virtuous, and Wise

If available virtue, wisdom, and knowledge are to be employed to benefit the state, one means of doing so would be to assemble a small council or synod of community leaders who are recognized to have such qualities. According to Plato, they would be an anchor that would give stability and salvation to the state:

Ath. Were we not saying that there must be in our city a council which was to be of this sort:– The ten oldest guardians of the law, and all those who have obtained prizes of virtue, were to meet in the same assembly, and the council was also to include those who had visited foreign countries in the hope of hearing something that might be of use in the preservation of the laws, and who, having come safely home, and having been tested in these same matters, had proved themselves to be worthy to take part in the assembly;– each of the members was to select some young man of not thirty years of age, he himself judging in the first instance whether the young man was worthy by nature and education, and then suggesting him to the others, and if he seemed to them also to be worthy they were to adopt him; but if not, the decision at which they arrived was to be kept a secret from the citizens at large, and, more especially, from the rejected candidate. The meeting of the council was to be held early in the morning, when everybody was most at leisure from all other business, whether public or private – was not something of this sort said by us before?

Cle. ... True.

Ath. Then, returning to the council, I would say further, that if we let it down to be the anchor of the state, our city, having everything which is suitable to her, will preserve all that we wish to preserve (960 E–961 D).[33]

After some remarks about the need to have a pilot who is concerned with directing a ship safely in all kinds of weather, a physician who is not ignorant about the health of the body, and a general who is not ignorant about victory, the Athenian Stranger continues his dialogue with Cleinias about a council or synod that would meet at night and give knowledgeable purpose and leadership to the state. It would have to be composed of just men who would look to promote the most desirable qualities and conditions in the state. In particular, the Athenian Stranger tells Cleinias, they should seek to promote the saving virtues of courage, temperance, wisdom, and justice (961 E–964 B).

Having set up this aristocratic body of ability and virtue to guide their divinely inspired state, the Athenian Stranger (i.e., Plato) is still concerned that its members be recognized as the ablest and that they receive some kind of special training and knowledge of virtue (964 B–966 B). This special training and knowledge of virtue is to come from religious insight. Just as a John Cotton, a John Winthrop, or an Increase Mather were later on, in New England, to require religious qualifications for public office, so does Plato in the *Laws* for those who would be guardians or wardens of the law (966 B–D). Such religious qualifications would include understanding that the soul is the oldest and most divine of all things that have existence, and that the visible heavenly bodies are not made of rock and earth and other lifeless substances, but are endowed with souls and are part of an orderly cosmos that is subject to divine rule. Therefore, the Athenian Stranger concludes, and Cleinias agrees, that:

> *Ath.* No man can be a true worshipper of the Gods who does not know these
> two principles – that the soul is the eldest of all things which are born, and is
> immortal and rules over all bodies; moreover, as I have now said several times,
> he who has not contemplated the mind of nature which is said to exist in the
> stars, and gone through the previous training, and seen the connection of music
> with these things, and harmonized them all with laws and institutions, is not
> able to give a reason of such things as have a reason[1] ([1] Cp. Rep. vii. 531 foll.).
> And he who is unable to acquire this in addition to the ordinary virtues of a
> citizen, can hardly be a good ruler of a whole state; but he should be the
> subordinate of other rulers. Wherefore, Cleinias and Megillus, let us consider
> whether we may not add to all the other laws which we have discussed this
> further one,– that the nocturnal assembly of the magistrates, which has also
> shared in the whole scheme of education proposed by us, shall be a guard set
> according to law for the salvation of the state. Shall we propose this?
> ...
> *Cle.* I agree, Stranger, that we should proceed along the road in which God is
> guiding us; and how we can proceed rightly has now to be investigated and
> explained (966 D–968 C).[34]

Seriousness of Purpose of the Laws

The ending of the *Laws* is typical of Plato: he is garrulous; his need to be
considered dazzlingly brilliant of mind and almost indispensable (i.e., to be
appreciated, needed, and wanted) is rather apparent; but, most of all, he does
inspire to seek greater virtue and improvement in personal lives and in the
governance of the state. Also, and perhaps most significant of all, is the
admission of his seriousness of purpose, that what has been voiced has not
been merely a long series of quasi-fantasy daydreams; for it is stated that the
more sophisticated *Laws* is meant to contain a reasonable, practicable plan
for the real world of the *polis*:

> *Ath.* As the proverb says, the answer is no secret, but open to all of us:– We
> must risk the whole on the chance of throwing, as they say, thrice six or ace, and
> I am willing to share with you the danger by stating and explaining to you my
> views about education and nurture, which is the question coming to the surface
> again. The danger is not a slight or ordinary one, and I would advise you, Cleinias,
> in particular, to see the matter; for if you order rightly the city of the Magnetes,
> or whatever name God may give it, you will obtain the greatest glory; or at any
> rate you will be thought the most courageous of men in the estimation of posterity.
> Dear companions, if this our divine assembly can only be established, to them

we will hand over the city; none of the present company of legislators, as I may call them, would hesitate about that. And the state will be perfected and become a waking reality, which a little while ago we attempted to create as a dream[1] ([1] Cp. Rep. ix. 592.) and in idea only, mingling together reason and mind in one image, in the hope that our citizens might be duly mingled and rightly educated; and being educated, and dwelling in the citadel of the land, might become perfect guardians, such as we have never seen in all our previous life, by reason of the saving virtue which is in them (968 C–969 D).[35]

Thus, our noble Plato, in his own words, reveals himself as somewhat a romantic dreamer who is generous and vain enough to share his dreams and yearning for a better humanity and a better state.

Assessments

In the *Laws*, we have variations on, and modifications of, a set of by-now-familiar themes. Plato's socio-politico-economic theory, to the very end, is predicated on a hierarchical, organological 'cosmos of callings' that is consonant with his 'divine plan of the universe'; and therefore it is designed to produce a united, strong, orderly, fraternal, and harmonious society and state, peopled by virtuous individuals who know their proper place and exercise their proper function in it. His constitutional approach, therefore, despite almost endless attention to detail, places less reliance on the structural organization and functioning of government – i.e., institutional checks and balances – than it does on the inherent limitations and potentialities provided by preventive and curative constitutional and social measures. Some of these basic principles, both institutional and personal, which organize society and the economy, rather than the government of the state, include: a balancing of four major socio-economic classes; a number of checks and balances in government; the principle of moderation; the spirit of friendship; eugenic marriage and breeding; the importance of leadership and discipline; a small size for the state and a fixed number of homesteads; an Iron Curtain for the state to keep out alien influences; and above all else, education (*paideia*) for moral development and obedience to law of a physically trained citizenry. All of these points flow from Plato's religious convictions that he views as consonant with God's hierarchical cosmic plan.

One of the most perceptive commentaries on what would be the practical effect of implementation of the recommendations and schemes to be found in the *Laws*, is that by Robert G. Bury in his Introduction to his translation of this work. Bury observes (Introduction to Plato, *Laws*, Vol. I, pp. xv f):

> The concentration of all the political power in the hands of the old is, in truth, one of the most characteristic features of the *Laws*, and another sign of its author's age. The Model City would be only too likely, one thinks, to strike the youth of to-day as a Paradise for the old but a Purgatory for the young.
>
> Since most of the power is thus given to a limited class, it is fair to describe the State of the *Laws* as a moderate oligarchy; although the historical survey in Book III, with its discussion of political types, might lead one to expect a rather different, and more liberal, combination of monarchy with democracy – the principle of order with the principle of freedom. As it is, the average citizen is given but little freedom, except the freedom to obey. And, though the State here pictured has been not unfitly described as "a mixture of Athenian constitutional forms and Athenian freedom with Spartan training and Spartan order, a practical *via media* between the two extremes of contemporary Greece,"[1] ([1] E. Barker, *Political Thought of Plato and Aristotle*, p. 202.) yet it must be confessed that there is much more of the Spartan element in the mixture than of the Athenian, much less of democracy than of aristocracy. The "Athenian Stranger" of the *Laws* is no less of an anti-democrat than the "Socrates" of the *Republic*; and his conviction of the natural perversity and stupidity of the average man has increased with the passing of the years. The saying *vox populi, vox dei* is, for Plato, the supreme lie.[36]

What, then, are some of the modifications that appear in the *Laws*? For one thing, there seems to be a difference of degree with respect to the desideratum of military strength: the *Laws* seems more truly concerned with matters of personal and civic virtue because more committed to interpersonal justice and seems to dwell less on military matters, although by no means ignoring or downgrading them. Nonetheless, the state is still patterned in many respects, as we have noted, on the Spartan model, especially with respect to physical training, indoctrination, and common tables.

There are important concessions to reality and practicability that are apparent in the early dismissal, as probably impractical, of some of the extreme ideas of common marriage and ownership for the Guardian class that were advocated in the *Republic*. The most outstandingly impractical scheme that is advanced – whether as a rhetorical device, in a spirit of playfulness, or perhaps because there is an irrational element in Plato – has to do with the idea of 5,040 family units for his model city-state.

Still more significant, Plato has moved closer to the existing Athenian system in two respects: concessions to the wealthy in the form of an imbalance of power so that they may feel secure in the preservation of their property, although their holdings would in some cases be reduced; and concessions to the mass of citizenry in the form of greater participation in some of the processes of government than he previously advocated, so that they may feel less under a sense of constraint and have a greater sense of the unity of the whole *polis* and their belonging to it. Plato's rule by wisdom and virtue has made some accommodations to wealth and numbers in the *Laws*, but he does not seem to take this as hard as he would have at the time of the writing of the *Republic*.

Thus, Plato has developed in the *Laws* a somewhat more sophisticated polity, which consists basically of a combination of aristocracy, plutocracy (oligarchy of the wealthy), and democracy.[37] He probably feels, however, that what he has set forth is more a combination of aristocracy and democracy that would become neither entirely one nor entirely the other, *but would be inclined by his mathematical arrangements to tilt and slide inevitably under greater aristocratic control.* Plato probably believes that virtue should yield some room to wealth and numbers because it should still be possible thereby to remain in control, dominate, and improve the state and society. And in some respects, the idea of a democratically selected aristocracy who are subject to constant re-examination and limited terms of office for the most part, is not so intolerable, although too much weighted in this case in favour of rule by the elderly and the wealthier: i.e., toward a plutocratic gerontocracy, while essentially a meritocracy.

What is disquieting in the *Laws*, however, as in the *Republic* and the *Statesman*, is a lack of light-hearted humour, rather than irony, in the writings themselves, a lack of understanding and appreciation of what women are really like in general, the retention of slavery, and a tendency to too harsh judgments and penalties. If, therefore, the philosophy and proposals of the *Laws* were put into practice, there would be in this city less of the kind of carefree joy, simple fun, warmth, and love of life and of others than is required to fulfil human nature, purposes, and happiness.

What is perhaps most constructive and hopeful in the *Laws* is the special emphasis Plato places on education to produce an aware, active, morally upright citizen who realizes his best human nature as a wise and virtuous person: i.e., *paideia* (παιδεία) or education in *areté* (ἀρετή: virtue). As Werner Jaeger has noted (1945, Vol. 1, p. 113):

> In the *Laws* Plato constructs just such an old Hellenic cosmos [as accepted in the early polis whose citizens held it to be 'something divine' because 'the sum of all the higher things in life'] based on law, a city in which the polis is the

spirit, and in which all spiritual activity is referred to the polis as its final end. There he defines the essence of all true culture, or paideia (in contrast to the specialized knowledge of tradesmen such as the shopkeeper and the travelling merchant), as 'the education in areté from youth onwards, which makes men passionately desire to become perfect citizens, knowing both how to rule and how to be ruled on a basis of justice'.

Jaeger writes further of the *Laws* and *paideia* (*ibid.*, Vol. III, p. 213):

> ... Plato thought that what he said in it was of central importance: it contains most profound discussions of the state, of law, of morals, and of culture. But all these subjects Plato subordinates to paideia. Therefore *The Laws* is a book of major importance in the history of Greek paideia. Paideia is Plato's first word, and his last.[38]

Thus, it may be concluded that Plato advocated, above all else, education for justice based on the rule of law as most apt to accord with God's will and to bestow the greatest benefits on citizen and state alike.[39]

But intent and advocacy do not always square with results. Also disquieting, therefore, are comparisons that suggest themselves between the advocated role of Plato's privileged class – still his Guardian class of the *Republic* – with 'the tutelage of the proletariat' exercised by the 'New Class' of the Communist Party of the Soviet Union and the advocated role of Plato's Nocturnal Council with that exercised by the Politburo, which also was given to nocturnal meetings. Plato and Marx may both never have intended such continuing unjust and unjustifiable results, but they are outcomes inherent in the principle and practice of hierarchical rule and the long-term thwarting of mass, democratic input and ultimate control.

The fundamental, constitutional choice then and now, therefore, remains that of hierarchical elitism or democratic egalitarianism – as both *means* and *ends*.

Notes

1   For the Greek text and opposite-page translation into English, as well as extensive commentary, see Plato, *The Laws*, 1967 and 1968.

Unless otherwise noted, all translations from the *Laws* in this chapter are from Jowett, 1892, contained in Vol. V.

On the role of religion and piety in Plato's political theory, see Pangle, 1976. Pangle observes (p. 1059):

I believe the chief reason why the *Laws* is so rarely studied by political scientists, and that when studied it seems so alien, is the emphasis on the gods and "religion" which pervades the work. The laws put forward by Plato's chief interlocutor (and old "Athenian stranger") are surely not revealed by god; but just as surely, they are proposed with an eye to god at all times. The *Laws* is the only Platonic work that literally begins with the word "god."

Cf. note 31 below.

For a wide-ranging discussion of various aspects of Plato's political theory that contains valuable insights, postulations, and features (e.g., the construction of a Platonic 'Constitution' in the Appendix, its bibliography, and numerous references to observations by other scholars interested in the text), see Stalley, 1983. Especially useful for the student is the frequent clarification of meaning and usage of various Greek terms. For increased comprehension of themes and ambiguities, Stalley recommends use of the translation and extensive commentaries in Saunders, 1970. However, for a more literal translation, see in its entirety, Pangle, 1980.

One cannot be certain when Plato agrees with any of the speakers in his Dialogues; but it is convenient to assume that the Athenian Stranger in the *Laws* is usually an accurate speaker of Plato's views.

2   Book II consists for the most part of a discussion of poetry, music, gymnastics, drinking, and similar subjects that is largely repetitive of earlier works and irrelevant to our main purposes (652 A–674 C).

Book III begins with a discussion of the regrowth of civil societies after all but some shepherds and their flocks have perished in deluges. Here, Plato discusses again, somewhat, the origin and evolution of government (676 A–683 E).

3   A *social contract*, often a *pactum unionis*, is a contract among equals agreeing to set up a civil society (i.e., a society living under civil rule, that is, under government). A *governmental contract*, often a *pactum subjectionis*, is a contract between unequals, between ruler and ruled, setting forth the obligations of each. These contracts may be only logical necessities to justify government, or they may mark actual historical occurrences (e.g., the Mayflower Compact of 1620 is a social contract). These contracts may exist separately or in a sequence in which a social contract (an agreement to set up a government) is followed by a governmental contract (an agreement which by its terms calls the government into being). Either contract or both may be supplemented by, or there may be instead, a *divine covenant* (*pactum divinum*) between God and man (with people or king, or with both the people and their ruler).

4   For application of the principle of proportionality to matters of compelling importance, see the pastoral letter of the National Conference of Bishops, 1983, e.g., Summary I.A.5 and B.2, p. iii. *Cf.* the generally misunderstood *limiting* principle of *only* a 'life for life, eye for eye, tooth for tooth', Exodus 21: 24.

5   The fourfold system was, in effect, a balancing of classes by giving each representation in the government. See the surviving portion of the analysis by Proclus (412–85), 'Examination of objection made by Aristotle in the second book of the *Politics* against Plato's *Republic*', in Stalley, 1995. Stalley discussed the sense of the unity that is in question and writes about Proclus' essay:

> Its primary aim is to defend Plato against Aristotle's charge that he goes astray in regarding unity as the goal of politics. Proclus believes that, providing we understand properly what is meant by 'unity' in this context, we should indeed seek to make the

state as much of a unity as possible. ... In doing so he commits himself to an unashamedly organic view of the state.

6   The same kind of approach calls for the Marxian 'dictatorship of [i.e., by] the proletariat' as, theoretically, the means of ushering in a non-coercive socialist society. See Polin, 1966, pp. 102–15.

It should be noted that it is advisable to make frequent comparisons of the Loeb Library editions and other translations with those of Jowett in any edition. E.g., in Plato, *The Dialogues of Plato*, translated and edited by Jowett, 1964, Vol. IV, at 709E, Jowett translates τυραννος (*tyrannos*) tyrant, while Bury translates it as monarch. In any event, the Jowett translation of 709 A–710 B seems to convey a more accurate sense of what Plato is saying in these passages.

See, accordingly, the explication of the nature of reason and tyranny and the liberating-constructive and limiting-destructive aspects of the latter in Saxonhouse, 1988.

7   Thus, it is to be noted that Plato recognizes the unavailability of a temperate, wise, and amenable tyrant and that desired improvements in government, therefore, will have to be worked out under other circumstances.

8   *Cf.* Wood and Wood, 1978, p. 184, who state:

> The fundamental principle of the laws in the 'Magnesian' polis, then, is that there are certain occupations and conditions in life that are corrupting and others that are not; and that inasmuch as many will have to pursue a corrupting course in life if the society's work is to be done and if others are to be able to lead an untainted life, there must be a clear and fixed separation between the two kinds of life, and citizenship must be confined to the untainted.

Wood, 1988, p. 144, directly challenges Plato and Aristotle on this point. Wood maintains that Protagoras, Aeschylus, and Sophocles are more correct and more representative of the prevailing views of Athenians, such as appreciation of proud, free craftsmen and tillers of the soil and the usefulness and merit of their skills and products. Indeed, Wood goes on to state that, in effect, Plato has distorted the truth of the situation by misappropriating the concept of *technē* as a means of downgrading artisans and farmers and excluding them from the *technē* of citizenship (p. 145). Wood also argues that freedom (*eleutheria*: ἐλευθερία) was in the main a peasant-artisan concept that Plato and Aristotle in addition misrepresented by clever rhetorical devices as a means of attacking Athenian democracy. A central message of her work is contained on pp. 134 ff.

9   See also note 31 below and Bk XII, 948 B–949 C.

For a similar viewpoint on justice and the relationship between God and justice in Plato, see in its entirety the definitive study of this subject by Rupert Clendon Lodge, 1928. See for the relationship Plato conceives of between God and justice especially pp. 119 ff. *Cp.* note 39 below.

See also the revealing summarization of conclusions in Manville, 1990, pp. 463–77, most notably the final sentences:

> The one item of new information which emerges from careful scrutiny of the *Philebus* is that the abstract, other-worldly contemplation to which the *Phaedo* and, at times the *Republic* incline, is now definitely rejected as being formal and one-sided, while the concrete idealization of the present world is accepted as the only adequate expression of the highest good.[24] ([24] *Phileb.* 60c. ff.) Our final conclusion is thus that the highest good for the universe consists in the ideal functioning of the whole so as to realize the

maximum of value-potentiality inherent in its elements, and that the highest good for a particular human being consists in so living as to constitute a consciously organic portion of this whole, and, in so living, to realize his own deepest happiness and well-being.

For an ambiguous view of whether Plato attributed a divine origin or relationship to law in the *Laws*, see Welton, 1995.

10 As a corrective to some of Plato's ideas on eugenics that have been proved incorrect, see again Karp, 1976.

11 Relevant speculation with reference to the *Republic* that came to the attention of the present writer after completion of the textual portion of this work is contained in Nichols, 1987, *passim* and especially pp. 3 ff and 191 ff, nn. 9–12. Nichols may, or may not, be compatible with the notion of the present writer that Plato (through the character of Socrates or the Athenian Stranger) *occasionally* uses the rhetorical device of presenting ideas or scenarios that are bound to be perceived as illogical, absurd, or impracticable, so that a more practical alternative (e.g., the rule of law instead of by a nonexistent, super-wise philosopher-ruler) which he really favoured from the start would become acceptable. Thus, in contrast to Aristophanes' portrayal in the *Clouds* of Socrates as an unrealistic theorist, Nichols believes of Plato that (p. 3):

> He portrays Socrates as talking to men in the market-place about what concerns them, while Aristophanes shows Socrates isolated in a "thinkery," where he investigates natural phenomena. ... Socratic political philosophy counteracts the attempt to escape from human life that Aristophanes depicts in the *Clouds*. Moreover, that temptation arises not primarily from philosophy, as Aristophanes claims, but from politics itself, as we see when the political community insists on an absolute solution to its problems.
>
> The city Socrates founds in the *Republic*, I shall argue, is meant to illustrate this extreme to which politics can be brought. In its communistic institutions, it detaches men from particular relationships and asks them to identify with the city as a whole. Plato thus replies to Aristophanes that it is politics rather than Socratic philosophy, especially a politics motivated by a desire for a perfect justice, that leads men to lose themselves in empty abstractions. He even suggests that politics is able to corrupt philosophy. The communistic city requires philosophic rulers in order to come into being. These philosophers, unlike Socrates, pursue mathematical studies with perfectly homogeneous objects. Their studies prepare them to institute communism in the city, which imitates the homogeneity of their mathematics.

But one may ask, why then should Plato put mathematical absurdities that Socrates does not believe in into the mouth of Socrates unless he has Socrates go on to indicate their preposterous nature? Is Plato being disingenuous or coy here and unfairly using Socrates? Alternatively, was there an unintended omission or incompleteness here of what would have brought out that both Plato and Socrates regarded these mathematical proposals as silly? Do we have any clear clue here that Plato is in disagreement with what he has Socrates saying here? Is it not a reasonable assumption, in any event, that Plato would be more concerned to show the absurdity of a foolish idea itself and not to present either Socrates or himself as really holding such ideas?

See, therefore, the extended treatment of Plato's use of mathematics for various purposes (including metaphorical analogy, humorous punning, ironical musing, and the straightforwardly serious) as presented in Brumbaugh, 1968. Gunnell, 1968, p. 211, states:

Brumbaugh's study of Plato's "mathematical" passages has done much to clarify Plato's intentions by recognizing that these sections are neither meaningless obscurities nor a trove of esoteric doctrine, but metaphorical illustrations which supplement and illuminate the discussion in the text.

Gunnell expatiates on this point, as follows (pp. 213 f):

It would be a mistake to interpret all this as the amusement of an old man who, having failed to change the world, decides to play imaginative games with it to satiate his manipulative urges, but neither is it correct to assume that this complexity of numbers and calculation is simply a "realistic" attention to detail. Finally, and most important, there is no need to delve behind the symbols for esoteric meaning. It is very clear that Plato has constructed the state as a cosmic analogy or a mathematical simile; in a very real sense the life of the state is a metaphor, a life in quotation marks like existence under the form of the myth. But now the myth is the conscious creation of reason, and the state becomes a work of art.

12   Thus, Plato here states again (see 745 E–746 D) the impracticability of the scheme of government he has been describing. In short, Plato's ideal form of government is again perceived by him, as in the *Republic*, as an unattainable plan whose pattern is heavenly; but although what may be realized by man in his earthly city is always imperfect, *yet it should have aim of, and strive towards, perfection*. See again *Republic*, 590 C–592 B and 621 B–D and pp. 66–8 above.

13   See again the illuminating discussion in Wood and Wood, 1978, pp. 162 ff, which finds justice, in Plato's view, not in arithmetical equality before the law (*isonomia*: ἰσονομία), but in an integrated, geometric (Pythagorean) proportional harmony (*harmonia*: ἁρμονία). See also Wood, 1988, p. 2, for the use of similar conservative ideas by Plato to oppose the Athenian democracy.

Plato finds not only justice in things proportional, and therefore harmonious, but also beauty and pleasure. For discussion of the dialectical, pluralistic approach to the good and the beautiful in Plato/Socrates that is based on measure and proportion as indispensable to wisdom and pleasure, see Cropsey, 1988–89. Cropsey notes (p. 190):

From his declaration that measure and proportion are indispensable to things and their mixtures, Socrates now (64e) draws a consequence: since measure and proportion are everywhere assimilated to beauty and virtue, the power of good may be said to have fled for refuge in the nature of the beautiful.

Cropsey elaborates on this theme (p. 192):

As if to help us to see the direction of the argument, Socrates is made to refer to the sufficiency of the reasoning by which wisdom and pleasure were proved to be insufficient: not enough, falling short in amount, number, or measure. Proportion points to measure and measure points to proportion. They exist in relation to each other like the twin bodies of a binary star, a one in two and two in one. If geometry is the science that encompasses measure and proportion, one might agree with the judgment that the diligent study of geometry is an appropriate preparation for inquiry after Good.

14   This passage is also illustrative of Plato's frequently voiced views on the importance of purity of family, legitimacy of birth, and limited tenure of office for most positions.

15   A reference to fortifications in the passage cited here is somewhat inconsistent with Plato's

general antipathy toward them expressed, e.g., in Bk VI, 778 C–779 D.

16 See again Bk V, 739 A–741 A, for more discussion about division into 5,040 households.

17 *Cf.*, however, Plato's assessment in the *Republic* (Bk V, 454 D–456 D) of the superiority of some women over some men and advocacy of classification in some cases by a shared equality instead of by sex; therefore he assigns similar roles and similar training to Guardians of both sexes. For discussion on this point, see Darling, 1986. See also Fite, 1934, pp. 64–8 and 158. Thus, we see that at times Plato expresses a scornful and callously contemptuous attitude toward women, while recognizing an inescapable dependence on them for procreation and, therefore, the necessity to see to their physical wellbeing and to attempt to control their behaviour equally as with men. Such scorn may have resulted from having been himself scorned or would certainly earn the reciprocal scorn and rejection of any wise woman, the type to whom Plato would probably have been attracted at least intellectually. But was Plato being a bit playful in these remarks?

In comparison, Socrates had a much more favourable view of women despite his despicable treatment of his wife, Xanthippe, even in his final hour. Perhaps thanks in part to the personal influence of Aspasia, Socrates had a more appreciative and accurate view of women – especially their thwarted potential – than Plato or Aristotle. See in its entirety the perspicacious study by Eva Cantarella, 1987, especially pp. 52–62.

A work that is much concerned with various forms of social, economic, and political injustice and exploitation, including conflicting interests of urban and rural areas of the polis, is Geoffrey E.M. de Ste Croix, 1981. Ste Croix is especially exercised about the age-old injustice of exploitation of women (pp. 98–111) and states (p. 101):

> Greek wives, I have argued, and therefore potentially all Greek women, should be regarded as a distinct economic class, in the technical Marxist sense, since their productive role – the very fact that they were the half of the human race which supported the main part of the burden of reproduction – led directly to their being subjected to men, politically, economically, and socially.

18 For extended discussion of *paideia*, see in its entirety Jaeger, 1945. For the ancient Greek view of *paideia* and its development of an elevated type of human being and citizen, see, e.g., Vol. III, pp. 79 ff. On Plato's view of *paideai*, see Vol. III, pp. 182–262, especially 223–6. *Paideia* may also be used, loosely, to refer to training of many kinds, such as shopkeeping or navigation. However, Jaeger specifies (p. 224):

> But when we look at it from our standpoint – that is, from the standpoint of an educator who wishes to implant a particular ethos or spirit in the state – we must take education to mean the teaching of areté, which begins in childhood, and makes us wish to become perfect citizens, knowing how to command and to obey in accordance with law. No type of training in special activities can strictly be called paideia, culture, or education. They are banausic, aiming at making money or at cultivating one particular skill which is devoid of a governing spiritual principle and right aim, and is merely a tool, a means to an end.

Thus, Jaeger further explains (p. 226) that *paideia* develops the use of *logos* (reason) instead of lust.

19 For discussion of Plato's views on education published more recently, see, e.g., Klosko, 1986, ch. VIII, pp. 117–32. Jaeger, 1945, remains the definitive study of *paideia* in Greek civilization from Homer through Plato and Aristotle to Demosthenes.

20 In effect, then, Plato espouses education for justice and citizenship as a process of acquisition of truth and consequent development of morality. For discussion of this theme see, e.g., Scolnicov, 1976. Indeed, Scolnicov declares (p. 50):

> I intend to show here that Plato's conception of learning is the focus towards which three of the most important themes of his philosophy converge: the unity of all knowledge, the tension between truth as given from the outside and as brought forth by the soul out of its own resources, and the moral value of knowledge.

Thus, Scolnicov concludes (p. 59):

> If one comes to be committed to truth one cannot help striving for it in thought and deed. The core of the educational process is in intellectual instruction – the "turning of the eye" in the right direction.

21 See again, n. 11 above.

22 See again, n. 11 above.

23 See in full the comment by the editor, Bury, Plato, *The Laws*, Vol. II pp. 222 ff, n. 2, which begins: 'In what follows, the *Athenian*, adopting the Socratic dictum that "vice is involuntary" (cp. *Tim.* 86 E ff.), applies it to the special vice of injustice ...'.

24 Note that Plato draws a distinction here between public good and private good, although he holds that placing the public good first is also to the greater advantage of the private good. Note also the concepts of individual free will and a related moral and practical law of retribution (reminiscent of Aquinas): that inevitably good actions ultimately beget positive rewards and happiness, while just as inevitably bad actions ultimately beget punishment and unhappiness. Defenders of Plato from his more extreme critics may therefore point to this passage as substantially consistent with the defence of Plato throughout Wild, 1953, especially pp. 57 ff. Wild, however, may have overlooked that the central point of his charge against detractors of Plato's political theory was somewhat the same error that Plato made with respect to democracy (p. 59): 'Plato's ideal may reasonably be described as deficient from a democratic point of view, but not as anti-democratic, unless the democratic ideal is uncritically identified with anarchism'.

25 There follows a lengthy recital of various crimes, offences, and recommended punishments, 876 E–882 C. For the definitive work on the system of punishments advocated by Plato, see Saunders, 1991. Saunders ends his work with the summary assessment that (p. 356): '... the institutions of the *Laws*, radically Platonic though they are, have flexibility and compromise built into them'. Prior to that, he notes (p. 353, n. 8): 'The death penalty occurs with sickening frequency in the pages of the *Laws*; would not a continuous reading of Athenian laws and practice be equally sickening?'.

Although Saunders points out that Plato is concerned to obviate the need for punishment and to rehabilitate the offender where possible and also restore friendship between the offender and his victim, he may not regard these desiderata as Plato's central concerns (pp. 350–5):

> He regards it as a major danger if an offender goes unpunished; for he becomes habituated to injustice and greater danger than before. Plato does not shrug his shoulders and think of the damage as only that of the injured party. Accordingly, without ceasing to rely on fundamentally the same system of law-enforcement and prosecution as was employed in Athens, he follows a decidedly interventionist policy: he often goes out of his way by back-up provisions such as incentives to prosecute when they should, to

ensure that no one shall offend without being duly punished. These provisions, so far as we can tell, are at least sometimes more stringent than the pressures applied in Athens.

As a companion-study to Saunders, see Todd, 1993, to provide in detail: the sources, shape, and adversarial-political mode of Athenian law; the jurisdiction, structure, officials, and procedures of its courts; the concept of citizenship and relations within and without the *polis*; and a useful, lengthy glossary. Procedure is emphasized.

26 So extensive are the prohibitions here against private worship in homes, they seem to conflict with contemporary Greek religious practice, which centred about the home and its perpetual sacred fire on the hearth. See again Fustel de Coulanges, 1864, especially Book First, pp. 13–48. We must therefore wonder about Plato's purpose or whether this passage is to be taken at face value, as Saunders, 1991, p. 313, n. 75, opines Plato does not mean to ban household worship of ancestral gods.

27 *Cf.* Bury translation for clarification.

28 Again, one must ask whether Plato is completely serious throughout this passage or at least in part spoofing, especially when he speaks of a one-price-only policy for merchants anywhere in the Mediterranean world.

29 The preceding Scriptural reference is to Exodus 20:12. *Cf.* Bury translation of this passage.

30 For the honours in life and death to be accorded the examiners, see 946 E–948 B.

31 This passage appears to support the view offered in Klosko, 1986, p. 171:

> It seems, then, that Bluck is incorrect in his assertion that the ideal state is a theocracy in which divine forces are responsible for all laws. A more proper view is that the philosopher-king is given an end at which to aim, while his political task lies in devising proper means. Though the end perhaps is rooted in mystically apprehended truths, the question of devising means involves prototypically rational considerations.

The reference here is cited (p. 180, n. 3 and n. 4) as: Richard S. Bluck, 'Is Plato's *Republic* a Theocracy?', *Philosophical Quarterly*, 5 (1955), 69 and 73.

For a monograph on classical Greek cosmological conceptions and especially those of Plato, see Vlastos, 1975, on his theistic revision of Greek naturalism. In a painstakingly careful treatment of his subject, Vlastos explains the central ideas and contributions of scientific-minded Ionian school of nature philosophers (especially Heraclitus, c. 540–c. 480 BC), including their theories of an eternal, infinite, orderly universe in a constant state of flux that consists of alternating forms of fire, water, earth, and air. Vlastos notes (pp. 23 f) the enormously tragic consequences of Plato's counter-argument and proposals for harsh punishment in Book X of the Laws (804–909 D) of those who voice heretical religious views, as more fully remarked upon by Morrow, 1960, with conditions Vlastos omits:

> In Book 10 of the *Laws* Plato drafts a statute against impiety which is without parallel in any surviving code of ancient Greece.[1] ([1] See the comment by G.R. Morrow, *Plato's Cretan City*, pp. 488–89: "Plato becomes the first political thinker to propose that errors of opinion be made crimes punishable by law ... with fateful consequences to Western history, for henceforth the punishment of errors of opinion could claim the sanction of one of the highest authorities.") The mildest of its penalties is five years' solitary confinement, to be followed by execution if the prisoner is still unreformed. A man of irreproachable character would get this sentence if it were proved that he believed that there are no gods or that they do not care for men (888C). As one reads the philosophical preamble (885Bff.) it dawns on one that the Ionian discoverers of the cosmos, the

physiologoi, are in Plato's eyes the main fomentors of the heresies from which his utopia must be purged. [There appears to be some confusion here: Plato's proposed sanctions are presented at 908 E–909 D – RP.]

For further treatment of Plato on religion, philosophy, and education and bibliographical suggestions, see Morgan, 1990. When posing the question of Plato's primary and determinative interests, Morgan answers (p. 2):

> What I would like to suggest is that one grand or overarching interest of Plato's is religious, in a broad sense. That is, Plato is interested in understanding the place of humankind in the cosmos, in relation to the polis, its values, commitments, traditions, and self-image, and to the gods, the divine. He comes to think that a certain kind of life, which includes a particular primary type of activity, is better than any other kind of life, precisely because of how it situates human beings in history, the world, and the polis, and vis-à-vis the gods.

Therefore, for Plato (p. 187): 'Ultimately, the philosopher desires to become divine or akin to divine, and he is hopeful that such transcendence is possible and not only temporarily so.'

32 This 'iron curtain' is reminiscent of a feature of the 'Nicholas System', the form of tyranny practised under Nicholas I in Russia, 1825–55. See, e.g., Pares, 1933, pp. 320–37, and the more contemporary account in Smucker, 1856, pp. 95 f, 153–71 and 237–58.

33 According to Plutarch, Solon spoke of the *Areopagus* and *Boulé* as two anchors of the ship of state. See Plutarch, 1932, p. 108.

34 *Cf.* Bury translation of this passage. For brief discussion of alternative views of the role Plato had in mind for the Nocturnal Council, see Klosko, 1988.

35 See Pangle, 1980, pp. 509 f, who concludes on the idea of virtue that 'this dialogue as a whole is devoted to that theme'.

36 Bury's perception of Plato's anti-democratic bias is supported throughout Wood and Wood, 1978, e.g., beginning on p. 129 with discussion of Plato's contrived, weighted argument in the *Protagoras*.

Morrall, 1977, p. 20, is in seeming agreement with Wood and Wood in their general view of the character and general accomplishments of Athenian democracy:

> By 460 all adult male native citizens were entitled to vote in the Assembly and be appointed to any official post in the *polis*, and the stripping of the last political privilege from the Areopagus, the Athenian 'House of Lords', the last bastion of the hereditary aristocracy, marked the final triumph of the Commons. It had been an age of revolution and upheaval and the more thoughtful adherents of the new democracy were anxious to remove the suspicion that *demokratia* was a veiled tyranny by numerical force. Aeschylus the dramatist, himself a veteran of the battle for freedom against the Persians at Marathon and Salamis, devoted much of his dramatic output (of which only a lamentably small fraction survives) to the problem of reconciling change with order and justice with freedom.

37 *Cf.* Davidson, 1969, ch. III, especially p. 149 f.

38 Among other reasons, the utopian objectives of Platonic political theory inevitably invite comparison with Marxism. Especially recommended as an example of Marxist interpretation of its subject is Rose, 1992. See especially ch. 6. Rose agrees (p. 369) with Okin, 1979, p. 57, that thanks to Plato's scheme of socialization, the natures 'of the guardians are in fact

socially *educationally* constructed – not the consequences of their genetic endowments'. To this finding, Rose adds the acute observation that:

> the radicalism of his attempted solution – his utopian negation of the whole range of democratic discourses as he posits an ideally rational state in which both birth and education are perfectly harmonized with the dictates of reason – represents an at least provisional ancient closure on the still hotly contested terrain of nature versus nurture.

39 But Plato's view of God and God's dispensation of justice remains a frightening one, for justice alone is inadequate for imperfect, fallible, and vulnerable human beings. Lord Byron grasps this point and dramatizes it in *Marino Faliero, Doge of Venice* (Act V, Sc. 1): 'He who is only just is cruel; who / Upon the earth would live were all judged justly?'

In prior agreement with Byron was the deist Charles Blount (1654–93), he of much insight and tragic emotional fragility. In 'A Summary Account of the Deists' Religion', Blount declares that God, '... for the Sins of the Penitent hath as well an inclination to Pity as Justice ...'. Available in the extract reprinted in Gay, 1968, pp. 48–51; quotation from p. 49. See also the concluding paragraph of Baring, 1960, p. 210, wherein he finds such qualities in Russian poetry but erroneously states they 'were unknown to the ancients and which only came to the world with Christianity'.

There is much agreement of Plato with Judaism on justice and law. To the end, Plato was committed to the belief that justice required conformity with God's will and that it was also a man's *duty* to make his life likewise conform to God's will, a view pithily stated by Bluck, 1951, p. 56: 'His lasting conviction was of a good and divine purpose in the world, and he believed that to conform his life to this purpose was at once a man's duty and his greatest privilege'. *Cp.* note 9 above.

What Plato really believed about the nature of justice and how to promote it, however, may be more substantiatedly perceived by examining the scale of offences, punishments, and so-called cures he proposes in his penological system. See again, therefore, the definitive work on this subject: Saunders, 1991, which argues that Plato prescribes essentially medical modalities for dealing with criminal behaviour and its pathological causes instead of a conventional basically retributive and punitive rationale. Indeed, one may suggest that Plato's proposed methods of dealing with the (presumed diseased) minds and bodies of those who have committed crimes (by a healing regimen for soul and body) is a programme of behaviour-modification, exercise, and diet that finally becomes a 'cure or kill' approach. Thus, Plato's penological system appears to be concerned primarily and proximately with utilitarian effectiveness of often observable deterrence of recidivism and is secondarily concerned with largely non-observable accord with claimed more distant, divinely ordained teleological matters, although they mesh.

Although famed for Aristotelian studies and musicology that earned him the sobriquet 'second teacher' (i.e., second to Aristotle), the Muslim-Turkish-Damascan scholar Alfarabi (c. 878–c. 950 CE), known also by other shortened names as Alpharabius, Avennasar, and Abu Nasr al-Farabi, produced a *Summary* of Plato's *Laws* that is the subject of Parens, 1995. Parens presents an important conclusion about a theologically oriented purpose that he finds in Alfarabi's treatment of Plato's *Laws* (pp. 144 f):

> Whereas metaphysical dogmatists attempt to replace the popular myths about the order of the divine and natural order with a demonstrative metaphysics, Alfarabi's Plato recognizes the futility of this objective. Plato, like Socrates, possesses knowledge of his ignorance above all about the order of the whole.[1] (1. *Apology* 19a–e.) Although he

lacks this knowledge, through an analysis of the needs of the human soul he becomes aware of the defectiveness of the popular myths. They fail to meet the human needs they promise to meet. Consequently, the theology in bk. 10 is intended not as an equally dogmatic replacement for the popular myths but merely as a corrective for their defects from the political or human point of view. The achievement of a demonstrative theology is not only futile but also unnecessary because of the heterogeneity of human nature and the nature of the whole.

VII Biographical Note on Aristotle

Early Years

Youth in Macedonia

Aristotle, or *Aristoteles* (Ἀριστοτέλης), was apparently born sometime during the summer or early autumn of the year 384 BC in Stagira, presently Stavro, son of the physician Nicomachus and his wife Phaestis.[1]

Stagira was probably located on the northern Aegean coast in Macedonia, in the newer, rougher world of Thrace, whose Chalcidic peninsula had long been colonized by Greeks. There is no certainty as to whether we should regard Aristotle as having been born in a Macedonian, Greek, or Thracian town, or one that represented a joint enterprise, perhaps by neighbouring Greek islands. In any event, the Greek cities of this region had banded together in a powerful league which struggled to keep Greek independence and ideals from being crushed by the rising power of Macedon. Constant support from the Greek cities to the South was necessary and influenced, no doubt, Aristotle's later contempt for non-Grecian ways and institutions.

Aristotle, however, was perhaps never to acquire Athenian citizenship, and his Macedonian connections were to prove not only a continuing embarrassment to him in Athens, but also a danger to his life following the death of Alexander the Great. Thus, immersed though Aristotle was in Greek culture and ideals, he was always to retain a degree of intellectual detachment from them that favoured him with a corresponding scientific objectivity about many matters.

Nicomachus was evidently a physician of considerable prominence who sprang from a long line of practitioners and traced his ancestry, as did most physicians of that day, to Asclepius, the son of Apollo and patron saint of medicine; but this lineal claim must be regarded as apocryphal at best. Nicomachus also seems to have been born in Stagira and was court physician to and, some biographers report, a close personal friend and adviser of Amyntas II, father of Philip of Macedon. He was also reputed to have been the author of six books on medicine and one on physics.

Aristotle's mother, Phaestis, also seems to have been born in Stagira, also with claimed descent from Asclepius and with more immediate forebears from Chalcis, on the island of Euboea. Phaestis apparently died when Aristotle was rather young, as did his brother Arimnestus (younger than Aristotle?), who died without issue. Aristotle also had an elder sister, Arimneste. After the death of her first husband (Demotimus or Callisthenes), with whom she seems to have had a daughter, Hero, Arimneste married Proxenus. Later on, upon the death of Nicomachus, Proxenus may have become the guardian of Aristotle. It is also possible that Theophrastus, his successor as Peripatus, or head, of the Lyceum, was Aristotle's second cousin. Theophrastus was also to become special guardian of Aristotle's daughter Pythias and his son Nicomachus.

Aristotle's parentage, then, was evidently one of aristocratic Greek descent. Their family background was probably one of culture and refinement, as well as of wealth and influential connections. This was continued by Nicomachus when he became closely associated with the Macedonian dynasty that was soon to bestride all of Greece and the extended Hellenic domain.

Upon acceptance by Nicomachus of the court post with Amyntas, it was necessary for the family to move to Pella, the new and beautiful Macedonian capital. Although Pella was otherwise surrounded by unhealthful swamps, it was situated on the shores of a freshwater lake and a navigable waterway that reached the Aegean a few miles to the south. Life in Pella, which had enjoyed a mushroom growth, was quite different from life in a Greek town; Macedon was the turbulent 'Wild West' of the times, beyond the pale of Hellenism and civilization. The Macedonians were country-bred, country-living – not dwellers in cities – and cared little for the niceties of urban existence so dear to the Greeks. The nobility lived a truly Homeric life, hunting, feasting, drinking, roistering, and 'shooting up' one another in baronial feuds and petty civil wars. The general anarchy prevailing has been likened to conditions in England in the 12th century and France in the 15th century.

Nicomachus and his wife must have pined for the law, order, comforts, and sightliness of Greek city life.

Early Years in Athens and Marriage

Aristotle's parents both died before he reached manhood, and so he was duly committed to the care of Proxenus. It is not known whether Nicomachus lived long enough to give his son any instruction in anatomy and medicine, nor have we further light on Aristotle's education or personality prior to his 18th year. At this age, Aristotle followed the fashion of many of the young intellectuals of his day by journeying to Athens and enrolling in Plato's Academy. This probably occurred when Plato was absent on his second trip to Sicily, seeking to turn the younger Dionysius into a philosopher-ruler, and his Academy was in the charge of such assisting professors as Xenocrates and Speusippus. Or it may well have been that the young Aristotle spent this time studying with Plato's foremost academic rival, Isocrates (436–338 BC), the brilliant orator, political essayist, and pro-Macedonian expounder of pan-Hellenism. However, another account states that in the year 367 BC, Proxenus brought Aristotle to Athens and personally entrusted him to Plato's tutelage.

There is an amusing and probably exaggerated and malicious account of Aristotle as a student at the Academy which has come down to us. According to this report, Aristotle is pictured as a precocious and ultra-smartly dressed fop who spoke with an affected lisp. Differing views have been asserted as to whether Aristotle was, in the main, in agreement with, or in opposition to, Plato's concepts. He remained a member of Plato's Academy for 20 years, but Plato himself is reputed to have said of Aristotle that, 'he kicked me away like a colt its mother'.

At the time of Plato's death (347 BC), Aristotle was 37 years of age. Charge of the Academy fell to Speusippus, a nephew of Plato endowed with only second-rate talents. Accordingly, Aristotle and Xenocrates (396–314 BC), the philosopher from Chalcedon who later on succeeded Speusippus as head of the Academy, accepted an invitation from Hermias (d. 342 BC) to visit with him. Hermias, a former schoolmate of Aristotle, was ruler of Assos and Atarneus in the Troad and altogether an abbreviated and milder version of Dionysius I of Syracuse, a self-made man of humble origin.

Aristotle spent three or four happy years as the guest of Hermias at Atarneus, and there he married Pythias, who has been variously reported as the sister, niece, and natural daughter of Hermias. They had a daughter, also named Pythias, for her mother. Shortly after his marriage, for reasons not known, Aristotle left the household of Hermias and went to the home of Theophrastus, his disciple. This was at Mytilene on the island of Lesbos.

A secret agreement had previously been entered into between Philip and Prince Hermias to use Assos and Atarneus as Asiatic bridgeheads for the Macedonian armies in case of war. Aristotle, an old playmate of Philip and a trusted confidante of Hermias, was in the good graces of both and perhaps had served as an unofficial ambassador between them. According to some accounts, at this time Philip was looking for a new tutor for his 14 year old son, Alexander, with the course of whose education he was dissatisfied; and so he offered the position to Aristotle, who accepted it.

Aristotle and Alexander

Tutorship

During the years since Aristotle had left the city, Pella had grown and developed into a respectable capital. Pella fairly bristled with troops. Philip had permanently established his treasury and war department there, and Pella now reflected the law and order which prevailed throughout the country since he had brought the insubordinate nobles to heel.

Aristotle's relations with Philip had always been cordial and, according to the popular accounts, he soon had the affection and confidence of his new pupil. The circle of Aristotle's friends also grew and came to include Antipater (398?–319 BC), who was to be European viceroy during Alexander's campaigns of conquest in Asia and finally king of Macedon and Greece upon Alexander's death. These friendships were also later to prove of great value to the Greek friends of Aristotle, upon whose behalf he made many successful appeals to the Macedonian conquerors.

At this time, also, occurred an incident which doubtlessly increased and inflamed Aristotle's hatred for the 'barbarians'. The Persians, after having got wind of the agreement between Philip and Hermias, invaded the principality, besieged Atarneus and succeeded in taking the prince by treachery. Hermias was sent to Susa, the Persian capital, where an attempt was made by torture to extort from him the terms of the secret treaty. Valiantly, Hermias refused to betray Philip, and was crucified. The last words of Hermias were reported as: 'Tell my friends and companions I have done nothing unbecoming or unworthy of philosophy'. Aristotle wrote the epitaph for the monument later erected to his memory at Delphi and also dedicated a hymn to Hermias.

While Philip was completing his conquest of Greece, Aristotle was at Pella, tutoring Alexander. Reports have it that Aristotle tried to overlay and control Alexander's character, so far as he could, with Greek ideals of self-control, moderation, and reasonableness. Aristotle taught his pupil history and statecraft, and attempted to develop within the future monarch a reflective and detached vision of his world.

Questionable Extent of Aristotle's Influence on Alexander

There is great dispute over the extent of Aristotle's influence on Alexander. Upon this subject, Benjamin A.G. Fuller (1930, pp. 9–12) has commented as follows:

> The young king seems in the first to have regarded the hero's sword an instrument not merely for conquest, but also for the dissemination of Hellenic culture among the barbarians, and in this ideal of himself as the bearer of Western civilization to "inferior" races it is maintained that Aristotle's hand can be clearly seen. But it has also been argued that the philosopher's influence was never very great. Certainly it was not enduring, for Alexander was soon to rise to the higher and wider vision of a fusing of Greek and oriental civilization that should transcend the distinction, so vital to Aristotle, between barbarian and Hellene – a vision prophetic of the cosmopolitanism of the Hellenistic and Roman worlds, and remotely foreshadowing the Stoic and Christian doctrine of the brotherhood of man. And as time went on, we shall soon see, the personal relations between the old pupil and his former teacher became uncomfortably strained.

Anton-Hermann Chroust presents and discusses the evidence to support the view that Aristotle was the chief preceptor of Alexander, and he also presents contrary evidence and reasoning. Chroust (1973, Vol. 1, p. 132) finally decides:

> In conclusion, it might be pointed out that the traditional and apparently widely accepted story which makes Aristotle the preceptor and, as a matter of fact, the chief tutor of Alexander, is by no means so firmly established as some people would like us to believe. It is quite possible, however, that between 434 [read 344 – RP]–42 BC and 340 (or 338) BC he gave some occasional instruction in one form or another .... Here, as elsewhere in the ancient biographical tradition of any prominent personage in antiquity, it is well-nigh impossible to separate fact from fiction in a satisfactory manner.[2]

There is also much dispute as to the influence on Aristotle of the growth of the Macedonian empire. Alfred E. Taylor (1955, p. 13) says that the march of contemporary events never budged Aristotle from the belief that the small, compact city-state of the *polis* was the only good type of government, and that Philip and Alexander might as well never have existed so far as the political theory of Aristotle is concerned.

On the other hand, we are told by Werner Jaeger that Aristotle was flexible and open-minded enough to move from Plato's position of ethical idealism as he gleaned much about the advantages of *Realpolitik* (i.e., beneficent tyranny here) from his association with Hermias. Jaeger further points out that Aristotle was fully alive to the dangers to Greece of disunity and weakness inherent in a city-state form of governmental unit; and that, therefore, although Aristotle still urged smallness, compactness, and a quasi-Platonic constitution upon the Greeks, he also saw the need for, and potentialities of, a larger governmental unit – the kingdom – of which various city-states would be the components. Indeed, Aristotle was aware that such a new political organization was rising before his eyes, and he dreamed of a Grecian empire, with Macedon as its core, fashioned into a single state with a single figure at its head. Jaeger (1948, pp. 120 f) believes that Aristotle purposefully trained Alexander to be the first sovereign of such an empire, able to transcend constitutional limitations and rule by virtue of an inborn quality of kingly nature. Thus did Aristotle believe political and moral domination of the world by Greek arms and Greek ideals might be accomplished.

According to Jaeger, Aristotle hoped, therefore, to find in Alexander a born monarch through whom 'Greece could rule the world' and did in fact influence Alexander to 'sometimes honestly think of his historical mission as a Hellenic project' (*ibid.*, pp. 121 f) After remarking on some of Alexander's wild, brutal, and hedonistic behaviour, Jaeger continues:

> Nevertheless, his remarkably high degree of personal and historical self-consciousness is a clear sign of the influence of Aristotle .... He was Greek in his literary and moral schooling. He was Greek in striving for 'virtue', i.e. for a higher and more harmonious individuality .... Of such a youth Aristotle might well expect that he would lead the Greeks to unity and establish their dominion in the east over the ruins of the Persian empire (the two things were inseparably connected in his mind). The community of ideas between the two men was obviously very close, not merely while Aristotle was living in Macedon, but down until long after the beginning of the Persian wars. Only when the expedition into Asia had immeasurably extended the horizon of the Iliadic landscape did Alexander begin to confound the bearing of Achilles with other and oriental roles. Then his Greek mission gave place to the new aim of reconciling peoples and equalizing races, and Aristotle opposed him strongly (*ibid.*, pp. 122 f).

On Jaeger's view of Aristotle's political aims, Fuller (1930, pp. 13 f) has commented:

> If this be true, Aristotle's provincialism lay not so much in a failure to rise above a multitude of petty city-states to the concept of a pan-Hellenic monarchy, as in an inability to take the last step with Alexander and to see that monarchy

in its turn as a component in a still wider federation and fusion of peoples and cultures. This step, however, was well-nigh impossible to anyone born and bred in the old-fashioned Greek tradition of disdain and dislike for everything that was "barbarian," that is to say, non-Greek. The distinction, we are told, meant almost as much as the "color-line" does in the southern United States to-day [1930]. It certainly meant as much as, if not more than the line the insular Englishman or the "one hundred per cent" American draws between himself and the rest of the world. Aristotle was deep-dyed in the prejudice, and Alexander's later cosmopolitanism did not soften, but only helped embitter it.

Years of Maturity

Aristotle and the Lyceum

Whether Aristotle continued to tutor Alexander until the latter's succession to power in 336 BC, therefore, is doubtful. In any event, Philip's having secured the surrender of Athens on honourable terms which left her an autonomous, though a vassal, entity, it was not unpropitious for Aristotle to return there. There is also the likelihood that Aristotle interceded successfully with Alexander to be magnanimous in his treatment of Athens. Thus, in the spring of 335–334 BC, the same spring in which Alexander crossed over into Asia, Aristotle set about starting his own school.

Aristotle's school, like Plato's Academy before it, grew from small beginnings. The first gatherings of Aristotle's followers took place in a park in the suburbs northeast of Athens. Dedicated to the Muses and Apollo Lyceus, the spot was known as the Lyceum and had been a favourite haunt of Socrates. Because Aristotle and his pupils were accustomed to walk about the Lyceum during their discussions, their school of thought has to this day been called 'peripatetic'.

The forenoon discussions were concerned in the main with the more technical and involved aspects of the sciences and were intended primarily for members of the school. Aristotle's afternoon classes in rhetoric and oratory attracted such large numbers that these sessions were held sitting down instead of peripatetically. Again it is to Fuller (1930, pp. 14–8) that we turn for a colourful description of Aristotle as teacher:

> We can see him there under the trees of the colonnades, just as we saw Socrates there eighty years before – a man just turning fifty, already bald, potbellied too, one unkind description says, thin of leg, small-eyed, extremely and even

ostentatiously well dressed, with a mocking and sarcastic way of speech, and still with his boyhood lisp. His manner, if he in any way lived up to his professed ideal of the distinguished man, must also have been somewhat self-conscious and pompous. Altogether, we may suspect him of having been somewhat of a dandy, a wit, and a snob.[3]

Final Years

The following 12 years were for Aristotle, inwardly, a period of intense intellectual activity, although outwardly peaceful. They were not, however, entirely peaceful, and certainly not without sorrow or important personal happenings. Some time after his arrival in Athens, Pythias, the wife to whom Aristotle was deeply attached, died, leaving him with their young daughter and an orphaned son of Proxenus, Aristotle's former guardian, whom he had adopted in gratitude for the kindness and care he had himself received in his own boyhood. Shortly after the death of Pythias, Aristotle became attached to a lady from Stagira, Herpyllis by name. Although Herpyllis bore Aristotle a son, Nicomachus, named after Aristotle's father, so far as is known, Aristotle never married her. Nicomachus became something of a philosopher himself and later edited the notes of one of his father's lecture courses now known to us as the *Nicomachean Ethics*.[4]

After the death of Alexander, persons known to have been sympathetic to Macedon were in danger. In the absence of any evidence against him, a suspect account has it, Aristotle was charged with an offence against the established religion. The reported charge was supposedly based on the hymn Aristotle had penned to Hermias of Atarneus. Fuller (1930, p. 26; *cf.* Chroust, 1973, Vol. 1, pp. 152 ff) comments that to the Athenians of Aristotle's day, religious intolerance was '... the blind spot in their intelligence, just as bigotry in sociology and ethics is the blind spot in ours'. Nor should it be forgotten that in the eyes of the irreconcilable Demosthenes (384–22 BC), Aristotle was a spy who continued to correspond with his old friend Antipater (c. 397–c. 319 BC), the Macedonian general.

Therefore, because of the hymn and the assertion he had also offered sacrifices to the martyred prince, Aristotle would be imperilled if found guilty of violating the established religion, '... a charge that inflamed much the same passions and prejudice in the conservative bosom then as the charge of questioning the established political, moral, or economic order inflames in it today' (Fuller, 1930, pp. 20 and 26).

Mindful of the fate that had befallen Socrates, and not wishing, as he said, 'to give the Athenians a second chance of sinning against philosophy', Aristotle fled from Athens, leaving Theophrastus in charge of the Lyceum. Aristotle retired to Chalcis, where he owned a country house which, perhaps, he had inherited from his mother.

Although Aristotle had eluded his Athenian accusers, an inescapable death lay close in store for him. The stomach trouble that for years had tortured the frail philosopher, now grew progressively worse. For a year, Aristotle lingered, bravely bearing up under his ailment, but finally he succumbed in the summer or very early autumn of 322 BC. This was little more than a year after Alexander's death, and was also just as the Greek revolt was collapsing and Athens was about to bow in unconditional surrender to Antipater (ibid., pp. 26 f).[5]

Aristotle was a comparatively wealthy man at the time of his death. His researches while in Macedon had been financed largely by Philip and Alexander in turn. Alexander, it has been said, perhaps with some exaggeration, contributed 800 talents (a sum amounting today to at least several million dollars) to these researches, and placed at Aristotle's disposal the services of all the fish, game, and forest wardens of the kingdom, with orders that they report to him anything novel or of interest. In fitting tribute to a truly remarkable man and mind, Fuller (ibid., p. 18) has stated:

> His writings were the outcome of a profound and minute study of an overwhelming mass of data drawn from every conceivable field of contemporary scientific research. Mathematics, physics, astronomy, biology, physiology, politics, ethics, logic, rhetoric, art, theology – all were grist to his mill. Nothing escaped his eye or ear, and everything he saw or heard of he investigated, from the philandering of elephants to the nature of God and the constitutions of one hundred and fifty-eight Greek cities. Never before or after has there been a human intellect that compassed at first hand and digested the whole body of existing knowledge, or one that held so vast a variety of fact in a single perspective. And, quite apart from the range and grasp of fact upon which it rests, this perspective still ranks in itself after the test of twenty-two hundred years as one of the supreme achievements of the mind of man.[6]

Thus, many centuries later, after Dante had once described him as 'the master of those who know', Aristotle appealed so much to the age of the Renaissance that he was referred to then simply as 'the Master'. And Aristotle still symbolizes the mind and unfolding character of the Renaissance, for this profound and wide-ranging scholar remains the classic example, *par excellence*, of the 'Renaissance man'.

Notes

1   The most critical and impressive study in a number of respects of the life of Aristotle and the *Vitae Aristoteles* is the work by Anton-Hermann Chroust, 1973. See especially Vol. 1, *Some Novel Interpretations of the Man and His Life*. However, the account followed for much of this brief biographical note was largely the shorter one presented in Fuller, 1930, Vol. III, pp. 1–27. Fuller includes popularly believed stories about Aristotle, although with some reservations expressed about them. Chroust is more careful, critical, and precise, and should be referred to as the more authoritative and specialized work on the subject; but the flow of principal events in the life of Aristotle is more easily followed in Fuller, and his generous appraisal of Aristotle also deserves our attention.

Additional sources consulted for this biographical note, and also for some of the analytical statements in this and subsequent chapters, include the following: Barker, 1975, portions of the Introduction, pp. xi–xlvi; Curteis, 1913; Ferguson, 1972; Jaeger, 1948; Moore, 1975; Morrall, 1979; Randall Jr, 1960, Taylor, 1955; and Veatch, 1974.

For a revealing verbal and pictorial glimpse of what life and culture must have been like in Macedonia in Aristotle's youth, see Prideaux, 1977, and cover illustration.

2   See entire ch. X, 'Was Aristotle Actually the Chief Preceptor of Alexander the Great?', pp. 125–32, including end-notes, pp. 358–64.

3   For another description of the Lyceum and Aristotle's activities there, see Jaeger, 1948, pp. 314 ff, for a briefer account; and for a more specialized account, see Chroust, 1973, *passim*.

4   For a detailed, yet lyrical, account of Aristotle's final stay in Athens, see Jaeger, 1948, ch. XII, pp. 311–23. It may be noted again, however, that the most trustworthy and properly qualified recent work, in its treatment of reputed events in the life of Aristotle, is Chroust, 1973, Vol. I, who may occasionally be at variance with Fuller.

5   Chroust, 1973, p. 177, argues very effectively against the report in Diogenes Laertius V. 6 that 'according to Eumelus, in the fifth Book of his Histories, [Aristotle died – Chroust] by drinking the hemlock, at the age of seventy'. See in its entirety, ch. XIV, pp. 177–82.

6   For an introductory appreciation of the life, work and contribution of Aristotle, see Edel, 1982, which considers especially his scientific philosophy and its roots in his logic, epistemology, and ethics.

VIII Concepts Aristotle Explicated: *The Athenian Constitution*

Overview

The Athenian Constitution or *Atheniaion Politeia* (Ἀθηναίων Πολιτεία) attributed to Aristotle, is one of 158 reports on the constitutional systems of contemporary states, largely Greek, that were prepared by Aristotle and his students. Although there may be divided opinion about his personal authorship of this work, its ancient ascription to Aristotle is vouchsafed by authoritative modern scholarship: 'There cannot be the slightest doubt ... that in the London papyrus we have the work which was considered in late antiquity as Aristotle's treatise on the *Constitution of Athens*' (von Fritz and Kapp, 1950, p. 4).[1]

The internal evidence seems to indicate that the *Athenian Constitution* (or *Polity*) was written later than the *Politics* and so the assumption that this work and its companion studies were used as the basis for Aristotle's *Politics* has been placed in doubt:

It had been generally assumed that the collection of constitutions was made as a basis which Aristotle was to use for writing his *Politics*. However, the latest date mentioned in the *Politics* is 336, while the *Constitution of Athens* mentions the Archonship of Kephisophon (329/8); it does not note either the loss by Athens of control of Samos or Antipater's modification of the Athenian constitution, both of which occurred in 322. Thus the writing of the *Constitution of Athens* seems to have fallen in the period 328–322; consideration of the types of warships discussed suggests that XLVI, 1 at least may have been completed before 325/4; see below on XLVI, 1. It is thus extremely unlikely that the *Constitution of Athens* as we have it was a preliminary study for the *Politics*, for it appears to have been written seven to ten years later. However, it is possible that the material was collected prior to the writing of the *Politics*, and put into its present shape at a later date (Moore, 1975, p. 144).[2]

The speculation that the 158 constitutional studies of *politeiai* (πολιτείαι) antedated the *Politics* in some fashion seems more plausible; for it is more likely that Aristotle would be involved in such a multifaceted enterprise at an earlier age and that he would write his political *magnum opus* subsequent to an evidence-gathering period. In any event, regardless of which was the earlier work and whether the *Athenian Constitution* was by the master himself (as we shall conveniently assume), it is more advantageous to an understanding of Aristotle's political theory to consider the *Athenian Constitution* first.

The *Athenian Constitution* is expository rather than advocatory and contains more historical development than contemporary description. Modern scholarship also indicates that for an earlier portion of this historical treatment, Aristotle relied to a substantial extent on Hellanicus of Lesbos, a sort of historian of the late fifth century BC.[3]

> The work falls into two sections. The first (chapters I–XLI) is a historical survey of the development of the constitution of Athens which is divided into eleven 'changes'; chapters XLII–LXII describe the constitution of Aristotle's own day in four sections, the franchise (XLII), legislation (XLIII–XLV), administration (XLVI–LXII), and the judiciary (LXIII–LXIX) (Moore, 1975, p. 144).

Also, the *Athenian Constitution* contains only a limited amount of material that, taken by itself, we may state with some assurance to be an expression of Aristotle's personal political theory and preferences. Only occasionally does he indicate in this work what may be regarded as definite approval or disapproval. An examination of it, however, will make us familiar with his general view of Athenian constitutional development and practice that must have had considerable influence on the constitutional formulae he presents in the *Politics* and the light in which he portrays them. This purpose may also be served by calling attention to a number of passages in the *Athenian Constitution* wherein Aristotle mentions certain cause-and-effect relationships or takes note of practices or arrangements that affect stability, safety, efficiency, freedom, and virtue in society and government.

Exposition

Council of Areopagus as Protector of Laws

Chapter 3 of the *Athenian Constitution*, which follows a fragmentary chapter 1 and very brief chapter 2, begins with a description of the constitution of

Athens as it existed before the reforms of Draco (c. 621 BC). Of interest is the role assigned to the Council of the Areopagus to protect the laws and carry out the most important administrative functions of the state:

> The Council of Areopagus had as its constitutionally assigned duty the protection of the laws; but in point of fact it administered the greater and most important part of the government of the state, and inflicted personal punishments and fines summarily upon all who misbehaved themselves. This was the natural consequence of the facts that the Archons were elected under qualifications of birth and wealth, and that the Areopagus was composed of those who had served as Archons; for which latter reason the membership of the Areopagus is the only office which has continued to be a life-magistracy to the present day (ch. 3).

Aristotle writes with some approval of Draco and his accomplishments in what may be an apocryphal or invented account. He recognizes there can be no true stability where there is injustice in government because the few who control it exploit the many. Thus, in discussing the previously existing system and the constitution drawn up by Draco, we see that Aristotle is aware of a degree of constitutional check in the functioning of public magistrates under the Draconian system, of economic causation of social tension and strife, and also of the right of public appeal for redress of grievances:

> The Council of Areopagus was guardian of the laws and kept watch over the magistrates to see that they executed their offices in accordance with the laws. Any person who felt himself wronged might lay an information before the Council of the Areopagus, on declaring what law was broken by the wrong done to him (ch. 4).[4]

Solon: Political and Economic Reforms to Abate Class Warfare

Aristotle sees, and understands the nature of, class warfare and seeks to abate it through the application of justice by the state and an appeal to individual virtue. The passages which deal with the reforms of Solon in the sixth century BC fasten most of the blame for such conditions on the greed for riches and power of the wealthy and show how Solon exhorted the rich through poetry to self-impose personal curbs on their impulses to acquire wealth and power. For example, Aristotle notes:

> But, as has been said before, the persons of the people were mortgaged to their creditors, and the land was in the hands of a few.

Now seeing that such was the organization of the constitution, and that the many were in slavery to the few, the people rose against the upper class. The strife was keen, and for a long time the two parties were face to face with one another, till at last,[1] ([1] The traditional date for Solon's legislation is 594 B.C.) by common consent, they appointed Solon to be mediator and Archon, and committed the whole constitution to his hands (chs 4–5).

Aristotle next discusses the reforms of Solon which cancelled debts, the *Seisachtheia* (σεισάχθεια) and prohibited all loans on the security of the person. Then follows a discussion that calls into play both the principle of a balancing of classes (four economic categories) and the principle of constitutional (institutional) checks:

Solon ratified his laws for a hundred years; and the following was the fashion of his organization of the constitution. He made a division of all rateable property into four classes, just as it had been divided before,[3] ([3] This division has hitherto been universally ascribed to Solon. What he actually did was apparently to take this property qualification, which hitherto had no direct connection with the political organization, and make it the basis of the constitution, substituting a qualification of wealth for the qualification of birth.) namely, Pentacosiomedimni, Knights, Zeugītae, and Thetes.[4] ([4] The name Pentacosiomedimnus means one who possesses 500 measures, as explained in the text below; that of Knight, or Horseman, implies ability to keep a horse; that of Zeugites, ability to keep a yoke of oxen; while the Thetes were originally serfs attached to the soil.) The various magistracies, namely, the nine Archons, the Treasurers, the Commissioners for Public Contracts [Polētae], the Eleven,[5] ([5] The superintendents of the state prison; see ch. 52.) and the Exchequer Clerks [Colacrētae],[6] ([6] These officers, whose original function was said to have been to 'collect the pieces after a sacrifice,' were the Treasury officials in early times, who received the taxes and handed them over to be kept by the Treasurers. In later times the Colacretae seem to have ceased to exist, and they are not mentioned in Aristotle's enumeration of the officials in his own day.) he assigned to the Pentacosiomedimni, the Knights, and the Zeugitae, giving offices to each class in proportion to the value of the rateable property. To those who ranked among the Thetes he gave nothing but a place in the Assembly and in the juries (ch. 7).

Interestingly enough, representation in some offices and processes of the state is not based on economic class but on tribal membership. It is important to note especially the part played by the tribes and representatives in naval preparedness and maintenance of the democracy, in some cases regardless of property class:

The elections to the various offices Solon enacted should be by lot, out of candidates selected by each of the tribes. Each tribe selected ten candidates for the nine archonships, and among these the lot was cast. Hence it is still the custom for each tribe to choose ten candidates by lot, and then the lot is again cast among these. A proof that Solon regulated the elections to office according to the property classes may be found in the law which is still in force for the election of the Treasurers, which enacts that they shall be chosen from the Pentacosiomedimni.[1] ([1] That this qualification was, in Aristotle's own time, purely nominal, appears from ch. 47, where it is stated that the person on whom the lot falls holds the office, be he ever so poor.) Such was Solon's legislation with respect to the nine Archons; whereas in early times the Council of Areopagus summoned suitable persons according to its own judgment and appointed them for the year to the several offices. There were four tribes, as before, and four tribe-kings. Each tribe was divided into three Trittyes [= Thirds], with twelve Naucraries[1] ([1] It appears from ch. 21 that the Naucraries were local divisions, which, under the constitution of Cleisthenes, were replaced by the demes. The division of tribes into Trittyes and Naucraries existed before the time of Solon, as appears from Herodotus [v. 71] and they are only mentioned here as continuing under Solon's constitution, not as created by him.) in each; and the Naucraries had officers of their own, called Naucrāri, whose duty it was to superintend the current receipts and expenditure. ... Solon also appointed a Council of four hundred, a hundred from each tribe; but he still assigned to the Areopagus the duty of superintending the laws. It continued, as before, to be the guardian of the constitution in general; it kept watch over the citizens in all the most important matters, and corrected offenders, having full power to inflict fines or personal punishment (ch. 8).

In modern states, failure to exercise the franchise usually does not result in a fine but may cause the nonvoter to be dropped from the election list. Solon, according to Aristotle, has a somewhat similar standard for those who refused to 'stand up and be counted' when there was a civil strife:

> Further, since he saw the state often engaged in internal disputes, while many of the citizens from sheer indifference waited to see what would turn up, he made a law with express reference to such persons, enacting that anyone who, in a time of civil factions, did not take up arms with either party, would lose his rights as a citizen and cease to have any part in the state (ch. 9).

Next, Aristotle takes cognizance of what he considers the most democratic aspects of Solon's reforms and the resultant power of the masses. They are, significantly, *individual*, rather than group, rights: of freedom, of legal action before a jury-court to correct injustice, and of legal appeal to law courts:

There are three points in the constitution of Solon which appear to be its most democratic features: first and most important, the prohibition of loans on the security of the debtor's person; secondly, the right of every person who so willed to bring an action on behalf of anyone to whom wrong was being done; thirdly, the institution of the appeal to the law-courts; and it is by means of this last, they say, that the masses have gained strength most of all, since, when the democracy is master of the voting-power, it is master of the constitution.[3] ([3] This was, unquestionably, one of the most important factors in the development of the Athenian democracy. The large juries [consisting of several hundreds of members] which sat in the Athenian courts, and appointed the sentence as well as decided on the guilt of the accused, practically represented the voice of the people; and as all magistrates had to submit to examination before the law-courts at the end of their term of office, the democracy had a ready means of securing obedience to its wishes. The 'voting power' is consequently that which was exercised in deciding the verdict and the sentence.) (ch. 9).

The above account, of course, stresses the approach of a balancing of the classes; and the chief constitutional safeguard lies in the individual right of appeal for redress of error or grievances, which is quite different from a mutual checking of each other's actions by the various organs of government. Aristotle continues along the same line of thought by pointing out that Solon, in his reforms, although fearful he might alienate both rich and poor, sought to balance their participation in government and to establish the best laws possible. At the same time, he emphasizes principles of moderation and temperance (chs 11–12).

Peisistratus: Stability through Agricultural Reform and Kindly Rule

Another widely-held belief of Aristotle's was that an agrarian citizenry tend to be more stable and that work and prosperity help to keep them satisfied and disinclined to engage in politics, especially if the laws be mild and humane. We see these ideas mirrored in his discussion of the administration of Peisistratus and its aftermath during much of the sixth century BC:

Such was the origin and such the vicissitudes of the tyranny of Pisistratus. His administration was temperate, as has been said before, and more like constitutional government than a tyranny. Not only was he in every respect humane and mild and ready to forgive those who offended, but, in addition, he advanced money to the poorer people to help them in their labours, so that they might make their living by agriculture. In this he had two objects, first that they might not spend their time in the city but might be scattered over all the face of the country, and secondly that, being moderately well off and occupied with their own business, they might have neither the wish nor the time to attend to public affairs. At the same time his revenues were increased by the thorough cultivation of the country, since he imposed a tax of one tenth on all the produce. For the same reasons he instituted the local justices, and often made expeditions in person into the country to inspect it and to settle disputes between individuals, that they might not come into the city and neglect their farms (ch. 16).

Continuing in a similar vein, Aristotle approves of some of Peisistratus' methods; for, although Aristotle extols a government wherein the rule of law is theoretically supreme, he understands the need for a discreet, kindly, and popular administrator of such a rule. Personal charm – charisma – no doubt enters into the picture; but one wonders whether the approach of Peisistratus upon which Aristotle reports so favourably is one of 'bribing' the poor, deactivating them, or giving them the opportunity to stand on their own feet (ch. 16).

Cleisthenes, Pericles, and Theramenes: Law, the Personal Equation, and Democracy

The role of ostracism is touched upon by Aristotle. It is a means of winning the good will of the masses and restraining the powerful; at the same time, it increases the influence of the masses in government. For example, in discussing the constitutional changes brought about by Cleisthenes, Aristotle notes their democratic influence and how ostracism was used by the mass of the citzenry:

> By these reforms the constitution became much more democratic than that of Solon. The laws of Solon had been obliterated by disuse during the period of the tyranny, while those which replaced them were drawn up by Cleisthenes with the object of securing the good will of the masses. Among these was the law concerning ostracism. ... It was originally passed as a precaution against men in high office, because Pisistratus took advantage of his position as a popular leader and general to make himself a tyrant; and the first person ostracised was one of his relatives, Hipparchus[,] ... the very person on whose account especially Cleisthenes had passed the law, as he wished to get rid of him. ... Megacles son of Hippocrates, ... was [also] ostracised. Thus for three years they continued to ostracise the friends of the tyrants, on whose account the law had been passed; but in the following year they began to remove others as well, including anyone who seemed to be more powerful than was expedient (ch. 22).

Thus, Aristotle never loses sight of the personal element. For him it is always of the first importance that there be good leaders, and one of the kind things he has to say about democracy is that democracy can develop, and bring to the fore, good leaders, although this is not invariably the case (ch. 28).

Hence, because he is aware that democracy does not automatically fulfil its promise of bringing forth leaders of ability and virtue, Aristotle places but limited trust in democracy. He justifies this position by pointing out, in a manner reminiscent of Plato, how democracy may be corrupted by demagogues and money (ch. 28).

Again and again, Aristotle returns to his theme of the supremacy of law, placing it above any transient constitution of government and stressing the duty of every good citizen to be law-abiding. Thus, in approval of Theramenes, one of the leaders in the succession following the death of Pericles who was one of the Thirty Tyrants and better known for his self-execution by the hemlock in 404 BC, Aristotle states:

> On the merits of Theramenes opinion is divided, because it so happened that in his time public affairs were in a very stormy state. But those who give their opinion deliberately find him, not, as his critics falsely assert, overthrowing every kind of constitution, but supporting every kind so long as it did not transgress the laws; thus showing that he was able, as every good citizen should be, to live under any form of constitution, while he refused to countenance illegality and was its constant enemy (ch. 28).

Again, we see Aristotle refusing to be blindly anti-democratic and pointing out that democracy does not necessarily fall because of inherent weakness. He points out, instead, and with sympathetic understanding, how it was dropped under the pressure of harsh circumstances in favour of the temporary oligarchy in an attempt to make Athens palatable to the Persians as an ally against Sparta (ch. 29). In like fashion, speaking of the return to power of the democracy a few years later, after the Thirty Tyrants were overthrown in 403 BC, Aristotle finds this form of government to be strong and effective. Thus, in his recapitulation of the 11 constitutional changes which brought about the Athenian constitution extant in his time, Aristotle gives an account of increasing popular participation in, and effective control of, the government:

> … [A]t the time of which we are speaking the people, having secured the control of the state, established the constitution which exists at the present day. Pythodōrus was archon at the time, but the democracy seems to have assumed the supreme power with perfect justice, since it had effected its own return by

its own exertions. This was the eleventh change which had taken place in the constitution of Athens. First of all came the original establishment by Ion and those who assisted him in forming the settlement, when the people was first divided into the four tribes, and the tribe-kings were created. Next, and the first organization of the constitution following this, was that which took place in the reign of Theseus, consisting in a slight deviation from absolute monarchy. After this came the constitution formed under Draco, when the first code of laws was drawn up. The third was that which followed the civil war, in the time of Solon; from this the democracy took its rise. The fourth was the tyranny of Pisistratus; the fifth the constitution of Cleisthenes, after the overthrow of the tyrants, of a more democratic character than that of Solon. The sixth was that which followed on the Persian wars, when the Council of Areopagus had the direction of the state. The seventh, succeeding this, was the constitution which Aristeides sketched out, and which Ephialtes brought to completion by overthrowing the Areopagite Council; under this the nation, misled by the demagogues, made the most serious mistakes on account of its maritime empire. The eighth was the establishment of the Four Hundred, followed by the ninth, the restored democracy. The tenth was the tyranny of the Thirty and the Ten. The eleventh was that which followed the return from Phyle and Piraeus; and this has continued from that day to this, with continual accretions of power to the masses (ch. 41).

In summing up the mastery of the democracy over Athens, Aristotle records two important developments: payment for attendance at Assembly meetings, followed by subsequent increases in the rate of payment; and passage of control of the Council into the hands of the mass of citizens as well. Aristotle can hardly have favoured such popular attendance at the Assembly and certainly not payment for it. A bit surprisingly, however, Aristotle approves of the increased influence of the general citizenry over the Council, as small bodies are more apt to become corrupted:

> The democracy has made itself master of everything and administers everything by its votes in the Assembly and by the law-courts, in which it holds the supreme power. Even the jurisdiction of the Council has passed into the hands of the people at large; and this appears to be a judicious change, since small bodies are more open to corruption, whether by actual money or by influence, than large ones. At first they refused to allow payment for attendance at the Assembly; but the result was that people did not attend, and often votes were passed by the Prytanes alone. Consequently, in order to induce the populace to come and ratify the votes, Agyrrhius, in the first instance, made a provision of one obol a day, which Heracleides of Clazomenae, nicknamed 'the king,' increased to two obols, and Agyrrhius again to three (ch. 41).

Council and Assembly: Checks and Balances or Division of Functions?

Aristotle was at least aware of the concept of checks and balances, and also of the constitutional safeguards provided by courts that function for the safety of the individual. It may be argued, however, that what is described as in actual operation represented more a division of duties rather than a mutual or countervailing check and countercheck system. But that is not entirely so. We find a law court acting as a check upon the Council. We find the Council acting as a check upon the magistrates. We find the right of a private individual to impeach any magistrate before the Council. We find the right of the magistrates to appeal to a law court. We find the Council examines its members for the ensuing year and the nine Archons. We also find control of public monies and the currency in the hands of the probouleutic Council (the *boulé*: βουλή) and the popular Assembly (the *ekklesiá*: ἐκκλεσία). Aristotle's report of this system is as follows:

> In former times the Council had full powers to inflict fines and imprisonment and death; and it was when it had dragged of Lysimachus to the executioner, and he was sitting in the immediate expectation of death, that Eumelides of Alŏpecē deprived it of its powers,[3] ([3] Or 'rescued him from its hands.') maintaining that no citizen ought to be put to death except after a hearing by a court of law.[4] ([4] It should be observed that throughout the treatise a 'law-court' [δικαστήριον] always means one of the large popular jury-courts ...) Accordingly there was a trial in law-court, and Lysimachus was acquitted, receiving henceforth the nickname of 'the man from the drum-head'; and the people deprived the Council thenceforward of the power to inflict death or imprisonment or fine, passing a law that if the Council condemn any person for an offence or inflict a fine, the Thesmothetae shall bring the sentence or fine before the law-court, and the decision of the jurors shall be the final judgment in the matter. The Council passes judgment on nearly all magistrates, especially those who have the control of money; its judgment, however, is not final, but is subject to an appeal in the law-courts. Private individuals, also, may impeach any magistrate they please for not obeying the laws, but here too there is an appeal to the law-courts if the Council declare the charge proved. The Council also examines those who are to be its members for the ensuing year, and also the nine Archons.[1] ([1] See ch. 55.) Formerly the Council had full power to reject candidates for office as unsuitable, but now these two have an appeal to the law-courts. In all these matters, therefore, the Council has no final jurisdiction. It has, however, a preliminary consideration [i.e., a probouleutic role – RP] of all matters brought before the Assembly, and the Assembly cannot vote on any question unless it has first been considered by the Council and placed on the

programme by the Prytanes; since a person who carries a motion in the Assembly is liable to an action for illegal proposal on these grounds (ch. 45).

Thus, close examination of the subject seems to reveal that the Council and the Assembly do not fundamentally act as checks upon one another, but rather do they divide functions between them. It would not be proper to make any hard and fast distinctions on this, however, because there are many borderline cases. For example, although the Council is largely a preconsidering body and is therefore a pipeline to, or a checkpoint before, the Assembly, it also acts as an indicting agency, and the arrangement seems to follow either a step-by-step or hierarchical pattern more than anything else. Yet there always seems to be a right of appeal in almost any matter to a jury- or law-court (*dikasterion*: δικαστήριον), a practice strongly reminiscent of Rousseau's idea of referring matters to a representative segment of the community. In short, the arrangement seems more suggestive of a row of monkeys, each holding on to and checking by the tail the monkey in front of him, rather than holding hands with their neighbours on both sides and able to check and bite in either direction. The passage is continued as follows:

> The Council also superintends the triremes that are already in existence, with their tackle and sheds, and builds new triremes or quadriremes, whichever the Assembly votes, with tackle and sheds to match. The Assembly appoints master-builders for the ships by vote; and if they do not hand them over completed to the next Council, the old Council cannot receive the customary donation, – that being normally given to it during its successor's term of office. For the building of the triremes it appoints ten ship-builders, chosen out of the whole body of the people. The Council also inspects all public buildings, and if it is of opinion that the state is being defrauded, it reports the culprit to the Assembly, and after itself condemning him hands him over to the law-courts (ch. 46).

Thus, it is apparent that Aristotle has a conception of various organs of government having the function of checking other bodies and officials, and that he has a visible, working example of this before him. But it is not on the basis of a division into three separate branches of government, each of which confines itself to one of the three basic processes of government. Rather do we see that each of the principle organs of government may be engaged in legislative, judicial, and executive (or administrative) processes. In other words, it is primarily an assignment of specific duties, rather than a discrete division of the trinity of processes of government.

Arbitration and Appeal to Jury-courts

In discussing the manner in which the Arbitrators function, Aristotle describes another important constitutional safeguard: the Arbitrators hear civil suits involving more than ten drachmas, but there is the right of appeal from their decision to a dikasterion. Their manner of operation is presented in lengthy, step-by-step detail. Aristotle gives here revealing insight into the legal system and dispensation of justice in classical Athens as illustrated by the role of the Arbitrator in the conduct of jury-courts:

> They [local justices – RP] have full powers to deal with cases in which the damages claimed do not exceed ten drachmas, but anything beyond that amount they hand over to the Arbitrators. The Arbitrators take up the case, and, if they cannot bring the parties to an agreement, they give a decision. If their decision satisfies both parties, and they abide by it, the case is at an end; but if either of the parties appeals to the law-courts, the Arbitrators enclose the evidence, the pleadings, and the laws quoted in the case in two urns, those of the plaintiff in the one, and those of the defendant in the other. These they seal up and, having attached to them the decision of the arbitrator, written out on a tablet, hand them over to the justices whose function it is to introduce cases on behalf of the tribe of the defendant. These officers take them and bring up the case before the law-court, to a jury of two hundred and one members in cases up to the value of a thousand drachmas, or to one of four hundred and one in cases above that value. No laws or pleadings or evidence may be used except those which were adduced before the Arbitrator, and which have been enclosed in the urns.
>
> The Arbitrators are persons of sixty years of age, as is clear from the Archons and the Eponymi, the ten [from each of four tribes, therefore 40 in all – RP] who give their names to the tribes, and the forty-two [one for each year between ages 18–59 inclusively – RP] of the years of [military – RP] service. ... [T]he Forty take the last of the Eponymi of the years of service, and assign the arbitrations to the persons belonging to that year, casting lots to determine which arbitrations each shall undertake; and everyone is compelled to carry through the arbitrations which the lot assigns to him. The law enacts that anyone who does not serve as Arbitrator when he has arrived at the necessary age shall lose his civil rights, unless he happens to be holding some other office during that year, or to be out of the country. These are the only persons who escape the duty. Anyone who suffers injustice at the hands of the Arbitrator may appeal to the whole board of Arbitrators, and if they find the magistrate guilty, the law enacts that he shall lose his civil rights. The persons thus condemned have, however, in their turn an appeal (ch. 53).

Prior, Continuing, and Post Examination of Top Officials

Examination of the accounts of holdings and transactions of public officials is meant to be rigorous, according to Aristotle's account. This examination is conducted prior to entering public office and, when deemed necessary or when charges are preferred, during and after the official tenure. Aristotle describes the work of the Auditors or *Logistae* (λογισταί) and Examiners of Accounts or *Euthunoi* (εὔθυνοι) as follows:

> The Council also elects ten Auditors [Logistae] by lot from its own members, to audit the accounts of the magistrates for each prytany. They also elect one Examiner of Accounts (Eūthunus] by lot from each tribe, with two assessors [Paredri] for each examiner, whose duty it is to sit in the market-place, each opposite the statue of the eponymous hero of his tribe; and if anyone wishes, on the ground of some private difference, to question the accounts of any magistrate who has given in his accounts before the law-courts, within three days of his having given them in, the assessor enters on a whitened tablet the name of this person[1] ([1] Or, reading τὸ αὑτοῦ as proposed by Prof. Blass, 'he [i.e., the complainant] enters … his own name.') and that of the magistrate prosecuted, together with the mal-practice that is alleged against him. Then he enters his claim for a penalty of such amount as seems to him fitting, and gives in the record to the Examiner. The latter takes it and hears the charge, and if he considers it proved he hands it over, if a private case, to the local justices who introduce cases for the tribe concerned, while if a public case he enters it on the register of the Thesmothetae. Then, if the Thesmothetae accept it, they bring the accounts of this magistrate once more before the law-court, and the decision of the jury stands as the final judgment (ch. 48).[5]

Not even the archons, kings, or polemarchs were above such prior examination, continuing accountability, and possible examination following their tenure of office. These practices are portrayed by Aristotle in graphic detail:

> When the examination has been thus completed, they proceed to the stone on which are the pieces of the victims [of sacrifices – RP], and on which the Arbitrators take oath before declaring their decisions, and witnesses swear to their testimony. On this stone the Archons stand, and swear to execute their office uprightly and according to the laws, and not to receive presents in respect of the performance of their duties, or, if they do, to dedicate a golden statue. When they have taken this oath they proceed to the Acropolis, and there they repeat it; after this they enter upon their office (ch. 56).[6]

Assessments

The *Athenian Constitution* is presented by Aristotle (or his student) as a piece of historical description, with only occasional statements of approval or disapproval. However, the choice of content and tone permit certain impressions to be gained that are reinforced by these occasional opinions. These impressions may therefore properly be offered as permissible conclusions if acknowledged to be somewhat tentative and not rigidly held.

Perhaps one of the most important impressions to be gained from the *Athenian Constitution* is that Aristotle is not so condemnatory of the record of democratic government in Athens or so depreciatory of its capacity to provide strong, stable, virtuous, and just government in a harmonious society as is Plato; yet these are desiderata that Aristotle shares with Plato. Perhaps because this work is not in the more dramatic form of dialogue, Aristotle not only favours, but also seems to express himself with, greater moderation, temperateness, and clarity, virtues that were preached but not always practised by Plato in his political dialogues.

Because it is descriptive rather than advocatory, the *Athenian Constitution* does not lend itself to a strong judgment of how important inherent limitations were to Aristotle, especially in comparison with constitutional checks and balances. Nonetheless, Aristotle does pay careful attention in this work to matters that involve the promotion of justice, virtue, stability, strength, and harmony in society and the state, especially when he approves of reliance on individual self-restraint as a means of curbing the greed for property and power that produces injustice, instability, weakness, and discord within the *polis*. Because the *Athenian Constitution* is largely a narrative description and account of the structure, organization, and functioning of a government, it deals primarily with institutional checks and balances; and so it may be that the nature of the work tended to preclude greater focus on aspects of inherent limitations that were, nevertheless, present in the Athenian constitutional system.

In any event, we may properly take note of the full and frequent description in the *Athenian Constitution* of the many instances in which accounts are audited and checked, of the right to appeal to jury-courts and to prefer charges against magistrates, of the careful provision for due process that required the *boulé* to act as a preconsidering body for the *ekklesia*, and of the balancing of the tribes and of socio-economic classes according to divisions imposed by the government. These, of course, are in the main, examples of institutional checks and balances. But lastly, and perhaps most important of all, was Aristotle's distinct commitment to the supremacy of rule according to principles of law, rather than according to personal preference, whim, or judgment.

Also, because the *Athenian Constitution* is not a complete manuscript, some note should be taken of what is not treated of, especially if it be relevant to the keystone point of the role of law. Thus, we should include attention to a recent study by Robert K. Sinclair (1988) that explains the process of enacting and revising laws (*nomothesia*: νομοθεσία) in ancient Athens and distinguishes a *nomos* in kind and weight from an assembly decree (*psēphisma*: ψήφισμα) of temporary and specific applicability:

> There were, it is true, some restraints on the power of the Ekklesia. The requirement that its decisions should not contravene existing law has already been noted.[23] ([23] See cg. 3.5.) Furthermore, specific procedures for the revision and making of laws (*nomothesia*), whereby all proposed changes were submitted to *nomothetai* (lawmakers), were instituted in the last years of the fifth century, largely in order to prevent snap votes in the assembly, such as had led to the repeal of key institutions in 411 and 404. ... The nomothetai ... were drawn from among the dikasts. ...
>
> Nomothesia has sometimes been regarded as a serious diminution of the sovereignty of the assembly, but it should be seen rather as a brake on the making of decisions which might affect the fundamental laws and institutions of the polis. ... Moreover, it would seem that the Ekklesia could prevent any proposals going forward to the nomothetai. ... The general view is that nomoi were conceived to be not only superior to psephismata, but more fundamental, more universal and more permanent (Sinclair, 1988, pp. 83 f).[7]

Again, it would seem that actual practice and the substance of the *Athenian Constitution* both call for meaningful checks and balances and the rule of law, not of whim.

Notes

1   Moore, 1975, pp. 143 f, also accepts the authenticity of this work and its ascription to Aristotle, as does Manville, 1990, p. xiii, note.

   For a definitive study of the text, extensive bibliography and commentary on the ms rediscovery and its authorship, see Rhodes, 1981. For the provenance of the ms, see pp. 1–5. For consideration of how content, purposes, and style mesh and lead Rhodes to believe that Aristotle did not personally write this work, see especially pp. 38 and 61 ff. *Cf.* von Fritz and Kapp, 1950, pp. 3–7. See also a more recent work that supports Aristotle as the direct author and its challenging review by Rhodes, 1992: Keaney, 1992. Both present cogent cases.

Unless otherwise noted, Kenyon, 1891, has been used for the quotations and citations from that work present throughout this chapter.

For the Greek text and opposite-page translation into English, as well as extensive commentary, see Rackham, 1952. Comparison may be made with the translations and commentary in von Fritz and Kapp, in Moore, and in Kenyon, 1961, *Atheniensum Respublica* (reprinted from Ross, 1908–82), Vol. X. Sandys, 1912, has also been relied upon to explain or caution about the Kenyon translation. See especially the comprehensive, detailed treatment of text and sources in Rhodes, 1981.

2   It is also conceivable that a few interpolations may have been added at various times after a first version had been completed.

3   Cited by von Fritz and Kapp, 1950, p. ix, from Felix Jacoby (1949), *Atthis: The Local Chronicles of Ancient Athens* (Oxford: Clarendon Press).

4   *The Cambridge Ancient History*, Vol. IV: *The Persian Empire and the West*, 1926, pp. 28 ff, focuses on Drako's reform of the law on homicide. N. 1, p. 31, reads: 'The constitutional order ascribed to Draco in Aristotle's *Constitution of Athens*, C. IV, is almost universally regarded as unhistorical ...'.

Sagan, 1991, states (p. 9): 'Cleisthenes' trumping of the Areopagus by the formation of a new, democratic Council effectively assured that, in the future, Athens would no longer be subject to aristocratic domination by a patrician senate'. Sagan adds concerning the role of Ephialtes, mentor of the young Pericles: 'In 462, he succeeded in passing measures that effectively put an end to the Areopagus as a political force'.

5   *Cf.* Rackham for terminology and explanations with respect to these officials; and also von Fritz and Kapp, 1950, pp. 122 f, especially footnote a, p. 122: 'These λογισταί [logistae: Auditors – RP], which are selected from the Council, are to be distinguished from the λογισταί mentioned in Chapter 54, 2, who are taken from the general body of citizens and who audit the accounts of all officials at the end of their terms'.

6   *Cf.* the translation and notes in Moore, 1975, p. 195 f and von Fritz and Kapp, 1950, pp. 130 f.

7   See Sinclair, 1988, in its entirety for background on the historical development, structure, and functioning of the society and government of the Athenian *polis*.

IX Concepts Aristotle Advocated: *The Politics*

Overview

The Politics (*Ta politika*: Τὰ πολιτικά) of Aristotle is the work in which we find the most extensive and systematic expression of his fundamental beliefs and espousals concerning the constitution and government of the *polis*.

In a sense, however, the *Politics* is not an integrated work, because: 'It is a collection or conflation of different essays rather than a single treatise – a collection assembled and arranged by Aristotle (or by some subsequent editor) under a single title, but not welded into a work' (Barker, 1975, p. xxxvii). Ernest Barker distinguishes these essays as six different sections or 'methods' concerned, respectively, with: (A) the management of the household; (B) ideal states in theory and practice; (C) the general theory of political constitutions; (D) problems of politics; (E) methods of ensuring stability in democracies and oligarchies; and (F) political ideals and the sketch of an ideal state. If the view be adopted that these six methods all were finally written during the time of Aristotle's teaching at the Lyceum, then they may be assigned to the period 335–322 BC (*ibid.*, pp. xxxvii–xxxiv and xli–xlv).[1]

In the *Politics*, Aristotle covers much the same ground as had Plato in his *Republic*, *Statesman*, and *Laws*. Indeed, the *Politics* may be regarded in good part as Aristotle's response to Plato's pronouncements on government and politics; for in many places it specifically addresses itself to the task of correcting, modifying, clarifying, or adding to Plato's writings on the same subject.

Beginning with their fundamental cosmological assumptions about the natural order of things and ending with their consequent recommendations, there is probably more often agreement than disagreement between the two on political and constitutional matters. In studying the *Politics*, therefore, it is useful always to bear in mind what Plato has written about whatever matter is being considered and to be aware of this substantial amount of agreement between them on both the nature of government and what it should strive to do. It is also useful, however, always to bear in mind that there were a few significant differences in personality and basic premises that affected their recommendations in such a way as to bring about some qualitative differences of attitude, spirit, and performance in the constitutional systems they respectively advocated. One of these significant differences, as Eduard Zeller (1952, Vol. II, pp. 211 f) has noted, is Plato's constant relating of everyone and everything of this world to the other world which is their common origin and destination of return. On the other hand, Aristotle was just as constantly concerned with the needs of the mundane world alone, or nearly so.

Now argued as ethical and practical instruction addressed primarily to lawgivers – of both the *polis* and family – the fundamental propositions that underlie the *Politics* include: Aristotle's belief in the superiority of the Greeks and their culture over the surrounding, and often threatening, non-Grecian world; the incompatibility of money-grubbing pursuits with the highest attributes of good citizenship and political virtue; and the general subordination of all else to the rule of law (Dunning, 1902–20, Vol. I, p. 93).[2]

Exposition

Organological, Hierarchical State Based on Human Nature and Reason: the Role of Law and Justice

In our direct examination of the text of the *Politics*, it becomes evident from the opening words wherein he defines the *polis*, that Aristotle's political theory, like Plato's, is built upon his conception of human nature, with all the potentialities and limitations that involves and in conformity with humanity's wants, drives, and aspirations. From the opening words of the *Politics*, the state is regarded as a supreme, all-inclusive community that embraces everyone in an association purposed to be and do good:

> Every state is a community of some kind, and every community is established with a view to some good; for mankind always act in order to obtain that which they think good. But, if all communities aim at some good, the state or political community, which is the highest of all, and which embraces all the rest, aims, and in a greater degree than any other, at the highest good (Bk I, 1252 a).[3]

This conception of human nature is, of course, basically a favourable and optimistic one when it regards humanity's capacity for virtue and wisdom; but Aristotle also recognizes humanity's capacity to be the worst and most savage of animals. This view is further elaborated on by Aristotle when he discusses the social impulse in humanity and the function of law and justice in enabling humanity to reach higher levels instead of lower depths. We find here a role for the state whereby the individual must be subordinated to the whole and whereby law and justice produce a decent, stable society. This follows from the premise that the state is a natural, indispensable prerequisite for both the survival of the individual and for the individual to realize one's humanity. Only 'a beast or a god' can be so self-sufficient as not to need, or not to be part of, a state. Regulation of the state and the group partnership it formalizes is by judicial procedure that decides what is just:

> Hence it is evident that the state is a creation of nature, and that man is by nature a political animal. ...
>   Thus the state is by nature clearly prior to the family and to the individual, since the whole is of necessity prior to the part .... The proof that the state is a creation of nature and prior to the individual is that the individual, when isolated, is not self-sufficing; and therefore he is like a part in relation to the whole. But he who is unable to live in society, or who has no need because he is sufficient for himself, must be either a beast or a god: he is no part of a state. A social instinct is implanted in all men by nature, and yet he who first founded the state was the greatest of benefactors. For man, when perfected, is the best of animals, but, when separated from law and justice, he is the worst of all; since armed injustice is the more dangerous, and he is equipped at birth with the arms of intelligence and with moral qualities which he may use for the worst ends. Wherefore, if he have not virtue, he is the most unholy and the most savage of animals, and the most full of lust and gluttony. But justice is the bond of men in states, and the administration of justice, which is the determination of what is just[a] ([a] Cp. N. Eth. v, 6. § 4.), is the principle of order in political society (1253 a).[4]

Aristotle also elaborates on his theme of an hierarchical society that follows from a universal principle that the superior should rule over the inferior. In particular, he justifies slavery for those who are destitute of enough reason to take care of themselves; and, *en passant*, declares the superior ruling relationship of male over female. A concomitant principle is that animate beings are composed of soul and body and therefore the soul, as the superior, should naturally rule over the body. The implication is that the rule of reason will lead to good, orderly government. Included in this discussion is the following passage:

> But is there any one thus intended by nature to be a slave, and for whom such a

condition is expedient and right, or rather is not all slavery a violation of nature? There is no difficulty in answering this question, on grounds both of reason and of fact. For that some should rule and others be ruled is a thing, not only necessary, but expedient; from the hour of their birth, some are marked out for subjection, others for rule.

And whereas there are many kinds both of rulers and subjects, that rule is the better which is exercised over better subjects – for example, to rule over men is better than to rule over wild beasts. The work is better which is executed by better workmen; and where one man rules and another is ruled, they may be said to have a work. In all things which form a composite whole and which are made up of parts, whether continuous or discrete, a distinction between the ruling and the subject element comes to light. Such a duality exists in living creatures, but not in them only; it originates in the constitution of the universe; even in things which have no life, there is a ruling principle, as in a musical harmony. ... And it is clear that the rule of the soul over the body, and of the mind and the rational element over the passionate is natural and expedient; whereas the equality of the two or the rule of the inferior is always hurtful (1254 a–1254 b).

Favours Diversity over Oneness

Aristotle begins Book II by posing the question of which form of political association would make the material conditions of life most as people would want them to be; and whether in this association all things should be in common, no things should be in common, or some things should be in common. He asks whether it is better to adopt Plato's plan of the *Republic* of a community of wives, children, and property or to continue the prevalent condition of separate families and private property (Bk II, 1260 b–1261 a).[5]

The objections of Aristotle to Plato's scheme of a community of wives are that: it is impracticable; and if it could be put into practice, it would produce uniformity, oneness, or homogeneity that is inimical to the nature, purpose, and strength of a state. A state consists of both numbers and variety; but Plato would reduce all to oneness and thereby he would not improve and strengthen the state, but would destroy it. It would seem that, in Aristotle's view, Plato has confused uniformity with unity (1261 a).

Favours Diversity, Equality, Freedom, and Rotation in Office

Next, Aristotle presents more sophisticated variations on Plato's more simplistic principle of division of labour which would have each man stick to that which he is best qualified to do. Firstly, Aristotle states that a fair exchange must be involved (each element should render as much as it receives); secondly, justice requires equal freedom and equal rotation of equals in office; and thirdly, Aristotle more clearly perceives that self-sufficiency is more apt to be achieved through greater variety, and that a greater degree of self-sufficiency is to be preferred even at the cost of a lesser degree of unity, for the state is not like a military alliance. Indeed, Aristotle believes a state is not fully a state until it has achieved self-sufficiency, something the individual and even the family cannot attain:

> Again, a state is not made up only of so many men, but of different kinds of men; for similars do not constitute a state. It is not like a military alliance, of which the usefulness depends upon its quantity even where there is no difference in quality. For in that mutual protection is the end aimed at; and the question is the same as about the scales of a balance: which is the heavier?
>
> In like manner, a state differs from a nation; for in a nation the people are not distributed into villages, but live scattered about, like the Arcadians; whereas in a state the elements out of which the unity is to be formed differ in kind. ... Again, in another point of view, this extreme unification of the state is clearly not good; for a family is more self-sufficing than an individual, and a city than a family, and a city only comes into being when the community is large enough to be self-sufficing. If then self-sufficiency is to be desired, the lesser degree of unity is more desirable than the greater (1261 a–b).

Favours Family Life and Private Property

Aristotle continues his argument with Plato's *Republic* by opposing a community of women and property as not conducive to the sought-for harmony, but resultive, instead, of actual loss:

> For that which is common to the greatest number has the least care bestowed upon it. Every one thinks chiefly of his own, hardly at all of the common interest; and only when he is himself concerned as an individual. For besides other considerations, everybody is more inclined to neglect the duty which he expects another to fulfill; as in families many attendants are often less useful than a few. Each citizen will have a thousand sons who will not be his sons individually, but anybody will be equally the son of anybody, and will therefore be neglected by all alike (1261 b–1262 a).

A note of derision enters Aristotle's argumentation against Plato as it becomes increasingly polemical and direct. Aristotle finds Plato illogical, inconsistent, and unaware or uncaring of certain incongruities and indecencies, such as incest, that are bound to result from a community of women and children among the Guardians. He adds, scornfully: 'How strange, too, to forbid intercourse for no other reason than the violence of the pleasure, as though the relationship of father and son or of brothers with one another made no difference' (1262 a).

Next, in repeating his assertion that a community of women and children would be counterproductive, Aristotle states that it would seem better calculated to serve Plato's purpose if it were applied to the governed agricultural class, rather than to the Guardians, because it would water down the spirit of fraternity and thereby make them more obedient and less given to revolution. Moreover, Aristotle holds that it is fraternity – i.e., a warm friendship and regard for one another among the people – that is the greatest good within a state because it is the best safeguard against civil disorder and conversely is therefore the chief source of stability and strength. In addition, he charges Plato with ignoring certain fundamental human motivations, namely, the sense of ownership and the preciousness of one's own:

> As a little sweet wine mingled with a great deal of water is imperceptible in the mixture, so, in this sort of community, the idea of relationship which is based upon these names will be lost; there is no reason why the so-called father should care about the son, or the son about the father, or brothers about one another. Of the two qualities which chiefly inspire regard and affection – that a thing is your own and that you love it – neither can exist in such a state as this (1262 a–b).

Continuing in polemical vein, Aristotle points out further oversights by Plato concerning the effects of a community of women and children. Illogical, unnatural, and indecent results would ensue because the beneficial motivations and deterrents conferred by a sense of kinship would be absent. The opening Aristotle sees to drive this thrust home is provided by Plato's allowance for a transposition of the rank of offspring where they prove of higher or lower endowment than their parents:

> And the previously mentioned evils, such as assaults, unlawful loves, homicides, will happen more often amongst those who are transferred to the lower classes, or who have a place assigned to them among the guardians; for they will no longer call the members of any other class brothers and children, and fathers, and mothers, and will not, therefore, be afraid of committing any crimes by reason of consanguinity. Touching the community of wives and children, let this be our conclusion (1262 b).

Aristotle's case against community of property is rooted in the nature of humanity, with both goodness and wickedness perceived as basic constituents of this nature. Thus, it is not the absence of a community of property that is the source of certain evils within the state, in Aristotle's opinion, but the inherent wickedness in humanity; and it is not self-love nor self-indulgence *per se* that is wicked but – as is generally true for Aristotle about almost anything – it is an excess of self-love and a misdirected self-indulgence that are wrong. A good part of the solution of the problem, therefore, is to make the holding and working of property private, and to direct to the common good the use made of its fruits (1262 b–1263 b).[6]

Opposes Plato's Emphasis on Unity

Aristotle continues to charge Plato with having laid too much emphasis on unity and says this would defeat the very ends Plato has in mind. Also, Aristotle finds Plato's programme utterly impossible of achievement. Therefore, Aristotle argues for a greater variety and a greater reliance upon education, social customs, and legislation. These proposals of Aristotle combine principles of the inherent limitations of conditioned human nature and the institutional checks provided by formal legislation. Aristotle declares that a state should not seek an impossible degree of unity and homogeneity, for then it would cease to be a state; for the nature and role of a state is to unite groups with lesser differing interests into a harmonious, self-sufficing community of greater common interests. Thus, Aristotle favours greater pluralism in society and would provide conditions and methods that would make for greater freedom in the *polis* than would Plato:

> Unity there should be, both of the family and of the state, but in some respects only. For there is a point at which a state may attain such a degree of unity as to be no longer a state, or at which, without actually ceasing to exist, it will become an inferior state, like harmony passing into unison, or rhythm which has been reduced to a single foot. The state, as I was saying, is a plurality[c] ([c] Cp. c. 2. § 22.), which should be united and made into a community by education; and it is strange that the author of a system of education which he thinks will make the state virtuous, should expect to improve his citizens by regulations of this sort, and not by philosophy or by customs and regulations … (1263 b–1264 a).

Favours Wider Participation and More Liberality

Aristotle continues his attack against Plato's *Republic* by pointing out an element of danger in the failure to balance participation in government by extending it to all classes of the citizenry and by rotating the holding of public office. Such a neglectful approach, he feels, is productive of sedition and other serious difficulties. Where all the ranks and categories of citizens participate in proper measure and turn in government, there is less discontent and greater happiness; and happiness is indivisible – the whole cannot be happy unless the parts of the state are happy:

> The government, too, as constituted by Socrates, contains elements of danger; for he makes the same persons always rule. And if this is often a cause of disturbance among the meaner sort, how much more among high-spirited warriors? ... Again, he deprives the guardians even of happiness, and says that the legislator ought to make the whole state happy[b] ([b] Rep. iv, 419, 420.). But the whole cannot be happy unless most, or all, or some of its parts enjoy happiness[c] ([c] Cp. vii. 9. § 7.). In this respect happiness is not like the even principle in numbers, which may exist only in the whole, but in none of the parts; not so happiness. And if the guardians are not happy, who are? Surely not the artisans, or the common people (1264 b).

Soon after shifting his attention from Plato's *Republic* to his *Laws*, Aristotle also finds fault with Plato's vagueness about the amount of property a man needs and his cultivation of temperance while neglecting the need for the balancing quality of liberality in the use of wealth and omitting any limitation of population for a fixed number of indivisible, entailed estates:

> A better definition would be that a man must have so much property as will enable him to live not only temperately but liberally[j] ([j] Cp. vii. 5. § 1.); if the two are parted, liberality will combine with luxury; toil will be associated with temperance. ... One would have thought that it was even more necessary to limit population than property ... (1265 a–b).

Favours Mixed, Balanced Government of Polity, but not Plato's Version

As Aristotle continues his examination of Plato's *Laws*, he offers a number of sharply barbed criticisms that are not always precise. For example, Plato argues in the *Laws* that the state and polity wherein there is a community of wives, children, and property [for the Guardians] is best (*Laws*, Bk V, 739 b–c). But Aristotle says that the plan offered in the *Laws* as the best form (but which seems not to be the one Plato so regarded?) is really a combination of democracy and tyranny; for Aristotle denies there are any features of kingship in the outline of the favoured plan of government in the *Laws* (1265 a). He finds therein only elements of oligarchy and democracy, and deems the whole scheme too inclined toward oligarchy. Aristotle appears to tilt here in favour of a 'mixed, balanced government' of the one (monarchy), the few (oligarchy), and the many (democracy):

> The whole system of government tends to be neither democracy nor oligarchy, but something in a mean between them which is usually called a polity, and is composed of the heavy-armed soldiers. Now, if he intended to frame a constitution which would suit the greatest number of states, be was very likely right, but not if he meant to say that this constitutional form came nearest to his first or ideal state; for many would prefer the Lacedaemonian, or, possibly, some other more aristocratic government. Some, indeed, say that the best constitution is a combination of all existing forms, and they praise the Lacedaemonian[d] ([d] Cp. iv. § 7; 7. § 4; 9. § 7–9.) because it is made up of oligarchy, monarchy, and democracy, the king forming the monarchy, and the council of elders the oligarchy, while the democratic element is represented by the Ephors; for the Ephors are selected from the people. Others, however, declare the Ephorality to be a tyranny, and find the element of democracy in the common meals and in the habits of daily life. In the Laws[e] ([e] vi. 756 E; cp. iv. 710.), it is maintained that the best state is made up of democracy and tyranny, which are either not constitutions at all, or are the worst of all. But they are nearer the truth who combine many forms; for the state is better which is made up of more numerous elements. The constitution proposed in the Laws has no element of monarchy at all; it is nothing but oligarchy and democracy, leaning rather to oligarchy (1265 b–1266 a).[7]

Favours Private Property, Moderation, Philosophy, Training, and Justice

In considering the proper distribution of property, Aristotle criticizes not only some of the proposals of Plato in the *Laws*, but also some views of one Phaleas of Chalcedon. He notes that there are those who consider the regulation of property to be the most important object of government because it is the greatest source of civil discord. Aristotle then observes that part of the problem is the failure to regulate simultaneously the amount of property and the number of children in the family; and that therefore there can be no just or stable system that gives each family a simple equality of property. It is also necessary to 'aim at moderation in their amounts', which presumably means moderate minimum and maximum limits (1266 a–b).

However, Aristotle does not find property to be the only important source of sedition and criminality; human nature is also a key source. The *masses* become revolutionary when the distribution of *property is unequal*; but *men of education* become revolutionary when the distribution of *power is equal*, rather than in proportion to their unsatisfied ambitions. Men do not commit crimes only out of desperate need for the necessities of life, but also to satisfy a desire or for the pleasure involved (1267 a).[8]

Consequently, in order to reduce sedition and crime, Aristotle makes proposals to fit each type of crime: for crimes of want, some modicum of property and some kind of employment; for crimes of desire or lust, temperance; and for crimes of pleasure, the aid of philosophy. Training and justice are needed to effect such remedies, not the simple equalization of property (1267 a–b).

Favours Sufficient, not Excessive, Military Strength and Wealth

Intertwined with his discussion of property and his criticism of Phaleas of Chalcedon for advocating equalization of property holdings, Aristotle points out the necessity for a state to be strong enough militarily to discourage attack by reason of being self-sufficient but not wealthy enough to invite covetous attack by other states. He wants it to be not worth the game in cost of lives or possible booty for others to attack, and concludes:

> Phaleas has not laid down any rule; and we should bear in mind that a certain amount of wealth is an advantage. The best limit will probably be, not so much as will tempt a more powerful neighbour, or make it his interest to go to war with you (1266 a–1267 a).

Favours Necessary Changes in Law and Custom

Aristotle pays attention not only to the constitutional proposals of Plato and Phaleas, but also to those of Hippodamus of Miletus, the architect who had been employed by Pericles to lay out the plan of roads, buildings, and fortifications of the Piraeus. Hippodamus was noted for his advocacy of a tripartite division of social classes, territory, and laws; reform of the method of tallying jury verdicts; and public honours for those who suggest an improvement of benefit to the state. In discussing this last suggestion, Aristotle expresses cautious reservations. More significantly, however, Aristotle shows that he puts no stock in the belief that whatever is, is right. He recognizes that conditions, customs, and even written laws can all be wrong. Therefore, the forthright recognition of reality, the common sense, and the sense of justice that are generally characteristic of Aristotle, lead Aristotle to allow for necessary change in law and custom:

> Even when laws have been written down, they ought not always to remain unaltered. As in other sciences, so in politics, it is impossible that all things should be precisely set down in writing; for enactments must be universal, but actions are concerned with particulars (1267 b–1269 a).[9]

Next, Aristotle is concerned to point out that laws should not be changed light-heartedly, but cautiously and only when there would be sufficient benefit to justify any interruption of habitual obedience – for he does not want the public thereby to fall into the dangerous habit of disobeying government. Also, he raises here, but does not answer in the *Politics*, the question whether all laws and constitutions should be open to change and whether anyone may be permitted to attempt such change, or only certain qualified persons. The passage concludes:

> For the law has no power to command obedience except that of habit, which can only be given by time, so that a readiness to change from old to new laws enfeebles the power of the law. Even if we admit that the laws are to be changed, are they all to be changed, and in every state? And are they to be changed by anybody who likes, or only by certain persons? These are very important questions; and therefore we had better reserve the discussion of them to a more suitable occasion (1269 a).

On Serfdom and Women as Sources of Trouble

When Aristotle considers the constitutions of Sparta and Crete, he must, perforce, deal with their treatment of serfs and women. He finds that either too gentle or too harsh treatment of serfs leads to their pressing of troublesome demands, conspiracy, and revolt. He acknowledges that the right mode of organization for dealing with serfdom has not been found. Although nothing more explicit is said on the subject, because he speaks of any state that has a system of serfdom as suffering from it, one wonders whether Aristotle does not possibly leave the door open for a system without serfdom as the means of eliminating the disorders that spring from it (1269 a–b).

With respect to Sparta, Aristotle strongly condemns the role played by their women. He believes they are too aggressive, too licentious, too outspoken, too influential, and the source of too much avarice and trouble there. Part of the reason is that the men are too busy with military adventures; and part of the blame is that military men develop great passion for their women, become too indulgent of them, and become dominated by them. The following criticism typifies Aristotle's discussion of the trouble he states women are in Sparta:

> This was exemplified among the Spartans in the days of their greatness; many things were managed by their women. But what difference does it make whether women rule, or the rulers are ruled by women? The result is the same. Even in regard to courage, which is of no use in daily life, and is needed only in war, the influence of the Lacedaemonian women has been most mischievous. The evil showed itself in the Theban invasion, when unlike the women in other cities, they were utterly useless and caused more confusion than the enemy (1269 b– 1270 a).[10]

Favours Property Reform, Mixed Constitution, Safeguards, and the Qualified

Aristotle finds great fault with, and danger in, the Spartan system of landholding and dowries that has permitted a concentration of two-fifths of the whole country in the hands of a few women and thereby reduced considerably the number of soldiers it could maintain. An equal, moderate distribution of land would have been better. Also, Aristotle finds the problem compounded by the law that exempts the father of three from military service and the father of four from all taxes, in an attempt to increase the birthrate and, presumably therefore, the available soldiery. Division of the same amount of land among a greater number of families, while at the same time much of it becomes concentrated in the hands of a few, necessarily reduces a large number of citizens to poverty (1270 a–b).

Aristotle has mixed feelings about the Ephorate at Sparta. He feels that election of the five Ephors, or 'Overseers', by all the citizenry means the elevation to office of men who lack wealth and are susceptible to bribery, and that the Spartan state has tended to turn into a democracy as the power of the Ephors has extended itself. However, despite additional shortcomings of the Ephorate that he notes, Aristotle acknowledges its unifying force:

> And so great and tyrannical is their power, that even the kings have been compelled to court them; through their influence the constitution has deteriorated, and from being an aristocracy has turned into a democracy. The Ephoralty certainly does keep the state together; for the people are contented when they have a share in the highest office, and the result, whether due to the legislator or to chance, has been advantageous. For if a constitution is to be permanent, all

the parts of the state must wish that it should exist and be maintained[a] ([a] Cp. iv. 9 § 10; v. 9. § 5.) (1270 b).

With respect to the Council of Elders, or Senate, at Sparta, the *Gerousia* (γερουσία), Aristotle criticizes their final election by a form of acclamation, the frequent bribery of them, their lifetime judgeship in certain cases, and the choice of unqualified, ambitious men. In effect, Aristotle would have the office seek the qualified, rather than have the unqualified but ambitious seek the office (1270 b–1271 a).

Criticism of Spartan Militarism and Public Finance

Before passing on to an examination of the Cretan constitution, which he finds generally similar and on the whole inferior because of certain defects in their system, Aristotle severely criticizes – and perhaps somewhat unfairly imputes to the Spartans a preference for goods over virtue – the excessive concern with military strength and conquest that characterizes the Spartan system. He believes such an excessive concern ultimately proves self-defeating; and he finds that the failure to see to payment of taxes reduced the Spartan state to penury and thereby also contributed to the downfall of Sparta (at the hands of the Thebans, led by the heroic Epaminondas, at the battle of Leuctra, 371 BC):

> The charge which Plato brings, in the Laws[d] ([d] (Laws, i. 630.), against the intention of the legislator, is likewise justified; the whole constitution has regard to one part of virtue only, – the virtue of the soldier, which gives victory in war. And so long as they were at war, their power was preserved, but when they had attained empire they fell[a] ([a] Cp. vii. 14 § 22.), for of the arts of peace they knew nothing, and had never engaged in any employment higher than war. There is another error, equally great, into which they have fallen. Although they truly think that the goods for which they contend are to be acquired by virtue rather than by vice, they err in supposing that these goods are to be preferred to the virtue which gains them.
>
> Once more: the revenues of the state are ill-managed; there is no money in the treasury, although they are obliged to carry on great wars, and they are unwilling to pay taxes. The greater part of the land being in the hands of the Spartans, they do not look closely into one another's contributions. The result which the legislator has produced is the reverse of beneficial; for he has made his city poor, and his citizens greedy (1271 a–b).

Criticism of Carthaginian Oligarchy

Although intended to be aristocratic ('election by merit'), Aristotle believes that in practice the Carthaginian system deviates in some respects towards democracy and in greater respects towards a plutocratic ('election by wealth') oligarchy. The principle that Aristotle favours most in this depiction is that offices should be filled by the truly qualified, something difficult to do when money can influence the election of the office-holder. One of the evils associated with the purchase of office is that the purchasers become venal as they try to make back their purchase-price plus a profit. Another shortcoming in the Carthaginian system is that there is too much plural office-holding by a few individuals; and to remedy that, Aristotle would adopt a 'one man, one office' rule by distributing each office to a different individual. Finally, Aristotle finds inadequate the voluntary distribution of wealth and emigration that Carthage is able to encourage; Aristotle believes in spelling out in law the necessary principles and procedures for effective government. He concludes about government at Carthage:

> The government of the Carthaginians is oligarchical, but they successfully escape the evils of oligarchy by their wealth, which enables them from time to time to send out some portion of the people to their colonies. This is their panacea and the means by which they give stability to the state. Accident favours them, but the legislator should be able to provide against revolution without trusting to accidents. As things are, if any misfortune occurred, and the people revolted from their rulers, there would be no way of restoring peace by legal methods (1272 b–1273 b).

Good Citizen and Good Man May Vary

For Aristotle, the good citizen and the good man may vary: 'In the perfect state the good man is absolutely the same as the good citizen; whereas in other states the good citizen is only good relative to his own form of government' (Bk IV, 1293 b). Different types of state, then, may require different qualities in their citizens; and within the same state, different functions may also require different qualities, especially as between ruler and ruled. In making this point, Aristotle employs a characteristically organological and hierarchical analogy:

> Again, the state, as composed of unlikes, may be compared to the human being: as the first elements into which a living being is resolved are soul and body, as

the soul is made up of reason and appetite, the family of husband and wife, property of master and slave, so out of all these, as well as other dissimilar elements, the state is composed; and, therefore, the virtue of all the citizens cannot possibly be the same, any more than the excellence of the leader of a chorus is the same as that of the performer who stands by his side. I have said enough to show why the two kinds of virtue cannot be absolutely and always the same.

But will there then be no case in which the virtue of the good citizen and the virtue of the good man coincide? To this we answer [not that the good citizen, but] that the good ruler is a good and wise man, and that he who would be a statesman must be a wise man. ...

... If then the virtue of a good ruler is the same as that of a good man, and we assume further that the subject is a citizen as well as the ruler, the virtue of the good citizen and the virtue of the good man cannot be always the same, although in some cases [i.e., in the perfect state] they may; for the virtue of a ruler differs from that of a citizen. ... But, on the other hand, it may be argued that men are praised for knowing both how to rule and how to obey, and he is said to be a citizen of approved virtue who is able to do both. Now if we suppose the virtue of a good man to be that which rules, and the virtue of the citizen to include ruling and obeying, it cannot be said that they are equally worthy of praise (Bk III, 1276 b–1277b; see also 1278 b).

What emerges, therefore, is in many fundamental respects in agreement with Plato's belief that each individual should fulfil the role for which he or she is qualified and contribute thereby to the health and efficiency of the body-politic. Some virtues (such as temperance, justice, and courage) will be common to all, and some will be appropriate for particular categories (such as wisdom for the ruler) and inappropriate for others (such as wisdom for the ruled), and in different degree (such as more courage for men and more modesty for women) (1277 b).

Definition and Types of Constitution

Aristotle is generally regarded as averse to democracy and he, too, so regarded himself. However, there are principles and practices he explicitly favoured that make him appear not altogether hostile to democracy, especially the modern understanding of democracy. He, too, was capable of some confusion of terms and an attack on an irrelevant position. His definition and descriptions of a constitution and of the six principal forms of government that he recognized, indicate this. For example, his definition of a constitution – using that term perhaps somewhat loosely and interchangeably with government –

and his distinction between a democratic and oligarchical state are by no means patently hostile to democracy:

> A constitution is the arrangement of magistracies in a state^c (^{c} Cp. c. 1. § 1; iv. 1. §. 10.), especially of the highest of all. The government is everywhere sovereign in the state, and the constitution is in fact the government. For example, in democracies the people are supreme, but in oligarchies, the few; and, therefore, we say that these two forms of government also are different: and so in other cases (1278 b–1279 a).

The classical sixfold categorization of forms of government distinguishes between good types as those that govern according to law and with a view to the common interest and bad types as those that govern according to will or whim and with a view to the narrow self-interest of those who rule. The good form of rule by one is kingship or monarchy, and its perversion is tyranny. The good form of rule by the few is aristocracy, and its perversion is plutocracy (referred to as oligarchy by Aristotle). The good form of rule by the many is polity (often translated by Jowett as 'constitutional government'), and its perversion is a corrupted form of democracy. Aristotle conforms in general to this classification in the passage that concludes:

> Of the above-mentioned forms, the perversions are as follows:– of royalty, tyranny; of aristocracy, oligarchy; of constitutional government, democracy. For tyranny is a kind of monarchy which has in view the interest of the monarch only; oligarchy has in view the interest of the wealthy; democracy of the needy: none of them the common good of all (1279 a–b).

Oligarchical and Democratic Confusion of Justice Lead to Rule of Law

Aristotle shows that he is fully aware that oligarchy and democracy are usually distinguished on a quantitative basis (i.e., how many rule) but maintains that number is not the correct criterion to be employed. He insists on making a qualitative distinction based on who benefits from such rule; and so he makes oligarchy out to be a form of plutocracy (i.e., rule by the wealthy for the benefit of the wealthy); and he makes democracy out to be a form of 'proletarianism' or 'povertyism' (i.e., rule by the poor for the benefit of the poor): 'Wherever men rule by reason of their wealth, whether they be few or many that is an oligarchy, and where the poor rule, that is a democracy' (1279 b–1280 a).[11]

Plato believes that the weak and inefficient state is so because his conception of justice (that each should do what he is qualified to do and not do what he is unqualified to do) has been violated. Aristotle seems to approach the matter somewhat differently. He, too, as we have seen, favours that each should do what he is qualified to do.[12] However, Aristotle seems to approach the matter of justice from a different viewpoint, saying that a denial of what one believes to be justice can lead to improper demands and instability. As Aristotle sees it, the problem is that in democracy, justice is taken to mean an equality of all, including unequals; and in oligarchy, justice is taken to mean inequality, but is applied on the erroneous basis of inequality of wealth, instead of inequality of ability (1280 a). However, the state is not formed to aggrandize wealth; for if it were, political power in proportion to property would justly prevail. Plato is in strong agreement with this view that unequals should not be treated equally, and no doubt also with Aristotle's statement that the confusion arises from the failure to appreciate that the purpose of the state is not mere survival but the good, just life:

> Whence it may be further inferred that virtue must be the serious care of a state which truly deserves the name: for [without this ethical end] the community becomes a mere alliance which differs only in place from alliances of which the members live apart; and the law is only a convention, 'a surety to one another of justice,' as the sophist Lycophron says, and has no real power to make the citizens good and just (1280 a–b).[13]

Accordingly, a state is not created overnight but comes into being through interactive social processes over a long period of time that bring forth 'the *good* society' – not just any society of individuals – whose shared life and purpose is to create the fraternal union of families that is the essence of a state. Indeed, Aristotle may be read to indicate that the process of political socialization that maintains a state also antedates and forms it:

> It is clear then that a state is not a mere society, having a common place, established for the prevention of crime and for the sake of exchange. These are conditions without which a state cannot exist; but all of them together do not constitute a state, which is a community of well-being in families and aggregations of families, for the sake of a perfect and self-sufficing life. Such a community can only be established among those who live in the same place and intermarry. Hence arise in cities family connexions, brotherhoods, common sacrifices, amusements which draw men together. They are created by friendship, for friendship is the motive of society. The end is the good life, and these are the means towards it. And the state is the union of families and villages having for an end a perfect and self-sufficing life, by which we mean a happy and honourable life[a] ([a] Cp. i. 2. § 8; N. Eth. i. 7. § 6.) (1280 b–1281 a).

Because of the difficulties and opportunities for spoliation of others each presents, Aristotle cannot accept any of the five alternatives he considers next as to who should rule: the many, the wealthy, the better sort, the one best, or the tyrant. His preference is for the rule of law; but even that presents the same inescapable difficulties, for the law itself may incline toward oligarchy or democracy (1281 a).

The Case for Popular Sovereignty

In considering the alternative of making the people at large sovereign, rather than the few best, Aristotle presents a strong case for this possible choice. He also points out how this can lead to an organological unity of the body-politic that has a number of demonstrated advantages. He notes, for example, what is called 'collective wisdom' and that group behaviour or judgment may be better than the individual behaviour or judgment of those who compose the group:

> The principle that the multitude ought to be supreme rather than the few best is capable of a satisfactory explanation, and, though not free from difficulty, yet seems to contain an element of truth. For the many, of whom each individual is but an ordinary person, when they meet together may very likely be better than the few good, if regarded not individually but collectively, just as a feast to which many contribute is better than a dinner provided out of a single purse. For each individual among the many has a share of virtue and prudence, and when they meet together, they become in a manner one man, who has many feet, and hands, and sense; that is a figure of their mind and disposition. Hence the many are better judges than a single man of music and poetry; for some understand one part, and some another, and among them, they understand the whole (1281 a–b).

In considering further what body of persons should be sovereign and the matters over which the general body of citizens should exercise powers of sovereignty, Aristotle weighs the alternative dangers of letting them exercise certain of these powers and of not letting them share in these powers. He favours excluding the common citizenry from executive office, while admitting them to participation in elective, legislative, and judicial processes:

> There is still a danger in allowing them to share the great offices of state, for their folly will lead them into error, and their dishonesty into crime. But there is a danger also in not letting them share, for a state in which many poor men are excluded from office will necessarily be full of enemies. The only way of escape

is to assign to them some deliberative and judicial functions. For this reason Solon[a] ([a] Cp. ii. 12. § 5.) and certain other legislators give them the power of electing to offices, and of calling the magistrates to account, but they do not allow them to hold office singly. When they meet together their perceptions are quite good enough, and combined with the better class they are useful to the state (just as impure food when mixed with what is pure sometimes makes the entire mass more wholesome than a small quantity of the pure would be), but each individual, left to himself, forms an imperfect judgment (1281 b).

Aristotle concludes, then, that the many have a greater right to decide issues more important then those delegated to the better sort of citizens and that their group judgment is generally better on matters that concern them. In a manner reminiscent of Plato, he also recognizes that the consumer or user may be a better judge of a product than its maker. In addition, the property of the many is collectively greater than that of any one or few individuals. In any event, it is rightly constituted laws that should be the final sovereign:

> The discussion of the first question[a] ([a] Cp. c. 10. § 1.) shows nothing so clearly as that laws, when good, should be supreme; and that the magistrate or magistrates should regulate those matters only on which the laws are unable to speak with precision owing to the difficulty of any general principle embracing all particulars[a] ([a] Cp. N. Eth. v. 10. § 4.). But what are good laws has not yet been clearly explained; the old difficulty remains[b] ([b] Cp. c. 10 § 5.). The goodness or badness, justice or injustice, of laws is of necessity relative to the constitutions of states. But if so, true forms of government will of necessity have just laws, and perverted forms of government will have unjust laws (1282 a–b; *cf. Republic*, Bk X, 601 C–E).

Dealing with the Superior Few

As it is his wont to examine an issue from all major alternative viewpoints, Aristotle proceeds to a consideration of how to cope with dangers that come from the ultra-superior few, those whom no law can hope to control. Whether it be a government in the hands of the many, the few, or one, he advocates ostracism and exile as just and necessary for such dangerous persons. He includes references to popular legends and familiar accounts of recent history, including Periander's unspoken advice for Thrasybulus to level the highest stalks of grain (1284 a). But what about the man whose outstanding eminence is in goodness; what is to be done with him? The advice of Aristotle is to make him king and give him willing obedience, much in the fashion advocated by Plato for the philosopher-ruler (1284 a). But one wonders whether Aristotle really regards the availability of such a superhumanly good and wise individual as an actual possibility.

Personal Rule of a King or Rule of Law and God?

Aristotle discerns four types of kingship (Spartan kingship, Asiatic hereditary legal monarchy, elective tyranny, and hereditary legal monarchy of the Greek heroic age); and then adds a fifth, namely, absolute monarchy, which he describes largely in terms of exercise of the executive power or direction of the administrative process:

> There is a fifth form of kingly rule in which one has the disposal of all, just as each tribe or each state has the disposal of public property; this form corresponds to the control of a household. For as household management is the kingly rule of a house, so kingly rule is the household management of a city, or of a nation, or of many nations (1284 b–1285 b).[14]

It is this fifth type of monarchy that Aristotle deals with when he attempts to answer the question whether it is better to have the rule of law or of one best man. In general, he supports the rule of law; but there are bound to be cases where the law cannot provide an adequate answer, and so a form of Equity provided by the king must take over. Thus, Aristotle asks, 'When the law cannot determine a point at all, or not well, should the one best man or should all decide?' (1285 b–1286 a). A choice that gives to an individual discretionary power beyond the application of known, relevant law, sits hard on Aristotle. He prefers to place his trust in an aristocracy of the few or more, instead of a kingship of one; and on some particular matters, the judgment of the multitude, especially a virtuous multitude, is also to be preferred:

> Or, if such virtue is scarcely attainable by the multitude, we need only suppose that the majority are good men and good citizens, and ask which will be the more incorruptible, the one good ruler, or the many who are all good? Will not the many? But, you will say, there may be parties among them, whereas the one man is not divided against himself. To which we may answer that their character is as good as his. If we call the rule of many men, who are all of them good, aristocracy, and the rule of one man royalty, then aristocracy will be better for states than royalty, whether the government is supported by force or not[a] ([a] Cp. infra, § 15.), provided only that a number of men equal in virtue can be found (1286 a–b).

Aristotle is cognizant of both the need to provide a king with an adequate bodyguard and of the danger to the state if this bodyguard be too great. His formula is to make it weaker than the multitude, but more than that commanded by any individual or group within the state (1286 b). Also, Aristotle desires to limit the authority of the king, and so he weaves together the strands of points he has previously discussed: it is not natural for one man to have sovereignty over a state composed of equals; justice therefore requires ruling and being ruled in rotation; where law cannot determine, an individual would be equally unable to determine; and therefore the rule of law and reason, unaffected by passion, should rule as an expression of God's will. The passage comes to an unfavourable judgment of the rule of an absolute monarch or *pambasileia* (παμβασιλεία) and a clear preference for the rule of law:

> There may indeed be cases which the law seems unable to determine, but in such cases can a man? Nay, it will be replied, the law trains officers for this express purpose, and appoints them to determine matters which are left undecided by it to the best of their judgement. Further it permits them to make any amendment of the existing laws which experience suggests. [But still they are only the ministers of the law.] He who bids the law rule, may be deemed to bid God and Reason alone rule, but he who bids man rule adds an element of the beast; for desire is a wild beast, and passion perverts the minds of rulers, even when they are the best of men. The law is reason unaffected by desire (1287 a).[15]

Additional arguments advanced by Aristotle against the rule of an individual, challenge the validity of the comparison with a physician's practice (a favourite analogy of Plato's) and point to the need for a neutral authority to provide justice ('the law is the mean'). As usual, Aristotle then falls back on a form of law to decide: 'Again, customary laws have more weight, and relate to more important matters than written laws, and a man may be a safer ruler than the written law, but not safer than customary law'. Also, he counters the claim of a better man to rule by saying that two good men are even better [and, presumably, still more good men are even better] (1287 a–b).

The discussion where to locate the sovereign powers of the state is not yet done with. There are societies where despotic rule, kingly rule, and constitutional rule are appropriate, but none which by its nature is meant to have tyranny. Indeed, sovereignty over his equals by an individual cannot be just under any circumstances; and there are specific conditions that are required for royal government, aristocracy, or polity:

> Neither should a good man be lord over good men, or a bad man over bad; nor,
> even if he excels in virtue, should he have a right to rule, unless in a particular
> case, at which I have already mentioned, and to which I will once more recur[b]
> ([b] C. 13. § 25, and § 5, infra.). But first of all, I must determine what natures are
> suited for royalties, and what for an aristocracy, and what for a constitutional
> government.
>   A people who are by nature capable of producing a race superior in virtue and
> political talent are fitted for kingly government; and a people submitting to be
> ruled as freemen by men whose virtue renders them capable of political command
> are adapted for an aristocracy: while the people who are suited for constitutional
> freedom, are those among whom there naturally exists a warlike multitude[e] ([e]
> Cp. c. 7. § 4.) able to rule and to obey in turn by a law which gives office to the
> well-to-do according to their desert (1287 b–1288 a).

Aristotle's discussion of where to locate the powers of sovereignty is about
to conclude with a description of circumstances that require it to be vested in
a single person. However, there is a questionable use of logic employed here
by Aristotle when he makes one greatly superior man stand in the same relation
to all others as the whole is to the parts. Also, Aristotle probably discussed the
right of a truly superior family or person to hold an absolute monarchy only
in a suppositional sense and as a logical – not an actual – necessity or
convenience for dialectical purposes, for Aristotle knows fully well that they
no more exist among mortal men than does Plato's utterly superior philosopher-
ruler. He would vest sovereign power in such a hypothetical person:

> For it would not be right to kill, or ostracise, or exile such a person, or require
> that he should take his turn in being governed. The whole is naturally superior
> to the part, and he who has this pre-eminence is in the relation of a whole to a
> part. But if so, the only alternative is that he should have the supreme power,
> and that mankind should obey him, not in turn, but always (1288 a).[16]

Where the Laws do not Govern, There is no Constitution

Aristotle writes of five different kinds of democracy: first, based on the
principle of equality; second, based on a property qualification, but a moderate
one; third, based on family descent, with the law sovereign; fourth, based
simply on citizenship, with the law still sovereign; and fifth, also based simply
on citizenship, but with the people, not the law, as the final sovereign. In this
fifth, other kind of democracy, where the law is not sovereign but the common
people collectively are sovereign and form a composite monarchy, demagogues
arise and the assembly overrides the law (Bk IV, 1291 b–1292 a).

Aristotle severely criticizes the demagogic leaders and the manner whereby under the fifth type of democracy they employ flattery and despotic behaviour to corrupt the democracy, undermine the authority of the magistrates and deny the sovereignty of the law, to the point that constitutional government becomes destroyed. Perhaps one of the most anti-democratic statements that Aristotle makes is when he raises here the question whether democracy really is a constitutional form of government; but it is asked of only this fifth type of democracy – which may not be a true democracy after all:

> The demagogues make the decrees of the people override the laws, and refer all things to the popular assembly. And therefore they grow great, because the people have all things in their hands, and they hold in their hands the votes of the people, who are too ready to listen to them. Further, those who have any complaint to bring against the magistrates say, 'let the people be the judges;' the people are too happy to accept the invitation; and so the authority of every office is undermined. Such a democracy is fairly open to the objection that it is not a constitution at all; for where the laws have no authority, there is no constitution. The law ought to be supreme over all, and the magistracies should judge of particulars, and only this should be considered a constitution. So that if a democracy be a real form of government, the sort of constitution in which all things are regulated by decrees is clearly not a democracy in the true sense of the word, for decrees relate only to particulars[a] ([a] Cp. N. Eth. v. 10 § 7.) (1292 a).[17]

Revolution, as well as gradually erosive change, may bring about disparity between the constitution and the actual workings of government. Sometimes, therefore, one may be democratic in form and oligarchic in practice; and there may be lags until form and practice become consonant with one another. This is another way of saying that inherent limitations, as embodied by the habits and customs of a people, are at times more important than constitutional forms or laws. Aristotle expresses his awareness of these occasional situations with reference to democracy and oligarchy (1292 b).

Constitutional Forms: Kingship, Oligarchy, Democracy, Aristocracy, and Polity

Aristotle distinguishes five forms of government – including democracy – which may be constitutional in nature: monarchy, oligarchy, democracy, aristocracy, and polity. The fifth, polity, he points out, is not usually noticed by writers and they limit themselves to the first four, as does Plato in the *Republic* (which, ironically, is entitled *Politeia*) (1293 a–b).

Before examining polity, Aristotle describes aristocracy as a government of the good, the able, and the morally best, and he identifies three forms of aristocracy: the first and perfect state; and under certain conditions, those which incline toward oligarchy or polity. If virtue be associated with wealth or the common people, then oligarchy and polity may under those circumstances be considered lesser forms of aristocracy (1293 b).

Aristotle also clearly states here his reason for not including tyranny on his list of constitutional forms: 'Last of all I will speak of tyranny, which I place last in the series because I am enquiring into the constitutions of states, and this is the reverse of a constitution' (1293 b).

Polity is described by Aristotle as a mixture of oligarchy and democracy; but he finds polity usually to be confused with democracy and some of the more oligarchically inclined polities to be confused with aristocracy. And here, as elsewhere, Aristotle uses the term oligarchy to identify what today would more likely be called plutocracy (rule by the wealthy). He writes, for example, with reference to polity (which is translated here by Jowett, and often elsewhere, as 'constitutional government'):

> Having explained why I have adopted this order, I will proceed to consider constitutional government; of which the nature will be clearer now that oligarchy and democracy have been defined. For polity or constitutional government may be described generally as a fusion of oligarchy and democracy; but the term is usually applied to those forms of government which incline towards democracy, and the term aristocracy to those which incline towards oligarchy, because birth and education are commonly the accompaniments of wealth (1293 b).

There has also been much confusion of aristocracy with rule by the wealthy (and, one may add, with rule by an hereditary, titled nobility); and so Aristotle is exercised to point out that oligarchies (as he and Plato are wont to term them, but really plutocracies because of rule by the wealthy) are not necessarily ruled out on the basis of merit. Aristotle is also concerned to point out that there is not truly a rule of law, even though there be obedience to law, unless the laws themselves be good. Aristocracy, it seems, requires both rule by the best of the citizenry and that this rule be according to truly good law. The passage continues with Aristotle ascribing to constitutionalism the fundamental characteristics of government by inherent limitations and what is today regarded as a central feature of democracy, namely, majority rule – although he maintains that aristocracies and oligarchies also live by majority rule. As a realist, Aristotle further notes that there is a distinction to be made between the attainable best laws and the absolutely best laws:

And there may be a further subdivision; they may obey either the best laws which are attainable to them, or the best absolutely.

The distribution of offices according to merit is a special characteristic of aristocracy, for the principle of an aristocracy is virtue, as wealth is of an oligarchy, and freedom of a democracy. In all of them there of course exists the right of the majority, and whatever seems good to the majority of those who share in the government has authority (1294 a).

Polity: a Realistic Theory of Human Nature and Politics

For Aristotle, the generally most practicable form of constitution is polity (*politeia*: πολιτεία), which is often not only loosely translated as 'constitutional government' but also more loosely as a 'republic'. He conceives of polity as a mixed, balanced form of government that combines democracy and oligarchy (for him, government respectively by the poor and the rich) and provides a mean between their separate extremes. In an overview of the forms of government he has been considering, Aristotle states that polity of some sort exists in most cities, and he takes pains to distinguish both among various forms of polity and how polity differs from aristocracy – which he finds it not very unlike. These distinctions are made here on the basis of freedom, wealth, and virtue:

> Generally, however, a state of this kind is called a constitutional government [not an aristocracy – BJ], for the fusion goes no further than the attempt to unite the freedom of the poor and the wealth of the rich, who commonly take the place of the noble. And as there are three grounds on which men claim an equal share in the government, freedom, wealth, and virtue (for the fourth or good birth is the result of the two last, being only ancient wealth and virtue), it is clear that the admixture of the two elements, that is to say, of the rich and poor, is to be called a polity or constitutional government; and the union of the three is to be called aristocracy or the government of the best, and more than any other form of government, except the true and ideal, has a right to this name.
>
> Thus far I have described the different forms of states which exist besides monarchy, democracy, and oligarchy, and what they are, and in what aristocracies differ from one another, and polities from aristocracies – that the two latter are not very unlike is obvious (1294 a).

In his consideration of how polity comes into being, Aristotle discerns three possible types of combination of democracy and oligarchy: first, one which combines the whole of both an oligarchical system and of a democratic system; second, one which strikes a mean between oligarchy and democracy;

and third, one which combines some features of oligarchy with some features of democracy:

> The nature of the fusion will be made intelligible by an example of the manner in which different governments legislate, say concerning the administration of justice. In oligarchies they impose a fine on the rich if they do not serve as judges, and to the poor they give no pay; but in democracies they give pay to the poor and do not fine the rich. Now (1) the union of these two modes[a] ([a] Cp. c. 13. § 6.) is a common or middle term between them, and is therefore characteristic of a constitutional government, for it is a combination of both. This is one mode of uniting the two elements. Or (2) a mean may be taken between the enactments of the two: thus democracies require no property qualification, or only a small one, from members of the assembly, oligarchies a high one; here neither of these is a common term, but a mean between them. (3) There is a third mode, in which something is borrowed from the oligarchical and something from the democratical principle. For example, the appointment of magistrates by lot is democratical, and the election of them oligarchical; democratical again when there is no property qualification, oligarchical when there is. In the aristocratical or constitutional state, one element will be taken from each – from oligarchy the mode of electing to offices, from democracy the disregard of qualification (1294 a–b).

In continuing his explanation of polity, Aristotle points to Sparta as an example of this form of constitution. As democratic features, Aristotle recounts Spartan equality and similarity of education, food, dress, and voting power for rich and poor alike. As oligarchical features, Aristotle recounts that magistrates are all selected by vote and none by lot, the power of inflicting the death penalty or banishment rests in the hands of a few, and the existence of many other similar practices. He also observes again that a polity contains both democratic and oligarchical features – but with the character of neither form seeming to be present – and that it is kept safe not by external support but by broadly based internal support:

> In a well tempered polity there should appear to be both elements and yet neither; also the government should rely on itself, and not on foreign aid, nor on the good will of a majority of foreign states – they might be equally well-disposed when there is a vicious form of government – but on the general willingness of all classes in the state to maintain the constitution (1294 b).[18]

Interspersed with Aristotle's discussion of polity, is a brief consideration of tyranny, which he has previously singled out for great condemnation (see 1293 b). Three forms of tyranny are distinguished by Aristotle: the elective monarch with absolute power, to be found among some uncivilized peoples; the elective monarch or dictator of similar type once to be found among the early Greeks; and the arbitrary tyrant. Aristotle's opposition to non-responsible tyranny because of its injustice and instability is manifest; he says of *pambasileia* (παμβασιλεία):

> There is also a third kind of tyranny, which is the most typical form, and is the counterpart of the perfect monarchy. This tyranny is just that arbitrary power of an individual which is responsible to no one, and governs all alike, whether equals or betters, with a view to its own advantage, not to that of its subjects, and therefore against their will. No freeman, if he can escape from it, will endure such a government (1295 a).

Aristotle is essentially a realist in his political theory: he is most concerned with a theory of politics adaptable to mortal humanity as he knows it and also within the limits of practicability. He therefore does not attempt to construct a framework and system of government that requires angels, rather than men, as leaders and led. Instead, he accepts humanity as it always is – a mixture of good and bad – and optimistically believes it possible to utilize and counteract, or counterbalance against one another, the basic drives and qualities of humankind; and he seeks to do so in such fashion as to achieve a maximum of goodness, stability, strength, artistry, efficiency, and happiness in the community. Aristocracy and polity share many of these qualities, purposes, and arrangements and may in some cases be approximately alike. Above all, it is necessary to promote his conception of the practice of justice and practicality that promotes the 'good life': i.e., the pathway of *eudaimonia* (ἐυδαιμονία), the virtuous middle way or golden mean between two extremes:

> For it has been truly said in the Ethics[a] ([a] N. Eth. vii. 13. 2.) that the happy life is the life according to the unimpeded virtue, and that virtue is a mean, then the life which is in a mean, and in a mean attainable by every one, must be the best. And the same principles of virtue and vice are characteristic of cities and of constitutions; for the constitution is in a figure the life of the city[b] ([b] Cp. iii. 3. §§ 7, 8.) (1295 a–b).[19]

Cogent reasons why the middle class contribute more to the stability, harmony, and strength of a state are advanced by Aristotle. Among them are the following: they are more willing to listen to reason; they suffer least from ambition; they are equals and peers; they are not plotters against others or plotted against by others, and therefore live free of danger. The wealthy, on the other hand, are unwilling to obey and also know how not to obey; the poor are dissatisfied and covet the possessions of others; and so a state of the rich and the poor is not one of freemen, but only of masters and slaves (1295 b–1296 a).[20]

Size is also an important factor according to Aristotle: large states (and democratic states) are generally more free from faction because they have a large middle class; but in small states where there are extremes of wealth and poverty, the result tends to be an extreme democracy or an unmixed oligarchy, both of which are more apt than middle class government to lead to tyranny. He also offers reasons why polity has seldom been achieved in practice, including the paucity in numbers of the middle class and the habit in many Greek cities of seeking class rule by the wealthy or by 'the people' (1295 b–1296 a).

For Aristotle, quality and quantity are determinants of the character of a government. Where the quantity of the poor is dominant, there will naturally be a democracy; where the quality of the rich and notables is dominant, there will naturally be an oligarchy; and where the neutral effect of the members of the middle class outweighs either or both of the other classes, a more lasting polity may be established. The passage concludes by advocating again a mixed constitution and warning, in words reminiscent of Alexander Hamilton, against encroachments of the rich as more ruinous than those of the people:

> The more perfect the admixture of the political elements, the more lasting will be the state. Many even of those who desire to form aristocratical governments make a mistake, not only in giving too much power to the rich, but in attempting to overreach the people. There comes a time when out of a false good there arises a true evil, since the encroachments of the rich are more destructive to the state than those of the people (1296 b–1297 a).

Another important discussion by Aristotle with respect to polity deals with practices that variously require, permit, fine, or ignore participation in five basic activities related to the needs of government: participation in the Assembly, holding of magisterial office, sitting on law courts, the keeping of arms, and physical training. Aristotle takes a dim view of how they may be manipulated to alter their character. His preference is duly to mix appropriate participation of both the wealthy and the poor and thus to bring about a just blend (1297 a–b).

Specialization in Processes of Government

Although Aristotle may not have a completely worked out system of checks and balances such as we find in a Polybius, Montesquieu, or John Adams, he clearly discerns the legislative, executive, and judicial processes in government. He also discerns specialization in one of these processes by various contemporary organs and officials of government. In an introductory statement to a consideration of how these three processes may be constituted in democratic, oligarchic, and aristocratic states, Aristotle refers to their assignment, respectively, to the 'deliberative element', the 'magisterial element', and the 'judicial element' (1297 b–1298 a).

The deliberative element may be seen to perform the usual role of a legislature. Exercise of all of its duties may be assigned to all of the citizens, all assigned to some of the citizens, or some assigned to all of the citizens and some to some of the citizens (1298 a).

There are four democratic ways in which all of the citizens may be organized to participate in the deliberative or legislative function. The first way has portions of the citizenry meet in rotation, especially to enact laws and deal with constitutional matters. The second way would have all of the citizens deal with a limited number of legislative functions directly, especially the enactment of laws, and have them assign others to magistrates drawn from their ranks by election or lot. The third way would make the examination of audits and of magistrates, who would carry on the other usual deliberative duties, the chief function of the citizens. The fourth way would have them all deliberate on all issues, with the magistrates having no power of decision and able only to make preliminary investigations; and 'that is the way in which the last and worst form of democracy, corresponding, as we maintain, to the close family oligarchy and to tyranny, is at present administered' (1298 a; see also 1292 a–1293 a).

There are three oligarchical modes in which the deliberative or legislative function may be organized. One mode, a form of constitutional oligarchy, would have a moderate property qualification, and therefore be fairly numerous and not be able to make changes where the law prohibits them. The second mode would limit the deliberative function to a group of selected eligibility, not to all persons, and these, too, should obey the law. The third mode, which inevitably means oligarchy, is to recruit the members of the deliberative body by co-optation or heredity and would give them the power to overrule the laws (1298 a–b). A third constitutional system may provide ways that tend more toward a polity, depending on which duties are assigned to some of the citizens and which to all of the citizens (1298 b).

The policy that is to the interest of a democracy because it improves the quality of the deliberative (legislative) body, is the oligarchical plan of compelling by threat of fine the attendance of those it is desirable have there; for when the common people and the notables deliberate together, they deliberate better (1298 b). In similar fashion, the policy that is to the interest of an oligarchy, is to provide by co-optation popular representation in the deliberative body or to erect a probouleutic, or pre-considering, council; also, the people should have the final power to reject proposals, but not for passing them, as they should be referred back for final passage to the magistrates (1298 b). On the other hand, in polities, the few have final authority to reject proposals, but not to pass them (1298 b–1299 a).

Next, Aristotle considers aspects of the executive element. These include identification of magistrates, their number, their duties, their tenure, and their manner of appointment. Not all public officials (e.g., priests, ambassadors, and producers of plays) are to be accounted magistrates or executives; but he does discern political, economic, and subordinate or menial categories of magistrates (1299 a).

In large states, Aristotle calls for a separate magistracy for each separate function; in small states, a few persons have to exercise a number of functions and develop versatility (1299 a–b). The existence, nonexistence, or duties of some magistracies may be peculiar to a particular type of constitution: democracy, oligarchy, or aristocracy. Aristotle touches, among others, on the *boulé* and officers for maintenance of order among women and children, and asserts that a probouleutic council would be an example of an undemocratic feature (1299 b–1300 a).

In similar fashion, the manner of appointment of magistrates befits, alternatively, a democracy, a polity, a polity inclining more toward oligarchy, a polity verging on aristocracy, an oligarchy, or an aristocracy. Aristotle recounts different ways of appointment that accord to each of these forms respectively: by lot, by vote, or by both modes (1300 a–b).

In his examination of the judicial element, Aristotle states that there are three points on which differences arise: their membership, or who is to sit on the courts; their competence, or the types of cases in which various courts have jurisdiction; and their machinery of appointment, or whether those appointed are to be drawn from all or parts of the citizenry, whether by vote or lot, and whether they decide on all matters or some matters (1300 b). First, continues Aristotle, the kinds of courts there are to be must be determined. These are to number eight, and their competence, or jurisdiction, is specified (1300 b).

Next, Aristotle therefore turns to matters of membership and machinery of appointment as well as jurisdiction of the courts: whether they are to include all or part of the citizenry; whether they are to be selected by vote or lot; and whether they are to deal with all cases or some cases. However, he does not here designate any of these methods of selection as characteristic of any of the forms of government he has been analyzing (1300 b–1301 a). Lastly, on the basis of their membership and whether or not they deal with all kinds of cases, Aristotle designates judicial systems as democratic if the judges be taken from the entire citizenry, oligarchical if few judges try all cases, and aristocratic or characteristic of polity if some courts have judges taken from all classes of citizens and some courts take judges from only certain classes (1301 a).

General Causes of Sedition, Revolution, and Constitutional Change

By now, Aristotle has considered four of the five subjects he outlines at the end of Book IV, ch. 2, 1289 b: (1) the various types of constitutions; (2) the most generally acceptable constitution; (3) the constitutional features respectively desirable for particular forms of government; and (4) how to establish or organize these various forms of government. Next, he is concerned with his fifth proposed subject of inquiry: how constitutions are destroyed or preserved and the causes of their destruction or preservation. In turning to this fifth subject, Aristotle remarks that different notions of equality give rise to democracy and oligarchy; and because these different notions are incomplete, they both fall short of absolute justice. Democracy assumes that because men may be equal in one respect (i.e., equally freeborn), they are equal in all respects; oligarchy assumes that because men may be unequal in one respect (i.e., in wealth), they are unequal in all respects; and Aristotle adds that there is some justice in giving a greater share to those who possess the advantage of good birth (i.e., ancestors of merit as well as wealth) (Bk V, 1301 a–b).

These assumptions, says Aristotle, explain the causes of *stasis* (στάσις) or sedition. Sedition may aim at two general types of change in the constitution: (1) to overturn the existing constitution; or (2) to modify it. If it be the latter, there are three modifications reformers may seek or institute: (1) that they gain control of administration of the state; (2) that its existing nature (e.g., oligarchy or democracy) be made more pronounced or more moderate; (3) that only one part of the constitution be changed (e.g., abolition of a particular magistracy) (1301 b).[21]

For Aristotle, therefore, incomplete, and thus erroneous, conceptions about equality and inequality are always a root cause of sedition. For Aristotle, proportionate equality is the correct kind of equality; but the simplistic approach of most men to being equal or unequal in all respects, makes them tend towards either democracy or oligarchy. Better than either democracy or oligarchy is a form of polity that properly combines numerical equality with equality proportionate to desert, and inclining toward democracy. In a choice between democracy and oligarchy, Aristotle judges in favour of democracy as safer and less seditious; he concludes:

> Still democracy appears to be safer and less liable to revolution than oligarchy[c] ([c] Cp. iv. 11. § 14.). For in oligarchies[d] ([d] Cp. c. 6.) there is the double danger of the oligarchs falling out among themselves and also with the people; but in democracies[e] ([e] Cp. c. 5.) there is only the danger of a quarrel with the oligarchs. No dissension worth mentioning arises among the people themselves. And we may further remark that a government which is composed of the middle class more nearly approximates to democracy than to oligarchy, and is the safest of the imperfect forms of government (1301 b–1302 a).

Specific Causes of Sedition, Revolution, and Constitutional Change

Aristotle specifies three factors to be examined in studying sedition and revolutionary change: the feelings or attitudes engendered; the motives of the leaders involved; and the origins and causes of the disputes and disturbances (1302 a).

The state of mind which brings on revolution is a passionate one, clearly a sense of outrage against presumed injustice because either a passion for equality or a passion for inequality is not satisfied (1302 a). The objects of sedition or revolution may be positive ones (to gain profit and honour) or they may be negative ones (to avoid loss or disgrace such as attaches to a fine or, we may reasonably infer, to a tax or to property or income depletion) (1302 a–b).

When it comes to dealing with the occasions of sedition and revolution, Aristotle's thoughts become a bit muddled. For example, he treats profit and honour as both objects and occasions of sedition and revolution. Next, he says that from one standpoint there are seven occasions that provoke seditious dissension, and that from another standpoint there may be more than seven. Then he seems to list eight occasions, without indicating which he had in mind for his basic seven: profit, honour, insolence, fear, election intrigues, wilful negligence, trifling changes, and dissimilarity of elements in the composition of the state (1302 a–b).

And in the next chapter, Aristotle seems to discern and discuss at least 13 occasions (or causes) of seditious conduct: insolence, profit-making, honour, some form of superiority for a person or body of persons, fear, contempt, a disproportionate increase of a part of the state, election intrigues, wilful negligence, neglect of trifling changes, heterogeneity of population stocks, heterogeneity of difference of interests between territorial parts (such as between island and mainland parts), and heterogeneity of various conditions (such as division between virtue and vice, and division between wealth and poverty) (1302 b–1303 b).

Demagoguery Changes Democracy to Oligarchy or Tyranny

According to Aristotle, demagoguery that attacks the rich is the principal cause for change-over from democracy. Such demagoguery may bring on oligarchy or tyranny. Aristotle describes first how oligarchy came about from democracy in a number of *poleis*, and then observes how demagogues may cause the notables to unite against them:

> For sometimes the demagogues, in order to curry favour with the people, wrong the notables and so force them to combine; – either they make a division of their property, or diminish their incomes by the imposition of public services, and sometimes they bring accusations against the rich that they may have their wealth to confiscate[c] ([c] Cp. infra. c. 8. § 20.) (1304 b–1305 a).

Next, Aristotle traces how tyranny may arise from democracy, especially when the offices of demagogue and general are held by the same man, when the state is small and the people are preoccupied with their farms, or when the suffrage is widely popular. He adds that changes take place when the magistrates are voted into office by an electorate who have no property qualification and have been set above the laws by ambitious aspirants for office. 'A more or less complete cure for this state of things is for the separate tribes, and not the whole people, to elect the magistrates' (1305 a).

Demagoguery and Sedition by the Excluded May Change Oligarchy to Tyranny, Polity, or Democracy

Oligarchy may be overthrown or altered for a variety of reasons and in a variety of ways. Unjust, exploitative treatment of the masses may enable one who champions their cause to make himself tyrant. Sometimes the excluded, who may be the rich, may bring sufficient pressure to bear to turn the government into more of a polity when they are finally given a share in office; and sometimes this enlargement of eligibility may go so far as to make the government over into a democracy (1305 a–b).

An oligarchy may be changed from within as well as from without, especially by practising demagoguery, whether such art be practised on the ruling group or on the masses. Aristotle includes a number of historical examples of such changes, including the experience of Athens with the rule of the Four Hundred in 411 BC and of the Thirty Tyrants in 404–3 BC. He adds: 'Again, oligarchies change whenever any attempt is made to narrow them; for then those who desire equal rights are compelled to call in the people' (1305 b).

A united oligarchy is not easily overthrown from within; but members of the oligarchy who waste their substance in riotous living may be trying to set up themselves, or someone else, as tyrant. An oligarchy may also be changed from within by creating an inner oligarchy by not admitting all of the citizenry to the highest offices. An oligarchy may also be changed from within when, whether in war or peace and whether from distrust of the people or of one another, they hire mercenaries and a neutral commander; and the latter then makes himself tyrant over all. In fear of such consequences, they may employ a popular force; and they may thereby come to give the masses some constitutional powers and, seemingly, introduce some democratic elements of polity (1305 b–1306 a). Aristotle also notes at the end of the chapter how democracies and oligarchies tend to swing towards and back from arbitrary forms of themselves:

> We must remark generally, both of democracies and oligarchies, that they sometimes change, not into the opposite forms of government, but only into another variety of the same class; I mean to say, from those forms of democracy and oligarchy which are regulated by law into those which are arbitrary, and conversely (1306 b).

Causes of Change in Aristocracy

Aristocracies may also change for a variety of reasons and into a variety of other forms. Some of the reasons why aristocracies are subject to change include: their limitation of office and honour to a narrow number, so that many feel resentment; an unjust balance or mixture of elements in the constitution itself; and unjust treatment of the outsiders and masses by greedy, grasping notables. Aristocracy may therefore change over, or evolve, into tyranny, polity, oligarchy, or democracy (1306 b–1307 a). Thus, in beginning this chapter, Aristotle points out how like-unto-oligarchies aristocracies are, and how they suffer the same defects of numbers and extremes of poverty: on the one hand, a vulnerability; and on the other hand, a source of seditious discontent (1306 b–1307 a).

Next, Aristotle discusses how polities and aristocracies, two good forms of government, may suffer downfall or change because of a deviation from justice in the constitution itself. This may result in the change-over, respectively, into democracy or oligarchy (1307 a).

Aristotle also points out, on the other hand, how aristocracy may change into democracy (especially because of an overconcentration of property and too great freedom of marriage); and how polity may change into oligarchy (especially because of obsession with property and being treated according to fancied desert). Some of these lapses would never occur, he claims, in a democracy or properly balanced aristocracy. The passage continues with Aristotle warning that aristocracies are prone to undergo revolutionary change by small steps (1307 a–b).

The chapter ends with Aristotle's observation that constitutions may be subverted from without, especially when confronted by a powerful neighbour with a different type of constitution; thus, 'the Athenians everywhere put down the oligarchies, and the Lacedaemonians the democracies' (1307 b).

Ten Methods of Preserving Governments

Having described the causes of sedition and revolution under various forms of government, Aristotle now presents a number of propositions, stated as conclusions, that deal with particular constitutional systems (1307 b–1309 a).

Proposition one deals with the need in mixed forms of government to guard vigilantly against all lawlessness, especially that of a petty sort that gradually erodes the constitution. Even a small beginning must be viewed as a dangerous one. Aristotle prefaces this proposition by stating that if we understand the reasons why constitutions are destroyed, we also know how they can be preserved (1307 b).

Proposition two, which deals with sham rights fobbed off on the masses (discussed in Bk IV, 1297 a), warns against trying to hoodwink the multitude with specious arguments, 'for they are refuted by the facts ...' (1307 a–1308 a).[22]

Proposition three advocates the cultivation of good relations between the officers and the unenfranchised and the enfranchised alike, and this is promoted by just sharing in constitutional rights, short terms of office, and rotation in office, because then oligarchies and aristocracies are less likely to become hereditary dynasties (1308 a).

Proposition four calls to attention that some dangers, when we are aware of them, may promote our safety by putting us on constant guard and making us take precautions. Therefore, when they are afraid of the government, the citizens may watch and control it more closely (1308 a).

Proposition five is a warning to guard against quarrels and seditions among the notables, and thereby to prevent the development of a spirit and practice of rivalry and contentiousness among them (1308 a).

Proposition six calls for periodic checking under oligarchies and polities that the property-qualification is in accord with current assessments and values. What Aristotle has to say here is very relevant in modern times when governments often fail to adjust tax rates and assessments to fluctuations in monetary and property values. They thereby radicalize significant portions of the population and the public becomes prepared to force revolutionary changes in government (1308 a–b).

Proposition seven cautions against granting too much honour or power at one time or precipitately. Honours and power should be granted gradually and slowly – especially for long terms of office – and should be taken away slowly; but best of all is to have the law regulate. If this cannot be achieved, then the powerful should be sent into exile while out of office (1308 b).

Proposition eight suggests that a magistracy be established to supervise those who live out of harmony with the constitution, and that it be manned by a different section of the populace in order to promote a proper balance or middle group. Again Aristotle is concerned to avoid radicalization, the causes of which may be governmental or non-governmental. In either case, it remains the enlightened role of government to regulate in such manner as to prevent the development of revolutionaries. It should be noted well that the harmonious constitutional system Aristotle seeks to establish by these means is a combination of democracy (the many poor) and plutocracy (the wealthy few) – clearly a polity (*politeia*). However, more to Aristotle's liking would be an alternative that would consist of a balance of a large middle class between the extremes of a wealthy class and an impoverished class:

> And since innovations creep in through the private life of individuals, there ought to be a magistracy which will have an eye to those whose life is not in harmony with the government, whether oligarchy or democracy or any other. And for like reason an increase of prosperity in any part of the state should be

carefully watched. The proper remedy for this evil is always to give the management of affairs and offices of state to opposite elements; such opposites are the virtuous and the many, or the rich and the poor. Another way is to combine the poor and rich in one body, or to increase the middle class: thus an end will be put to the revolutions which arise from inequality (1308 b).

Proposition nine is advanced as an important rule under all types of constitutions, but especially under oligarchy, that provision be made by law to have transfer of funds take place in public; and by workings of the economic system, that magistrates be prevented from using their office for personal gain. We should also note well here Aristotle's observation than an improved form of polity is one that mixes democracy and aristocracy (instead of democracy mixed with plutocratic oligarchy). But the main point of this proposition is to prevent officials from making use of their office for profit (1308 b–1309 a).[23]

Proposition ten is a dual one: in democracies the rich should be spared and their property protected; and in oligarchies, the poor should be given much consideration and opportunity to become prosperous, while wealthy malefactors should be punished more severely. Inheritances and estates should be regulated to prevent overconcentration of property, and honours and offices should be distributed with due care. The highest offices of state, however, as much as possible should be assigned as prescribed by the constitution (1309 a).

Qualifications of Chief Officers and More General Principles to Ensure Stability

In somewhat repetitive fashion, or perhaps in summarization, Aristotle lists and discusses the general qualifications he believes necessary for the 'supreme magistrates' (i.e., the decision-making officers) of the state; and then he adds on five more general principles that are also intended to ensure stability and duration. He begins this chapter by stating the need for these supreme officers to be loyal, able, virtuous, and just. However, the sort of justice consonant with each type of constitution differs according to the nature of the constitution (1309 a).[24]

The five additional general principles and practices Aristotle has in mind are: the observance of rules that tend to preserve all constitutional forms; taking precautions that those in favour of an existing constitution outnumber those opposed; avoidance of deviate or extreme forms and policies in favour of moderate, middle-of-the-way choices; the well-to-do and the multitude must coexist for either democracy or oligarchy to be possible, and therefore neither of these forms can endure if the different classes are destroyed by an even level of property ownership; and most important of all, suitable education of the citizenry to preserve the existing constitution. In effect, Aristotle advocates a policy of leaning over backwards to protect the interests of the rich under democracy and of the poor under oligarchy, with a warning against the divisive actions of demagogues under both systems. Aristotle's advice here, however, concludes with a ringing statement that places the greatest reliance on education – *paideia* – to secure the stability of constitutions:

> But of all things which I have mentioned that which most contributes to the permanence of constitutions is the adaptation of education to the form of government[a] ([a] Cp. i. c. 13. § 15.), and yet in our own day this principle is universally neglected (1309 a–1310 a).

The emphasis here is interesting and quite revealing in two respects: it shows a fundamental agreement with Plato on the role and importance of suitable, supportive education (but with both of them, is it not often inculcation rather than education?); and it thereby places a greater reliance on the constitutional safeguard of inherent limitations rather than on institutional and structural safeguards. Democracy loses out because the citizenry incorrectly define justice as equality in the form of whatever the majority may decide, and because they confuse liberty with being able to do whatever one pleases. They fail to realize that doing whatever one likes is not liberty and that obedience to law is not slavery, but salvation:

> The best laws, though sanctioned by every citizen of the state, will be of no avail unless the young are trained by habit and education in the spirit of the constitution, if the laws are democratical, democratically, or oligarchically, if the laws are oligarchical. For there may be a want of self-discipline in states as well as in individuals. Now, to have been educated in the spirit of the constitution is not to perform the actions in which oligarchs or democrats delight, but those by which the existence of an oligarchy or of a democracy is made possible. Whereas among ourselves the sons of the ruling class in an oligarchy live in luxury[a] ([a] Cp. iv. 11. § 6.), but the sons of the poor are hardened by exercise and toil, and hence they are both more inclined and better able to make a revolution[b] ([b] Cp. Pl. Rep. viii. 556 D.) And in democracies of the more extreme type there has arisen a false idea of freedom which is contradictory to the true interests of the state. For two principles are characteristic of democracy, the government of the majority and freedom. Men think that what is just is equal; and that equality

is the supremacy of the popular will; and that freedom and equality mean the doing what a man likes. In such democracies every one lives as he pleases, or in the words of Euripides, 'according to his fancy'. But this is all wrong; men should not think it slavery to live according to the rule of the constitution; for it is their salvation (1310 a).

Causes of Destruction of Monarchy, Whether Kingship or Tyranny

Monarchy, for Aristotle, may take either of what he states are two diametrically different forms; kingship (or royal government) or tyranny. Kingship is akin to aristocracy; and tyranny can be made up of two bad forms, oligarchy and democracy – yet note, so may polity be composed – and therefore can combine the bad features of both. On the different composition and origins of these different forms of monarchy, Aristotle says that royalty comes into existence from the assistance of the better classes against the people, and tyranny from the support of the people against the notables. The passage continues:

> The appointment of a king is the resource of the better classes against the people, and he is elected by them out of their own number, because either he himself or his family excel in virtue and virtuous actions; whereas a tyrant is chosen from the people to be their protector against the notables, and in order to prevent them from being injured (1310 b).

As to their difference of aims, Aristotle sees the king as a guardian of society and therefore aiming at good; while the tyrant covets his own advantage and riches. Therefore a king has a civic guard; while a tyrant has a foreign guard of mercenary troops (1310 b–1311 a).

The vices of tyranny that Aristotle notes include the oligarchic ones of amassing of wealth, distrust and disarming of the masses, and oppression of the common people and expulsion of many of them from the city to the countryside. From democracy, tyranny derives such vices as its hostile treatment that secretly or openly ruins the notables and drives them into exile because of their hindrances and their opposition that stems from their own desire for power and not wanting to be slaves; therefore the advice of Periander to Thrasybulus to remove outstanding citizens (1311 a).

The causes of revolution against the person or office of the tyrant derive from the common effects of anger. These include various forms of insult, confiscation of property, fear, hatred, contempt, avarice, and quarrels between partner-tyrants. These abhorrent doings are to be understood as the behaviour of adventurous military men with ambitious lust for fame who are willing to disregard utterly their personal safety and the preservation of their regimes, satisfied as they are to die in a moment of glory (1311 a–1312 b). External forces may also destroy any form of government; and in the case of tyranny, a rival state that has an opposing form of government, such as democracy, kingship, or aristocracy, may overthrow a tyranny (1312 a–b). Internal causes, especially hatred and contempt, are more usual causes of ruin to tyrannies; and the tyranny of one man arouses the same type of opposition as the collective tyrannies of unmixed oligarchy or extreme democracy. The manner in which hatred and contempt work to overthrow tyranny is explained by Aristotle as follows:

> There are two chief motives which induce men to attack tyrannies – hatred and contempt. Hatred of tyrants is inevitable, and contempt is also a frequent cause of their destruction. Thus we see that most of those who have acquired, have retained their power, but those who have inherited[b] ([b] Cp. Plato, Laws, iii, 695.), have lost it, almost at once; for living in luxurious ease, they have become contemptible, and offer many opportunities to their assailants. Anger, too, must be included under hatred, and produces the same effects. It is often times even more ready to strike – the angry are more impetuous in making an attack, for they do not listen to reason. And men are very apt to give way to their passions when they are insulted. To this cause is to be attributed the fall of the Peisistratidae and of many others (1312 b).

Kingship or royal government (*basileia*: βασιλεία) is the form of government Aristotle believes is least liable to external destruction. Its internal causes of destruction include quarrelling among its administrators and attempting to govern like a tyrant, without legal restrictions. In any event, Aristotle finds kingship outmoded in his own day because of a lack of support and its being regarded as a form of tyranny:

> There are now no royalties; monarchies, where they exist, are tyrannies. For the rule of a king is over voluntary subjects, and he is supreme in all important matters; but in our own day men are more upon an equality, and no one is so immeasurably superior to others as to represent adequately the greatness of dignity of the office. Hence mankind will not, if they can help, endure it, and any one who obtains power by force or fraud is at once thought to be a tyrant. In hereditary monarchies a further cause of destruction is the fact that kings often fall into contempt, and, although possessing not tyrannical but only royal power, are apt to outrage others. Their overthrow is then readily effected; for there is an end to the king when his subjects do not want to have him, but the tyrant lasts, whether they like him or not (1313 a).

Methods of Preservation of Monarchy, Whether Kingship or Tyranny

The observations Aristotle makes about how a kingship may be preserved are few and short. The observations he makes about preserving tyranny are many and longer. He begins the subject of preserving monarchical government with a declaration that may well be applied to the monarchical system of Great Britain across the past three centuries:

> And they are preserved, to speak generally, by the opposite causes; or, if we consider them separately, (1) royalty is preserved by the limitation of its powers. The more restricted the functions of kings, the longer their power will last unimpaired; for then they are more moderate and not so despotic in their ways; and they are less envied by their subjects (1313 a).

Methods of maintaining tyranny involve the varying types of action that deal with such matters as treatment of the general public, friends, women, slaves, and aliens by the two opposite methods: traditional measures of repression; and pretence of royal legitimacy. The first type of tyrannical approach to ruling includes: repression of the general populace and removal of outstanding men; separation, division, and estrangement of individuals from one another; compulsory constant reporting in person at the palace gates, to make them humble and servile; employment of secret police, informers, and eavesdroppers; and impoverishment of subjects by taxation and lavish public works that leave no means, leisure, or energy for sedition. 'The tyrant is also fond of making war in order that his subjects may have something to do and be always in want of a leader' (1313 a–b).

A tyrant must be careful to see that his friends are not his undoing, and so Aristotle pays separate attention to how a tyrant should treat them. In general, tyranny is a system which chooses bad friends and makes special use of women, slaves, and aliens; and as with democracy where the common people also wish to be the sole ruler and must be flattered, so is it profitable to flatter the tyrant:

> Hence tyrants are always fond of bad men, because they love to be flattered, but no man who has the spirit of a freeman in him will demean himself by flattery; good men love others, but they do not flatter anybody. Moreover, the bad are useful for bad purposes; 'nail knocks out nail', as the proverb says. It is characteristic of a tyrant to dislike every one who has dignity or independence; he wants to be alone in his glory, but any one who claims a like dignity or asserts his independence encroaches upon his prerogative, and is hated by him

as an enemy to his power. Another mark of a tyrant is that he likes foreigners better than citizens, and lives with them and invites them to his table; for the one are enemies, but the others enter into no rivalry with him (1313 b–1314 a).

In summarizing the foregoing, Aristotle discerns three basic purposes in the behaviour of the tyrant who is openly repressive: to keep the public broken-spirited, distrustful of one another, and powerless to act (1314 a).

Next, Aristotle treats of the second general type of approach that may be used to preserve tyrannies, or at least to try to preserve a tyrant in office. This second method is for the tyrant to pretend to be a public steward who is acting within the law and in the public interest, and so to act as much as he can. Of course, if he become this in fact, the tyranny is no longer maintained, for it changes over into kingship. He must especially take care to spend and collect monies for obviously legitimate purposes of state and not to excess. His central concern, however, is to protect his power to rule with or without the approval of the public (1314 a–b).

The tyrant should take great care to create and maintain a favourable public image. He must appear grave, without being harsh; he should give the impression of military efficiency; he and his family, including the women, should avoid all sexual offences, especially against the chastity of others, for the insolence of women has often brought about the ruin of tyrannies; and he should be moderate in enjoying the pleasures of the table. Best of all, not only should he be moderate in taking his pleasures, but he should also do so out of sight of his fellows; for the sleeping drunkard is easy to despise and attack – but not the sober and alert (1314 b).

Continuing his discussion of how the tyrant may project a favourable public image, Aristotle points out how the appearance of being god-fearing may suit his purposes well. Also, we may recognize here advice repeated centuries later by Machiavelli when the Florentine wrote that the Prince should associate himself personally with the distribution of honours, but should leave all punishments to the officials and the courts. Nor should the tyrant contribute to making anyone else great enough to become his rival, but if need be he should elevate two who would oversee each other; and when he decides to deprive anyone of power, it should not be done all at once, but by stages (1314 b–1315 a).

Aristotle states that a tyrant should 'abstain from all outrage' and in particular not inflict physical indignities or violate the chastity of the young. He should be most careful about attempts at assassination, for they are difficult to prevent when a hot-blood is willing to pay with his life to do the deed

(1315 a). Finally, in a manner reminiscent of both Plato and Machiavelli, Aristotle gives astute advice on how the tyrant should deal with the poor and the rich so that both of these groups feel that it is the tyrant who is protecting them from the other, and also how he and the state can benefit from his seeking the company of the notables and courting the favour of the masses:

> For then his rule will of necessity be nobler and happier, because he will rule over better men[b] ([b] Cp. i. 5. § 2.) whose spirits are not crushed, over men to whom he himself is not an object of hatred, and of whom he is not afraid. His power too will be more lasting. Let his disposition be virtuous, or at least half virtuous; and if he must be wicked, let him be half wicked only (1315 a–b).

Nature and Preservation of Democracy

For Aristotle, liberty is the basic aim that underlies democracy, and equality is the fundamental principle involved in the practices that are efficient methods of achieving this goal. Inherent in this principle of equality is the conception of justice as a form of arithmetical equality that today is expressed by the slogan 'one person, one vote'. Liberty itself may take two forms: one requires rotation in office, and the other consists in being free from control so that a man may live as he likes. Aristotle encapsulates his view of the democratic state in the following passage:

> The basis of a democratic state is liberty; which, according to the common opinion of men, can only be enjoyed in such a state;– this they affirm to be the great end of every democracy[e] ([e] Cp. Plato, Rep. viii. 557 foll.). One principle of liberty is for all to rule and be ruled in turn, and indeed democratic justice is the application of numerical not proportionate equality; whence it follows that the majority must be supreme, and whatever the majority approve must be the end and the just. Every citizen, it is said, must have equality, and therefore in a democracy the poor have more power than the rich, because there are more of them, and the will of the majority is supreme. This, then, is one note of liberty which all democrats affirm to be the principle of their state. Another is that a man should live as he likes[a] ([a] Cp. v. 9. § 15.). This, they say, is the privilege of a freeman, and, on the other hand, not to live as a man likes is the mark of a slave. This is the second characteristic of democracy, whence has arisen the claim of men to be ruled by none, if possible, or, if this is impossible, to rule and be ruled in turns; and so it coincides with the freedom based upon equality [which was the first characteristic] (Bk VI, 1317 a–b).[25]

Aristotle then specifies a number of practices of democracy that follow from its basic assumptions of liberty and equality. These include: general selection of officials and judiciary from the citizens at large without property qualifications; rotation in office; brief tenure in office; public auditing of accounts; supremacy of the popular assembly (or of a council) in all matters (including constitutional questions); and payment for governmental service (1317 b). Aristotle also stresses as democratic features: the importance of the assembly and council (and whether they receive pay); use of common-mess tables; and avoidance of life tenure in public office. One of the key passages in the *Politics* lists at length in Book VI specific practices and features that Aristotle finds to be usual under democracy:

> Such being our foundation and such the nature of democracy, its characteristics are as follows:– the election of officers by all out of all; and that all should rule over each, and each in his turn over all; that the appointment to all offices, or to all but those which require experience and skill[c] ([c] Cp. iv. 14. § 6.), should be made by lot; that no property qualification should be required for offices, or only a very low one; that no one should hold the same office twice, or not often, except in the case of military offices; that the tenure of all offices, or of as many as possible, should be brief; that all men should sit in judgement, or that judges selected out of all should judge in all matters, or in most, or in the greatest and most important,– such as the scrutiny of accounts, the constitution, and private contracts; that the assembly should be supreme over all causes, or at any rate over the most important, and the magistrates over none or only over a very few. Of all institutions, a council is the most democratic[e] ([e] Cp. iv. 15. § 11.) when there is not the means of paying all the citizens, but when they are paid even this is robbed of its power; for the people then draw all cases to themselves, as I said in the previous discussion[a] ([a] Cp. iv. 6. § 5.). The next characteristic of democracy is payment for services; assembly, law-courts, magistrates, everybody receives pay, when it is to be had; or when it is not to be had for all, then it is given to the law-courts and to the stated assemblies, to the council and to the magistrates, or at least to any of them who are compelled to have their meals together. And whereas oligarchy is characterized by birth, wealth, and education, the notes of democracy appear to be the opposite of these,– low birth, poverty, mean employment. Another note is that no magistracy is perpetual, but if any such have survived some ancient change in the constitution it should be stripped of its power, and the holders should be elected by lot and no longer by vote (1317 b–1318 a).

The section that follows may not contain as favourable a finding by Aristotle about democracy as may appear at a first reading, but simply his observation on what adherents of democracy believe. It may very well not mean that Aristotle is hopeful here that democracy, and what he regards as a simplistic practice of equality, would lead to proper equality and genuine liberty. Thus, its conclusion may be sarcastic rather than Aristotle's real opinion:

> These are points common to all democracies; but democracy and demos in their truest form are based upon the recognized principle of democratic justice, that all should count equally; for equality implies that the rich should have no more share in the government than the poor, and should not be the only rulers, but that all should rule equally according to their numbers[c] ([c] Cp. iv. 4. § 22.). And in this way men think that they will secure equality and freedom in their state (1318 a).[26]

For what Aristotle demonstrably favours is not a *numerical equality* based on 'one person, one vote', but what he and Plato regarded as a *proportional equality* whereby voting strength would be equal to measure of presumed merit. Accordingly, Aristotle goes on to consider carefully the rival demands of democrats that decisions be made on the basis of a majority of persons, and of oligarchs that they be made on the basis of a majority of qualifying property-owners. He also examines alternative schemes that would combine persons and property, some of which would also take into account the total amount of property of various groups, rather than a per capita minimum. The perceptive observation is made that it is the weaker who always seek equality and justice, while the stronger ignore them:

> But although it may be difficult in theory to know what is just and equal, the practical difficulty of inducing those to forbear who can, if they like, encroach, is far greater, for the weaker are always asking for equality and justice, but the stronger care for none of these things (1318 a–b).

Aristotle describes three occupational kinds of democracy: the one of farmers, which is the best; the one of pastoral herdsmen, which is the next best; and the one of mechanics, shopkeepers, and labourers, which is the least best. Farmers are too busy farming to get too involved in politics, they are seldom in the city, and they do not covet what does not belong to them. The masses covet profits more than honours and power, and will be satisfied if given the right to elect magistrates and call them to account. Aristotle therefore proposes that this best form of democracy, which presumably is best because of the strength of character of its agrarian populace, employ a system that would couple accountability with a balance of rights and qualifications:

Hence it is both expedient and customary in such a democracy that all should elect to offices, and conduct scrutinies, and sit in the law-courts, but that the great offices should be filled up be persons having a qualification; the greater requiring a greater qualification, or, if there be no offices for which a qualification is required, then those who are marked out by special ability should be appointed. Under such a form of government the citizens are sure to be governed well, (for the offices will always be held by the best persons; the people are willing enough to elect them and are not jealous of the good). The good and the notables will then be satisfied, for they will not be governed by men who are their inferiors, and the persons elected will rule justly, because others will call them to account. Every man should be responsible to others, nor should any one be allowed to do just as he pleases; for where absolute freedom is allowed there is nothing to restrain the evil which is inherent in every man. But the principle of responsibility secures that which is the greatest good in states; the right persons rule and are prevented from doing wrong, and the people have their due. It is evident that this is the best kind of democracy, and why? Because the people are drawn from a certain class (1318 b–1319 a).

To help achieve this just government by what we would call 'the better sort', Aristotle proposes that there be limits to the size of land-holdings, entailment of family portions, limitation of mortgages, and assessment for political rights that would qualify even the poorer landowners (1319 a). Aristotle says little here about the pastoral populace except, in passing, that in many ways they are like the farmers and that their life trains and hardens them into good condition for war (1319 a).

The description that Aristotle has for a lower and middle class urban populace is reminiscent of Thomas Jefferson's strictures against the urban populace in his *Notes on Virginia*. He would therefore neutralize the urban 'mob' by arrangements that would compel the mass of the citizenry to live outside the city, and at the same time have a rule that there be no assembly meetings that could not be attended by rural residents because of inconvenient scheduling (1319 a).

The remarks that Aristotle makes about the democratic urban class are even more reminiscent of Plato. They repeat his distrust of them, of human nature, of women, of slaves, and of children; and yet they are somewhat more optimistic than Plato because they include the hope that schemes may be able to be set up to keep democratic government within tolerable bounds despite his conclusion that 'most persons would rather live in a disorderly than in a sober manner' (1319 b).

For Aristotle, the priorities and bases of judgment of a constitution, its founders, and its legislators, are its durability and stability, rather than its democratic or oligarchic features and character. To achieve this durability and stability, Aristotle states the need for inherent limitations as well as constitutional safeguards when he writes of the need for customary, as well as enacted, laws (1319 b–1320 a).

As an example of how contemporary demagogues attempt to please the populace, Aristotle mentions their use of the law-courts to confiscate a large amount of property for public use. Aristotle presents these and other practices as illustrations of what should be guarded against, and advises such measures as: turning over confiscated property to religious use instead of to the public treasury; making trials public, short, and before law-courts (dicasteries) of many members; and having prosecutions on an impartial basis. Aristotle offers both suggested practices and their rationale to show how they can work to safeguard democracy realistically and equitably (1320 a).

However, as is customary with Aristotle, he does not present only one side or aspect of an issue or problem. He also recognizes that democracy cannot be maintained as truly democratic unless it attempt to end excessive poverty; and he finds that it is to the interest of all classes, including the prosperous and notables, to enlist themselves in sensible efforts to do this. He presents this task of all forms of government – but particularly of democracy – and some suggested economic remedies, including the distribution of public funds for public service in order to enable the needy to survive or, better still, to acquire small landholdings. The Carthaginians and Tarentines have won the friendship of the common people by such measures as subsidizing business efforts and emigration to nearby territories. The Tarentines are praised both for making certain property communal and for setting up a category of public office filled by vote and another category filled by lot (1320 a–b).

Preservation of Oligarchy

Interestingly enough, unlike the case with tyranny and democracy, where Aristotle points out that if certain policies are followed, they will lose their tyrannical or democratic character, Aristotle simply advises that the best sort of oligarchy is one that is not very oligarchic. It would seem that this is achieved by having some features of aristocracy and moving in the direction of democracy, so that the practical result is a form of oligarchy that is akin to polity and has more participating supporters of the constitution than there are excluded citizens. This requires a moderate property qualification (1320 b).[27]

With respect to the extreme form of oligarchy that corresponds to extreme democracy, Aristotle finds it more akin to tyranny; and, therefore, because it is a worse form of oligarchy, its preservation requires greater vigilance and greater strength of organization. The passage concludes.

> The nature [in terms of quantity – RP] of those admitted should be such as will make the entire governing body stronger than those who are excluded, and the new citizen should be always taken out of the better class of the people. The principle, narrowed a little, gives another form of oligarchy; until at length we reach the most cliquish and tyrannical of them all, answering to the extreme democracy, which, being the worst, requires vigilance in proportion to its badness. For as healthy bodies and ships well provided with sailors may undergo many mishaps and survive them, whereas sickly constitutions and rotten ill-manned ships are ruined by the very least mistake, so do the worst forms of government require the greatest care. The populousness of democracies generally preserves them (for number is to democracy in the place of justice based on proportion); whereas the preservation of an oligarchy clearly depends on an opposite principle, viz. good order (1320 b–1321 a).

One form of superior organization that militates to permit the more limited numbers of an oligarchy to prevail, is the military. In treating of this, Aristotle lists four segments of the population (farmers, artisans, retailers, and labourers) and four branches of the military (cavalry, heavy infantry, light infantry, and marines). He correlates the cavalry with oligarchy; but warns that the sons of the oligarchy must also be trained in light infantry drill and weapons, or they will be creating a potential danger within the ranks of the masses, for the light infantry and naval element are wholly democratic (1321 a).

Finally, Aristotle advises that oligarchy is supported by reserving the most important offices to full citizens who can meet high property qualifications for them, who will draw no pay, and who will offer magnificent sacrifices and erect public monuments. Aristotle also regards some of the oligarchy's more corrupt features as earmarks of democracy (1321 a).

Categories of Public Officials

Aristotle lists various categories of public officials he believes necessary to a state (1321 b–1322 b). In his introduction of the subject, he notes certain general rules: without various indispensable magistracies, a state cannot even exist; without those that maintain law, order, and good appearance, a state cannot be well governed; and in smaller states, they are fewer in number, and in larger states they are greater in number (1321 b).

The first category of public officials that Aristotle presents here, lists the six executive (or administrative) offices he regards as the most indispensable: (1) a superintendent of markets to supervise contracts and maintain public order; (2) a superintendent of streets and buildings (often entitled a city-controller) to supervise urban private and public properties to see they are maintained in good order and correct boundaries observed; (3) a superintendent of rural areas to perform the same duties in the countryside and also to act as forest-warden; (4) receivers of accounts or treasurers to receive, hold and disburse public monies; (5) public recorders to register private contracts and court decisions; and (6) a superintendent of gaols to execute sentences on offenders, recover debts due the state, and have custody of prisoners, who exercises 'perhaps the most indispensable and most difficult of all' offices and that should be a plural one (1321 b–1322 a).

The second category of public officials that Aristotle presents here, lists four additional offices he regards as of a higher grade of dignity: (1) the generals and naval commandants; (2) the auditors, accountants, examiners, or advocates of the treasury; (3) the preliminary council, a probouleutic or preconsidering body (*probouloi*); and (4) the priests and custodians of temples. There may also be a separate fifth office here, an archon, king, or prytanis, who manages public sacrifices (1322 a–b).

At this point, Aristotle summarizes by function the essential administrative officials of a *polis* by listing them according to substantive area of activity:

> These, then, are the necessary offices, which may be summed up as follows: offices concerned with matters of religion, with war, with the revenue and expenditure, with the market, with the city, with the harbours, with the country; also with the courts of law, with the records of contracts, with the execution of sentences, with custody of prisoners, with audits and scrutinies and accounts of magistrates; lastly, there are those which preside over the public deliberations of the state. There are likewise magistracies characteristic of states which are peaceful and prosperous, and at the same time have a regard to good order: such as the offices of guardians of women, guardians of the laws, guardians of children, and directors of gymnastics; also superintendents of gymnastic and Dionysiac contests, and of other similar spectacles (1322 b–1323 a).

In bringing the subject to a close, Aristotle identifies some of the officials peculiar to more prosperous *poleis* (1322 b–1323 a). But of greatest interest here is his association of the Guardians of the Law *Nomophulakes*: Νομοφυλάκες) with aristocracy; the Preconsidering Council (*Probouloi*: Πρόβουλοι) with oligarchy; and the Council (*Boulé*: Βουλή) with democracy. The principle of mixed, balanced government is implicitly evident in the following passage:

Once more: there are three forms of the highest elective offices in states – guardians of the law, probuli [a pre-considering council group – RP], councillors,– of these, the guardians of the law are an aristocratical, the probuli an oligarchical, the council a democratical institution (1323 a).

Size and Location of the City-state

Aristotle is much concerned with the size and quality of both the population and territory of his city-state. He places no arbitrary restriction upon the number of its citizens and inhabitants or the extent of its territory (whereas Plato, time and again refers to 5,040 landowning families: e.g., *Laws*, 918 A–920 C). Aristotle's approach emphasizes the human material over the territorial material, is concerned in both respects with quality rather than quantity, and prefers an optimum, or sufficiency, of size rather than a greater amount:

First among the materials required by the statesman is population: he will consider what should be the number and character of the citizens, and then what should be the size and character of the country. Most persons think that a state in order to be happy ought to be large; but even if they are right, they have no idea what is a large and what a small state. For they judge of the size of the city by the number of the inhabitants; whereas they ought to regard, not their number, but their power. A city too, like an individual, has a work to do; and that city which is best adapted to the fulfilment of its work is to be deemed greatest, in the same sense of the word great in which Hippocrates might be called greater, not as a man, but as a physician, than some one else who was taller (Bk VII, 1325 b–1326a).

Included in Aristotle's objections to a state of over-large population are the difficulties therein of obtaining habitual obedience to law, of communication, and of rightly judging the merits of unfamiliar candidates and disputants. Neither too large a maritime vessel nor too large a ship of state can be properly or safely controlled, for only a divine power can control what is unlimited in size. Therefore an optimum size – probably middling – of due proportion that can provide the essential factor of self-sufficiency is the quantitative desideratum. For Aristotle, quantity is not to be confused with quality, especially the quality of greatness:

For law is order, and good law is good order; but a very great multitude cannot be orderly: to introduce order into the unlimited is the work of a divine power – of such a power as holds together the universe. Beauty is realized in number and magnitude[a] ([a] Cp. Poet. 7. § 4.), and the state which combines magnitude with good order must necessarily be the most beautiful. To the size of states there is a limit, as there is to other things, plants, animals, implements; for none of these retain their natural power when they are too large or too small, but they either wholly lose their nature, or are spoiled. For example, a ship which is only a span long will not be a ship at all, nor a ship a quarter of a mile long; yet their may be a ship of a certain size, either too large or too small, which will still be a ship, but bad for sailing. In like manner a state when composed of too few is not as a state ought to be, self-sufficing; when of too many, though self-sufficing in all mere necessities, it is a nation and not a state, being almost incapable of constitutional government. For who can be the general of such a vast multitude, or who the herald, unless he have the voice of a Stentor (1326 a–b)?

In similar fashion, the state requires a large enough territory, large enough to have a maximum of self-sufficiency; and therefore it should be able to provide a life of leisure that combines liberality with temperance: i.e., a life of moderation. Additional requirements are that the location of the central city facilitate dispatch of military aid to all points, and that it be a convenient commercial centre (1326 b–1327 a).

Unlike Plato, Aristotle would place his city-state near the sea. As against the objection that this would introduce more strangers and therefore more disorder, Aristotle argues that it would provide better security and a good supply of necessary imported materials, for he does not seem to feel that a maximum of self-sufficiency is tantamount to autarchy. Therefore, unless it wish to engage in commerce for the sake of profit and to benefit foreigners instead of itself, it need not have a great port (1327 a).

There are additional advantages of greater safety and greater potentiality for leadership if a state has naval power. Aristotle includes in this passage a pertinent observation about the frequent placement of cities somewhat apart from their ports. Besides providing masses of hardy agricultural serfs and labourers to man the ships as oarsmen, this arrangement is more defensible (as in the case of Athens and its Piraeus that was separated from the main city by the 'Long Walls' that were some five miles in length) (1327 a–b).

In discussing the personal qualities that Aristotle prefers in the population of his city-state, he mentions spirit (courage) and intelligence. The first quality, a characteristic of peoples of a cold climate, makes for the freedom of a people; the second quality, a characteristic of Asian peoples, makes for their leadership over others. The Greeks have a middle geographical position, and their consequent combination of spirit and intelligence – as is characteristic of the middle position – leads to freedom and goodness (1327 b–1328 a).[28] In the final analysis, it is passion – spirited courage – that Aristotle seems to prefer most as a human quality, because it is commanding and unconquerable. But men of passionate spirit, even when moved by righteous indignation, ought to be magnanimous and not harsh even to strangers (*cp*. Plato, Laws, 731 D–732 B), for:

> ... a lofty spirit is not fierce by nature, but only when excited against evil-doers. And this, as I was saying before, is a feeling which men show most strongly towards their friends if they think they have received a wrong at their hands: as indeed is reasonable; for, besides the actual injury, they seem deprived of a benefit by those who owe them one. Hence the saying,
> 'Cruel is the strife of brethren[b] ([b] Eurip. Frag. 51 Dindorf.);'
> and again,
> 'They who love in excess also hate in excess.' (1328 a)

Necessary Elements and Services of a State

Aristotle writes of both necessary conditions and parts of the state and also of the highest good of the state. Some of the elements of a state, such as property, are needed by a state but are not part of the state *per se*; and this evidently includes animate forms of property such as slaves, beasts of burden, and livestock that are necessary to a state and its citizens but are not organic parts of the whole system. The state requires that its members share a common condition, even if their shares be not equal. Thus, for membership in a state (i.e., the condition of citizenship), there must be an equal, similar, or common condition that involves participation in the processes of sovereignty; but some may participate more fully in these processes that are supposed to seek the highest good of the state and its inhabitants, namely the happiness that results from virtuous activity in keeping with the peculiar needs and resultant modes of the particular state:

> And so states require property, but property, even though living beings are included in it[a] ([a] Cp. i. 4. § 2.), is no part of a state; for a state is not a community of living beings only, but a community of equals, aiming at the best life possible. Now, whereas happiness is the highest good, being a realization and perfect practice of virtue, which some can attain, while others have little or none of it, the various qualities of men are clearly the reason why there are various kinds of states and many forms of government; for different men seek after happiness in different ways and by different means, and so make for themselves different modes of life and forms of government (1328 a–b).

To attain this felicity and goodness, a state must have continued existence;

and for continued existence a state requires six basic elements: food; handicrafts; arms; money; a priesthood; and a means of deciding questions of interests and rights. Therefore, in order to function properly and to endure, a state must be organized along the lines of these requirements (1328 b).[29] The production of all of these goods and services needed by the state and its inhabitants may be shared by all; they may each be assigned to a different group of persons; or some may be furnished by all and others by different sets of persons. The differing manner in which these modes of production may be organized and make decisions about duties, rewards, materials, and processes, also makes – in rather Marxian fashion – for correspondingly different constitutions; but there is a common absolute justice:

> Having determined these points, we have in the next place to consider whether all ought to share in every sort of occupation. Shall every man be at once husbandman, artisan, councillor, judge, or shall we suppose the several occupations just mentioned assigned to different persons? or, thirdly, shall some employments be assigned to individuals and others common to all? The question, however, does not occur in every state; as we were saying, all may be shared by all, or not all by all, but only by some[b] ([b] Cp. iv. c. 4 and 14.); and hence arise the differences of states, for in democracies all share in all, in oligarchies the opposite practice prevails. Now, since we are here speaking of the best form of government, and that under which the state will be most happy (and happiness, as has been already said, cannot exist without virtue[c] ([c] Cp. c. 8. § 5.]), it clearly follows that in the state which is best governed the citizens who are absolutely and not merely relatively just men must not lead the life of mechanics or tradesmen, for such a life is ignoble, and inimical to virtue[d] ([d] Cp. Plato Laws xi. 919.). Neither must they be husbandmen, since leisure is necessary both for the development of virtue and the performance of political duties (1328 b–1329 a).[30]

Thus, again we pause to note a most revealing statement that presents a touchstone attitude of Aristotle that should be given due consideration: hard physical labour and commercial activity engaged in to make a living debase the individual and render him unfit for citizenship in the *polis* Aristotle most desires. Aristotle, by today's standards, shows himself at bottom a snob who makes too close a relationship between leisure to study and reflect with nobility of character and views and consequent qualification for citizenship. Accordingly, Aristotle's political ideas must all be judged with the thought in mind that, however sincere and disinterested, they come from one predisposed to elitism, albeit of an intelligentsia in whom virtue and knowledge have been so developed that they are to some extent all to be regarded as philosophers.

In a similar vein, Aristotle sets forth an order of participation in the military, deliberative (legislative), and judicial processes: war is for the young and vigorous; and deliberation on matters of public interest and participation in judicial activity are for the mature and wise. Such an arrangement also satisfies the requirements of justice by awarding roles and rights in proportion to desert and in rotation (1329 a). Those who participate in exercise of powers of sovereignty should, ideally, be a leisure class of property owners who can devote to political activities the time and goodness needed to promote the felicity of the state and of all its inhabitants. This is in direct contradiction of Plato, who would have deprived the Guardian class of any individually owned, private property (1329 a).

In addition to an opportunity for those who have done military service to perform as councillors, Aristotle would limit priestly service to an elder part of the citizenry and he would assign it to those drawn from the military and councillor classes. He specifically excludes farmers and artisans from priestly service, and then reprises the functional groups within the state as *parts* (warriors and councillors) or *appurtenances* (husbandmen, craftsmen, and labourers):

> We have shown what are the necessary conditions, and what the parts of a state: husbandmen, craftsmen, and labourers of all kinds are necessary to the existence of states, but the parts of the state are the warriors and councillors. And these are distinguished severally from one another, the distinction being in some cases permanent, in others not (1329 a).[31]

Land-division to Provide Classes, Common-messes, and Military Security

In Egypt, says Aristotle, is where the practice of dividing the population into separate classes, especially into the military class and the farming class, began. In Italy, he also says, is where common-messes originated. A formula for the distribution of land that is intended to support both classes and common-messes is then offered. It would divide the land into four parts: two public parts, one to support the gods and the other to support the common meals; and two for each private holder, one on the frontiers and one near the city. Aristotle argues in support of this plan (borrowing in good part from Plato, despite earlier criticisms of it) on the ground that it would satisfy demands for equality, justice, and military security (1329 b–1330 a). However, any notion that Aristotle is libertarian or egalitarian in the modern sense, should be dispelled by the manner in which he proposes to use public and private slaves and serfs to work the land for the benefit of the state and private owners:

> The very best thing of all would be that the husbandmen should be slaves, not all of the same race[b] ([b] Cp. Plato Laws vi. 777.) and not spirited, for if they have no spirit they will be better suited for their work, and there will be no danger of their making a revolution. The next best thing would be that they should be perioeci of foreign race[c] ([c] Cp. c. 9. § 8.), and of a like inferior nature; some of them should be the slaves of individuals, and employed in the private estates of men of property, the remainder should be the property of the state and employed on the common land[d] ([d] Cp. ii. 7. § 23.). I will hereafter explain what is the proper treatment of slaves, and why it is expedient that liberty should be always held out to them as the reward of their services (1330 a).[32]

Considerations of health and military matters are of primary importance to Aristotle. Indeed, he regards health as the first and most indispensable of the four considerations he has in mind (the other two being, it seems, the needs of political life and beauty). Cities that slope towards the east and are exposed to the east winds and have a supply of good drinking water provided by natural streams are preferable, because air and water are the elements we use most and therefore can contribute most to our good health. The construction of large, beautiful reservoirs of rain-water that will not fail in case of siege is an available substitute. For reasons of military advantage, the site should permit easy egress of inhabitants but should be difficult for enemies to approach or blockade. It would seem that when he speaks of strongholds or fortified points, Aristotle has in mind a potential enemy-within-the-gates as well as outsiders. Thus, he may only seemingly not make consistent military sense when he writes:

> As to strongholds, which is suitable to different forms of government varies: thus an acropolis is suited to an oligarchy or a monarchy, but a plain to a democracy; neither to an aristocracy, but rather a number of strong places (1330 b).

In continuing his discussion of military matters, Aristotle advocates a plan that may combine the advantages of beauty found in the straight streets of Hippodamus that are suited to peacetime with the military advantages of streets that are not continuingly straight. He proposes that some sections employ the gardener's diamond-shaped plan (also to be found in natural beehives) that makes for more efficient use of space and would, in addition, make it more difficult for a foreign garrison to fight its way out and for attackers to fight their way in (1330 b).

Aristotle concludes his discussion of military considerations with a devastating attack against Plato's suggestions that the walls of a city not be fortified. He says that modern weapons and tactics have made this notion antiquated and concludes: 'for when men are well prepared no enemy even thinks of attacking them' (1330 b–1331 a).

Man's Rational and Ethical Nature Make him Educable and the Good State Possible

Aristotle's political theory rests ultimately on the assumption that although man is an animal, he is different from and superior to the other animals by virtue of his being endowed with reason and a soul. Man, therefore, should not live a simply naturalistic existence, as do the other animals. His natural endowment and desires should be tempered by the ennobling influence of his reason and the cultivation of good habits, so as to result in virtuous purpose and behaviour; for it is virtue, not blind adherence to custom or desire, that should lead to happiness, the supreme aim of the legislator. Therefore, it is up to the legislator to make use of the available elements and help to educate and direct the population into paths of righteousness and civic activity in much the same manner as would Plato by his system of *paideia*; for the goodness of all and the goodness of each are interrelated. Accordingly, aside from the given elements and the formal structure of the constitution, it is still necessary to develop, especially by education, the human limitations and potentialities (i.e., 'inherent limitations') that make for the good man and the good state, for:

> There are three things which make men good and virtuous; these are nature, habit, reason[a] ([a] Cp. N. Eth. x. 9. §6.). In the first place, every one must be born a man and not some other animal; in the second place, he must have a certain character, both of body and soul. But some qualities there is no use in having at birth, for they are altered by habit, and there are some gifts of nature which may be turned by habit to good or bad. Most animals lead a life of nature, although in lesser particulars some are influenced by habit as well. Man has reason, in addition, and man only[b] ([b] Cp. i. 2. § 10.). Wherefore nature, habit, reason must be in harmony with one anther [for they do not always agree]; men do many things against habit and nature, if reason persuades them that they ought (1332 a–1332 b).

It is necessary, therefore, to realize the central role that education (*padeia*) must play within a state, and to develop the educational institutions and methods that will produce the desired kind of people and government. If governors and governed were essentially different in quality, their education would have to be different; but there are no gods or race of supermen available, and so justice requires that all who are essentially alike take turns in ruling and being ruled. On the other hand, there should be a difference between governors and governed. The just and practical solution, therefore, is to have the generically same citizenry divided by age, and the young await their turn to rule. Aristotle's ideas about the tractability of the young and their willingness to wait for their own maturity before taking over control of government – or of education – however, is not that correct an observation today (e.g., their pressure to reverse roles and evaluate teachers); and this, no doubt, contributes to the *stasis* that afflicts society today. When the system works so that it is in the interest of the governed, Aristotle opines that it is a government of freemen and it is then honourable for them to perform even menial work in the public interest. The passage concludes with reliance on the legislator to discover how to achieve fulfilment in life and to bring it about:

> But since we say^c (^{c} Cp. iii. 4. and 5. § 10.) that the virtue of the citizen and ruler is the same as that of the good man, and that the same person must first be a subject and then a ruler, the legislator has to see that they become good men, and by what means this may be accomplished, and what is the end of the perfect life (1332 b–1333 a).

Aristotle distinguishes two parts of the soul: a higher part that is intrinsically rational; and a lower part that has the capacity to accept and obey what is rational. The intrinsically rational and higher part is in turn subdivided into two parts: a higher part that is speculative and concerned with wise objectives; and a lower part that is concerned with practical activity directed towards realization of wise objectives (e.g., even war should have peace as its purpose). Since we always prefer the highest we can attain, our preferences and activities in life should therefore be directed toward attainment of the highest goods of the soul, namely, wise (i.e., good and noble) objectives (1333 a–b).

Aristotle is led, next, to challenge recent writers who have lauded the Spartan constitution and its concentration on war, conquest, and empire, with the expectation of consequent great material prosperity. For Aristotle, it is a policy that leads to ultimate failure and involves great internal risks:

> But surely they are not a happy people now that their empire has passed away, nor was their legislator right. How ridiculous is the result, if, while they are

continuing in the observance of his laws and no one interferes with them, they have lost the better part of life! These writers further err about the sort of government which the legislator should approve, for the government of freemen is noble, and implies more virtue than despotic government[a] ([a] Cp. i. 5. § 2.). Neither is a city to be deemed happy or a legislator to be praised because he trains his citizens to conquer and obtain dominion over neighbours, for there is great evil in this. On a similar principle any citizen who could, would obviously try to obtain the power in his own state .... No such principle and no law having this object is either statesmanlike or useful or right (1333 b).

Thus, none of the arguments in favour of training that is directed solely to empire over others is correct or right. It must lead inevitably to collapse of empire and inability to use peace and leisure properly. Training for war should emphasize prevention of becoming enslaved; and enslavement of those who do not deserve such a fate should not be practised; but Aristotle does argue in favour of enslavement of those who do deserve to be slaves (e.g., uncivilized peoples):

Neither should men study war with a view to the enslavement of those who do not deserve to be enslaved; but first of all they should provide against their own enslavement, and in the second place obtain empire for the good of the governed, and not for the sake of exercising a general despotism, and in the third place they should seek to be masters only over those who deserve to be slaves. Facts, as well as arguments, prove that the legislator should direct all his military and other measures to the provision of leisure and the establishment of peace. For most of these military states are safe only while they are at war[c] ([c] Cp. ii. 9. § 34.), but fall when they have acquired their empire; like unused iron they rust[d] ([d] Lit. 'they lose their edge.') in time of peace (1333 b–1334 a).[33]

For Aristotle, occupation with work is a means to the enjoyment of leisure. The activities of occupation require the combined quality of courage and endurance (i.e., fortitude); the activities of leisure require wisdom; and temperance and justice are required at all times. A state, to achieve felicity and goodness, must therefore promote especially the qualities of wisdom, temperance, and justice (1334 a).[34]

The problem of how to achieve excellence remains. It is not to be done by a narrow form of training such as the Spartan, which cultivates the single quality of military courage and, like the rest of the world, pursues external goods. It is the whole of excellence, not a part of excellence, that should be pursued. This will require the means of natural endowment, habit, and rational principle, as previously noted. It will also require determination of the proper order of training necessary to realize ultimately the highest fulfilment of man: namely, for man to employ a disciplined mind or soul to reason properly and a disciplined character to act accordingly. However, this is brought about by a reversed order of training: training of the body preceded training of the mind or soul; and training of the irrational part of the mind (which is concerned with appetite and desire) must precede training of the rational part of the mind (which is concerned with intelligence and intellect). Therefore, good habits must be developed in the young before the ability to reason sets in:

> Now, in men reason and mind are the end towards which nature strives, so that the birth and moral discipline of the citizens ought to be ordered with a view to them. In the second place, as the soul and body are two, we see also that there are two parts of the soul, the rational and the irrational[c] ([c] Cp. N. Eth. i. 13. § 9 ff.), and two corresponding states – reason and appetite. And as the body is prior in order of generation to the soul, so the irrational is prior to the rational. The proof is that anger and will and desire are implanted in children from their very birth, but reason and understanding are developed as they grow older. Wherefore, the care of the body ought to precede that of the soul, and the training of the appetitive part should follow: none the less our care of it must be for the sake of the reason, and our care of the body for the sake of the soul[d] ([d] Cp. Plato Rep. iii. 410.) (1334 a–1335 b).

Eugenical Marriage and Procreation

As does Plato, Aristotle outlines a plan for eugenical mating and procreation in order to provide a stock of the healthiest possible children for the nurseries of the state. Unlike Plato, however, Aristotle does so within the framework of highly moral, monogamous marriage. He begins, accordingly, with the requirement that marriage be between partners whose period of fertility overlap; the second requirement is that there not be too great or small a gap between the ages of parents and children, so that the children may benefit from parental guidance and the parents in return receive filial piety; and the third requirement is that a stock of healthy children be provided (1334 b–1335 a).

Therefore, because the period of procreation usually ends for men at the age of 70 and for women at the age of 50, a man should marry at about the age of 37 and a woman at about the age of 18. Too early marriage is bad because young mothers tend to have children who are imperfectly developed, small of stature, and more often female, and to experience harder labour and more frequent death in childbirth. Also, sexual restraint of daughters will be encouraged because young women are supposed to be more intemperate once they have experienced sexual intercourse; and the physique of young men is supposed to become stunted if intercourse be started before the seed has finished its growth. Winter is regarded by Aristotle as the proper season of the year for marriage and it seems to be a good time to bring children into the world when a more favourable wind, the north wind, is blowing. Proper habits of exercise, diet, prayer, and attitude are then prescribed for both sexes, with good prenatal influence a priority:

> The temperament of an athlete is not suited to the life of a citizen, or to health, or to the procreation of children, any more than the valetudinarian or exhausted constitution, but one which is in a mean between them. A man's constitution should be inured to labour, but not to labour which is excessive or of one sort only, such as is practised by athletes; he should be capable of all the actions of a freeman. These remarks apply equally to both parents.
> Women who are with child should be careful of themselves; they should take exercise and have a nourishing diet. The first of these prescriptions the legislator will easily carry into effect by requiring that they shall take a walk daily to some temple, where they can worship the gods who preside over birth[a] ([a] Cp. Plato Laws vii. 789.). Their minds, however, unlike their bodies, they ought to keep unexercised, for the offspring derive their natures from their mothers as plants do from the earth (1335 a–b).

Aristotle expresses non-equivocal views on the exposure to death of deformed newly-born, abortion, and adultery. Aristotle would have a law to prevent the rearing of deformed children; but he would also have a law to prevent exposure merely to limit population. Induced miscarriage (i.e., abortion) is preferred for the latter purpose, provided sense and life have not yet begun (1335 b). Before stating his opinions on adultery, Aristotle mentions the age at which he advocates men stop engaging in procreation: four or five years beyond the age of 50, the time he regards as their mental prime. Aristotle then expresses the strongest kind of unqualified contempt for adulterers, be they man or woman, of any age; and he unqualifiedly states that they must be punished with suitable disgrace or loss of privilege when it occurs during childbearing years (1335 b–1336 a).

Some Principles of Education of the Young

The system of education which Aristotle advocates is similar to Plato's *paideia* in its fundamental objectives and methods; it differs in greater degree of moderation rather than in kind. It is by no means a system of liberal education, but rather a combination of physical development and inculcation.

Some of the advice which Aristotle offers about diet and physical training for the first few years of life still holds good, such as a diet abundant in milk, the less wine the better, physical movement, and habituation to endure cold, although he may recount an example of the last recommendation that goes beyond sensible bounds (1336 a).

During the next few years, until the child reaches five, the child should not be subjected to any set lessons or compulsory tasks, so as not to hinder its growth. However, physical activity and games that are neither laborious nor effeminate, and therefore appropriate to freemen, should be carried on. Careful attention should also be given by the superintendents of education to the sort of tales and stories told to children of this age, and to the play they engage in that will mimic their occupations of later years. Aristotle, a physician's son and a father himself, also takes time to jibe at Plato with what he says is a correction of the *Laws* on the matter of children's crying:

> Those are wrong who [like Plato] in the Laws attempt to check the loud crying and screaming of children, for these contribute towards their growth and, in a manner, exercise their bodies[a] ([a] Plato Laws vii. 792.). Straining the voice has an effect similar to that produced by the retention of the breath in violent exertions (1336 a).

For similar reasons, it is also important to Aristotle that the superintendents of education exercise a general control over children. Children should be so controlled as to pass very little time in the company of slaves; and since until the age of seven their education is bound to be home training, they should not contract vulgar habits there. He makes a particular point against the deleterious effects of the use of bad language and bad examples set by elders, and the need to punish these offenders:

> Indeed, there is nothing which the legislator should be more careful to drive away than indecency of speech; for the light utterance of shameful words is akin to shameful actions. The young especially should never be allowed to repeat or hear anything of the sort. A freeman who is found saying or doing what is forbidden, if he be too young as yet to have the privilege of a place at the public tables, should be disgraced and beaten, and an elder person degraded as his slavish conduct deserves (1336 a–b).

Aristotle is similarly very much concerned to prevent the exhibition of indecent pictures, statuary, and plays (with the exception of certain festivals of deities where the use of scurrility is allowed); and the seeing of mimes should be forbidden until they reach an age of discretion (i.e., old enough to recline and take wine with the older men at the common-mess), when their education would have made them immune to the evil influences of the mimes' performances. Meanwhile, the sight of good example is a positive form of education; and so, when children have reached the age of seven, they may become spectators of the lessons in gymnastics and music given the older children that they will in turn have to learn (1336 b).

In a preliminary summation, Aristotle states that the problem is both to conform to nature and to correct her deficiencies. Therefore, since seven-year periods seem to conform to nature, education of the child from seven to puberty should be followed by another period lasting until the age of 21. Thus, it is necessary to consider: first, whether some regulation of boys should be instituted; whether it be advantageous to have education conducted by the state or to have it conducted on a private basis as in most contemporary states; and the proper nature of any such regulations (1336 b–1337 a).

Book VIII, the final book of the *Politics*, opens with a very significant, recapitulative discussion of the nature and purposes of a constitution and of education within a state, that accords neatly with the Marxian principle of the structural unity of every culture. Thus it is that, in complete agreement with Plato as to aims, Aristotle calls here for a pervasive system of state regulation that would train and indoctrinate the young to support the state and its constitutional system:

> No one will doubt that the legislator should direct his attention above all to the education of youth; or that the neglect of education does harm to states. The citizen should be moulded to suit the form of government under which he lives[a] ([a] Cp. v. 9. §§ 11–16.). For each government has a peculiar character which originally formed and which continues to preserve it. The character of democracy creates democracy, and the character of oligarchy creates oligarchy; and always the better the character, the better the government.
>
> Now for the exercise of any faculty or art a previous training and habituation are required; clearly therefore for the practice of virtue. And since the whole city has one end, it is manifest that education should be one and the same for all, and that it should be public, and not private,– not as at present, when every one looks after his own children separately, and gives them separate instruction of the sort which he thinks best; the training in things which are of common interest should be the same for all. Neither must we suppose that any one of the citizens belongs to himself, for they all belong to the state, and are each of them a part of the state, and the care of each part is inseparable from the care of the

whole. In this particular the Lacedaemonians are to be praised, for they take the greatest pains about their children, and make education the business of the state[b] ([b] Cp. Nic. Eth. x. 9. § 13.) (Bk VIII, 1337 a).

Having delivered himself of this statement about the proper purposes and principles of education, Aristotle declares it is now evident that there should be regulation of education by the state and that education should also be conducted by the state:

That education should be regulated by law and should be an affair of state is not to be denied, but what should be the character of this public education, and how young persons should be educated, are questions which remain to be considered (1337 a).

Thus, what the state should teach and the order of educational priorities are at this point still unresolved. Aristotle therefore asks pertinent questions: what are the subjects of education? Should the emphasis have in mind: plain goodness or the best life possible; understanding or moral character development; or to advance the bounds of knowledge? Also, he points out that virtue or goodness has different meanings to different people (1337 a–b).

Close examination of Aristotle's dicta regarding the curriculum that is fit for freemen reveals – according to present-day standards – a simply snobbish, and at times simply foolish, character to some aspects of his educational philosophy and programme. Firstly, he divides occupations into the categories of those that are fit for freemen to pursue. Next, he declares that the total amount of useful information imparted to children should never be enough to make them *banausos* (βάναυσος): literally, 'mechanically-minded'; and metaphorically, low, vulgar, or illiberal. The term 'mechanical' is used metaphorically by Aristotle to apply to any occupation, art, or instruction that makes the body, soul, or mind unfit for goodness (and therefore makes the person unfit, in Aristotle's eyes, for citizenship). Accordingly, 'mechanical' is applied to activity that adversely affects physical fitness and to employment pursued for gain that keeps minds too much occupied with mean thoughts. Moreover, too intense pursuit of even liberal arts and studies in the attempt to attain perfection has similar illiberal, evil results. In effect, Aristotle seems to be saying that one should never lose the easy-going grace of the amateur or dilettante, for one cannot continually work slavishly for oneself or others without becoming slave-like. Thus, Aristotle concludes this passage with advice that would liberate and distinguish liberal education from servile habits and results:

The object also which a man sets before him makes a great difference; if he does or learns anything for his own sake[a] ([a] Cp. iii. 4. § 13.) or for the sake of his friends, or with a view to excellence, the action will not appear illiberal; but if done for the sake of others, the very same action will be thought menial and servile. The received subjects of instruction, as I have already remarked[b] ([b] § 3 supra.), are partly of a liberal and partly of an illiberal character (1337 b).[35]

Educational Subjects: Reading, Writing, Drawing, Gymnastics, and Music

The educational curriculum, according to Aristotle, has two preparatory purposes: for occupational activity; and for leisure activity. Leisure is the higher of these two forms of activity; indeed, occupations are carried on so that they may provide the wherewithal for leisure. The established studies that one engages in while preparing for occupational and leisure activity are reading and writing, physical training, and music, and some would add drawing. Reading, writing, and drawing are regarded as practical (i.e., occupational in purpose); physical training is supposed to develop courage; and musical training is undertaken as though it were for pleasure, but its original educational purpose is something higher (1337 b–1338 a).[36]

Ultimately, therefore, education and occupation are both directed toward filling our leisure with appropriate activity; and this does not mean with play, for that would make play the be-all and end-all of life. Play, for Aristotle, is a restorative or a relaxation from occupation, or exertion and is associated with work, not leisure. Leisure, unlike occupation and play, is an end in itself: it provides an intrinsic felicity, accompanied by pleasure and not by pain. However, despite his downgrading of occupation in comparison with leisure, Aristotle expresses a realization that both are requisite to fulfilment of our human nature and its drives. But for Aristotle, the enjoyment of leisure is the source of greatest felicity, human fulfilment, and pleasure: 'the pleasure of the best man is the best, and springs from the noblest sources' (1337 b–1338 a).

Although attention is paid to the loftier purposes of education, pragmatism and dualism (or pluralism) prevail whenever Aristotle deals with a fundamental question – or at least they are his starting point. Thus, following discussion of how the study of useful subjects (such as reading, writing, and drawing) can help in general in the acquisition of form and figure, Aristotle deals realistically with the questions of whether to cultivate habits or reason first, and whether to cultivate body or mind first. His responses are that with respect to children, cultivation of good habits and development of the body come first. But basically pragmatic though he be, the dualistic Aristotle never overlooks that single-minded attention to these related factors can be self-defeating and that even the utilitarian requires something higher also be present – as does human fulfilment. He accordingly writes, in repetition of what he has said before, a prescription for virtue that calls for 'a sound mind in a sound body':

> It is evident, then, that there is a sort of education in which parents should train their sons, not as being useful or necessary, but because it is liberal or noble. Whether this is of one kind only, or of more than one, and if so, what they are, and how they are to be imparted, must hereafter be determined. Thus much we are now in a position to say that the ancients witness to us; for their opinion may be gathered from the fact that music is one of the received and traditional branches of education. Further, it is clear that children should be instructed in some useful things,– for example, in reading and writing,– not only for their usefulness, but also because many other sorts of knowledge are acquired through them. With a like view they may be taught drawing, not to prevent making mistakes in their own purchases, or in order that they may not be imposed upon in the buying or selling of articles, but perhaps rather because it makes them judges of the beauty of the human form. To be always seeking after the useful does not become free and exalted souls[a] ([a] Cp. Plato Rep. vii. 525 ff.). Now it is clear that in education habit must go before reason, and the body before the mind; and therefore boys should be handed over to the trainer, who creates in them the proper habit of body, and to the wrestling-master, who teaches them their exercises (1338 a–b).

Despite the need to train the body before the mind, Aristotle does not place overly great value on physical training. Indeed, excessive, animalistic physical training of the Spartan kind does not even produce the greater manly courage or victory in games and war. Excessive physical training produces vulgarity; but the higher end served by liberal education is that it produces men of honour and statesmanship. The following passage highlights Aristotle's educational objective to produce spirited men of noble character and performance who fulfil human potential and requirements, rather than individuals of 'an athletic habit':

> Of those states which in our own day seem to take the greatest care of children, some aim at producing in them an athletic habit, but they only injure their forms and stunt their growth. ... It is notorious that the Lacedaemonians, while they were themselves assiduous in their laborious drill, were superior to others, but now they are beaten both in war and gymnastic exercises. For their ancient superiority did not depend on their mode of training their youth, but only on the

circumstance that they trained them at a time when others did not. Hence we may infer that what is noble, not what is brutal, should have the first place; no wolf or other wild animal will face a really noble danger; such dangers are for the brave man[a] ([a] Cp. Nic. Eth. iii. 6 § 8.). And parents who devote their children to gymnastics while they neglect their necessary education, in reality vulgarize them; for they make them useful to the state in one quality only, and even in this the argument proves them to be inferior to others (1338 b).

Assessments

Thus, the central purpose of the state as revealed in Aristotle's *Politics* is to enable humanity to fulfil its nature by living the good life, a felicitous life of virtue rather than of material success and conquest. Among the virtues and qualities of the good life that contribute to the good state and society are: temperance, justice, and courage, shared by all; and prudence and modesty, as they befit others. The basic social unit on which this state is built is the monogamous family, with adultery proscribed. The economy is essentially one of private property and enterprise, supplemented by state enterprise, and with slavery and serfdom also present. The state, whatever its form of government, should be a meritocracy.

The state should be neither too large nor too small; and it should be strategically located, in a healthful situation, preferably with some access to the sea and with good prevailing winds and natural water supply. It should be populous and extensive enough to be self-sufficing and strong enough – but not overly so – to defend itself and so to discourage attack. As a corollary, it should be wary of seeking to conquer others, for that is usually ignoble and counterproductive.

The principles and practices that cause instability and sedition are rooted in injustice and improper conceptions of equality. Equality of treatment should be proportionate to equality of condition: i.e., equals should be treated equally and unequals should be treated unequally, but in a ratio proportionately equal to their merit or condition. Therefore, the state should be constituted on the basis of an organological, hierarchical class structure predicated on ownership of private property, but with extremes of wealth and poverty eliminated among the citizens, who share in the exercise of the powers of sovereignty. The superior should rule over the inferior: e.g., notables over common folk, elders over juniors, parents over children, men over women, masters over slaves and serfs, and especially soul, mind, and reason over body and passion.

The rule of law, rather than personal rule, should prevail. Therefore, the favoured forms of government-according-to-law are kingship, aristocracy, and polity; and the corresponding opposed forms of personal rule are tyranny, oligarchy (really plutocracy), and extreme democracy. Rule of large numbers is better than the rule of one or a few, especially if unrestrained by law; and so democracy is preferable to tyranny and oligarchy at least in some instances, for it has at times produced substantial liberty. Although it is difficult to pin down because he considers the strengths and weaknesses of each form and their suitability for various circumstances, Aristotle's preference seems to be aristocracy, a government according to law by the meritorious few. However, in terms of more practicable forms, he seems to feel that most governments tend toward either democracy or oligarchy; and so the best achievable form is usually polity, a constitution which has various formulas for combining the wealthy (always an oligarchy, or government by the few) and the poor (always a democracy, or government by the many) in a balanced relationship based on dispensing a substantial amount of power, benefits, and honours to both. Under the polity Aristotle favours, unequals would not be treated arithmetically equally, but would be treated in ways considered proportionately equal to their merit and therefore just. It is in the final analysis a polity tilted in favour of plutocracy (government by the wealthy few). The non-citizen categories of the population – such as resident aliens, serfs, and slaves – would, of course, be denied the franchise, as well as the women. But Aristotle would go much farther, if he could, to prearrange his polity to favour what in practice would be a plutocratic oligarchy and away from democracy. Thus, in his ideal state, he would deny the status of citizen to large groups of agricultural workers, artisans, and urban labourers who in his day constituted the bulk of the Athenian democracy. Although the disenfranchised are to be treated with firmness, they are not, however, to be brutalized.

The highest purpose of the state, which aims to be a self-sufficient commonwealth, is to help and permit man, a sociable political animal, to fulfil his political, social, moral, and spiritual nature in concert with the rest of the community. According to the *Politics*, that requires a form of justice that may be substantially the same as that advocated by Plato – that each do what each is qualified to do. There are some differences, however: Aristotle is less concerned with specialization, unity, and uniformity, and feels that more freedom and rotation or periodic participation in government actually make for a more harmonious, stable, and enduring state and government. (But bear in mind always that in his ideal state, Aristotle would severely restrict the number of participants by depriving most of the working population of the status of citizen, as ignoble because of their banausic activity.) Also, his chief reliance for development and maintenance of a good *polis* is not on constitutional checks or structural aspects of government. Ultimately, as does Plato, Aristotle calls for a eugenically cultivated and carefully educated citizenry who have been soundly developed in soul or mind (reason), character (morals), and body (health) by a system of education (*paideia*) specially designed to support its particular form, and in accordance with God's will.

Thus, Aristotle's political system, in the final analysis, is founded on the optimistic assumption that enough of the population can be educated to be virtuous and active enough to provide a state that is satisfactorily efficient, safe, and just – and therefore promotes the happiness of those who dwell therein. This can be nothing other than a striving for constitutionalism, a verity recognized by Ernest Barker (1975, p. lxi) when he wrote:

> If we ask ourselves at the end of this summary review of the substance and argument of the *Politics*, 'What has been, and still is, the nature of the legacy which it bequeathed to the common thought of Europe?', the answer may almost be compressed in a single word. The word is 'constitutionalism'.[37]

But as with Plato, the disquieting question that does not go away is whether an arrangement of state and society that is based on hierarchy and exclusivism will not ineluctably lead to the injustice and consequent dissatisfaction, disorder, and revolt they firmly purposed to avoid. Aristotle's 'councillors' are too reminiscent of Plato's 'Guardians', and both philosophers sought to thwart too much the general will and impose a system of elitist rule that perhaps could maintain itself in power only by ultimately – or even habitually – resorting to the brutal use of force.

Notes

1   *Cf.* the translation from Zeller, 1845–52, of Part II, Division II, currently available as *Aristotle and the Earlier Peripatetics* (Costelloe and Muirhead, 1962): Russell and Russell, 1962, Vol. II, ch. XIII, which treats of the *Politics* as follows: 1. Necessity, Nature, and Function of the State; 2. The Household as a Constitutional Element of the State; 3. The State and the Citizens; 4. Forms of Constitution; 5. The Best State; 6. Imperfect Forms of Government.
    Additional works consulted in the preparation of this chapter include, as well as those listed in the preceding chapter, VII, 'Biographical Note on Aristotle', n. 1, pp. 181–2, the following: Bambrough, 1963 and 1965; Barker, 1959; Chance, 1968; Kort, 1952; Le Boutillier, 1950; Lloyd, 1968; Ross, 1964; Sinclair, 1968; Taylor, 1955; Troeltsch, 1931; Ullman, 1961, 1965, and 1975; and Voegelin, 1956–74, Vol. III, 1957. For a concise,

illuminating treatment of Aristotle's political writings, see especially Morrall, 1977, and Mulgan, 1977.

Nichols, 1992, was not available until after the present work had been submitted for publication. It merits careful, unhurried reading in its entirety. Nichols explains the purpose of her study when she writes in her Preface (p. viii) about Aristotle's *Politics*: 'The community between the philosopher and the city is a version of that between statesmen and citizens, as they rule and are ruled in turn. *Citizens and Statesmen* thus examines the meaning of Aristotle's argument that human beings are by nature political animals'. A partial summation of the conclusions reached in this examination reveals both appropriately grave and optimistic findings for a humanity constantly engaged in a multifaceted struggle with life wherein political conflict and rule inescapably play central roles (p. 169):

> Aristotle presents a vision of human life torn by conflict. Human beings try to enslave them. The poor seek the goods of the rich and the rich seek to increase their wealth at the expense of the poor. Virtuous individuals who want to rule unencumbered by their inferiors become tyrants. Competition and even war characterize the foreign relations of political communities. If tragedy is not in the foreground of politics, it lurks in the background, threatening to make an appearance. The necessity against which tragic heroes unsuccessfully rebel remains a limit to human life; slavery exists in Aristotle's best regime, and the concerns of defense must become an object for philosophy. Yet Aristotle's vision is not a tragic one. Aristotle objects to the *Republic*'s teaching that regimes inevitably degenerate and that founding is a tragic undertaking. His political theory depends on deliberate choice, law and equity, political rule, and friendship. Human beings can deliberate about their alternatives; there is a realm in which events can happen one way or another as a result of human choices and actions (*NE*, 112a15–b11). Law is not an imperfect substitute for the absence of statesmanship but the framework in which statesmen and citizens operate and the means by which they accomplish their common purposes. Political rule and the friendship it reflects, not mastery of slaves or overall kingship, manifests freedom (1325a23–30).

Thus, substantial attention is paid by Nichols to Aristotle's *Nicomachean Ethics* because, as opined in her Introduction (p. 7): 'The Politics is a continuation of, or at least a sequel to, the *Nicomachean Ethics*'. But as pointed out in the Preface to this work, the choice was made to concentrate herein on Plato and Aristotle's major works dealing more specifically with constitutionalism. Therefore, for extended consideration of fundamental philosophical assumptions that underlie Aristotle's entire range of political theory as presented especially in the *Nicomachean Ethics* and for reference to other related sources, see in its entirety Kraut, 1989.

For a monograph that treats of Aristotle's ethical views, with emphasis on justice and politics, see Tessitore, 1996. Tessitore states (p. 120) that Aristotle acknowledges a life of radical inquiry cannot be completely harmonized with the ethical doctrines contained in the *Ethics* and concludes that:

> Aristotle demonstrates rather than recommends a way through the impasse: The practice of political philosophy is characterized by both a concern for politics and an awareness of something beyond politics. Rather than prescribe a formula or propose a solution, Aristotle brings to light the competing demands of two ways of life that most merit attention and effectively invites his audience – philosophers and nonphilosophers alike – to find a balance or combination appropriate to their circumstances and abilities.

A highly relevant, comprehensive, well reasoned, and well supported study that is also recommended for its extensive bibliography, source notes, and habitually convenient inclusion of useful (save for non-identification of publishers) clarifying information and opinion, is a work that appeared after completion of the present one: Miller Jr, 1995. The task Miller set for himself and accomplished is described in the very first paragraph of his Preface (p. vii):

> Aristotle maintains that there is only one constitution which is everywhere according to nature the best (*Ethica Nichomachia* V 1135ª5). This book is a study of what I take to be the central argument of his *Politics* in support of this thesis: that constitution is best according to nature which is unqualifiedly just and which guarantees the rights of its citizens according to this standard. The best constitution serves as a standard by which politicians can establish, preserve, and reform different political institutions appropriate to a wide variety of social circumstances. I offer a reconstruction of Aristotle's political philosophy based upon examination of his texts, along with an assessment of his argument in the light of modern theories and concerns. I argue that Aristotle is a precursor of modern theorists of justice, that it is not anachronistic to understand him as concerned with individual rights, and that he makes an important contribution to our understanding of these concepts.

Among additional significant observations, Miller states (p. 55): '*Politics*, VIII 8, makes clear that the polis is a community rather than an organism.' Further citation is provided to support this conclusion: II 2 1261ª18–21 and 1261ᵇ10–15.

2 The subject of Aristotle's intended audience for the *Politics* and related writings is treated of in well-supported fashion in Bodéüs, 1993. In his epilogical 'Conclusion: Education, Ethics and Politics', Bodéüs finds (p. 123):

> The preceding investigations have shown that Aristotle's discussion of ethical problems corresponded to his most important concern, the instruction of the lawgiver. This concern will not seem peculiar if one remembers that the thinking of our philosopher places itself in the tradition of Plato, whose last important work is the *Laws*. Indeed, for Aristotle, as for Plato, legislation is the tool required for the realization of the ends pursued by life in the city, that is, not only political life but life in general as lived in the framework constituted by political organization.
>
> Put into perspective in this way, Aristotelian ethics, far from describing an individual ethics alien to politics, presents, on the contrary, the essential body of learning with which the lawgiver must fortify himself when legislating. Conversely, one might say that the main body of political issues discussed by the philosopher also presents learning which is to provide direction for heads of household, who are often responsible for the education of children and thus need to act, in a restricted context, as if they were lawgivers.

Although the advice given therein is often quite different from that offered by Plato or Aristotle, Bodéüs' comments here are reminiscent of a passage in the Introduction to *Lao Tzu: Tao te ching* [c. 500 BC], Lau, 1963, p. 32, that begins:

> Almost all ancient Chinese thinkers were concerned with the way one should lead one's life, and this was never confined to conduct in the personal sense, but covered the art of government as well. Politics and ethics, for the Chinese as for the ancient Greeks, were two aspects of the same thing, and this the Chinese thinkers called the

tao. One who has the *tao* will, in the words of the *T'ien hsia* chapter of the *Chuang tzu*, be 'inwardly a sage and outwardly a true king'.

3   Unless otherwise noted, the translations from Aristotle's *Politics* presented throughout this chapter are from Jowett, 1885. Translation of the text is contained in Vol. I. For the Greek text of the *Politics* and a opposite-page translation into English, as well as extensive commentary, see Rackham, Vol. XXI, 1972. It may also be useful at times to compare the Jowett and Rackham translations and comments with those provided by Barker by reference to the same column and page division (chapters and chapter sections of these editions do not always correspond because of editorial changes made by Barker). If available, for the Greek text and discussion of the development of the manuscript, its contents, its authenticity, attempts to insert spurious sections and various extant copies and editions, see Newman, 1887–1902, especially the general introduction in Vol. I and the volume introduction to Vol. II. The critical notes and commentary are copious and extremely useful for elucidation of probable intent and meaning of words and phrases.

See also the discussion of why the household (*oikos*: οἶκος) is absolutely necessary for an aristocracy and how concord (*homonia*: ὁμονία) unites this lesser association or community (*koinonia*: κοινωνία) into the larger *koinonia* – the *polis* – necessary to realize human potentiality fully, in Wood and Wood, 1978, pp. 227–37. See also the discussion of *eunomia* (εὐνομία), which is often translated as 'good order', in Garner, 1987, p. 26.

4   See in its entirety the treatment given the important question of what Aristotle regarded as public or private and what he believed was the role of each sphere in Swanson, 1992. It may be argued by some that Swanson's view of liberalism is too narrow because of its individualistic characterization (e.g., p. 207); but see for citation of key passages and plausible speculation, including general conclusion reached, especially pp. 204 ff:

> In sum, Aristotle makes clear that human beings are not simply political animals (in the sense of inclined toward others) but, insofar as they have a divine element in them, also intensely private beings. 'Happiness extends just so far as contemplation does' (*NE*, 1178b28–29). Of course, 'the happy person is a human being, and so will need external prosperity also' – that is, 'bodily health, food, and [human] attention [*tēn loipēn therapeian*]' (1178n33–35). Nature compels the philosophical and all those who aspire to happiness to use the resources of both the public and the private. But in contrast to the noble citizen or ruler, who draws on the private to serve the public, the philosopher draws on the public to serve the private.

For consideration of Aristotle's philological, ethical, and action-oriented views on justice, see the essay by Bambrough, in Bambrough, 1965. See also Masters, 1990, especially the conclusions on 'The Implications of Naturalism in Political Theory' (pp. 204–7) which posit that views of human nature, virtue, and natural justice may have rationally intelligible foundations: i.e., essentially what Aristotle maintained. For a collection of contemporary philosophical viewpoints and argumentation on the subject of women's capacity for the objective use of evidence and valid use of reason, see Antony and Witt, 1993; and see especially the discursive review of its contents and related topics by Nussbaum, 1994.

Rawls, 1971, pp. 10 f, comments:

> It is evident that this definition is framed to apply to actions, and persons are thought to be just insofar as they have, as one of the permanent elements of their character, a steady and effective desire to act justly. Aristotle's definition clearly presupposes,

however, an account of what properly belongs to a person and of what is due to him. Now such entitlements are, I believe, very often derived from social institutions and the legitimate expectations to which they give rise. There is no reason to think Aristotle would disagree with this, and certainly he has a conception of social justice to account for these claims. The definition I adopt is designed to apply directly to the most important case, the justice of the basic structure.

For wider treatment of Aristotle on justice and related ideas, see Hardie, 1968, especially ch. X, 'Justice', pp. 182–211.

For some consideration of how Aristotle concludes it can be just and right, instead of arbitrary, for one to rule over others – i.e., 'in virtue of his rational superiority' in their relationship – see Everson, 1988, especially p. 97.

For a view of contemporary currents of thought, globally, see ideas presented by Fay, 1990, an ethicist, in a thoughtful article which cogently argues the applicability of Aristotelian principles in attempting to reach just determination of current issues such as even the 'right to life of the foetus' versus the 'right to abortion of the woman' (pp. 90–4):

> We have rights alleged, literally from the cradle, or more properly before the cradle, to the grave, and even beyond. Thus Right to Life groups assert rights for the fetus on one end of the spectrum and on the other end some rights theorists even claim rights for the dead.[1] ([1] See for example Loren Lamasky, *Persons, Rights and the Moral Community* [New York: Oxford University Press, 1987], pp. 212–221.) ...
>
> ... And of course, as is well known, Jeremy Bentham thought of the whole idea of rights as 'nonsense on stilts'. ...
>
> And so it seems a useful course is to try to seek out an Aristotelian mean[6] ([6] Lomasky, *op. cit.*, p. 14.) between the Scylla of moral and legal discourse which is rendered difficult or impossible by the explosive creation of asserted rights on the one hand, and the Charybdis of the total abnegation of rights which safeguard our individual liberties on the other.

For a concise account of the central role the concept of the law (*nomos*) plays in Aristotle's political theory and his belief that what is lawful and what is just may at times be different, see Schroeder, 1981–82. Note the six types of law – consisting of three paired categories – that Schroeder finds in Aristotle's writings (pp. 19 f):

> It is possible to identify six types of law in Aristotle's writings. Each of these categories is not exclusive of all the others, but there are three pairs of mutually exclusive categories. Laws may be: customary or enacted; written or unwritten; and particular or general (or common) law. These pairs of categories intersect, so we may speak of written or unwritten customary laws and particular or common written law.
>
> In the distinction between customary and enacted law the former appears more important.

See also Schroeder's discussion of Aristotle's views on 'Natural Law' (pp. 23–6) and 'The Means and End of Law' (pp. 26 ff).

5 Aristotle would appear to believe here that Plato advocated a community of women, children, and property that was not limited to the Guardian class; however, he states at 1262 a that 'it seems more serviceable for the Farmers to have this community of wives and sons than the Guardians ...'.

Saxonhouse, 1992, appeared after draft of the present work had been completed, but must be noted. See in its entirety, especially with reference to Aristotle, pp. 189–232, and Plato, pp. 93–183, and an apt comparison, pp. 234 ff. Saxonhouse explains her purpose and presents her basic finding in her Preface, pp. x f:

> This book is about the fear of diversity – a fear that differences bring on chaos and thus demands that the world be put into an orderly pattern. Part of that order is to see the unity underlying the apparent variety of the world we experience with our sense. It is the poetic art and philosophic reason that can go behind the observed, the physical differences, or the cultural differences between a Priam and an Achilles and make us recognize their common humanity. At the same time, though, the pursuit of unity can create a world that tries to eliminate that which is not easily accommodated into this underlying unity, a world that finds diversity so threatening that it collapses all into one, avoids the multiplicity of human experience, and leaves us immobile and sterile.
>
> I do not intend in this book to suggest that the Greeks lead us to one or the other perspective. Rather, we see them grappling with the dangers of the extremes on either side. With the exception of the pre-Socratics, all the Greek authors with whom I deal warn of the danger of striving for too much unity; human beings are separate bodies, they emerge from particular families, they develop particularized relationships. The city will always be limited by that which it cannot fully assimilate into itself – for the Greeks, in particular, this was the female, sexuality, and the family. While the others warn us, however, it is only Aristotle who, accepting the centrality of sight for understanding, is able to overcome the fear and welcome the diverse.
>
> … He acknowledges the sense and uses them to explore a multiplicity of political regimes and the multiplicity of parts that comprise the regime – and thus he gives birth to political science. Epistemologically, Aristotle allows us – and encourages us – to see the many with our eyes and to build a polity out of differences rather than unity.

For consideration of the methodology – rhetoric – that Aristotle often employs to give reasoned support to his political ideas and purposes and to make them more persuasive, see in its entirety Arnhart, 1981. The specific rhetorical device habitually relied upon by Aristotle – the enthymeme – involves reasoning that is less rigorous than the strictly deductive syllogism because it is in part based on inductive inference derived from commonly held views or information; and so the enthymeme may contain as one of its premises some looser, implicit, or intuitive kind of argumentation as well as 'more scientific' forms of logical demonstration.

6 *Cf.* a decidedly darker judgment of Aristotle and his opinion of humankind found in a reading of the same portion of the *Politics*, Wood and Wood, 1978, e.g., pp. 215 f.

7 It should be noted that Aristotle here, as does Plato before him, uses the term oligarchy to identify government by the wealthy, although plutocracy would be more correct, especially today. Care should also be taken not to confuse aristocracy, which is government by the able (who are presumed to be few), with either plutocracy (also presumed to be a government by the few) or with oligarchy in the general sense (simply government by the few). See also the observations in Miller, 1995, p. 253, n. 3, that:

> Plato, *Statesman*, 302^{d}3–5, distinguishes between a good and bad form of democracy, the former corresponding to Aristotle's polity, the latter to his democracy. Polybius, [*Histories* – RP] VI 4 6, uses 'democracy' for the good form and 'ochlocracy' for the deviation.

For consideration of the future influence of Aristotle's ideas on mixed, balanced government, a good starting point is Blythe, 1992.

8 For Aristotle's contribution to legal theory, including the Roman system of law, see Sorabji, 1980, pp. 288–98, with emphasis on 'tragic error'.

For clarifying treatment of Aristotle's politico-economic ideas, see Polanyi, 1968. Polanyi (pp. 78 f) rebuts charges of simplisticism on the part of Aristotle, who rejected the unlimited 'unnatural urge of money-making' and favoured that 'prices should conform to justice'. See also philological discussion, pp. 112–5.

9 See also Winthrop, 1978, who states (p. 1201): 'to be sure, he had a theory of justice, and from this fact we might infer that he thought it necessary to have one. But the argument I shall make is that Aristotle thought all theories of justice, including his own, to be insufficient.' Accordingly, Winthrop notes (p. 1203, n. 5): 'While less willing to attack the law publicly, Aristotle is less convinced than many of us that there are universal principles of justice in the name of which to attack laws that appear to deviate from the just.' Instead, Aristotle is represented (p. 1206) as believing: 'The rule of a law which distinguishes in a formulaic manner the just from the unjust is preferable to the rule of human beings who would presumably make such distinctions with only their own good in mind.'

Cf. Wiltshire, 1992, especially pp. 12 f, who asserts an independent existence of natural law in Aristotle and calls on John Locke in support of her viewpoint:

> Aristotle insists, first, that there is a distinction between laws that merely have been enacted, which may or may not be good laws, and those that have been enacted well, that is, enacted according to the higher law of nature. In the same context he distinguishes between laws that are best for the individuals for whom they are enacted and laws that are absolutely best.[16] ([16] Aristotle, *Politics* 1294a7–9 [4.8.6].) Thus, for Aristotle, natural law has an existence apart from the conventional or positive laws that human beings enact to deal with matters of everyday justice.

The tripartite system of division of classes (artisans, farmers, and warriors) and of landholding (religious, public and private) attributed by Aristotle to Hippodamus (1267 b) bears interesting comparison to Plato's subsequent scheme set forth especially in the *Republic* (376 B–434 C).

10 For a revisionist approach to Aristotle on women and politics, see the carefully argued position in Levy, 1990.

For further discussion, sources, and bibliographical references concerning Aristotle's views on women, see Okin, 1979, especially pp. 5 f, 73–96, 233–6 and 347–51. See also Saxonhouse, 1986, who perceives (p. 416): 'The artificial equality of citizens in a polity is a practical solution, but one which means the failure of Aristotle's theory, for such equality denies what he would understand as the rule of the best'.

For a discussion of congruent and contrasting views of Plato and Aristotle on the subject and for reference to additional relevant articles, see Smith, 1983, who declares (p. 477):

> Unlike Plato, Aristotle does not believe the soul to be essentially sexless; the souls of women and men are as different by nature as their bodies are. Also unlike Plato, therefore, Aristotle does not restrict the natural differences and inferiorities of women to merely physical capacities, such as strength. As their bodies are too weak for some purposes, so their souls are too weak for others, each weakness an effect of the same basic causes, which occur in the reproductive process. Hence, what is an unnatural domination in Plato – that of men over women – becomes a natural one in Aristotle.

This last statement, however, may be subject to some challenge with respect to Plato. See, e.g., ch. VI, 'A Natural Right to Rule', pp. 101–4 above, discussing *Laws*, 690 A–C.

For a work that treats of much the same topic and considers as well the impact of Aristotle's views on medieval society and present-day activists, see also Coole, 1988, especially pp. 19–48.

Both Plato and Aristotle would, no doubt, have been confounded by such a modern document as 'An Act to establish a Human Rights Commission and to promote the advancement of human rights in New Zealand in general accordance with the United Nations International Covenants on Human Rights', 21 November 1977. Typical of the purposes of this act is the prohibition contained in Part II, 15 (2): 'It shall be unlawful for any person concerned with procuring employment for other persons or procuring employees for an employer to treat any person seeking employment differently from other persons in the same or substantially similar circumstances by reasons of the sex, marital status, or religious or ethical belief of that person'. The text and analysis of this document are included in Roger S. Clark (1987), *Constitutions of the Countries of the World: New Zealand* in Blaustein and Flanz, 1971–, pp. 407–60; see p. 415 for provision quoted. See also the Supplement (1988) which contains the text of the Constitution Act 1986 (No. 114) that came into force on 11 January 1987 and consolidated the dominion's 'constitution'.

Of similar character is the Basic Law of the Federal Republic of Germany (promulgated 21 May 1949), especially Article 3 (Equality before the law), as amended 19 March 1956. For constitutional chronology, 1954–84, and the text of this document as amended and updated through 1983, see Flanz (1985), *Constitutions of the Countries of the World: Federal Republic of Germany* in Blaustein and Flanz, 1971–, especially p. 44.

Even more forthright in its advocacy of equality – in all respects – is the Constitution of the Kingdom of the Netherlands (1983), which begins with Chapter 1, Fundamental Rights, Article 1. For constitutional chronology, 1974–83 and the text of this document, see Flanz (1984), *Constitutions of the Countries of the World: The Netherlands* in Blaustein and Flanz, 1971–, especially p. 3.

See also Polin, 1979, pp. 66–71, on the 'Modern Classification of Human Rights and the Role of the Universal Declaration of Human Rights' (10 December 1948).

For treatment of conflicting conceptions of justice from the Homeric to the present era, see MacIntyre, 1988. MacIntyre makes a case for confirmation of the practical rationality – and hence the continuing relevance – of the Aristotelian-Thomistic tradition of justice.

11 See also Bk IV, 3, 1290 a, where Aristotle declares:

> It must not be assumed, as some are fond of saying, that democracy is simply that form of government in which the greater number are sovereign, for in oligarchies, and indeed in every government, the majority rules; nor again is oligarchy that form of government in which a few are sovereign.

12 See again Bk III, 1277 b. See in its entirety, including notes and sources, von Leyden, 1985, especially the following statement (p. 3):

> For Aristotle recognised that a truly defensible definition of equality depended on a compromise between the two doctrines of distributive justice prevalent in his day. One was the democrats' assertion that equality in respect of free birth, or that each man was to count for only one, represented the principal aspect of equality, and hence could be generalized so as to mean equality in any respect whatsoever. The other was the oligarchs' thesis that superiority in one respect (e.g. wealth, or nobility of birth) meant

superiority on all counts.

See also the assessment of restrictions on equality by Aristotle as perceived by von Leyden, n. 17, p. 127; and the review of von Leyden by Mulgan, 1987, who writes (p. 143): 'Aristotle is therefore properly described as a natural justice theorist but not as a natural law theorist'.

Glassman, 1989, *passim*, justifiably focuses on Aristotle's ideas concerning proportionate equality, justice, and democracy, with comparatively minor attention given to those of Plato (although in some respects they are quite similar and Plato expounded them earlier). Perhaps the principal value of this work is that it shows some of the great issues of social order, justice, and efficiency addressed in classical times to be essentially the same as those related to major problems of our own times.

For some of the classical roots of what Glassman treats of, see O'Neil, 1995. Especially relevant here is Appendix 3, 'Aristotle's Classification of Democracies', pp. 181–4, where he discerns that:

> Within democracy, Aristotle recognises four classifications. First democracy (also called ancestral - *patria* - at 1305a29) is Aristotle's preferred form. Its magistrates are chosen from those who have a high census-class (*timêma*) (1292b29, 1318b29), and the people are made up of a farming population (*to geôrgikon*) which does not desire frequent assembly meetings (1292a25, 1319a4). At 1291b39 Aristotle recognises a separate subdivision of this type in which the census requirements for office are lower.
>
> Aristotle twice divides his intermediate types of democracy into two. The second democracy is where all citizens are eligible to hold office, subject to checks (*euthynê*) that they are qualified by birth (*kata genos*), and the law, not the people, rules (1292b34, cf. 1292a1). In the third type, all citizens (1292a2) or all free men (1292b28) are eligible and the law, not the people, rules. ...
>
> His last type is final democracy (also called 'newest' at 1305a24). This term implies Aristotle's teleological theory, in that this constitution is the logical (if regrettable) development of democracy. In it the masses, and not the law, rule (1292a4, 1293a9, 1298b14, 1305a24). There is pay for office, so that all citizens are not only eligible to participate but also can afford to do so (1292b41), the people are made up of craftsmen (*banausoi*) and wage-earners (1296b28), and such democracies have large populations, again requiring pay for office (1320b17).

O'Neil as well points out that:

> In recent years M.H. Hansen[1] ([1] *The Sovereignty of the People's Court*, 13–14. R. Sealy [*The Athenian Republic*] accepts his arguments.) has argued that fourth-century Athens should not be considered a 'final' democracy in Aristotle's terms, in view of the stress laid by Athenians on their respect for the rule of law and the existence of rules for changing law, not by the assembly but by careful consideration by a panel of jurymen acting as *nomothetai*. This, he argues, shows the laws ruled, not the people.

See also O'Neil's definitions and criteria, pp. 1 ff.

13 It is useful, again, to compare the translation of this passage with that provided by Barker, 1975, including his explanatory notes (e.g., concerning *eudaimonia*, n. 1, p. 118).

14 Again, *cf.* Barker's (1975) translation of this passage.

Cf. also a work that has some challenging views of Aristotle's treatment, and claimed lack of treatment, of executive power, despite his extensive consideration especially of various forms of monarchy or royal power including tyranny, its corrupt form: Mansfield, 1989. Mansfield states (p. 24): 'In fact, his book contains only one passage [cited as 1321b2–1323a11] that directly addresses executive power'. Some may find this questionable (e.g., *cf.* 1285 b–1288 a), and the examples given may be viewed as officials entrusted more with administrative duties. However, Mansfield's ideas merit attention throughout and offer more than the ambivalence of executive power; for he presents dilemmas and paradoxes that Aristotle himself would say do not admit of any absolute or 'fail-safe' formulas but do require executive adherence to the law and its intent. See, therefore, also Mansfield, 1985, where a strong case is made for constitutionalism.

Indeed, Aristotle clearly holds that the proper exercise of the executive power requires above all else the proper attitude toward law and its intent; and this entails a sympathetic attitude toward the needs and sense of the community (see again n. 3 above on the nature of the community, the *koinonia*, as viewed by Aristotle) and its members. Thus, an essentially Aristotelian approach to law that is probably just as applicable to the proper role of its chief executive, is to be found in the concluding words of Dworkin, 1986, p. 413:

> Law's attitude is constructive: it aims, in the interpretative spirit, to lay principle over practice to show the best route to a better future, keeping the right faith with the past. It is, finally, a fraternal attitude, an expression of how we are united in community though divided in project, interest, and conviction. That is, anyway, what law is for us: for the people we want to be and the community we aim to have.

15 Note the allowance for something similar to the English legal principle and practice of an Equity proceeding. See also Barker, 1975, n. 4, p. 146.

16 See also Barker, 1975, n. 2, p. 151. Since the topic of a 'god-like' king of superlative virtue who would be entitled to rule absolutely according to his own judgment and aside from provisions of law is discussed seemingly *en passant* and perhaps only hypothetically, is Aristotle here casting an anxious glance over his shoulder at the awesome figure of Philip II of Macedon, or latterly his son Alexander? *Cf.* in its entirety Newell, 1991.

17 It is also to be noted that Aristotle himself also raises the question whether such a simplistic type of rule by majority vote is really democratic. It is even more important to understand that Aristotle's strictures against simple majority rule miss the mark if applied to modern democracy. Indeed, modern democracy is characterized by both the principle of majority rule and its correlative principles of *limited government*: i.e., government limited by a constitution and the rule of law in letter and spirit, and wherein fundamental rights of the individual or group are thus not subject to infringement by majority vote. See, e.g., Polin, 1979, especially chs 2, 5, and 16. More especially, see *idem*, 1981a, pp. 49 ff.

Again, *cf.* Barker's 1975 translation of this passage.

18 There is an interesting similarity in this conclusion to John C. Calhoun's 'theory of the concurrent majority'. Verbatim presentation of Calhoun's argument in favour of this concept of a '*constitutional* majority' is widely available, e.g., in Mason and Baker, 1985, particularly p. 494, taken from *A Disquisition on Government* (1850). One may regard the negatively determining action of the provincial legislature of Manitoba by their refusal to ratify the Meech Lake Accord in June of 1990 as an example in practice of Calhoun's principle by a significant element of Canada's population, her aborigines, who felt their rights were being ignored by the politically more powerful 'English' and 'French' elements. Note the tactics and remarks of Elijah Harper, a legislative member of Ojibwa-Cree origin, as recorded in Maybury-Lewis, 1992a, and as reported upon in the accompanying book, Maybury-Lewis, 1992b, pp. 253–64.

For concise, systematic explication of its subject, see in its entirety Johnson, 1990. Johnson raises central questions (e.g., 'what is the state or constitution', pp. xi f and 47–65) and provides basic distinctions and descriptions (e.g., of 'polity' and of the 'middle regime', pp. 143–54; and of the 'best state absolutely', pp. 155–69) that are clearly posed and discussed. For example, Johnson explains:

> Polity is consistently defined as a *mix* of wealthy and poor in the regime, but it is a mix of a specific sort, namely one in which the poor are at least wealthy enough to supply themselves with arms and possess at the same time that part of virtue called courage. The middle regime, by contrast, is not a mixture but rather a 'middling part'.

19 The middle course, way, or position so favoured by Aristotle, and also Plato (see, e.g., *Laws*, Bk III, 694 A, 701 E and especially Bk VI, 757 A), is termed *meson* (μέσον). For a many-faceted recent treatment, see in its entirety Salkever, 1990, especially pp. 76–9, 116–9, 139–42, and 239–44, most especially the listings in chart from on p. 240.

Eudaimonia (ευδαιμονία) is explicated by Barker, 1975, pp. lxxv f:

> It has been noted, more than once, that the Latin element in our English speech is not always a good conductor of the sense with which Greek words are charged. But there are times when Latin may stand us in good and happy stead. The Greek word *eudaimonia* may furnish us with an instance. It is generally translated by the word 'happiness'. But happiness carries with it the material association of pleasure; and *eudaimonia* is a word of different and higher associations. Literally it means the condition of being under a good genius [or rather, demon – RP]; and it is defined in the *Politics*[3] ([3] Book VII, c. xiii, § 5.) as a state of activity (and not of enjoyment), which consists in the energy and practice of goodness. It is thus a conquest rather than a happening or good hap; and it may be better expressed by the Latin word 'felicity' than by any other word. 'Bliss' and 'blessedness' might perhaps serve; but they raise philological difficulties, and they import the religious associations of Christianity. 'Felicity' has the felicity of matching most nearly the shade of meaning in the original Greek.

For discussion of the 'doctrine of the mean', see Lloyd, 1968, especially pp. 217–27, and also 192 f, 255 and 290 f. Also see the insightful discussion of the 'golden mean' by Elliott and McDonald, 1949, pp. 175–9. The place of this doctrine in ancient Greek culture and attitudes is indicated by Durant, 1926, p. 88: 'The Seven Wise Men had established the tradition by engraving, on the temple of Apollo at Delphi, the motto *medeñ agan* – nothing in excess'. For a brief observation on its carry-over in Cicero in Roman times and St John of Salisbury in medieval times, including consideration of its relationship to virtues and forms of vice, see Nederman, 1986. For an observation on its role in Jewish religious thought, see Levíne, 1976. Levine states (pp. 192 f):

> [I]f one wishes to gain a proper understanding of the Bible and later rabbinic writings, one has to study Greek philosophy which Falaquera [Shem Tob Ben Joseph, 1225–90 – RP] and other Jewish and non-Jewish savants maintain was originally derived from teachings of Solomon and other Jewish sages. ... As far as human conduct was concerned, Falaquera advocated the golden mean which Maimonides had adopted from Aristotle: 'If a man constantly guards his actions,' said Maimonides, 'so that he maintains the proper balance between excess and deficiency, he will gain the highest degree of excellence and will come nearer to an understanding of the Creator and partake of His blessing.'

An earthier view of the mean that follows hard upon a similar elucidation (p. 251) of the 'passionate joy' of *erôs* (ἔρως), is to be found at the conclusion (p. 252) of a very instructive, lively work: Kitto, 1957:

> The Greek had little need to simulate passion. He sought control and balance because he needed them; he knew the extremes only too well. When he spoke of the Mean, the thought of the tuned string was never very far from his mind. The Mean did not imply the absence of tension and lack of passion, but the correct tension which gives out the true clear note.

Continuing note should also be taken that the Mean is associated in Aristotle's mind with polity, which for him is the most practicable form of government and one for which he is willing to settle. Miller, 1995, pp. 252 f, also makes this point and discerns it in Plato as well as in argumentation that supported adoption of the Constitution of the United States of America:

> The 'constitution of our prayers', though possible in principle, was unattainable in Aristotle's view ... He accordingly proposes an alternative constitution in which he thinks most polises could partake (*Politics*, IV 11 1295ª30–1). He remarks that Plato had a similar aim in the *Laws* (*Pol.* II 2 1265ª3; cf. *Laws*, V 739ª1–ᵇ7). Such a constitution is the 'second sailing' or second-best solution.[1] ([1] 'Second sailing' (*deuteros plous*) refers to the use of oars when there is no wind to fill the sails. See *Pol.* 13 1284ᵇ19; *Ethica Nichomachea* II 9 1109ª34–5; Plato, *Statesman*, 300ᶜ2; cf. Plato, *Phdo.* 99ᶜ9–ᵈ1 and *Phlb.* 19ᶜ2–3.) The leading example of this is polity, which, despite its shortcomings, Aristotle includes as one of the three types of correct constitution in *Politics*, III. *Politics*, IV, in effect extends the 'second-best' category to include a group of mixed constitutions which are not deviations but fall short of the most correct constitution (IV 8 1293ᵇ22–7).

20 See the discussion of Aristotelian forms of justice, especially 'distributive' justice (the *proportional* allotment of honours, benefits, and burdens) and 'rectificatory' justice (the righting of commercial injuries), in Wood and Wood, 1978, pp. 237–43. The Woods conclude elsewhere (p. 209) that: 'Aristotle's doctrines seem to reflect an aristocratic and oligarchic bias as clearly as do the teachings of Socrates and Plato ... Aristotle's social and political ideas are fundamentally ideological, forged as weapons to be used in the political struggles of the age'. Perhaps this is correct if we adhere to use of 'fundamentally' as a matter of general intent and design, but not as exclusively so or simplistically tendentious. Some of the Aristotelian pro-agrarian ideas about urban capitalistic economics touched on by the Woods (e.g., pp. 227–37) may quite properly be viewed as proto-Marxian as well as anti-democratic, anti-egalitarian, and anti-libertarian.

See also Barker, 1975, pp. lxix–lxxii, a source cited by Wood and Wood which expands on the subject of justice in Aristotelianism in a number of different directions; and Garner, 1987, especially pp. 2–30, including source notes and the extensive bibliography, pp. 145–51.

In a concise, analytical work that makes a number of illuminating observations about Aristotle's underlying political principles, Michael Davis (1996) postulates that Aristotle attributes a paradoxical nature to justice and also advances a principle for its reconciliation (pp. 121 f):

> In Book 3, the *pambasileus* is so superior because he has a kind of knowledge that no

one else in the city has. But his knowledge of distributive justice, of political philosophy, so distinguishes him that, were he to receive his just deserts, all others in the city would be deprived of political life. In democracy, articulating and acting on the principle of the regime – freedom leading to equality – undermines the principle of the regime. And polity is actually constructed on the basis of the regime's misunderstanding of itself. Books 7 and 8 are meant to reconcile these two strands of the argument of the *Politics*: the emphasis on the good or wisdom in Books 1–3 that culminates in *pambasileia* and the emphasis on the just or freedom in Books 4–6 that culminates in democracy.

The instrument of this reconciliation is the beautiful – the *kalon*. The regime that preserves itself because the good it aims at is education for the sake of something more than its own preservation will be a regime where knowing and doing can be reconciled.

The present writer, however, believes this passage should be read in a light that allows for the *pambasileus* to be an unavailable – rhetorically and hypothetically posed – figure necessary to compete the logic of Aristotle's case in favour of a polity tilted towards oligarchy (and hopefully towards aristocracy) as a reasonably practicable and practical form of government when a theoretically more nearly ideal form can not be had.

21 See again the discussion of *stasis* in ch. I, n. 1 above; in Burnet, 1900, pp. xlvi f, n. 2; and in Wood and Wood, 1978, pp. 237–49. Wood and Wood conclude (p. 243) that, in addition to supportive modes of education: 'Aristotle's fundamental prescription for the disease of *stasis* can be reduced to the ideas of combining in a polity the oligarchic principle of proportionate equality in such a way with the democratic principle of numerical equality as to oligarchize democracy'. One may ask if this is not the same plan Plato offers in the *Laws*, 643 B–645 C and 741 E–750 A.

For a positive view of the role of *stasis*, see the essay by Finley, 1976, reprinted in Shaw and Saller, 1982, especially pp. 80 ff:

Changes in the matrix of rights that prevail in any society normally begin in a struggle over specific issues, not over abstract concepts or slogans. The rhetoric and the abstractions come later, and then are reified. Consider *stasis*, civil strife, in the Greek world. Although the dominant line of Greek writers, from Thucydides to Aristotle, called it the greatest of evils, they had little impact on the Greek people, who went on with their *staseis* unrelentingly. Why? Because, Aristotle concluded in our textbook on Greek *stasis*, the fifth book of his *Politics*, one sector of the community sought more *kerdos* [κέρδος –RP], profit, gain, material advantage, and more *time*, honour (1302a32): two concrete, definable objectives. The methods employed ranged from normal political means to open civil war; the intellectual argument, when there was one, centred round the concept of equality, the only abstraction which Aristotle introduced into his analysis.

...

One of the most important privileges of the Greek citizen was the freedom to engage in *stasis*. I am being neither frivolous nor perverse. A quarter of a century ago Loenen made the acute, and still generally neglected, observation that 'illegality is simply not the *constant* hallmark of *stasis*. The label *stasis* was also applied to completely legal groups, existing or arising, between whom there were permanent oppositions and tensions which did not burst into spectacular forms.'[9] ([9] Loenen [1953] 5.] Freedom that does not include the freedom to change is empty. So is the freedom of advocacy that does not include the freedom to combine with others. And change, as I have already said, entails the loss of some rights by some members of the community. They resist, hence *stasis.*

The paper quoted from by Finley, in translation from the Dutch, is Loenen, 1953.

22 This seems to be a thrust at the arrangements Plato advocated that would weight matters against the many. One may then ask if Aristotle is not engaged in the same type of enterprise.

23 Aristotle seems to have put his finger directly on the hope of modern democratic elections: for the many to participate in a selection of the best; i.e., an aristocracy of ability chosen by democratic process.

24 Also relevant here is a comment contained in V, x, 1316 b: '... although when some of the leaders have lost their properties they stir up innovations, when men of the other classes are ruined nothing strange happens ....' *Cf.* Barker's 1975 translation: 'What *is* true is that when any of the leading men lose their property, they become revolutionaries.'

25 The beginning of the above quotation is, of course, reminiscent of Pericles' Funeral Oration, attributed by some to Aspasia, his consort. Kagan, 1991, p. 182, does not take seriously this attribution by Plato in the *Menexenus* [236 b and 249 d]; and uncertainty that Plato was even the author of the *Menexenus* is expressed by Benjamin Jowett in his Introduction to this short work (1953, Vol. I, pp. 677 ff).

26 See also Barker's 1975 translation here. This would seem to be an admission by Aristotle that democracy conceivably could be a government of the many, rather than of the poor; but the authenticity of this passage has been questioned.

For a cogent discussion of Aristotle on democracy that presents a convincing description of the Athenian *politeia* that on some points is decidedly not in agreement with Aristotle's views on the workings of democracy, see Strauss, in Lord and O'Connor, 1991. E.g., Strauss disputes (p. 221) Aristotle's contention (*Ath. Pol.* 41.2) that the common people were exercising 'ever-increasing power' and adds (p. 222):

> Furthermore, Aristotle goes too far when he denies that Athenian democracy was a regime of the rule of law. The opposite – that fourth century democracy did respect the rule of law – has been cogently argued in recent research, particularly that of M.H. Hansen. Hansen lays great emphasis on the careful Athenian distinction between *nomos* and *psēphisma*, demonstrating that the Assembly was careful not to pass general and permanent rules (*nomoi*), but to reserve them for the separate process of *nomothesia.* Hansen also stresses the importance of the *graphē paranomon,* the public indictment for proposing in the Assembly an illegal law or decree, and the prosecution *nomon mē epitēdeion theinai,* for 'making an unsuitable law.' Hansen concludes, therefore, that fourth-century Athens was indeed ruled by law.

This entire collection of essays is relevant to the subject of Aristotle on constitutionalism, and all of them present noteworthy sources in the supporting footnotes. For revealing additional speculation and analytical assessments by Strauss, see especially pp. 229–33. For probing analysis of Aristotle's own conception of justice, which relies especially on the *Nicomachean Ethics* and is based on principles other than 'the recognized principle of democratic justice, that all should count equally', see also in this collection O'Connor, 1991. See especially the conclusions on pp. 162 ff that include the following remarks;

> From the perspective of virtue in relation to others, the just man's limited interest in external goods makes it possible for him to share with others, since he is not bent on getting as much as he can from them. He will be satisfied with a 'median' amount in the sense that he demands an amount sufficient for living well and virtuously (and thus won't accept being deprived unjustly of a share commensurate to his virtue) but not an

amount that brings him into conflict with the reasonable claims of others.

Since justice is virtue considered in relation to others, it is this second, 'external' mean that is of primary importance. This is why justice is a mean primarily between suffering and committing injustice, not between too little and too much concern for external goods. But this 'interpersonal' mean is in no sense prior to the 'intrapersonal' mean defined by the requirements of virtuous activity. Indeed, it is defined with reference to the 'intrapersonal' mean; for the aim of the community is to promote the virtue (and thus the happiness) of each of its members. In a sense, then, the just man is conceptually prior to the just distribution: he is prior *qua* virtuous simply, not *qua* just. As a result, in Aristotle's view an indifference to just distribution is based on an underlying misorientation, since a man's unwillingness to abide by the mean in his relations with others is just the 'political' manifestation of his failure to abide by the mean psychically.
...

... The only guarantee of good citizenship is the proper psychic disposition toward the pleasures and pains that motivate human action.

For a variety of insightful views, including commentary that deals especially with the more important role of the larger community of the *polis* and the corollary role of family life in the *oikia* in developing the defining qualities of humanity and the just ordering of life, see also in this collection Salkever, 1991.

27 See also Barker's 1975 translation of this passage in the text and in n. 1, p. 270.
28 See the discussion of the broader import of Aristotle on geographical position in Saxonhouse, 1983, especially pp. 35 ff, who clearly states the greater importance Aristotle assigned to 'inherent limitations' (see p. 6 above) as against 'institutional arrangements' (see pp. 5–6 above):

The two extremes of heat and cold represent the two extremes of political life. It is only in the moderation between the two that we can find our best city. It is in the character of the people, more than in the political structure (about which Aristotle says strikingly little here considering his elaborate earlier detailing and classification of regimes) that the unity necessary for the existence of the best *politeia* resides. That character is the result of many interacting variables. Climate is, as Aristotle knows well, only one. The power of education over nature is a subject of a later chapter in Book 7 (Chapter 17, esp. 1336a15–21); it is a section which will call into question all his generalizations here. Both *ethos* and *logos* (habit and reason) are capable of transforming what is given by nature. With the proper training, the men from both the north and the south could learn to moderate the climatically determined traits and become similar to what the Greeks are by nature. The advantage which the Greeks have is simply one which comes from chance, not from moral worth. Aristotle is not simply glorifying the Greek city in which he often finds much that is faulty. Rather, he is suggesting how political communities of all sorts and all times must be built on the reconciliation of opposing forces and needs: isolation and interaction (war); freedom and domination.

Cf. the response by Davis, 1986, who demurs on a number of points, e.g., as follows (pp. 35 f):

My impression ... is that Saxonhouse excessively intellectualizes Plato and that concomitantly she views Aristotle's stance as more purely impassioned than the data warrant. Plato, after all, was trying to build a city with broadened familial ties, and his approach to higher education required daring leaps of imagination. By contrast, Aristotle was certainly not unaware of the high place that intellect would occupy in his best system; hence, for example the references to *philosophia* (1334a23 and 32) and to *nous* [mind or reason – RP] (1334b15 and 27).

29 *Cf.* the discussion of occupational and class groups in Wood and Wood, 1978, pp. 220–5.
30 For discussion of the Marxian principle that the mode of production ultimately determines the form of government and the ultimate course of history, see Polin, 1966, especially ch. IV, 'Historical Materialism', pp. 53–85 and more especially pp. 53–60. Marx was originally a classical philosopher. The doctoral dissertation he submitted to the University of Jena was a comparative treatment of the ideas of Democritus and Epicurus, and his ideas of justice and equality (especially those expressed in his *Critique of the Gotha Programme*) are at times quite similar to those advanced by Plato especially and also by Aristotle. See Polin, 1966, n. 30, p. 118.

Also of interest concerning this passage is the observation of Barker, 1975, p. 301, n. 4:

> 'The wisdom of the scribe cometh by opportunity of leisure; and he that hath little business shall become wise. How then shall he become wise that holdeth the plough ... whose discourse is of the stock of bulls?' Ecclesiasticus xxxviii. 24–5. The 'scribe' of Ecclesiasticus is the guardian and interpreter of the law of the Jewish community. The book, written about 200 B.C., 'exhibits unmistakably some of the permanent effects of Greek influence' (G.H. Box, *Judaism in the Greek Period*, p. 162).

Box, 1953, is concerned almost entirely with the influence of Greek culture on Judaism and Christianity. Aside from frequently present *cultural parallelism*, one may be given to wonder, however, whether there might not also have been some influence flowing in the other direction as two cultures interacted. See Kimpel, 1981, *passim*. Kimpel, who is concerned almost entirely with parallels and similarities rather than matters of *cultural diffusion* and who influenced whom, denies a 'philosophical uniqueness' to the content of Greek thought or 'a revelation to one people to the exclusion of others' to the Jews (p. xiii).

Especially to be recommended in its entirety is the discussion of similarities and differences in Boman, 1960, e.g., pp. 27, 53–8 and 205–8. Boman ends (pp. 227 f) with the conclusion that:

> Our attempt to represent the unitary Hebraic manner of thinking and the unitary Greek manner of thinking as two possible and equally necessary reactions to one and the same reality can possibly offer a contribution toward illuminating a problem which atomic physics has passed to contemporary epistemology. The Nestor of modern physics, Niels Bohr, has continually emphasized that the findings of atomic physics are *complementary*, i.e. they cannot be correctly described without resorting to expressions which are logically irreconcilable. Thus, some experiments show that the atom has wave structure, and others show that it consists of particles (quanta). If both are right, reality possesses opposite properties which complete each other, Bohr calls the unitariness of opposite manifestations of a phenomenon *complementarity*.[1] ([1] Niels Bohr, 'Discussion with Einstein on Epistemological Problems in Atomic Physics', *Albert Einstein: Philosopher-Scientist*, ed. Paul Schilpp ('Library of Living Philosophers', vol. 7 [New York, 1951]), pp. 199–241. *Idem*, 'The Unity of Knowledge', *The Unity of Knowledge*, ed. Lewis G. Leary ('Columbia University, Bicentennial Conference Series' [New York, 1955]), pp. 47 ff. An extensive treatment of the problem is to be found also in Neils Bohr, *Atomic Physics and Human Knowledge* (London and New York, 1958);

> [the last-named title is a continuation of a previous set of papers, Niels Bohr, *Atomic Theory and the Description of Nature* (Cambridge: at the University Press, 1934.). Tr.].) In that sense, Hebrew and Greek thinking are complementary; the Greeks describe reality as *being*, the Hebrews as *movement*. Reality is, however, both at the same time; this is logically impossible, and yet it is correct.

I am not sure this is logically impossible; also, wave structure and particles conceivably could be alternating or paired *different* states or activities, unlike the DNA double-helix.

Finally, our attention to the correspondence between aspects of Judaism and Aristotelianism would be incomplete if mention were not made that the similarities of values and viewpoint were on some points strong enough to give rise among some Jews to the belief that Aristotle had Jewish ancestry and had become a convert to Judaism. Under its entry on 'Aristotelianism', we thus find this concluding passage in *The Encyclopedia of Judaism*, 1989, p. 74, that appears not to endorse as historical fact what may be only wish-inspired speculation or creative imagination that was influenced by the perceived affinity between Judaism and Aristotelianism:

> Aristotle is one of the few non-Jews to figure in Jewish legend. Josephus records traditions that he was affected by contact with Jews (Josephus, *Apion*, 1:176–182). Several medieval and Renaissance Jewish writers claim that Aristotle actually converted to Judaism and one story even tells of his natural Jewish origin from the tribe of Benjamin. A number of aprocryphal notes ascribed to Aristotle brought him esteem in kabbalistic circles.

More important are the Introductory remarks about Falaquera's *Iggeret ha-Vikkuah* (Treatise of the Controversy) in *The Book of the Seeker* (Levine, 1976), p. xl:

> Presented in the form of a dialogue between a pietist and a philosopher, this book attempts to prove that "philosophy is Torah's twin sister." Falaquera concludes that the study of philosophy is not only permissible but essential for the true understanding of Judaism.

31 *Cf.* Barker's 1975 translation of this passage in the text and n. 1, p. 303.
32 However, Aristotle did provide by will to emancipate his slaves upon his death.
33 See also the further comments about the defects of the Spartan system of education contained in Aristotle's discussion of physical training and the dangers of over-athleticism in VIII, iii–lv, 1338 b–1339 a.
34 For extended discussion of Aristotle's ideas on education, see two works by Davidson: 1969 and 1978. The vitality of these ideas is further indicated by the Paideia Proposal advanced by Mortimer J. Adler and his associates. See, e.g., Adler, 1982, and occasional issues of *Paideia* beginning in 1972; Gregory, 1984; and Spear, 1984. Of particular reference here is the Special Aristotle Issue, *Paideia* (1978), especially Section VI, 'Education and Political Philosophy', pp. 172–201.
   The events of 1989–91 in Eastern Europe that must have resulted in part from the liberating *goals* of Marxism and the educational systems that accordingly were put in place by Marxist regimes professedly exercising a 'tutelage' role, correspond neatly to some of the conclusions reached in Polin, 1966, p. 181, and in Brumbaugh, 1978, p. 179:

> If the apparent or effective revolutionary potential is measured by the angle between the direction of the state and the *apparent* good, the natural potential remains measured by the angle between the direction of the state and the *true* good.

Thus, for an Aristotelian, one central problem is the constant contest between propaganda and education; between Sophistry and philosophy. And education offers a very powerful means of bringing about political revolution, when such a revolution is in fact needed for human betterment.

... We often think of Aristotle, in contrast to Plato, as a sensible middle-class defender of the *polis* as a status quo. But the final proposal of *Politics* VIII – a compulsory public education that will be liberal as well as vocational – is a built in program for revolution in any state where the actual is out of phase with the ideal.

35   See also the translation and explanatory notes provided by Barker, 1975, pp. 334–5.

For further discussion of Aristotle's views on *banausos* and its significance in the political theory of Aristotle, see West, 1994, e.g., p. 78: 'He believes that extreme democracy fails because it gives political power to those who are ill-equipped to use it, namely the banaustics ....'

36   For further discussion by Aristotle of the aims and methods of musical education, see VIII, iv–vii, 1339 a–1342 b. We may note in these passages points on which he takes issue with Plato about musical forms and principles. For some interesting speculation about a 'paradox involved in Plato's hostility toward literature and the arts', see Lord, 1982, pp. 19 f, where the observation is also made that: 'For Aristotle and for the classics generally, literature and the arts constitute the core of an education designed to form the tastes, character, and judgment of good citizens and free men'. Lord returns to this point at the conclusion of his Introduction, p. 35, where he states:

I shall try to show that the argument of the final books of the *Politics* – so far from prefiguring either liberal or totalitarian ideas – constitutes the classic exposition of the classical view of literature or culture as at once the vehicle of civic education and the central component of a kind of leisure that is essential in any decent political order precisely because it serves to moderate the claims of politics.

The notion that grown men – particularly educated and leisured gentlemen – stand in need of a continuing education in virtue or prudence may be thought to bear the stamp of Plato rather than of the mature Aristotle. That music or poetry rather than science or philosophy forms the core of a moral or political education will strike some as an idea that is more at home in archaic or tragic Greece than in the thought of a follower of Socrates. ... They do not see that Plato and Aristotle were unable to dispense with poetry precisely because they recognized that, given the limits imposed on man by nature, philosophy or reason could never be fully effective in political life.

37   Note should also be taken of a relevant study of widespread popular interest, but to be read with constant caution, that appeared after most of the manuscript of the present work had been prepared for publication: Stone, 1989. Although there are a number of judgments in this work that have not been substantiated, the recently demised Stone lends supportive evidence and argumentation to some of the viewpoints I have expressed and also to the message of writings by Ellen Meiksins Wood and Neal Wood. The following statement (p. 38) is also in apparent agreement with Bury about a basic position of the 'Socrates' of Plato's *Republic* and the Athenian Stranger of his *Laws* (see again p. 144 above):

So we conclude our first point in demonstrating the fundamental philosophical divergences between Socrates and Athens. He and his disciples saw the human community as a herd that had to be ruled by a king or kings, as sheep by a shepherd. The Athenians, on the other hand, believed – as Aristotle later said – that man was "a political animal," endowed unlike the other animals with *logos*, or reason, and thus capable of distinguishing good from evil and of governing himself in a *polis*. This was no trivial difference.

We may add to Stone's autodidactic opinion the scholarly conclusion (about a narrow range of topics) of Morrall, 1977, p. 105:

> Aristotle's main criticism of Plato, within these limits, is that in an exaggerated zeal for unity with his communities, both in the *Republic* and the *Laws*, Plato had virtually swallowed up the individual in the *polis*. In doing so, Aristotle contended, Plato had not only stunted the individual but had seriously crippled the *polis* itself because the happiness of the community depended on that of its members. ...

However, Morrall also finds (pp. 104 f) that Aristotle is 'arbitrarily selective' in his criticism of Plato's *Republic* and *Laws*: 'Aristotle concentrates entirely on Plato's suggestions for communism of property and wives [for the Guardian class only – RP], matters which seem to be secondary elements of Plato's general argument'. And more importantly, Morrall charges (pp. 95 ff) that the anti-democratic Aristotle purposely omitted from consideration [if such material be not missing from the surviving manuscript – RP] a number of effective constitutional safeguards that indicate the Athenian democracy was not legally arbitrary but essentially conservative, orderly, and just. As support for these views, Morrall lists and explains the role of a number of 'brakes' that militated against hasty or improper action by the government or powerful personages. These checks included: (1) the probouleutic Council, the *boulé*, which set the proposals on which the popular Assembly, the *ekklesia*, was permitted to act; (2) the *graphe paranomon* (γραφή παρανόμον), a written appeal that could be brought by any citizen against the validity of a law or decree and prevent its implementation until tried before a tribunal of 1,000 to 6,000 jurors; the *eisangelia* (εισαγγελία), an impeachment for subversive or treasonous activity, triable before the Assembly (the form of prosecution of Socrates); and (3) the introduction in the fourth century BC of *nomothetai* (νομοθέται), 501 or 1,001 members of the Assembly to whom power was delegated annually to decide whether to make, and if so the wording of, revision in any sections of the laws. Thus, Morrall concludes:

> In order to serve this main objective, Aristotle was ready to modify actually existing facts in such a way as to present, if not actually a caricature, at any rate an incomplete picture of the democratic type of constitution as exemplified at Athens.

For detailed treatment of the historical development and procedural workings of a broad array of classical Athenian political and judicial institutions, including those mentioned in this note, see especially Ostwald, 1986. For a more specialized study of relevance for the succeeding century, see Hansen, 1987. The information presented in both Ostwald and Hansen is supportive of the assessment by Morrall of the Athenian democracy. For the 'paramount importance' of Aristotle's contention that man is a political animal and the *polis* a living creature – a thesis that also finds expression in his theory of justice – see Miller, 1995, p. 15:

> An organism such as a human being or a horse has within it an organizing and guiding formal principle: its soul. The polis also has within it a formal principle by which it is organized and governed: its constitution. As the orator Isocrates (436–338 BC) pronounced, 'The soul of a polis is nothing other than its constitution.'[25] ([25] *Areopagiticus* 14 I. Cf. Aristotle, *Pol.* III 3 1276^{b}7–8 and IV 4 1291^{a}24–8. The analogy between soul and constitution is also central to Plato's *Republic*.)

X   Comparisons and Conclusions

Overview

Plato and Aristotle are securely established as towering figures in the intellectual development of Western civilization. However, because some of their fundamental assumptions and methodology cannot stand against modern knowledge and criticism, and because their outlook was much too circumscribed and Hellenic for even the requirements of their own day, the contributions of Plato and Aristotle should not be overstated with reference to the scientific-industrial age. Science, philosophy, ethics, religion, and government have in important respects all passed them by, most notably with regard to women, slaves, and democracy.[1]

What, then, is the key factor in our enduring interest in them? In important measure it is because they addressed great persistent questions and problems of mankind. They discussed basic wants, needs, and fears of us all. They understood our vulnerability, especially the central one of mortality, and the terror that overcomes us when we realize how defenceless we become when faced by possible deprivation of justice. Therefore, they highlighted humanity's constant passion for justice and the universal Old Testament message that man is born for justice, because they understood the relationship between available justice and much of human happiness. The happiness that comes from a sense of security of person and property and continuing enjoyment of the familiar, is inseparable from available, affordable, and swift justice. Hence their focus of attention on education for morality, on law, on competent magistrates, and on consequent greater justice.

Also, Plato and Aristotle were often dissatisfied with humankind and its habitual ways; and so we share with them a longing for something better and are attracted to the glimpses they offer of possible improvement in ourselves and in the world about us. There is a combination of uplifting higher purpose and resolve accompanied by some practicable suggestions that frequently give hope of implementation and, therefore, at least the occasional triumph of virtue and justice. We are all dissatisfied with ourselves and with the world about us, and Plato and Aristotle continue to offer inspiration and instruction aimed at the betterment we long for.

Thus, we are dealing with basic human qualities and aspirations that in each age and clime face similar difficulties and disappointments. To continue to touch us and to be relevant across millennia, the human factor must be ever present and clearly visible especially when dealing with government. For government is a very human thing: it is men and women who govern and are governed; and government is the agency through which humanity may best hope to exercise effective and rational control on the direction and rate of development of its civilization.

Both Plato and Aristotle always kept the human factor in mind even when treating of unrealized visions: they recognized the rational intellectual faculty in humanity, its moral faculty of will, and its consequent capacity for self-ennoblement of its conditioned nature. There is something optimistic rather than pessimistic in their belief in humanity's capacity to improve itself individually, its institutions, its technology, and its environment; and humanity is generally attracted to – and lives by – hope rather than despair. It is manifest that Plato and Aristotle believed that proper use of human faculties can lead to greater knowledge, greater understanding, and development not only of an enlightened theory and practice of government but also of science and religion (see Wild, 1946, p. 19).[2] Thus, they constantly paid close and perceptive attention to problems of human nature and government, and although our solutions may differ, the basic problems (e.g., how to render government effective yet safe) remain; and so we continue to turn to them to increase our own *understanding* of human problems, rather than for solutions. Note, for example, John Wild's observation (1946, p. 88) about Plato's contribution to our understanding of the nature and role of a culture in any age that applies equally to Aristotle: 'With the aid of Plato, we have now perhaps gained some genuine insight into the complex structure of human culture or *technē* – the care or cultivation of something rationally guided for the sake of achieving some legitimate end'.

Yet something very human – and humane – seems to be missing in the political writings of both Plato and Aristotle. Perhaps it is because of their academic manner of expression or the dictates of good taste in their social circles – which was certainly not the case with the coarsely spoken dramatists of classical Athens – for their expressions of human emotion do not run the gamut. They are indeed too calculated and rational even when they seem to be voicing concern for those who have been wronged because they have been treated beneath or above their worth. Where is there the truly heartfelt sympathy – *Mitleid* – for suffering that one may find in the writings of Aeschylus and

Euripides or in the declamations of Demosthenes? Where is there appreciation of the agony of the downtrodden of their day? One looks in vain in the works we have examined here for a single statement that conveys the same kind of exquisite sensitivity and humanity one may find, for example, in the tragedies of Sophocles. Thus, one may question the degree of warmth of love for one's fellow humans that Plato and Aristotle professed to foster through their political proposals that they claimed would promote friendship (i.e., fraternity) and bonding within the *polis*. There is a beauty of genuine warmth and personal caring to be found in the Old Testament, the New Testament, and the Qur'an, all of which unceasingly preach the need for justice, *but tempered with mercy and forgiveness despite the horrendous material to be found in them*. All of these Scriptures, as well as those of more-Eastern civilizations, contain a message of *misericordia* that seems to be deficient in Plato and Aristotle. Perhaps this lack was also an aspect of the prevailing spirit of Greece in their times, despite the Athenian traits of pity (*eleos*: Ἔλεος) and kindliness toward humankind (*philanthropia*: φϊλανϑώπία) (see, e.g., Wood and Wood, 1978, p. 262).

In all fairness, however, in both Plato and Aristotle there is essential nobility of purpose and reliance on reason in the pursuit of effective means of constraining government to do what is pragmatic and just and restraining it from what is counterproductive, unjust, and cruel. Most of all, they are to be appreciated because they provide insightful examination of a wide range of classical problems in political theory that we have with us always in some form or degree. For example, one of the basic problems treated of by political theory concerns the relative claims of society, the state, or the group on the individual and those of the individual on society, the state, or the group.

In the past, especially in an age of more enduring kinship ties, such as the family and tribe, there was little doubt that the claims of the individual were secondary. In order for the family, the tribe, the nation, or the religious group to protect its members and survive, the individual had to be prepared to offer one's all. One's individual life was of limited importance, and it was recognized that it was the group that made one's life and that of one's kin possible to begin with. Therefore, survival of the group and its greatest good (or that of its rulers, all too often) was the highest order of priority even when the group closed ranks to try to save the individual. It was recognized that species of the animal kingdom that live in packs, herds, hives, flocks, and colonies also follow this principle as a matter of instinct and habit. Thus, family and group loyalty was unquestioningly regarded as a *sine qua non* of survival – and of morality. Increasingly, however, especially as humanity improved its technology in modern times and nature's obstacles to survival and communication were reduced or eliminated, there has been a breakdown of family, religious, and political loyalties. The emphasis has tended to go simultaneously in two opposite or divergent directions: towards universality and towards individualism.

The trend towards universality often takes political expression in a cry for the elimination of sovereign states and the development of a global state; and those who favour this change may tend to view national patriotism as disloyalty to humankind in general. They say the choice is 'patriotism or peace',[3] as fierce ethnic wars still go on.

Beginning much earlier, for example, in the 16th century with the Protestant Reformation and in the 17th and 18th centuries with the British, American, and French Revolutions, the demand for individual religious and political rights and freedoms grew; and in the 19th and 20th centuries, various socialist, social democratic, and reform movements extended the demand to include economic and social benefits for the individual of both sexes. The mixing of different national, religious, ethnic, and social groups in this global age of mass, instantaneous means of communication, ever-changing place of employment, study, jet-travel, and resultant rootlessness that really began with the introduction of the train and then the automobile, has contributed apace to the breakdown of the family, job loyalty, professionalism, and social boundaries which formerly were less often crossed.

A most significant example that symbolizes this breakdown of all kinds of past barriers is the increasing number of inter-faith and inter-ethnic marriages that are now taking place because the partners involved consider themselves as individuals first and members of a common humanity rather than of separate groups. However laudable at times in certain respects, this priority of consideration of self, of self-gratification, and of universal fraternity, has also contributed to the frequent breakdown of marriages and the increased rate of divorce as the commitment to any kind of partner or group has been downgraded in favour of the individual and narrow personal desires. The concern is primarily with self: one avoids getting involved in helping or defending others; and so, many become alienated, lonely, and homeless. The inevitable result of such swollen priority for self – exemplified by road rage – and lack of commitment to others of one's group, of course, is that just as too much evil practised against others becomes self-destructive, so does too much concern with self become self-defeating, and the selfish individual is no longer safe, benefited, or fulfilled – i.e., happy. There develops a society wherein service to others breaks down as inefficiency, lawlessness, greed, and indifference – i.e., *dysnomia, anomie,* and *stasis* – become widespread. These habits of indifference, misbehaviour, and non-performance extend throughout government, commerce, industry, the media, the arts, and education, and even unto the clergy; and the priorities for too many become profits, power, and fame. 'Nothing works', as appearance and image are substituted for substance, and jargon for proper language. Part of the problem is that individual duties and responsibility have not been paired with individual rights and freedom and there has not been developed the kind of self-controls and imposed controls on the individual that make the rights and freedom of the individual safe and justifiable. Small wonder that individuals, opposition groups, and states engage in terrorism as acceptable behaviour. Thus, there is today both within and among nations a substantial degree of *dysnomia, anomie,* and *stasis* such as Plato and Aristotle were familiar with and were concerned to prevent and cure. They understood, as do ultimately the members of any endangered group, the need for active loyalty and cooperation to make possible the survival and greater welfare of both the individual and of the associated group. The traditional wisdom that understood the consequences of failure to support group and state with a higher priority than self were understood and dramatically underscored by Plato and Aristotle (see again, e.g., Plato, *Laws,* X, 903 B–905 D; Aristotle, *Politics,* I, i, 1252 a–1253 a).

The vision that Plato and Aristotle had of a better society derives from understanding that overselfishness is not productive of stability, survival, or fulfilment. The individual in any age remains dependent on, and under consequent obligation to, others for the development of one's human nature; for one's daily needs of food, clothing, and shelter; and for one's protection. And although Plato especially may have overemphasized the priority of the group over the individual, both Plato and Aristotle also looked beyond the state and its needs, back to the individual and one's needs, and hoped to use the state in order to cultivate and improve the individual citizen's character, achievements, and condition. No doubt, for both, the highest achievement of a man is to become a knowing, virtuous individual in control of his disciplined mind and body – i.e., a philosopher. For this to come about, proper education and training are necessary; for right knowledge (for Plato, of 'divine forms') is requisite to virtuous behaviour. Accordingly, their writings contain essentially the same message that Vannevar Bush (1890–1974) (1954, p. 232) delivered himself of in an address before the American Philosophical Society in Philadelphia: 'faith that it is man's mission to learn to understand'. The role of the state for Plato and Aristotle in helping to bring this about through law (*nomos*) and education (*paideia*), is discussed by Eduard Zeller (1962,

Vol. II, p. 211), who provides a perspective from which to view the shared central political purpose of the two philosophers:

> Aristotle himself regards the peaceful occupations as the true object of social life; war he permits only as a means to peace, only, therefore in so far is it is necessary for self-defence or for the subjugation of those whom Nature has destined to serve. He demands, accordingly, that besides bravery and constancy, which are necessary in order that the State may assert its independence, the virtues of peace – namely, justice, temperance, and scientific culture (φιλοσοφία) [philosophy – RP] should also be cultivated. It cannot be denied that the aim of the State is thus placed sufficiently high. It is not, indeed, to Aristotle the absolutely highest, as it was to the Greeks of an earlier age. To him as to his teacher the highest is that scientific activity which in itself can dispense with the society of others. This alone it is, in which man attains the highest perfection permitted him by his nature, in which he transcends the limits of humanity and lives the life of God. Only as man does he require practical virtue and the community in which it manifests itself. As man, however, these are wholly indispensable to him. But the highest form of community, embracing and completing every other, is the State. Its aim comprehends every other moral aim, while its institutions not only give security and stability to the moral life by means of law and education, but extend it over a whole people. We thus arrive at a definition of the highest function of the State as that of making the citizens happy by means of virtue. This is essentially the same view of civil life that we have already met with in Plato.[4]

Points of Constitutional Agreement

Indeed, fuller appreciation of the nature of Plato's theory of man and the state is gained by recognition that it is in fundamental respects quite similar to that less mystifyingly set forth by Aristotle. Thus, John Wild (1946, pp. v–vi) remarked that it is their similarity, rather than their differences, that should be emphasized:

> I have tried to call attention to such points of congruence which, in spite of undeniable differences, would seem to accord with the view of the ancient commentators that Platonism and Aristotelianism are not fundamentally opposed but are rather to be understood as two modes of one and the same realistic philosophy.

On the basis of the available evidence – it should be borne in mind that, in addition to other works, certain sections of Aristotle's *Politics* are missing –

the conclusion appears justified that Plato and Aristotle placed only a secondary, however important, emphasis upon a system of constitutional checks and safeguards.

It is true that they did attempt to render governmental power safe by dividing it on a functional basis and providing for a system of constant examination and check upon the various organs and officials of government. There was also in almost all cases the right of appeal by the citizen or public official who had been decided against. However, there was not a fully developed theory of mutual checking and countervailing balance of power among the important organs of government. The legislative, executive, and judicial functions and processes of government were clearly discerned by Aristotle, and specialization in them was assigned by him to particular governmental bodies and officials; but there was nowhere an attempt by either Plato or Aristotle to formulate a theory of government in which three separate and distinct branches of government were delineated.

This was probably because Plato and Aristotle believed in an organological, hierarchical arrangement of society and government, with the higher commanding and supervising the lower, and being in turn answerable to its own superior; although in the case of equals or age differences, Aristotle advocated rotation and service according to age brackets. Ultimately, it is expected by both that the rule of a combination of law, mind, reason, and soul will prevail: that, in effect, God will be the all-high commander. Closely examined, however, the structure of the state described by Plato and Aristotle in neither case follows such a pattern. It is an amorphous structure wherein superiority is not always sure, but wherein assignment of function is somewhat more distinguishable.

What, then, are the broad general principles upon which Plato and Aristotle depended to secure stability and safeguards in government and community?

First of all, they sought to achieve an harmonious socio-economic structure through an hierarchical arrangement of society wherein each individual found his proper niche and practised his proper vocation according to the nature and measure of his talents. Slavery was therefore regarded as necessary and proper for those who were born with slave natures. Such specialization, it was felt, would lead to harmony and strength, and was in itself a form of justice by virtue of its being in harmony with the cosmos and giving each man his due and asking proportionate obligations in return in a system of organological symbiosis.

Secondly, they sought to balance the participation of the classes in government, seemingly; but it was by unbalanced arrangements and discriminatory qualifications that tilted against labouring and commercial groups. They hoped by this method to minimize class warfare, to secure the loyalty of all social groups to the government by giving each a sense of sharing in it to an extent equal to one's status, and, consequently, to dispense justice and foster friendship and a warm regard for one another among all ranks of the population. Aside from their ideal preferences, they hoped to achieve this through the practicable form of government known to them as polity or *politeia* (πολιτεία), a combination of oligarchy (so they termed it, but it was, more precisely, plutocracy) and democracy (government by the many, and therefore by the poor, as they defined it). Both Plato and Aristotle, however, because they overweighted their practicable proposals to give the wealthy few – although they spoke in terms of meritorious notables – effective practical control and would overly limit or debar participation by the labouring many and commercial groups, really advanced a prescription for some kind of oligarchy (government by the few). Quite contrary to their intention, however, such a narrow government could be maintained only by constantly available military force and would have to be ever-ready to engage in violent suppression. On this point they were more clever than wise.

Thirdly, they placed secondary reliance on constitutional checks and balances; for they sought to put in place as the keystone to their structure of society and government a system of education (*paideia*: παιδεία) which was designed to produce alert, virtuous, courageous, and capable citizens and populace who would be staunchly loyal to their state and to its particular form, and fraternal with one another. (One suspects that a good part of this plan of education would call for tendentious indoctrination and inculcation.) It was purposed that the resultant unity, strength, and merit of its inhabitants would be reflected in the consequent unity, strength, and good character of the state. This is to be regarded, then, as a system based more upon the inherent potentialities of humankind as developed and moulded, rather than upon their inherent limitations.

Fourthly, they hoped for a rule of justice through law and custom as the embodiment of the wisdom of the community, superior to the wisdom of any individuals and guarding against the consequent loss of virtue of even the wisest and best when unrestrained by law. The law was not to be entirely static, however, as provision was made for its re-examination and change when deemed necessary.

Fifthly, they sought to promote spiritual and moral qualities, such as temperance, honesty, decency, courage, prudence, and piety, through other conditioning factors in addition to education. Some of these other approaches dealt with the proper location and size of the community; the avoidance of extremes of poverty and wealth; the attempt to keep women, children, and slaves under control; utilization of religion; the voidance of profit-making in trade; eugenical breeding; and body-strengthening exercise.

Sixthly, they attempted to render governmental power safe by dividing it on a functional basis and providing for a system of constant examination and check upon the various organs and officials of government. Aristotle went beyond Plato, however, in assigning specialization in the deliberative, magisterial, and judicial functions to particular governmental bodies and officials.

Seventhly, a fundamental hope for every form of government they treated of was that it would be basically a meritocracy. No matter which system they discussed, they tried to see how it could function at its best and how the best qualified could be placed in office. Neither confused wealth or numbers with merit or ability. They both regarded the truly qualified and able as limited in number, but Aristotle believed the judgment of the many more apt to be correct than the judgment of one or of the few.

Eighthly, they proposed no final, dogmatic plan of government as to details or the provisions of particular laws. They both made specific suggestions but also made allowance for correction, adjustment, and updating in the light of the lessons of experience, new knowledge, and changed conditions. However, these are modifications within parameters dictated by their basic cosmological assumptions, and in neither case do they clearly represent openness to fundamental or revolutionary changeover. Of the two, Aristotle was more flexible. Perhaps, therefore, he was more susceptible than Plato to acceptance of the kind of fundamental or revolutionary change in the direction of mass, limited, constitutional government that we now call modern democracy and which is in great part a consequence of the scientific-industrial revolution.

Points of Constitutional Disagreement

What are the significant differences in the political theory of Plato and Aristotle? First, it seems Aristotle *at all times* advocated the supremacy of the rule of law, rather than rule by the judgment of a super-wise man he knew to be nonexistent or by an elite group unrestrained by law; but Plato always tried so to hedge that his system would produce at least in *hypothetical theory* the rule of a savant or of a council of elite elder statesmen or philosopher-rulers whose qualifications were supposedly wisdom and virtue and who would have the ultimate political power in the state. Because of the manner in which Plato would 'load the dice' to produce pro-oligarchical imbalance, the mixed government of *politeia* he finally came to advocate in the *Statesman* and the *Laws* was more the appearance of polity, rather than the substance of polity, for the democratic segment would not under his scheme have a sufficient share of the decision-making power. Thus, more so than did Aristotle, Plato speculated at times in terms of rule by a super-wise man he knew to be nonexistent; and as did Aristotle, he favoured control by an elite group that, from our viewpoint, might prove not to be properly restrained by law.

In short, Plato never really gave up completely his dream of the *Republic* that an all-wise philosopher-ruler – i.e., a projection of his self-image? – or a superior Guardian group would rule according to higher knowledge and principles of reason and justice. Such ruler or rulers seemingly would be guided by, but not be rigidly restrained by, positive law or custom. Perhaps a careful reading of key passages confirms, however, that Plato understood the dream of an all-powerful, superman philosopher-ruler was but a dream and that it was therefore only a rhetorical device to promote acceptance of his available alternative, what may have been his real purpose. This intent was advocacy of what was indeed practicable and generally preferable even to him: *the rule of law rather than of men*. For one may simultaneously have fanciful daydreams to play with and work at making practical plans.

One suspects, also, that Plato's Nocturnal Council of elders proposed in the *Laws* would have been more than a bit out of tune with their people and times, and would have been characterized by the following traits, rather than wisdom and virtue: asceticism, conservatism, intolerance, a lack of sympathy for human failings and desires, a lack of understanding of and respect and sympathy for women, a lack of a sense of kindly humour, and a cold, intellectual ruthlessness that would have led to extreme regimentation and frequent purging of so-called heretics and traitors. Plato would not have wanted things to go so far from moderation; but that would have been the practical result of his proposals, just as Marx's plans have miscarried in a number of 20th century states.[5] One cannot see as the prevailing mode people being free, spontaneous, happy, and laughing – and truly enjoying their leisure – under a Platonic rule. Sombreness, such as characterized much of the Middle Ages, would likely be the tone of such a society; yet Plato, as did Aristotle, said he aimed chiefly at human happiness and friendship.[6]

Secondly, Aristotle was more cosmopolitan in his outlook. For example, in his professed political theory, he allowed for location of his desired city-state near the sea and the carrying on of commerce that was of benefit to one's state. More importantly, we see how Aristotle reacted to the great events of his own day when in his lifetime supremacy passed from Greece to Macedonia: Aristotle was not so much in opposition to the Macedonian movement as he was attuned to and part of it. Plato had sought to strengthen Athens and the Greek city-states by establishing strong, authoritarian, elitist kingships or republics within them. Aristotle, on the other hand, sought a fusion of Macedonia and Greece, and was more temperate in aim, tone, and method than Plato with respect to the internal government of their *poleis* (e.g., he seldom mentioned the death penalty, whereas Plato frequently advocated it).

Thirdly, Plato was willing to introduce convenient myths in support of his beliefs and instill them in the minds of all – unless he is not to be taken seriously and literally on this matter. The trouble with untruth, falsehood, or even a well-intentioned myth that is meant to be understood as myth, however, is that it usually cannot stand alone and requires a multitude of lesser and greater myths or falsehoods in support; and by creating a credibility-gap when finally understood to be unbelievable, it makes even truth suspect. This must inevitably lead in the direction of corruption, dishonesty, specious rationalization, and force. Plato said he advocated virtue, truth, and reason above all else, and myths and parables are capable, in varying degree, of containing them all, especially when not presented as literal accounts; but even the best of myths can prove enormously dangerous and evoke unrestrained evil, especially when accepted or acted upon as if literally true – as does happen with myths.[7]

Fourthly, Plato was more concerned to use the state for other-worldly religious purposes, whereas Aristotle was essentially mundane in his political theory and paid but limited, *pro forma* attention to the role of religion within the state. This is an important difference which helps to explain differences in tone and emphasis between them, especially the greater zeal of expression and methods called for that are to be found in Plato. Indeed, Eduard Zeller (1962, Vol. II, pp. 211 f) has remarked on it as the single difference he finds between them:

> In only a single feature do the two philosophers differ from one another, but it is a fundamental one. In Plato the State, like everything else upon earth, is essentially related to the other world, whence all truth and reality spring. This is the ultimate source of his political idealism. Just as the Ideas belong to the supersensible world, so the philosophical rulers to whom he entrusts the realization of these Ideas in the State have their home there also, and only unwillingly descend to take part in earthly affairs. The State, therefore, serves

not only for moral education, but also as a preparation for that higher life of the disembodied spirit into which a beautiful glimpse is opened to us at the end of the *Republic*. Of this view of the State and of human life in general, we find no trace in Aristotle. We have simply and solely here to do with the present life and with that happiness which is the immediate outcome of moral and spiritual perfection. It is not the aim of the State to represent an ideal world beyond or to prepare for another life, but to satisfy the wants of the present.[8]

Platonic and Aristotelian Contributions to Constitutionalism

Aristotle, as did Plato, advanced a basically conservative and ascetic programme. However, the degree to which he differed from Plato must be considered a qualitative difference as well. And so there are greater ultimate possibilities of freedom, happiness, and reliance upon individual self-control and expression in Aristotle.[9] Indeed, Aristotle's 'ideal' or 'perfect' state is really an imperfect one that requires constant adjustment and balancing. We all-too-frequently tend to project ourselves into any situation; and so perhaps Aristotle presented a more tolerant and favourable view of human nature and women because he was more such a person than Plato and had enjoyed fulfilment in marriage and parenthood. But in Plato there is a surfeit of control and severe punishments he would impose upon the individual and the group if we are to take his words at their face value in most cases.

Thus, the practical-minded colonial American intelligentsia, who were characterized by 'common sense' as well as lofty idealism, were drawn more to Aristotle by their general agreement with basic tenets of his statecraft, and probably also by his greater comprehensibility. Consequently, when it came time to construct their own Republic, it was to Aristotle's *Politics* they turned, rather than to Plato's *Republic*. John Corbin's pithy declaration (1930, pp. 465 ff) to this effect is found in a critical observation wherein he advocates 'a middle way' he finds in the American Constitution, 'the theory of which derives from Aristotle and was put into successful practice in ancient Rome, in eighteenth century England, and in our early state constitutions, before it was given perhaps its most perfect embodiment by the Convention of 1787'.[10]

That there is a growing awareness of the importance of this direct and indirect contribution of Aristotle to the American constitutional system is later exemplified in the work of John G.A. Pocock that is called to attention by George F. Will (1992, p. 155 f):

In the 1960s classical republicanism became a rival of Lockean liberalism as an explanatory concept in the writing of early American history. The crucial difference with Lockean liberalism is the emphasis classical republicanism gives to man's natural sociability. That sociability entails both a need and a disposition to participate in civil life and to develop and display public virtue. In 1969, J.G.A. Pocock, backed by rich and persuasive scholarship, said, in effect: Mr. Locke, move over and make room for credit to be given to another philosophic contribution to the making of the first modern nation. Pocock extracted from the writings of Aristotle, Cicero, Machiavelli and others a coherent political philosophy that first appeared in Ancient Greece and Rome, later resurfaced in Renaissance Italy, then resonated in eighteenth-century England and became a fighting faith in revolutionary and postrevolutionary America. ... But in America it was alloyed with Lockean liberalism and was often lost sight of.

Classical republicanism is rooted in Aristotle's notion that man is a political animal. Man, to Aristotle, is not political in the tentative, limited and diffident manner of the Lockean man who enters into political society only negatively, as a necessary concession to inconveniences. Rather, said classical republicanism, man is political in the sense that his nature can not be realized, and his natural inclinations can not be fulfilled, without active involvement in a political order – a particular kind of political order. It is a kind that makes possible political participation, which Aristotle considered a defining attribute of citizenship. Such a political order is right for man's nature. Which is to say, it is a natural right.[11]

The case has also been made by Paul Stern that in his *Statesman*, Plato similarly recognizes that human nature requires political communities for its proper fulfilment, and that the imperfect form and functioning of any actual political community in turn needs the application of wisdom to its rule of law:

What keeps the city from perishing, from sinking into disorder – into "the sea, which is limitless, of dissimilarity" – is the wisdom of its captains and crews (273d6–e1). By nature, we require political communities for our flourishing, but this very nature dictates that the political community is a human production. Most important, if such production is informed by wisdom, then it does not aim to approximate the one true regime which must be distinguished "from all the rest as a god from human beings" (303b4–5) ... To do so is to emulate the defective rulers whose defect lies in their being ignorant of their ignorance (302a8–b3). Its production must rather be guided precisely by recognition of why imitation is necessary, why the community's wholeness is only approximate. This recognition, finally, differentiates the statesman from his "greatest imitators," "the sophists of sophists" (303c2–5). It is not that the statesman is true and genuine while the sophist is imitative, but rather that the statesman is guided by awareness of why imitation is unavoidable, why the perfectly harmonious community must be unavailable (Stern, 1997, pp. 273 ff).[12]

Aristotle urged only truth, decency, and human nature as the basis of his system. Less the mystic than Plato, and at least seemingly less compulsive or driven than Plato, Aristotle felt no need to use fabrications or myths as a prop for his system as a matter of serious discussion, although he might pay passing heed to some already held as popular legend. Therein lies critical difference between them.

While Plato and Aristotle both contributed to the organological conception of society, politics, and religion that was to find its classical expression in Medievalism, Aristotle was much the stronger proponent of this viewpoint. But by adhering to principles of truth, practicability, and the inductive use of empirical evidence that gave more valid general conclusions, and by his development of deductive rules that gave more valid particular conclusions, Aristotle also was eventually to contribute through St Thomas Aquinas and the Humanists of the Renaissance to the breakdown of Medievalism and the rise of modern science with all of its potentialities for a better life. Aquinas, the Humanists in general, and Erasmus notably, were all in agreement with Aristotle on the importance of the use of human reason to aid in the discovery of truth; and Aquinas himself played no small part in introducing the recently rediscovered (from the Arabic) Aristotle to Western Europe. Thus, there was good cause why Aristotle outshone Plato as the supreme intellectual authority of the Middle Ages – and was universally known as 'the Master' – just as Medievalism began to progress toward higher levels of understanding and material accomplishment. A pivotal role in bringing this about was played by the great Arabian scholar Ibn Rushd (1126–98), a native of Cordoba popularly known as Averroes, whose commentaries on Aristotle widely influenced Jewish and Christian, as well as Muslim, scholars. Among ensuing Christian scholars of Aristotle should be noted the remarkable Spanish monarch Alfonso X (1221?–1284).

This better life in a better society that humankind has always sought, requires the practice of constant re-examination and re-evaluation. It requires both retention of what continues to be valid and work well, and being constantly geared for rational and desirable change through principles of dynamic equilibrium. It requires a greater focus of attention and effort on the development of good people, the be-all and end-all of government, while not neglecting the sound structure and effective functioning principles of government. Hence the continuing supremely important role of education and political socialization. And for these reasons, the political theory of Plato and of Aristotle, especially with their emphasis on education, contains essential ideas and wisdom about constitutionalism that, as is true of all classical writing, have enduring values and messages that are worth the attention of every age and of every seeker of political truth. This is particularly so today in an age that has the momentous problems of *dysnomia, anomie,* and *stasis* that now confront society and the state in our developing global village.

Thus, more so than ever before, and increasingly so, we have need of genuinely effective *paideia* to produce strong, virtuous, and capable individuals who could properly fulfil themselves through decent values, habits, and achievements that would be so pervasive they would maintain social, political, and economic systems wherein justice, fraternity, and harmony would prevail.[13] However imperfectly and incompletely both perceive how to bring it about, Plato and Aristotle present a vision of a better and happier humanity living and working under more rational politico-socio-economic arrangements and processes. Plato and Aristotle continue to be relevant, therefore, because we also seek that kind of vision and political inspiration and perforce regard constitutionalism as an indispensable instrumentality for realization of the good life in the good society for us all.

Finally, could we in a single word epitomize the purpose, methodology, or message of Plato or Aristotle in their writings on constitutionalism? First, they were teachers who shared the common didactic purpose to enlighten through instruction, so δίδαζις: (*didaxis*: teaching) is the word here. Next, the refutational methodology of Plato in his Socratic dialogues features ἔλεγχος (*elenchos*: disproving cross-examination, elenchus). And the teleological message of Aristotle is expressed in his doctrine of εντελεζέια (*entelecheia*: entelechy, actualization of innate, potential form, as when an acorn becomes an oak).

Plato's Socratic methodology is therefore largely negativistic: intended to sweep away the beliefs and processes that support a socio-political system he opposes. Aristotle's message, however, is essentially affirmative: man is a socio-political animal that fulfils its human nature by constructing a state in which to nest collectively that embraces particular family nests. For both Plato and Aristotle, the *polis* is a construct woven – and held together – by the never-ceasing process of the political art of government that becomes an expression of utility, justice, beauty, and philanthropy when the compound term *constitutional statesmanship* is the traditional credo and ruling practice.

Notes

1   The conclusion that with respect to their attitudes about women, slavery, and democracy, Plato (more especially with respect to slavery and democracy) and Aristotle (more especially with respect to slavery and women) have been passed by, is supported by the generally received principles contained in the basic documents of modern states. It should be useful in the evaluation of Plato and Aristotle's ideas on constitutionalism, therefore, to present verbatim a broad array of relevant provisions to be found in constitutions or equivalent statutes especially of English-speaking nations and others that have been influenced by British or American occupation or strong cultural contacts.

These provisions indicate increasing acceptance at least in principle of the following propositions: (1) the abolition of slavery and involuntary servitude; (2) full equality for women; and (3) the mundane, direct origin of sovereignty in the people and their corollary right to democracy. Their text and accompanying commentaries may be found in the ongoing series edited by Blaustein and Flanz, 1971–. See especially the volumes dealing with the recent or current constitutions or basic laws of Canada, France, the Federal Republic of Germany, India, Israel, Italy, Japan, New Zealand, Pakistan, Sweden, the United Kingdom, and Yugoslavia. Some pertinent provisions from present and former Commonwealth states are as follows:

Canada

(1) B.I.7. Everyone has the right to life, liberty and security of the person and the right not to be deprived thereof except in accordance with the principles of fundamental justice.
(2) B.I.15. (1) Every individual is equal before and under the law and has the right to the equal protection and equal benefit of the law without discrimination and in particular, without discrimination based on race, national or ethnic origin, colour, religion, sex, age or mental or physical disability.
(3) B.I. The *Canadian Charter of Rights and Freedoms* guarantees the rights and freedoms set out in it subject only to such reasonable limits prescribed by law as can be demonstrably justified in a free and democratic society.

Ghana

(1) 16 (1) No person shall beheld in slavery or servitude.
    (2) No person shall be required to perform forced labour.
(2) 12 (2) Every person in Ghana, whatever his race, place of origin, political opinion, colour, religion, creed or gender shall be entitled to the fundamental human rights and freedoms of the individual contained in this Chapter but subject to the rights and freedoms of others and for the public interest.
(3) Preamble: The Principle that all powers of Government spring from the Sovereign Will of the People …
    1 (1) The Sovereignty of Ghana resides in the people of Ghana in whose name and for whose welfare the powers of government are to be exercised in the manner and within the limits laid down in this Constitution.

India

(1) III.23.(1) Traffic in human beings and *begar* and other similar forms of forced labour are prohibited and any contravention of this provision shall be an offence punishable in accordance with law.

(2) III.15.(1) The State shall not discriminate against any citizen on grounds only of religion, race, caste, sex, place of birth or any of them.

(3) Preamble. WE, THE PEOPLE OF INDIA, having solemnly resolved to constitute India into a SOVEREIGN SOCIALIST SECULAR DEMOCRATIC REPUBLIC ...

New Zealand

(2) 1979, No. 49, An Act to Establish a Human Rights Commission and to promote the advancement of human rights in New Zealand in general accordance with the United Nations International Covenants on Human Rights, II.15(1). It shall be unlawful for any person who is an employer, or any person acting or purporting to act on behalf of any person who is an employer,–

(a) To refuse or omit to employ any person on work of any description which is available and for which that person is qualified; or

(b) To refuse or omit to offer any person the same terms of employment, conditions of work, fringe benefits, and opportunities for training, promotion, and transfer as are made available for persons of the same or substantially similar circumstances on work of that description; or

(c) To dismiss any person, or subject any person to any detriment, in circumstances in which other persons employed by that employer on work of that description are not or would not be dismissed or are not or would not be subjected to such detriment –

by reason of the sex, marital status, or religious or ethical belief of that person.

Pakistan

(1) I.3. The State shall ensure the elimination of all forms of exploitation and the gradual fulfilment of the principle, from each according to his ability[,] to each according to his work.

(2) II.1.25.(2) There shall be no discrimination on the basis of sex alone.

(3) Preamble. [T]he State shall exercise its powers and authority through the representatives of the people;

Wherein the principles of democracy, freedom, equality, tolerance and social justice, as enunciated by Islam, shall be observed ....

United Kingdom

(1) Act Abolishing Slavery 1833, 1833 Chapter 73. An act that ... from and after the ... first day of August, 1834, slavery shall and is hereby utterly and forever abolished and declared unlawful throughout the British colonies, plantations, and possessions abroad ....

(2) Sex Discrimination Act 1975, 1975 Chapter 65. An Act to render unlawful certain kinds of sex discrimination on the ground of marriage, and establish a Commission with the function of working towards the elimination of such discrimination and promoting equality between men and women generally; and for related purposes.

With respect to point (2) above, the definitive work is Flanz, 1983. In addition to historical treatment and analysis of the subject that begins with the eighteenth century, Flanz presents an extensive bibliography of printed sources in English and other languages as well as an appendix that includes the text of 30 keystone national and international documents produced in Europe between 1970 and 1981.

Unfinished tasks with respect to the elimination of discrimination against women unto even the use of language are addressed by Flanz in the multilingual essay contributed to the *Festschrift für Felix Ermacora*, 1988. Flanz is concerned especially to eliminate what he calls 'male-oriented linguistic discrimination' (MOLD) (p. 452). Flanz turns Aristotle against himself when he states (p. 452): 'More than two thousand years ago Aristotle defined law as reason unencumbered by passion [*Politics*, 1287 a – RP]. If one applies this definition to the field of women's rights, it means that the law and its administration would be gender-neutral.' Thus, it is Flanz's advocacy that not only should there be full equality and protection in the intent and operation of the law with respect to the *sex* (male or female) of the individual, but there should also be replacement of hurtful language based on unnecessary use of *gender* (masculine or feminine). For an apt illustration of implementation of Flanz's proposals, see report of the American Association of University Professors, 1990.

2   Because the present writer's own approach to government is also based in good part on the 'nature' and potentialities of humankind, he is using this work as a partial frame of reference for this section of overview, without regard to agreement or disagreement. But therefore see also the conclusion in Adkins, 1960, p. 350, of the hoped-for type of moral citizens with developed nobility of character and efficient virtues that Plato and Aristotle purposed their politico-socioeconomic systems to produce:

> To Aristotle and the Plato of the *Laws*, the city required proves to be one composed essentially (but by no means entirely) of *agathoi politai* [αγαϑοι πολιται: good citizens – RP], each of whom possesses all the *aretai* [ἀρετάι: efficient virtues – RP], moral, intellectual, social, and economic: a city in which this term of political efficiency commends the quiet moral virtues as manifestations, among others, of this efficiency, or as means to the desired end.

For a wide-ranging treatment of important aspects of the subject of theory and practice, see also Lobkowicz, 1967, especially pp. 3–57 with reference to Plato and Aristotle.

For an incisive treatment of Plato and Aristotle's philosophical and cosmological systems, including commentary on the more mundane, materialistic, and empirical thrust of Greek philosophy in the ensuing century that was both somewhat a reversion to pre-Socratic views and somewhat more consonant with prevailing modern views, see also Gould, 1970, ch. 3. See especially pp. 23–7 and Gould's conclusion that, 'In Strato the tendency towards observation culminates and philosophy turns into scientism. Wehrli, the most recent commentator on the text, speaks of Strato's positivistic science ...'. Gould cites here: Benjamin Farrington (1949), *Greek Science* (Baltimore: Penguin Books), p. 171; and Fritz Wehrli (1950), *Die Schule des Aristotles. Texte und Kommentar*. Heft V. *Straton von Lampsakos* (Basel: Benno Schwabe and Co.), p. 46.

For a comprehensive survey of Plato's ideas, see Crombie, 1962–63.

3   Advocates of this viewpoint became increasingly articulate during and shortly after World War II, many of them pinning their hopes on the infant United Nations. See, e.g.: Doman, 1942; Reves, 1945; and de Hegedus, 1947.

4   This exaltation of the state by Plato is, of course, reminiscent of Hegel: see Georg W.F. Hegel (1821), *Philosophy of Right and Law, or Natural Law and Political Science Outlined*,

especially paragraphs 257–65, in Friedrich, 1953. For more extended discussion of Hegel's life and ideas, see Findlay, 1958. See also in its entirety Reeve, 1988.

For a more specialized, relevant work that provides substantial explication of its subject and extensive bibliography and sources, see Browning, 1991. In referring to a reformulation of his own understanding of their political philosophies in his article on 'Plato and Hegel: Reason, Redemption and Political Theory', 1987, Browning presents an underlying theme of his work (p. x):

> The integrative role assigned to a 'rational' political community in uniting individuals and in framing a shared cultural identity in both their political philosophies is highlighted. On the other hand their political philosophies are seen as being sharply divided by the contrasting features of their conceptions of reason. Plato is explained to be concerned to re-design the structures of political life according to the dictates of ideal, transcendent principles of reason whereas Hegel is shown to be aiming to 'redeem' the imperfections of political life by recognising the reason underlying actual political experience.

Thus, Hegel may be more attuned to Aristotle's more empirical and more inductive approach to political theory than to Plato's more deductive approach. All three philosophers, however, share the methodological role of their philosophies assigned by Browning to Plato and Hegel (p. 100): 'In distinctive, but related ways, their respective philosophical works locate the source of philosophy's explanatory powers within its self-critical procedure, that is to say, its commitment to question and justify all the concepts which are invoked in the course of its investigations.'

But Plato's and Hegel's differing assumptions and differing dialectical systems, Browning concludes, are designed to produce fundamentally different results (p. 105): 'Whereas Plato considered that a rational political community demanded the subordination of human freedom to the transcendent criteria of philosophical cognition, the political order of the *Philosophy of Right* is designed to secure and express the freedom of its citizens'. Yet how much freedom would Hegel's conception of freedom provide?

5   See the Introduction by Robert M. MacIver to Polin, 1966, especially pp. xvii ff.

Also, we should never lose sight of the proposition supported by Havelock, 1957, that Plato and Aristotle were philosophically allied reactionaries. Thus, for example, Havelock writes in his Preface (pp. 6 f) especially with reference to their political theory:

> The very different theories of Plato and Aristotle, so far from being a summation of previous Greek thinking in this department, were designed to counteract its effects, or more properly to call up the forces of an older order of Greek ideas to correct the balance of the new .... The documentation of what, for want of a better word, I have styled the "liberal" position, is admittedly tortuous and difficult. But that there was such a position, in whatever variety of versions, is attested by the central fact, and that is the vehemence with which Plato and Aristotle sought to discredit it. To take their polemics at face value is, as I have written elsewhere, equivalent to accepting an estimate of the philosophy of Hume as that philosophy is refracted through the arguments of Kant.

6   Although the previous paragraph of evaluation is obviously not one which views Plato as an advocate of democracy, neither is it to be taken as an indictment of Plato as a prototype totalitarian. We know quite accurately what was contained in most of the dialogues of Plato; but as indicated earlier, we do not know with certainty which of the ideas present in the Platonic dialogues were offered in such a way as to be a means of undercutting them

with the trenchant tool of irony. (Aristotle, who wrote his chief political works that have survived in essay form, is, of course, almost never given to ambiguous ironical remarks in them, if ever.)

To attempt to treat of Plato's intentions in greater depth would require at least another volume and would have to include much of the material and views already available in other works. The attention of the reader is therefore suggested, e.g., to the collection of judgments presented in Thorson, 1963, and also to the quasi-polemical defence of Plato's motives contained in Randall, 1970, e.g., pp. 6 f and 162–9. It should be cautioned, however, that Thorson, pp. 5 f, omits from his discussion that natural law has been used to justify slavery as well as freedom.

Other works that deal with the same subject at least in part include the very well-reasoned one by Shorey, 1933; the favourable work by Levinson, 1970; and the very perceptive work by Fite, 1934. See also the carefully argued article in defence of Plato that addresses intent rather than probable result: Hall, 1988.

The present writer is rather well convinced that the underlying concepts of organism and hierarchy present in both Plato and Aristotle's discussion of the state, were congruent with accepted religious, cosmological, and political beliefs of their time in Greece; and without both of these concepts there would be too much missing from Plato and Aristotle's political framework of ideas for it to hold together – and it is doubtful that either would have committed such an oversight. Therefore, because the organological and hierarchical concepts are inherently non-democratical when applied to social organization and the qualifications for political participation and position, neither Plato nor Aristotle should be viewed as essentially democratic. Indeed, one cannot lightly dismiss, therefore, the conclusion reached by Wood and Wood, 1978, p. 261: 'The Socratic ideal has no place for democratic values and consequently allows no discrimination between good and evil in democratic practice, no real distinction between, on the one hand, democratic freedoms, equality, and self-rule, and on the other hand, licentiousness, mediocrity, and unprincipled, amoral caprice'. Aristotle, however, was to a significant degree less extreme in his negative appraisal of democracy.

We may also take cognizance of the irony present in the paragraphs with which Wood (1988) concludes her work, pp. 171 f:

> Plato sought a universal and permanent order underlying the world of experience and flux; he looked for a universal principle of justice and the good to set against the conventions of popular morality; he elaborated a principle of hierarchy to challenge democratic aspirations to equality, and a theory of justice diametrically opposed to the democratic concept of *dikē*; he used the analogy of the practical arts to exclude their practitioners from the specialized 'art' of politics; he hoped to restore the age-old division between rulers and producers, developing a theory of knowledge and a concept of the soul which corresponded to it. Virtually all the philosophical problems he confronted were questions raised by the new social order. Plato was anything but a peasant or craftsman; but it is difficult to imagine his invention of philosophy without the provocation offered by peasant-citizens and all their 'banausic' compatriots, whose very political existence challenged eternal verities, the truths and values 'universally recognized everywhere under Heaven' – at least, almost everywhere.

7   Again, this judgment is based on the assumption that Plato was not talking with tongue-in-cheek or indulging in illuminating make-believe when he was discussing how to 'contrive one of those opportune falsehoods' (e.g., *à la* the earth-mother myth, III, xxi, 414 B–415

D), although obviously it would not continue to be believed beyond the impressionable years of early childhood when Plato would want it to work its lasting effect. In any event, how much gentle humour is in the Platonic dialogues? If very little, then Plato probably should be adjudged as more in earnest than ironical on most questionable issues of interpretation. Perhaps a variation of the same conundrum has been set before us, without hope of more than a conjectural answer, by a scholar who devoted considerable thought to it. Gilbert Ryle, 1966, p. 7 states: 'The question was Plato a Hume or a Kant? is an open question'. *Cp.* Havelock, 1957.

That the problem of how to interpret Plato has been addressed by Rosen, 1995, has been noted above (ch. III, n. 17). See also his discussion (pp. 132 ff) of methodological and purposive differences between Plato and Aristotle that one may take to represent respectively more despairing and more hopeful expectations for respectively more philosophically and more pragmatically oriented political arrangements and practices.

8   For an evaluation of the contribution of Aristotle to the scientific attitude and method, see also Davidson, 1968, Book III, especially the appraisal on p. 162:

> Instead of appealing, like Plato, to the individual consciousness, and trying to discover ultimate truth by bringing its data into harmony among themselves, Aristotle appeals to the historic consciousness, and endeavours to find truth by harmonizing and complementing its data through a further appeal to the outer world, in which these data are realized. He maintains that the truths reached by the dialectic process are merely formal, and therefore empty,– useless in practice, until they have been filled by experience from the storehouse of nature. In consequence of this changed attitude, he sets aside the dialectic process, and substitutes for it the *Method of Induction*, which he was the first man in the world to comprehend, expound, and apply, becoming the father of all true science.

For a concise commentary on Aristotle's religious viewpoint, see the review by John Glucker of John Dudley, 1989. Glucker states (p. 70): 'It seems clear that Aristotle does not believe in the gods of popular religion, and that he does take the Unmoved Mover of *Metaphysics* to be 'o δεός [the God – RP] (A1072b 24–30).'

Also quite apt is the appraisal by Luce, 1992, p. 130:

> He was reluctant to advance or support any view that was flagrantly at variance with common sense, but at the same time his speculations were far from trite or obvious. He almost always managed to impose a powerfully novel interpretation on any body of material that he handled. The bias of his mind was empirical rather than idealistic. He was a true successor to the early Ionians in his devotion to research and his concentration on particular objects in the external world. 'In every product of nature', he said, 'there is something to arouse our wonder'.

To this we may add an observation contained in an analytical view focused on the thought of Marsilio Ficino (1433–99) presented in Mebane, 1989, p. 24:

> Unlike the lower animals, we are not limited to the practice of a single art to which our species is subject; instead, since the human soul contains the powers of all of the species, we can choose to perform whatever creative activity we please. Moreover, since parts of the human soul transcend the physical world, we not only imitate nature, we compete with it or even excel it. It is here that the Renaissance Neoplatonist departs from the Aristotelian tradition, which had limited humankind to the imitation of nature, and

asserts a vision of humanity which is a necessary part of an atmosphere conducive to the birth of science ....

See also Bartlett, 1994, which begins:

This essay contends that Aristotle's scientific account of the best form of government or "best regime" in the *Politics* deserves serious reconsideration today because, quite apart from its specific conclusions or prescriptions, it brings to light a nearly forgotten but hardly settled dispute between reason and faith as to what the best way of life and its political embodiment are. In brief, can human beings by their own lights discover the good life, or are they necessarily dependent on the divine to reveal this to them?

9   An exception should be noted with respect to women, or at least to women of the Guardian class. E.g., see again ch. IX, n. 10 above, and Smith, 1983, which begins: 'In the *Republic*, Plato argues that women (at least those in the upper classes) must be assigned social roles in the ideal state equal (or approximate) to those of men. Only one generation later Aristotle, in his *Politics*, returns women to their traditional roles in the home, subserving men'.

10 Also quoted in part if Gummere, 1963, p. 176. See Gummere in its entirety, especially ch. X, 'wherein he explains (p. 178): 'These three authorities – Aristotle, Cicero, Polybius – are given special emphasis here because of their underlying and essential relationship to the American Constitution'. Gummere finally narrows it (p. 192) to: 'In the end, they settled for the *Politeia* of Aristotle ....' Gummere also declares (pp. viii f): 'We shall see that the democratic element in the *Politics* of Aristotle was anathema to John Winthrop but a panacea to James Otis and Samuel Adams. Plato as a political scientist was not taken seriously by the colonial statesmen, notably so in the case of Jefferson and Adams'. (See again notice of the unfavourable view of Plato in ch. IV, n. 26, above.)

11 The substance of what Will presents here appeared in Pocock 1975, e.g., pp. 68–73, 316– 20, and 328 ff. It also appears in Sheldon, 1991, pp. 8–13, 51, 150–3, and 166–70, taken largely from Pocock.

For further discussion of the role of classical political thought, especially Aristotle's, in the founding of the American republic, see in its entirety Rasmussen and Den Uyl, 1991. The general thrust of their main argument may be excerpted from their chapter of conclusion, as follows (pp. 221 and 225):

Liberal political theory grew out of a tradition other than the Aristotelian one. For the most part, liberalism can be roughly categorized as an outgrowth of British empiricism, since liberalism's founding fathers include such figures [as] Hobbes, Locke, Hume, and Adam Smith. Nevertheless, certain continental thinkers – such as Voltaire, Kant, and Spinoza – have also factored into the development of the liberal political tradition. Virtually all of these thinkers share a rejection of Aristotelianism, although the degree and explicitness of that rejection varies. We, on the other hand, have tried to lay the foundations for a liberal political theory within the Aristotelian tradition. The liberalism for which we have chosen to seek a moral foundation is one which justifies itself by reference to natural justice. ...

In the end, our project might be understood as an effort to resuscitate the founding philosophy of the American political tradition. For it is evident from the Declaration of Independence that our Founding Fathers were committed to moral truth (through natural rights) and liberal political institutions. At present the connection between them has been severed.

Thus, although ce.tain wording in the Declaration of Independence may be accidental, one may speculatively compare Aristotle's emphasis on *eudaimonia* ('happiness') with Jefferson's celebrated phrase about 'the pursuit of happiness'. At the same time, credit for the ideas contained in this representative document should also be accorded many others, as Jefferson himself stated. E.g., George Mason (1725–84), Richard Bland (1710–76), and John Morin Scott (c. 1730–84) come to mind. For concise treatment of some obvious and some neglected sources of the Declaration, see Polin, 1981b. Clearly, then, classical Aristotelianism played an important role alongside liberal Lockeanism in the movement for Independence and the creation of the American constitutional system.

12 See also the examination of the claimed shortcomings of contemporary scholars in their analyses and assessments of 'the very elements of Aristotle's thought that can assist in promoting prudence' in Ruderman, 1997. Ruderman concludes (p. 418):

> The renaissance of interest in Aristotle's concept of *phronesia* proves, in the final analysis, to be motivated less by desire to recover Aristotle than by the felt need to accommodate both postmodernism's critique of reason and democracy's dislike of political distinctions. Conceived by the thinkers discussed as an antidote to reason (viewed as both harmful and illegitimate for politics), *phronesis* so understood will (by design) undermine both the science of politics and representative democracy. But if Aristotle's *Politics* stands for anything, it is not republicanism, but the science of politics. Aristotle's whole undertaking is premised on the view that the gap between theory and practice is *not* unbridgeable but, in fact, can be bridged by his political science.

13 For a succinct statement that reports aright the same message of constitutionalism as that advanced by Plato and Aristotle, see the contribution by William J. Bennett, 1979, to the symposium on *Constitutionalism, Nomos XX*, wherein he declares (p. 213): 'In the view of the people who founded this government, the purpose of civil society is not merely to preserve life but to provide an occasion and condition for living a good life. ... I would like to make a point relating education, constitutionalism, and virtue'.

A collection of essays that considers in depth the Athenian and contemporary democratic ideas of constitutionalism is Euben, Wallach, and Ober, 1994. The concluding section by Wallach, pp. 319–40, is particularly relevant. Wallach raises basic questions, e.g. (p. 319): 'We ask Can democracy be virtuous? Can virtue be democratic? and Can anything common be actually good?' Wallach concludes (p. 340) that stories of ancient Athens cannot provide us simple guideposts, 'But they surely can offer us myriad lessons for enabling the new American virtue to become a democratic friend', while 'the question of how to relate democracy and virtue has assumed paramount importance'.

A statement that strikingly presents what may be the core issue of constitutionalism in all ages has been reported by Thomas Babington Macauley in the first chapter of his *History of England*. As the life of Richard Rumbold (1622–85) was about to come to an unfortunate end, he expressed a credo that epitomized the principles for which he fought and was about to give up his life. Whether one holds that Rumbold was mistaken or not in the cause he supported, these last words could be taken as a tersely cogent response to those who argue for unjustly restricting principles or practice injustice and as an affirmation of the viewpoint from which this work has been written: 'I never would believe that Providence had sent a few men into the world, ready booted and spurred to ride, and millions ready saddled and bridled to be ridden'.

There has been a recent increasing interest in Aristotle's thought in China that may prove to have significant results there also. For a brief overview of Aristotelian studies in

China from the introduction of his thought by Jesuit missionaries beginning in 1623 and down to the present, see Mi, 1997. There is much in common between the values and teachings of Aristotelianism and those of traditional Chinese Taoism, Confucianism, and Buddhism. Aristotle's thought was therefore long apt to be regarded in China as unoriginal. A new translation into Chinese of Aristotle's works began to appear during the regime of the People's Republic of China in 1957, culminating in (p. 256):

> (The complete) *Aristotle's Politics*, translated by Wu Shoupeng from the original Greek edition (The Commercial Publishing House, Beijing, 1965, reprinted in 1983).

The translation by Wu Shoupeng marked a new height of China's translation level. It was translated from the original Greek at a high level of scholarship. It retained the Bekker numbers and added a good bibliography, two sorts of elaborate appendices, and two detailed indices. The most valuable parts of the book may be the notes where the translator has absorbed almost all the achievements of famous western scholars such as W.L. Newman, W.H. Jaeger, B. Jowett, W.D. Ross, and E. Barker. Although there are still some mistakes in the book, its contribution and influence have received high praise from scholars within and without China.

Epilogue

It is now in order to set forth a number of significant implications that the political ideas of Plato and Aristotle have for governance and constitutionalism today and in the future. There are salient lessons to be learned from consideration of what Plato and Aristotle sought to call to our attention and convince us of about the origin, nature, purposes, structure, and functioning of the state and government. This may be best accomplished by bearing in mind important events and developments of the modern historical period and recent past that deal with democracy, communism, and fascism.

Thus, before going further, it is requisite to provide at least some concise analysis of these three major ideologies; and it is methodologically convenient to begin with democracy. There is, of course, only general agreement even among its leading expositors about the tenets usually assigned to the democratic ideology; but a good case can be made for the following descriptive analysis of democracy.

Democracy as *a way of life* is, as it were, a three-legged stool, supported by the interactive principles and practices of *political* freedom of person and participation in government, *social* equality and fraternity, and *economic* opportunity and security. Thus, democracy, in this view, is not a purely political concept or term. However, the political process is now the most important one in the overall maintenance of democracy; for the political process has recently proved a more efficacious means of promoting social and economic reforms and justice than grand social and economic experiments have been in promoting political reform and justice. To support this last conclusion, all one need do is point to the history in this century of the United States of America and of the Soviet Union and the recent outcome of the competition between them by their emphasis respectively on the political and on the economic approach to building a better society. There is no more Soviet Union, and its former parts are being supported in their groping for a democratic way by Marshall Plan-like aid spearheaded by America.

Democracy as *a form of government* is a *direct type* (participatory) when the eligible citizenry themselves make decisions about selection of major officials and issues through elections, referenda, and popular assemblages such as town meetings; an *indirect type* (representative) when it is done in their name through the agency of elected or appointed legislators and officials who are to an assured meaningful degree responsive to their wishes and answerable to them; and in most cases a *mixed type* where it is partly direct democracy and partly indirect democracy.

Democracy as *a set of aims and practices* – ends and means that are imperfectly realized and practised by imperfect humans – asserts the following principles and conforms to the following kinds of behaviour:

1   majority (or plurality) rule, limited by minority and individual rights that is based on a system of adversarial political parties;
2   equality of kind, opportunity, rights, and before the law;
3   the spirit of truth, fair play, and the rule of law;
4   freedom and privacy;
5   a happy, respected, uncoerced enjoyment of life that features warm, active fraternity, good humoured fun, and useful fulfilment through occupation and recreation.

Fraternity, we should pause to make special note of, makes democracy or any other form of substantially decent government possible.

Marxian communism is therefore incompatible in theory, and even more so in the practices of its past and present votaries, with the credo of democracy just expressed, despite claims often made by its espousers that it represents 'economic and social democracy' with more beneficial prospects. And also despite additional claims that it is a type of 'scientific socialism', Marxist-Leninist communism is a pseudoscientific body of socio-politico-economic historical doctrine that only imagines it proposes how it is theoretically possible to bring about a classless, stateless communist society. Yet this imagination is somewhat weak, for it does not guarantee the statelessness of its hoped-for utopian society in which freedom, equality, material plenty, and an end of humanity's alienation from its beneficent true nature will actually be realized. Thus, rational anarchy is the ultimate goal and hope of Marxist-Leninism, but is stated to be only logically possible and not definitely assured of achievement.

Basic flaws of Marxian communism include: too strong reliance on bloody revolution and the probability of civil war to lead up to it and on a 'temporary' dictatorship of the proletariat that would use increased coercion to lead supposedly to its promised good society. Secondly, there is the great irony that the system of control by voluntary committees they envision under communism constitutes even in theory only a less coercive and more just system of state and government, but not their demise. All of this stems from the frequent abuses by governments especially in the early stages of the factory system that led them to believe the state is always an instrument of coercive control for the benefit of an exploiting ruling class. Therefore the early proponents of Marxian communism made the fundamental mistake of believing the harsh and repressive misuse of the state on behalf of the owning class they called the bourgeoisie was its role and *raison d'être*.

Fascism, on the other hand, is an ideology that is openly and avowedly anti-democratic as well as a pretended saviour from communism or other forms of socialism, its chief talking point. Even worse than the ideas of the communists were the still-not-dead even falser, more dangerous, meaner, and more unjust principles and practices promoted especially by Adolf Hitler, who preached racial supremacy and supernationalism and practised genocide, and by Benito Mussolini, who preached cultural supremacy and made war on weaker nations. Whereas the communists said their ultimate goals were to bring into being a just, kindly society based on peace, freedom, and equality, including especially of the sexes, the fascists argued that 'freedom is forever impossible'; they advanced elitist, hierarchical, and organological views and correspondingly organized and operated their state, with a tyrannical dictator as the capstone. They gloried in violence, war, conquest, terrorism, and totalitarian control over the population and media, without remorse or pity and with deliberate use of 'the big lie' – and many lesser ones – of all kinds. Fascism is an immoral, reactionary ideology based essentially on force and violence, despite its saturation of the population with propaganda and constant distortion of the educational process by tendentious indoctrination. It is committed to propositions, practices, and supporters from which and from whom one cannot expect decency. Thus, fascism is a retrogressive or 'dead end' ideology in terms of hope for truth, equality, freedom, universal fraternity, impartial justice, kindness, and internal or international peace: i.e., the enlightenment and progress of humanity.

What, then, are the lessons to be learned from comparative examination of Plato and Aristotle's political ideas and of the tenets and record of democracy, communism, and fascism in our own century? The lessons to be learned from such an exercise include what may simply be regarded as political and constitutional truisms; and as is true of the Commandments of the Decalogue, they are mostly negative ones: what not to believe or do. For the chief value of such a comparison does not lie in the applicability of Plato and Aristotle's political recommendations to our own time – for, to say it again, they have little such practical relevance – but in helping us reject what is feckless and false from what is bruited about today and also from what they had advocated in their day.

We can easily begin with an outright rejection of fascism for our own time or any time by saying that a desirable amount of law, order, and strength can be maintained by a civilized society without going to such indecent, evil extremes in terms of both ideas and practice.

Similarly, we can reject Marxian communism by saying that a more rational, more productive, more just, kinder, and less coercive society, state, and economy can be realized other than by eliminating the state and substituting an anarchy that is impracticable for any technologically advanced civilization.

We can follow with rejection of dictatorship by a Platonic tyrant or a Marxist promised-to-be-temporary one by the proletariat as an easier – or preferable – way to introduce change in the state and society. One need only briefly mention that the Marxist-Leninist-Stalinist 'dictatorship of the proletariat' did not create a dictatorship *by* or *for* the proletariat, but a dictatorship *over* the proletariat. Nor was it short-lived, but substantially self-perpetuating for the benefit of a bureaucratic ruling 'new class'; and it had greater success in producing a largely military-servicing economy, mass repression and exploitation, and advances in space; but it produced little in the way of 'democratic socialism' in the Union of Soviet Socialist Republics. And it should be added that the experimental regimes introduced by Hitler and Mussolini perished even sooner with them, as did tens of millions by the global war they precipitated and such consequences as mass starvation.

Plato, Aristotle, and fascism must also be rejected with respect to their general arguments against democratic equality and in favour of elitest inequality. There is genuine need and therefore rational justification for selection for certain status, role, office, or service on the basis of aristocratic merit deriving from such factors as ability, training, skill, strength, and accomplishment or experience; but this does not have unlimited applicability. We should be wary of any kind of hierarchical schemes based especially on weighted voting, debarment from – or preference for – the franchise, office, or service because of gender, race or ethnicity, religion, occupation, hereditary rank, or other usually irrelevant factor. We should be especially wary of anything rooted in myth, mysticism, pseudoscience, or – most important of all – in any claim of divine or hereditary right to be head of state or for separation of the population into estates, whether hereditary or appointive. The guiding principle of 'one person, one vote' should prevail – and votes be counted, not weighed – along practices of similar intent and effect.

Not only should we be especially wary of anything rooted in myth, mysticism, or pseudoscience, but we should also enforce 'separation of church and state' and observe the rule that 'no religious test shall ever be required as a qualification to any office or public trust' (Constitution of the United States, X, 3; Australia Constitution Act, V, 116)). When state and church are one, or the latter an establishment of the former, religion is almost always subordinated to purposes of state, be they moral, amoral, or immoral; and freedom of conscience and availability of truth are thereby diminished. Although Aristotle was more mundane than Plato in outlook and purpose, both endorsed in general the contemporary association of the state with religious rites and practice, and their ideas on this relationship simply cannot apply in an age of diversity. The best approach for any state to religion and things sacred in the long run, is a combination of separation from formal association and a friendly neutrality (e.g., tax exemptions).

On the positive side, an important message we may discern from both Plato and Aristotle is a call for use of expertise and 'true knowledge', and that means today the state – whether we speak of a national, multi-national, or global state – should rely to an important degree particularly on scientists and scientific knowledge. But could it now be otherwise in our technologically advanced era (i.e., in comparison with the past) of the unfolding subatomic-space age and its awesome, intensifying problems?

Any organological or mechanological explanation of the state or society can be used for specious rationalizations and consequent dangerous practices, even if they be regarded as figurative (i.e., forms of simile or metaphor that indicate only comparability) rather than literal (i.e., actual organisms or machines). This is because the individual – including even numerous members of large groups – becomes then an expendable, replaceable unit who should be 'liquidated', removed, or 'cleansed' from the body politic when he or she becomes a so-called diseased or infected source of disaffection or political heresy. This is akin to some of the more pernicious activities of the Inquisition and of the Reformation that stained a sheaf of pages of the recorded history of religion, in contradistinction to its uplifting mission, examples, and accomplishments. James Burham persistently taught that, 'An analogy is valid proof of nothing', and so we should accordingly beware of any argument of the sort that, 'It is better to get rid of a rotten apple than to let it spoil the whole barrel'. We should therefore beware of not only any kind of religious or political 'correctness', but also of any idea that tends to promote invidious and undue constraints. Thus, the concept of an organic nature of the state that is strongly present in the doctrines of fascism and Aristotle, and also present in those of Plato, should as well be rejected.

There remains the matter of slavery and slave labour. One suspects that Plato and Aristotle were not as strongly in favour of slavery as they seemed to profess and that they largely and discreetly simply went along with contemporary Athenian attitudes and practices, in good part because of the dependence of the economy and military establishment on the evil institution. If ever there were justification for slavery, even of limited severity or duration, it has come to an end with the availability of machines and robots. 'Virtuous' human beings (i.e., in the original sense of 'manly' persons of integrity characterized by pride, courage, strength, and the capacity for bold, decisive action, as taken from the Latin word for a male, *vir*) do not make good slaves, and slavery does not make persons virtuous in this sense – but a general population of persons substantially virtuous in this sense is a *sine qua non* for a good society and state, and particularly a democratic one.

The horrendous and detrimental treatment of slave labourers in the Soviet gulags and in the Nazi concentration camps, factories, and mines – and today in Chinese 'correctional' prisons to a lesser degree – need not be recounted here. But it is inadequate understatement simply to say that it too often destroyed virtuous qualities of the spirit and behaviour of the slave labourers and then too often killed them physically. The greatest evil in American history was slavery, and the greatest tragedy in American history was the Civil War it led to. Whether practised out of supposed military necessity (the generals of the Imperial German army in World War I believed voluntary, uncoerced German labour was much more productive), for profit, and/or for supposed 'correctional' purposes to 'rehabilitate' political opponents or criminals, slave labour is now prohibited by every contemporary constitution and not practised by any genuinely democratic state or society. This point of prohibition of slavery and slave labour – whether voluntary or involuntary servitude – may indeed well be the most important of the lessons to be learned from studying Plato and Aristotle's political ideas and 20th century ideologies: for the freedom from slavery and safety of none of us is secure if anyone at all can be enslaved, whether for cause or not.

Lastly, the lesson to be learned that goes to the very essence and foundation of the sort of constitutional system we should support, is that it should be predicated on the tenets of democracy presented near the beginning of this Epilogue. Note well how such a system of democracy – although they would not have embraced it because they would not have thought it very suitable for the Athens of their day – accords with Plato and Aristotle's advocacy of *meson*, the middle way between two extremes. The democratic practice of *limited government* as expounded here can be 'a golden mean' between the extreme

Marxian communist call for *no state* and the extreme fascist call for the *superstate*.

Such a democratic type of constitutionalism could well – as Plato and Aristotle advocated – reconcile the classes within a state and derive spirited, loyal service from all of them because of their recognition of their common interests and that a genuine effort was being made that all should receive a fair share of recognition, participation, burdens, and benefits. This would be far more preferable than the unworkable Marxian communist programme for the elimination of classes – which could only produce a different ruling class, as has been evidenced – and the unendingly harsh fascist programme whose principal role may well be to attempt to freeze the status quo for the continuing advantage of any exploiting ruling class.

En fin de compte, the overall lesson to be learned from the study of Plato and Aristotle's political ideas, the history of constitutionalism, and the record of competing ideologies in the 20th century is a simple but compellingly important one: the great advantages of modern democracy are that it can provide nonviolent, healing means of arriving at acceptable and workable decisions – not ideal solutions – and that it is, accordingly, the only known system of government and society that can remain soft yet strong, caring, self-curing, and enduring. And so more people are happiest under democracy because it affords the maximum of opportunity to fulfil oneself, the minimum sense of restraint, and the maximum of feeling comfortable, secure, and hopeful that any system of constitutionalism can help to promote. Democracy is the preferable choice of 'mother-form' of constitution set before us by Plato (*Laws*, Bk III, 693 D).

Bibliography

Aristotle's Writings

Aristotelis Opera (1960 facsimile of 1831 edition), from the redaction of the Greek text by August Immanuel Bekker as prepared by Olof Alfred Gigon, 5 vols, Berlin: Walter de Gruyter and Co.

Barker, Ernest (tr. and ed.) (1975), *The Politics of Aristotle*, London, Oxford (1958), New York: Oxford University Press.

Fritz, Kurt von and Kapp, Ernst (trs and eds) (1950), *Aristotle's Constitution of Athens and Related Texts*, New York: Hafner Publishing Co.

Jowett, Benjamin (tr. and ed.) (1885), *The Politics of Aristotle*, 2 vols, Oxford: Clarendon Press.

Kenyon, Frederic George (tr.) (1891), *Aristotle on the Athenian Constitution*, London: George Bell and Sons.

Moore, John M. (tr. and ed.) (1975), *Aristotle and Xenophon on Democracy and Oligarchy*, Berkeley and Los Angeles: University of California Press, 1975.

Newman, William Lambert (ed.) (1887–1902), *The Politics of Aristotle*, 4 vols (Greek text), Oxford: Clarendon Press.

Ostwald, Martin (tr. and ed.) (1962), *Nicomachean Ethics*, Indianapolis: Bobbs-Merill Co.

Rackham, Harris (tr. and ed.), *Aristotle*, 23 vols: Vol. XX (1971), *The Athenian Constitution. The Eudemian Ethics. On Virtues and Vices* (Loeb Classical Library No. 285, 1935, reprinted in 1971 from 1952 revision); Vol. XXI (1972), *Politics* (Loeb Classical Library, No. 264, 1932, reprinted in 1972 from 1944 corrections), Cambridge, Mass.: Harvard University Press; London: William Heinemann.

Rhodes, Peter J. (tr.) (1984), *Aristotle: The Athenian Constitution*, Harmondsworth: Penguin Books.

Ross, William D. (ed.) (1908–1952), *The Works of Aristotle*, 12 vols, Oxford: Clarendon Press.

Sandys, John Edwin. (ed.) (1912), *Aristotle's Constitution of Athens*, 2nd edn, with redaction of the Greek text, London: Macmillan.

Plato's Writings

Adam, James (ed.) (1963), *The Republic of Plato*, 2nd edn, 2 vols, with an Introduction by David A. Rees, Cambridge: Cambridge University Press.

Benardete, Seth (tr. and ed.) (1984), *The Being of the Beautiful: Plato's Theaetetus, Sophist, and Statesman*, Chicago and London: University of Chicago Press.

Burnet, John (ed.) (1961–62), *Platonis Opera*, 5 vols (reprinted from 1900–07), Oxford: Clarendon Press.

Jowett, Benjamin (tr. and ed.) (1892), *The Dialogues of Plato*, 3rd edn, 5 vols, London: Oxford University Press.

Jowett, Benjamin (tr. and ed.) (1964), *The Dialogues of Plato*, 4th edn, 4 vols, Oxford: Clarendon Press.
Pangle, Thomas L. (tr. and ed.) (1980), *The Laws of Plato*, New York: Basic Books.
Plato, 12 vols. Vols V–VI, *Republic*, 2 vols (Loeb Classical Library, No. 237, 1930, reprinted in 1978 from 1937 revision; No. 276, 1935, reprinted in 1970), tr. and ed. Paul Shorey: Vol. VIII, *Statesman. Philebus*, tr. and ed. Harold N. Fowler; *Ion*, tr. and ed. Walter R.M. Lamb (Loeb Classical Library, No. 164, 1925, reprinted in 1975): Vols X–XI, *The Laws*, tr. and ed. Robert G. Bury, 2 vols (Loeb Classical Library, No. 187, 1926, reprinted in 1967; No. 192, 1926, reprinted in 1968), Cambridge, Mass.: Harvard University Press; London: William Heinemann.
Saunders, Trevor J. (tr. and ed.) (1970), *Plato, the Laws*, Harmondsworth: Penguin Books.

Other Sources

Adam, Adela M. (1913), *Plato: Moral and Political Ideals*, Cambridge: Cambridge University Press.
Adcock, Frank E. (1964), *Roman Political Ideas and Practice*, Ann Arbor: University of Michigan Press.
Adkins, Arthur W.H. (1960), *Merit and Responsibility: A Study in Greek Values*, Oxford: Clarendon Press.
Adler, Mortimer J. (1958–61), *The Idea of Freedom*, 2 vols, Garden City, NY: Doubleday & Co.
Adler, Mortimer J. (1982), *The Paideia Proposal: An Educational Manifesto*, New York: Macmillan Co.
Adorno, Theodor W. et al. (1950), *The Authoritarian Personality*, New York: Harper & Brothers.
Allen, Reginald E. (1980), *Socrates and Legal Obligation*, Minneapolis: University of Minnesota Press.
American Association of University Professors (1990), 'Gender-Specific Language Being Eliminated from Older Policy Documents', *Academe*, Vol. 76, pp. 36–48.
Annas, Julia (1981), *An Introduction to Plato's Republic*, Oxford: Clarendon Press.
Antony, Louise M. and Witt, Charlotte (eds) (1993), *A Mind of One's Own: Feminist Essays on Reason and Objectivity*, Boulder, Colorado: Westview Press.
Armstrong, Arthur Hilary (ed.) (1967), *The Cambridge History of Later Greek and Early Medieval Philosophy*, Cambridge: Cambridge University Press.
Arnhart, Larry (1981), *Aristotle on Political Reasoning: A Commentary on the* Rhetoric, DeKalb: Northern Illinois University Press.
Arnheim, Michael T.W. (1977), *Aristocracy in Greek Society*, London: Thames and Hudson.
Averroes [Ibn Rushd] (1966), *Averroes' Commentary on Plato's* Republic, text and translation from the Hebrew with editing by Ervin J. Rosenthal, Cambridge: Cambridge University Press.
Bambrough, Renford (1963), *Aristoteles*, New York: New American Library, Mentor Classics.
Bambrough, Renford (ed.) (1965), *New Essays on Plato and Aristotle*, New York: Humanities Press.
Baring, Maurice (1960), *Landmarks in Russian Literature*, London: Methuen.
Barker, Ernest (1959), *The Political Thought of Plato and Aristotle*, New York: Dover Publications.

Barker, Ernest (1960), *Greek Political Thought: Plato and His Predecessors*, rev. edn, London: Methuen & Co., University Paperbacks.

Bartlett, Robert C. (1994), 'Aristotle's Science of the Best Regime', *American Political Science Review*, Vol. 88, pp. 143–55.

Benardete, Seth (1989), *Socrates' Second Sailing: On Plato's* Republic, Chicago: University of Chicago Press.

Bennett, William J. (1979), 'A Comment on Cecilia Kenyon's "Constitutionalism in Revolutionary America"', *Constitutionalism, Nomos XX*, pp. 210–4, eds James Roland Pennock and John W. Chapman, New York: New York University Press.

Berry, Christopher J. (1989), 'Of Pigs and Men: Luxury in Plato's *Republic*', *Polis*, Vol. 9, pp. 2–24.

Berve, Helmut, (1967), *Die Tyrannis bei den Griechen*, 2 vols, Munich: C.M. Beck'sche Verlagsbuchhandlung.

Blaustein, Albert P. and Flanz, Gisbert H. (eds) (1971–), *Constitutions of the Countries of the World*, ongoing series, Dobbs Ferry: NY: Oceana Publications.

Bluck, Richard S.H. (1949), 'Plato's Biography: The *Seventh Letter*', *Philosophical Review*, Vol. 58, pp. 503–9.

Bluck, Richard S.H. (1951), *Plato's Life and Thought: With a Translation of* The Seventh Letter, Boston: Beacon Press.

Bluestone, Natalie H. (1988), *Women and the Ideal Society: Plato's* Republic *and Modern Myths of Gender*, Amherst: University of Massachusetts Press.

Blythe, James M. (1992), *Ideal Government and the Mixed Constitution in the Middle Ages*, Princeton, NJ: Princeton University Press.

Boas, George (1961), *Rationalism in Greek Society*, Baltimore: The Johns Hopkins Press.

Boas, George and Cherniss, Harold (1948), 'Fact and Legend in the Biography of Plato', *Philosophical Review*, Vol. 57, pp. 439–57.

Bodéüs, Richard (1933), *The Political Dimensions of Aristotle's* Ethics, tr. from the French by Jan Edward Garrett, Albany: State University of New York Press.

Boman, Thorleif (1960), *Hebrew Thought Compared with Greek*, tr. from the German 2nd edn (1954) by Jules L. Moreau, Philadelphia: The Westminster Press.

Bonner, Robert J. (1967), *Aspects of Athenian Democracy*, New York: Russell & Russell.

Bonner Robert J. and Smith, Gertrude (1930), *The Administration of Justice from Homer to Aristotle*, 2 vols, Chicago: University of Chicago Press.

Botsford, Goerge W. and Robinson, Charles A. (1956), *Hellenic History*, 4th edn, New York: Macmillan Co.

Bowler, Peter J. (1989), *The Mendelian Revolution: The Emergence of Hereditarian Concepts in Modern Science and Society*, London: Athlone Press; Baltimore: Johns Hopkins University Press.

Bowra, Cecil M. (1958), *The Greek Experience*, New York: World Publishing Co.

Box, George H. (1953, reprinted from 1932), *Judaism in the Greek Period: From the Rise of Alexander the Great to the Intervention of Rome (333 to 63 B.C.)*, Oxford: Clarendon Press.

Bradshaw, Kenneth and Pring, David (1981), *Parliament and Congress*, rev. edn, London: Quartet Books.

Brickhouse, Thomas C. and Smith, Nicholas D. (1994), *Plato's Socrates*, New York and Oxford: Oxford University Press.

Browning, Gary K. (1991), *Plato and Hegel: Two Modes of Philosophizing about Politics*, New York and London: Garland.

Brumbaugh, Robert S. (1962), *Plato for the Modern Age*, New York: Crowell-Collier Press.

Brumbaugh, Robert S. (1968), *Plato's Mathematical Imagination: The Mathematical Passages in the Dialogues and Their Interpretation*, New York: Kraus Reprint (Bloomington: Indiana University Press, 1954).

Brumbaugh, Robert S. (1978), 'Revolution, Propaganda and Education: Aristotle's Causes in Politics', *Paideai*, Special Aristotle Issue, pp. 172–81.

Buber, Martin (1967), *Kingship of God*, 3rd edn, tr. from the German by Richard Scheimann, New York and Evanston, Ill.: Harper & Row.

Burn, Andrew R. (1965), *The Pelican History of Greece*, Harmondsworth, Penguin Books.

Burnet, John (1900), *The Ethics of Aristotle*, London: Methuen & Co.

Burnet, John (1930), *Early Greek Philosophy*, 4th edn, London: A. and C. Black.

Burnet, John (1964), *Greek Philosophy: Thales to Plato*, New York: St Martin's Press.

Bury, John Bagnell (1937), *A History of Greece to the Death of Alexander the Great*, New York: Modern Library, Random House.

Bush, Vannevar (1954), *Proceedings of the American Philosophical Society*, Vol. 98, p. 232.

Caird, Edward (1968), *Evolution of Theology in the Greek Philosophers*, 2 vols in one, New York: Kraus Reprint (Glasgow: James MacLehose and Sons, 1904).

Calhoun, John C. (1953), *A Disquisition on Government and Selections from the Discourses*, Indianapolis, Ind.: Bobbs-Merrill Co.

The Cambridge Ancient History (1923–39), 12 vols, Vols I–VI, eds John Bagnall Bury, Stanley A. Cook and Frank E. Adcock, Cambridge: Cambridge University Press.

The Cambridge Ancient History, 2nd edn (1993), Vol. V: *The Fifth Century BC*, eds David M. Lewis, John Boardman, John K. Davies, and Martin Ostwald, Cambridge: Cambridge University Press.

Campbell, Blair (1982), 'Poliatrics: Physicians and the Physician Analogy within Fourth-century Athens', *American Political Science Review*, Vol. 76, pp. 810–24.

Campbell, Blair (1986), 'Constitutionalism, Rights and Religion: The Athenian Example', *History of Political Thought*, Vol. 7, pp. 239–73.

Cantarella, Eva (1987), *Pandora's Daughters: The Role and Status of Women in Greek and Roman Antiquity*, tr. from the Italian by Maureen B. Fant, Baltimore and London: Johns Hopkins University Press.

Cappon, Lester J. (ed.) (1959), *The Adams–Jefferson Letters: The Complete Correspondence Between Thomas Jefferson and John and Abigail Adams*, 2 vols, Vol. II, Chapel Hill: University of North Carolina Press, for the Institute of Early American History and Culture at Williamsburg.

Cartledge, Paul, Millett, Paul and Todd, Stephen (eds) (1990), *Nomos: Essays in Athenian Law, Politics, and Society*, Cambridge and New York: Cambridge University Press.

Chance, Roger (1968), *Until Philosophers Are Kings: A Study of the Political Theory of Plato and Aristotle in Relation to the Modern State*, Port Washington, NY: Kennikat Press.

Cherniss, Harold F. (1962), *The Riddle of the Early Academy*, New York: Russell & Russell.

Chroust, Anton-Hermann (1973), *Aristotle, New Light on His Life and Some of His Lost Works*, 2 vols, South Bend, Ind.: University of Notre Dame Press.

Congwen, Shen (1995), *Imperfect Others*, ed. Jeffrey C. Kinkley, Honolulu: University of Hawai'i Press.

Connor, Walter R. (1970), *The New Politicians of Fifth-Century Athens*, Princeton, NJ: Princeton University Press.

Coole, Diana H. (1988), *Women in Political Theory: From Ancient Misogyny to Contemporary Feminism*, Sussex: Wheatsheaf Books; Boulder, Colorado: Lynne Rienner Publishers.

Corbin, John (1930), 'That Other Liberty', *Saturday Review of Literature*, Vol. 7, pp. 465–7.

Cornford, Francis M. (1968), *Before and After Socrates* (1932), Cambridge: Cambridge University Press.

Craig, Leon H. (1994), *The War Lover: A Study of Plato's* Republic, Toronto: University of Toronto Press.

Creed, John (1989), 'Aristotle's Middle Constitution', *Polis*, Vol. 8, pp. 2–27.

Crombie, Ian M. (1962–1963), *An Examination of Plato's Doctrines*, 2 vols, London: Routledge and Kegan Paul; New York: Humanities Press.

Cropsey, Joseph (1988–89), 'On Pleasure and the Human Good: Plato's *Philebus*', *Interpretation*, Vol. 16, pp. 167–92.

Cropsey, Joseph (1995), *Plato's World: Man's Place in the Cosmos*, Chicago and London: University of Chicago Press.

Cross, Robert C. and Woozley, Anthony D. (1964), *Plato's Republic: A Philosophical Commentary*, New York: St Martin's Press.

Curteis, Arthur M. (1913), *Rise of the Macedonian Empire*, London and New York: Longmans, Green and Co.

Darling, John (1986), 'Are Women Good Enough? Plato's feminism re-examined', *Journal of Philosophy of Education*, Vol. 20, pp. 123–8.

Davidson, Thomas (1969), *Aristotle and Ancient Educational Ideas* (reprinted from 1892), New York: Franklin, Burt; Lenox Hill.

Davidson, Thomas (1978), *Education of the Greek People and Its Influence on Civilization* (reprinted from 1894), New York: AMS Press.

Davis, Michael (1996), *The Politics of Philosophy: A Commentary on Aristotle's* Politics, Lanham, Md: Rowman & Littlefield.

Davis, Morris (1986), 'On Saxonhouse's "Further Reflections on The Peoples of Europe and Asia"', *Polis*, Vol. 6, pp. 31–9.

Demetriou, Kyriacos (1995), 'The Sophists, Democracy, and Modern Interpretation', *Polis*, Vol. 14, pp. 1–29.

Dent, Nicholas J.H. (1987), 'Plato and Social Justice', *Polis*, Vol. 6, p. 78–115.

d'Entreves, Alessandro P. (1965), *Natural Law: An Historical Survey*, New York: Harper & Row, Harper Torchbooks.

Develin, Robert (1989), *Athenian Officials 684–321 B.C.*, Cambridge and New York: Cambridge University Press.

Dicey, Albert Venner (1982), *Introduction to the Study of the Law of the Constitution* (reprinted from 8th edn, 1915, London: Macmillan and Co.), Indianapolis, Ind.: Liberty Classics.

Doman, Nicholas (1942), *The Coming Age of World Control*, New York: Harper & Brothers.

Dumézil, Georges (1988), *Mitra-Varuna: An Essay on Two Indo-European Representations of Sovereignty*, 2nd edn, tr. from the French by Derek Coltman, New York: Zone Books.

Duncan, Christopher M. and Steinberger, Peter J. (1990), 'Plato's Paradox? Guardians and Philosopher-Kings', an exchange, *American Political Science Review*, Vol. 84, p. 1317–21.

Dunning, William Archibald (1902–20), *A History of Political Theories*, 3 vols, New York: Macmillan Co.

Durant, Will (1926), *The Story of Philosophy*, New York: Simon and Schuster.

Düring, Ingemar (1957), *Aristotle in the Ancient Biographical Tradition*, Göteborg: Elanders Boktrychkeri Aktiebolag.

Dworkin, Ronald (1986), *Law's Empire*, Cambridge, Mass.: Belknap Press of Harvard University Press.

Edel, Abraham (1982), *Aristotle and His Philosophy*, Chapel Hill: University of North Carolina Press.

Edelstein, Ludwig (1966), *Plato's Seventh Letter*, Leiden: E.J. Brill.

Ehrenberg, Victor (1962), *The People of Aristophanes: A Sociology of Old Attic Comedy*, 3nd edn, New York: Schocken Books.

Ehrenberg, Victor (1968), *From Solon to Socrates: Greek History and Civilization during the Sixth and Fifth Centuries B.C.*, London: Methuen.

Ehrenberg, Victor (1969), *The Greek State*, 2nd edn, London: Methuen & Co.

Elliott, William Y. and McDonald, Neil A. (eds) (1949), *Western Political Heritage*, New York: Prentice-Hall.

Emerson, Ralph Waldo (1983), *Essays and Lectures*, ed. Joel Porte, New York: Library of America; Cambridge: Cambridge University Press.

Euben, Jay Peter (1990), *The Tragedy of Political Theory: The Road Not Taken*, Princeton, NJ: Princeton University Press.

Euben, Jay Peter, Wallach, John R. and Ober, Josiah (eds) (1994), *Athenian Political Thought and the Reconstruction of American Democracy*, Ithaca, NY: Cornell University Press.

Everson, Stephen (1988), 'Aristotle on the Foundations of the State', *Political Studies*, Vol. 36, pp. 89–101.

Farrar, Cynthia (1988), *The Origins of Democratic Thinking: The Invention of Politics in Classical Athens*, Cambridge: Cambridge University Press.

Fay, Thomas A. (1990), 'Rights and Natural Law', *Archiv für Rechts und Sozialphilosophie*, Beiheft 42, pp. 90–4.

Ferguson, John (1972), *Aristotle*, New York: Twayne Publishers.

Ferguson, William Scott (1963), *Greek Imperialism*, New York: Biblo and Tannen.

Field, Gary Cromwell (1967), *Plato and His Contemporaries: A Study in Fourth Century Life and Thought*, 3rd edn, London: Methuen & Co.

Findlay, John N. (1958), *Hegel: A Re-Examination*, New York: Oxford University Press.

Finley, Moses I. (1976), 'The Freedom of the Citizen in the Greek World', *Talanta*, Vol. 7, pp. 1–23.

Finley, Moses I. (1985), *Democracy: Ancient and Modern*, rev. edn, New Brunswick, NJ: Rutgers University Press.

Finley, Moses I. (1982), *Economy and Society in Ancient Greece*, edited with an Introduction by Brent D. Shaw and Richard P. Saller, New York: Viking Press.

Fite, Walter (1934), *The Platonic Legen*d, New York and London: Charles Scribner's Sons.

Flanz, Gisbert H. (1983), *Comparative Women's Rights and Political Participation in Europe*, Dobbs Ferry, NY: Transnational Publishers.

Flanz, Gisbert H. (1988), 'Gender-Based Discrimination in Spite of Equal Treatment Laws? Legal and Linguistic Aspects', *Festschrift für Felix Ermacora*, eds Manfred Nowak, Dorothea Steurer and Hans Tretter, Strassburg: N.P. Engel Verlag.

Forrest, William G. (1966), *The Emergence of Greek Democracy*, New York and Toronto: McGraw-Hill, World University Library.

Franklin, Julian H. (comp. and ed.) (1969), *Constitutionalism and Resistance in the Sixteenth Century: Three Treatises by Hotman, Beza, and Mornay*, New York: Pegasus.

Friedländer, Paul (ed.) (1958), *Plato, Vol. I: An Introduction*, tr. from the German by Hans Meyerhoff, New York: published for the Bollingen Foundation by Pantheon Books.

Friedrich, Carl J. (1950), *Constitutional Government and Democracy*, rev. edn, Boston: Ginn and Co.

Friedrich, Carl J. (ed.) (1953), *The Philosophy of Hegel*, New York: Modern Library, Random House.

Friedrich, Carl J. (1958), *The Philosophy of Law in Historical Perspective*, 2nd edn, Chicago: University of Chicago Press.

Fritz, Kurt von (1954), *The Theory of the Mixed Constitution in Antiquity: A Critical Analysis of Polybius' Political Ideas*, New York: Columbia University Press.

Fuller, Benjamin A.G. (1923–30), *A History of Greek Philosophy*, 3 vols, New York: Henry Holt and Co.

Fustel de Coulanges, Numas-Denis (1956), *The Ancient City: A Study on the Religion, Laws, and Institutions of Greece and Rome* (1864), tr. from the French by Willard Small, Garden City, NY: Anchor Books, Doubleday & Co.

Gadamer, Hans-Georg (1980), *Dialogue and Dialectic: Eight Hermeneutical Studies on Plato*, tr. from the German with an Introduction by P.Christopher Smith, New Haven and London: Yale University Press.

Garner, Richard (1987), *Law and Society in Classical Athens*, New York: St Martin's Press.

Gay, Peter (ed.) (1968), *Deism: An Anthology*, Princeton, NJ: D. Van Nostrand.

Gehrke, Hans-Joachim (1985), *Stasis: Untersuchungen zu den inneren Kriegen in den griechischen Staaten des 5. und 4. Jahrhunderts v. Chr.*, Munich: C.H. Beck'sche Verlagsbuchhandlung.

Glassman, Ronald M. (1989), *Democracy and Equality: Theories and Programs for the Modern World*, New York: Praeger Publishers.

Glotz, Gustave (1929), *The Greek City and Its Institutions*, tr. from the French by Nora Mallinson, London: Alfred A. Knopf.

Glover, Terrot R. (1966), *Democracy in the Ancient World* (1927), New York: Cooper Square Publishers.

Glucker, John (1989), review of John Dudley, *Gott und Θεωρία bei Aristoteles. Die metaphysische Grundlage der Nikomachischen Ethik*, *Philosophia*, Vol. 19, pp. 63–71.

Gomperz, Theodor (1901–12), *Greek Thinkers: A History of Ancient Philosophy*, 4 vols, tr. from the German by George G. Berry and Leonard A. Magnus, London: J. Murray.

Gould, John (1980), 'Law, Custom and Myth: Aspects of the Social Position of Women in Classical Athens', *Journal of Hellenic Studies*, Vol. 100, pp. 38–59.

Gould, Josiah B. (1970), *The Philosophy of Chrysippus*, Albany: State University of New York Press.

Gould, Thomas (1963), *Platonic Love*, New York: Free Press of Glencoe.

Gouldner, Alvin W. (1965), *Enter Plato: Classical Greece and the Origins of Social Theory*, New York: Basic Books.

Gramsci, Antonio (1973), *Letters from Prison*, comp., tr., and ed. by Lynne Lawner, New York: Harper & Row.

Grant, Michael (1989a), *The Classical Greeks*, New York: Charles Scribner's Sons.

Grant, Michael (1989b), *The Rise of the Greeks*, New York: Charles Scribner's Sons.

Graves, Robert (1997), *The White Goddess* (1948), redacted with an Introduction by Grevel Lindop, Manchester: Carcanet.

Greenidge, Abel H.J. (1896), *A Handbook of Greek Constitutional History*, London: Macmillan and Co.

Gregory, Marshall W. (1984), 'A Response to Mortimer Adler's *Paideia Proposal*', *Journal of General Education*, Vol. 36, pp. 70–2.

Grene, David (1965), *Greek Political Theory: The Image of Man in Thucydides and Plato*, Chicago and London: Phoenix Books.

Grofman, Bernard et al. (eds), (1993), 'The 2500th Anniversary of Democracy: Lessons of Athenian Democracy', *PS: Political Science and Politics*, Vol. 26, pp. 471–94.

Gross, Barry (ed.) (1968), *The Great Thinkers on Plato*, New York: G.P. Putnam's Sons.

Grote, George (1971), *A History of Greece from the Earliest Period to the Close of the Generation Contemporary with Alexander the Great*, 10 vols, New York: AMS Press, reprinted from the London edition, 1888.

Grube, Georges M.A. (1958), *Plato's Thought*, Boston: Beacon Press.

Gummere, Richard M. (1963), *The American Colonial Mind and the Classical Tradition: Essays in Comparative Culture*, Cambridge, Mass.: Harvard University Press.

Gunnell, John G. (1968), *Political Philosophy and Time*, Middletown, Conn.: Wesleyan University Press.

Guthrie, William K.C. (1962–75), *A History of Greek Philosophy*, 4 vols, Cambridge: Cambridge University Press.

Hackforth, Reginald (1913), *The Authorship of the Platonic Epistles*, Manchester: Manchester University Press.

Hall, Robert W. (1981), *Plato*, London: George Allen & Unwin.

Hall, Robert W. (1987), 'Platonic Justice and the *Republic*', *Polis*, Vol. 6, pp. 116–26.

Hall, Robert W. (1988), 'Plato and Totalitarianism', *Polis*, Vol. 7, pp. 105–14.

Hallowell, John H. (1954), *The Moral Foundation of Democracy*, Chicago: University of Chicago Press.

Hammond, Nicholas G.L. (1976), *The Classical Age of Greece*, New York: Barnes & Noble; Harper & Row.

Hankins, James (1990), *Plato in the Italian Renaissance*, 2 vols, Leiden and New York: E.J. Brill.

Hansen, Mogens H. (1987), *The Athenian Assembly*, Oxford: Basil Blackwell.

Hardie, William F.R. (1968), *Aristotle's Ethical Theory*, Oxford: Clarendon Press.

Hare, Richard M. (1982), *Plato*, Oxford and New York: Oxford University Press.

Havelock, Eric A. (1957), *The Liberal Temper in Greek Politics*, New Haven and London: Yale University Press.

Havelock, Eric A. (1978), *The Greek Concept of Justice: From its Shadow in Homer to Its Substance in Plato*, Cambridge, Mass. and London: Harvard University Press.

Hawgood, John A. (1939), *Modern Constitutions since 1787*, London: Macmillan and Co.

Hegedus, Adam de (1947), *Patriotism or Peace?*, New York: Charles Scribner's Sons.

Herz, John H. (1976), *The Nation-State and the Crisis of World Politics*, New York: David McKay Co.

Hignett, Charles (1962), *A History of the Athenian Constitution to the End of the Fifth Century B.C.*, Oxford: Clarendon Press of Oxford University Press (corrected reprint from 1952 edition).

Hobbs, Angela (1996), 'Socrates' Searches', review of Richard B. Rutherford, *The Art of Plato: Ten Essays in Platonic Interpretation* (London: Gerald Duckworth), *Times Literary Supplement*, 9 February, p. 32.

Hoernlé, Reinhold F.A. (1938), 'Would Plato Have Approved of the National Socialist State?', *Philosophy*, Vol. 13, pp. 166–82.

Howland, Jacob (1993), The Republic: *The Odyssey of Philosophy*, New York: Twayne/ Macmillan.

Hyland, Drew A. (1988–89), '*Republic*, Book II, and the Origins of Political Philosophy', *Interpretation*, Vol. 16, p. 247–61.

Jaeger, Werner W. (1948), *Aristotle: Fundamentals of the History of His Development*, tr. from the German with the author's corrections and additions by Richard Robinson, 2nd edn, Oxford: Clarendon Press of Oxford University Press.

Jaeger, Werner W. (1945), *Paideia: The Ideals of Greek Culture*, 3 vols, tr. from the German by Gilbert Highet, 2nd edn, New York: Oxford University Press.

Johnson, Curtis N. (1990), *Aristotle's Theory of the State*, New York: St Martin's Press.

Jonas, Hans (1979), *Das Prinzip Verantwortung: Versuch einer Ethik für dei technologische Zivilisation*, Frankfurt am Main: Insel Verlag.

Jonas, Hans (1981), *Macht oder Ohnmacht der Subjektivität?: Das Leib-Seele-Problem im Vorfeld des Prinzips Verantwortung*, Frankfurt Am Main: Insel Verlag.

Jonas, Hans (1984), *The Imperative of Responsibility: In Search of an Ethics for the Technological Age*, tr. from the German by Hans Jonas and David Herr, Chicago and London: University of Chicago Press.

Jones, Arnold H.M. (1957), *Athenian Democracy and Its Critics*, Oxford: Basil Blackwell.

Joravsky, David (1970), *The Lysenko Affair*, Cambridge, Mass.: Harvard University Press.

Kagan, Donald (1991), *Pericles of Athens and the Birth of Democracy*, New York: Free Press, Macmillan Co.

Karp, Lawrence E. (1976), *Genetic Engineering: Threat or Promise?*, Chicago: Nelson-Hall Co.

Keaney, John J. (1992), *The Composition of Aristotle's* Athenian Politeia: *Observation and Explanation*, New York and Oxford: Oxford University Press.

Kimpel, Ben (1981), *Philosophies of Life of the Ancient Greeks and Israelites: An Analysis of Their Parallelism*, New York: Philosophical Library.

Kitto, Humphrey D.F. (1957), *The Greeks*, rev. edn, Baltimore, Md: Pelican Books.

Klosko, George (1986), *The Development of Plato's Political Theory*, New York and London: Methuen.

Klosko, George (1988), 'The Nocturnal Council in Plato's *Laws*', *Political Studies*, Vol. 36, pp. 74–88.

Konvitz, Milton R. and Murphy, Arthur E. (eds) (1948), *Essays in Political Theory*, Ithaca, NY: Cornell University Press.

Kort, Fred (1952), 'The Quantification of Aristotle's Theory of Revolution', *American Political Science Review*, Vol. 46, pp. 486–93.

Kraut, Richard (1989), *Aristotle on the Human Good*, Princeton, NJ: Princeton University Press.

Krohn, August A. (1876), *Der Platonische Staat*, Halle: Richard Mühlmann.

Lao Tzu (supposititious?) (1963), *Lao Tzu: Tao te ching*, tr. from the Chinese and ed. with an Introduction by Dim Cheuk Lau, Harmondsworth: Penguin Books.

Larsen, Jakob A.O. (1948), 'Cleisthenes and the Development of Democracy at Athens' in Konvitz and Murphy, *op. cit.*

Le Boutillier, Cornelia G. (1950), *American Democracy and Natural Law*, New York: Columbia University Press.

Lévêque, André (1940), *Histoire de la civilisation française*, New York: Henry Holt.

Levine, Mordecai H. (1976a), 'Falaquera's Philosophy', *Proceedings of the Association of Orthodox Jewish Scientists*, Vol. 3–4, pp. 191–6.

Levine, Mordecai H. (tr. and ed.) (1976b), *The Book of the Seeker (Sefer Ha-Mebaqquesh)*, New York: Yeshiva University Press.

Levinson, Ronald B. (1970), *In Defense of Plato*, New York: Russell & Russell.

Levy, Harold L. (1990), 'Does Aristotle Exclude Women from Politics?', *Review of Politics*, Vol. 52, pp. 347–416.

Leyden, Wolfgang von (1985), *Aristotle on Equality and Justice: His Political Argument*, New York: St Martin's Press.

Liddell, Henry George and Scott, Robert (comp. and eds) (1985), *A Greek–English Lexicon*, 9th rev. (reprinted from 1940), Oxford: Clarendon Press.

Lintott, Andrew (1981), *Violence, Civil Strife and Revolution in the Classical City 750–330 BC*, Baltimore, Md: Johns Hopkins University Press.

Lloyd, Geoffrey E.R. (1968), *Aristotle: The Growth and Structure of His Thought*, London: Cambridge University Press.

Lobkowicz, Nicholas (1967), *Theory and Practice: History of a Concept from Aristotle to Marx*, Notre Dame, Ind.: University of Notre Dame Press.

Lodge, Rupert C. (1928), *Plato's Theory of Ethics: The Moral Criterion and the Highest Good*, London: Routledge and Kegan Paul.

Loenen, Dirk (1953), *Stasis, enige aspecten van de begrippe partif-en klassenstrijd in oud-Griekenland*, Amsterdam: Noord-Hollandische Utig.

Loraux, Nicole (1993), *The Children of Athena: Athenian Ideas about Citizenship and the Division between the Sexes*, tr. from the French by Caroline Levine, Princeton, NJ: Princeton University Press.

Lord, Carnes (1982), *Education and Culture in the Political Thought of Aristotle*, Ithaca and London: Cornell University Press.

Lord, Carnes and O'Connor, David K. (eds) (1991), *Essays on the Foundations of Aristotelian Political Science*, Berkeley, Los Angeles, and Oxford: University of California Press.

Luccioni, Jean (1958), *La Pensée de Platon*, Paris: Presses Universitaires de France.

Luce, John V. (1992), *An Introduction to Greek Philosophy*, New York: Thames and Hudson.

Lycos, Kimon (1987), *Plato on Justice and Power: Reading Book I of Plato's* Republic, Albany: State University of New York Press.

MacDowell, Douglas M. (1978), *The Law in Classical Athens*, Ithaca, NY: Cornell University Press.

McIlwain, Charles H. (1939), *Constitutionalism and the Changing World: Collected Papers*, Cambridge, Cambridge University Press.

McIlwain, Charles H. (1947), *Constitutionalism: Ancient and Modern*, rev. edn, Ithaca, NY: Cornell University Press.

MacIntyre, Alasdair (1988), *Whose Justice? Which Rationality?*, Notre Dame, Ind.: University of Notre Dame Press.

MacIver, Robert M. (1940), 'The Political Roots of Totalitarianism', *The Roots of Totalitarianism*, James-Patten-Rowe Pamphlet Series No. 9, Philadelphia: The American Academy of Political and Social Science, pp. 5–8.

MacIver, Robert M. (1947), *The Web of Government*, New York: Macmillan Co.

Maguire, Joseph P. (1947), 'Plato's Theory of Natural Law', *Archives of the Temple of Soknobraisis at Bacchias*, ed. Alfred R. Bellinger, *Yale Classical Studies*, Vol. 10, pp. 151–77, New Haven: Yale University Press; Cambridge: Cambridge University Press.

Mahoney, Timothy A. (1995), 'Plato's Practical Political-Rhetorical Project: The Example of the *Republic*', *Polis*, Vol. 14, pp. 30–52.

Mansfield, Harvey C. Jr (1985), 'Constitutionalism and the Rule of Law', *Harvard Journal of Law and Public Policy*, Vol. 8, pp. 323–6.

Mansfield, Harvey C. Jr (1989), *Taming the Prince: The Ambivalence of Modern Executive Power*, New York: Free Press, Macmillan.

Manville, Philip B. (1990), *The Origins of Citizenship in Ancient Athens*, Princeton, NJ: Princeton University Press.

Marx, Karl and Engels, Friedrich (1947), *The German Ideology*, ed. Roy Pascal, New York: International Publishers.

Mason, Alpheus T. and Baker, Gordon E. (eds) (1985), *Free Government in the Making: Readings in American Political Thought*, 4th edn, New York: Oxford University Press.

Masters, Roger D. (1990), 'Evolutionary Biology and Political Theory', *American Political Science Review*, Vol. 84, pp. 195–210.

Maybury-Lewis, David (moderator) (1992a), '*Millennium: Tribal Wisdom and the Modern World*: The Tightrope of Power/At the Threshold', Los Angeles: Biniman Productions, Adrian Mole Productions, KCET Los Angeles and BBC-TV.

Maybury-Lewis, David (1992b), *Millennium: Tribal Wisdom and the Modern World*, New York: Viking Penguin.

Mebane, John S. (1989), *Renaissance Magic and the Return of the Golden Age: The Occult Tradition and Marlowe, Jonson, and Shakespeare*, Lincoln and London: University of Nebraska Press.

Meese, Edward III, Brennan, William J. Jr and Polin, Raymond (1986), 'Interpreting the Constitution', *USA Today*, Vol. 115, pp. 36–45.

Meier, Christian (1990), *The Greek Discovery of Politics*, tr. from the German by David McLintock, Cambridge, Mass. and London: Harvard University Press.

Mi, Michael C. (1997), 'The Spread of Aristotle's Political Theory in China', *Political Theory*, Vol. 25, pp. 249–58.

Michels, Robert (1958) *Political Parties: A Sociological Study of the Oligarchical Tendencies of Modern Democracy* (1911), tr. by Eden and Cedar Paul, Glencoe, Ill.: Free Press.

Miller, Fred D. Jr (1995), *Nature, Justice, and Rights in Aristotle's* Politics, Oxford: Clarendon Press of Oxford University Press.

Miller, Mitchell H. Jr (1980), *The Philosopher in Plato's* Statesman, The Hague: Martinus Nijhoff.

Mion, Mario (1986), 'Athenian Democracy: Politicization and Constitutional Restraints', *History of Political Thought*, Vol. 7, pp. 219–38.

Moors, Kent F. (1978–79), 'Plato's Use of Dialogue', *Classical World*, Vol. 72, p. 77–96.

Moors, Kent F. (1981), *Glaucon and Adeimantus on the Just: The Structure of Argument in Book 2 of Plato's* Republic, Washington, DC: University Press of America.

Moors, Kent F. (1982), *Platonic Myth: An Introductory Study*, Washington, DC: University Press of America.

Moors, Kent F. (1984–85), 'Justice and Philosophy in Plato's *Republic*', *Interpretation*, Vol. 12, pp. 193–223.

Moraux, Paul (1957), *A la Recherche de l'Aristotle Perdu: La Dialogue 'Sur la Justice'*, Louvain: Publications Universitaires de Louvain; Paris: Beatrice-Nauwelaerts.

More, Paul Elmer (1926), *Platonism*, 2nd rev. edn, Princeton, NJ: Princeton University Press.

Morgan, Michael L. (1990), *Platonic Piety: Philosophy and Ritual in Fourth-Century Athens*, New Haven and London: Yale University Press.

Morrall, John B. (1977), *Aristotle*, London: George Allen & Unwin.

Morrow, Glenn R. (1960), *Plato's Cretan City: A Historical Interpretation of the Laws*, Princeton, NJ: Princeton University Press.

Mulgan, Richard G. (1977), *Aristotle's Political Theory: An Introduction for Students of Political Theory*, Oxford: Clarendon Press.

Mulgan, Richard G. (1987), review of Wolfgang von Leyden, *Aristotle on Equality and Justice: His Political Argument*, *Polis*, Vol. 6, pp. 139–44.

Muller, Herbert J. (1961), *Freedom in the Ancient World*, New York: Harper & Row.

Murphy, Neville R. (1951), *The Interpretation of Plato's* Republic, Oxford: Clarendon Press.

Mustacchio, Paul F. (1972), 'The Concept of Stasis in Greek Political Theory', dissertation, New York: New York University, Graduate School of Arts and Science.

Myres, John Linton (1927), *The Political Ideas of the Greeks*, London: Edward Arnold.

National Conference of Catholic Bishops (1983), *The Challenge of Peace: God's Promise and Our Response*, Publication No. 863, Washington, DC: United States Catholic Conference.

Nederman, Cary J. (1986), 'The Aristotelian Doctrine of the Mean and John of Salisbury's Concept of Liberty', *Vivarium*, Vol. 24, pp. 128–42.

Nettleship, Richard L. (1963), *Lectures on the Republic of Plato* (1897), London: Macmillan and Co.; New York: St Martin's Press.

Nettleship, Richard L. (1966), *The Theory of Education in Plato's* Republic (1880) (reprinted from 1935 edn) with an Introduction by Spencer Lesson, London: Oxford University Press.

Nichols, Mary P. (1964), 'The Republic's Two Alternatives: Philosopher-Kings and Socrates', *Political Theory*, Vol. 12, pp. 252–74.

Nichols, Mary P. (1987), *Socrates and the Political Community: An Ancient Debate*, Albany: State University of New York Press.

Nichols, Mary P. (1992), *Citizens and Statesmen: A Study of Aristotle's* Politics, Savage, Md: Rowman & Littlefield.

Nicholson, Peter and Rowe, Christopher J. (eds), 'Plato's Statesman: Selected Papers from the Third Symposium Platonicum', *Polis*, Vol. 12, pp. 3–217.

Nietzsche, Friedrich (1964), *Complete Works of Friedrich Neitzsche*, 18 vols, ed. Oscar Levy, New York: Russell & Russell.

Nussbaum, Martha (1987), 'Undemocratic Vistas', review of Allan Bloom, *Closing of the American Mind*, *New York Review of Books*, Vol. 34, pp. 20–6.

Nussbaum, Martha (1994), 'Feminists and Philosophy', review of Louise M. Antony and Charlotte Witt, *A Mind of One's Own: Feminist Essays on Reason and Objectivity*, *New York Review of Books*, Vol. 41, pp. 59–63.

Ober, Josiah (1989), *Mass and Elite in Democratic Athens: Rhetoric, Ideology, and the Power of the People*, Princeton, NJ: Princeton University Press.

O'Connor, David K. (1991), 'The Aetiology of Justice', in Lord and O'Connor, *op. cit.*

Okin, Susan M. (1979), *Women in Western Political Thought*, Princeton, NJ: Princeton University Press.

Oncken, Wilhelm (1964), *Die Staatslehre des Aristoteles in Historisch-Politischen Umrissen* (1870–75), 2 vols in 1, Darmstadt: Scientia Verlag Aalen.

O'Neil, James L. (1995), *The Origins and Development of Ancient Greek Democracy*, Lanham, Md: Rowman & Littlefield.

Ophir, Adi (1991), *Plato's Invisible Cities: Discourse and Power in the* Republic, London: Routledge.

Ostwald, Martin (1969), *Nomos and the Beginnings of Athenian Democracy*, Oxford: Clarendon Press.

Ostwald, Martin (1986), *From Popular Sovereignty to the Sovereignty of Law: Law, Society, and Politics in Fifth-Century Athens*, Berkeley, Los Angeles and London: University of California Press.

Paideia (1978), Special Aristotle Issue, ed. George C. Simmons.

Pangle, Thomas L. (1976), 'The Political Psychology of Religion in Plato's Laws', *American Political Science Review*, Vol. 70, pp. 1059–77.

Parens, Joshua (1995), *Metaphysics as Rhetoric: Alfarabi's Summary of Plato's 'Laws'*, Albany: State University of New York Press.

Pares, Bernard (1933), *A History of Russia*, New York: Alfred A. Knopf.

Pater, Walter (1912), *Plato and Platonism* (1893), London: Macmillan Co.

Pennock, James Roland and Chapman, John W. (eds) (1977), *Constitutionalism, Nomos XX*, New York: New York University Press.

Peters, Francis E. (1967), *Greek Philosophical Terms: A Historical Lexicon*, New York: New York University Press; London: University of London Press.

Peters, Francis E. (1968), *Aristotle and the Arabs: The Aristotelian Tradition in Islam*, New York: New York University Press; London: University of London Press.

Pierce, Christine (1973), 'Equality: *Republic V*', *The Monist*, Vol. 57, pp. 1–11.

Planinc, Zdravko (1991), *Plato's Political Philosophy: Prudence in the Republic and the Laws*, Columbia and London: University of Missouri Press.

Plutarch (1932), *The Lives of the Noble Grecians and Romans*, tr. John Dryden, rev. Arthur Hugh Clough, New York: Modern Library, Random House.

Pocock, John G.A. (1975), *The Machiavellian Moment: Florentine Political Thought and the Atlantic Republican Tradition*, Princeton, NJ: Princeton University Press.

Polanyi, Karl (1968), *Primitive, Archaic, and Modern Economies: Essays of Karl Polanyi*, ed. George Dalton, Garden City, NY: Anchor Books, Doubleday & Co.

Polin, Raymond (1966), *Marxian Foundations of Communism: An Introduction to the Study of Communist Theory*, introduction by Robert M. MacIver, Chicago: Henry Regnery.

Polin, Raymond (1979), *Modern Government and Constitutionalism: A Concise Textbook and Reference Source*, Chicago: Nelson-Hall.

Polin, Raymond. (1981a), 'Simple Majority Rule at the UN: An Inadvisable Proposition', *USA Today*, Vol. 110, pp. 49 ff.

Polin, Raymond (1981b), 'George Mason: Father of the Bill of Rights', *The Freeman*, Vol. 31, pp. 734–9.

Pollitt, Jerry J. (1974), *The Ancient View of Greek Art: Criticism, History, and Terminology*, New Haven and London: Yale University Press.

Popper, Karl R. (1963), *The Open Society and Its Enemies*, 2 vols, 4th edn, Princeton, NJ: Princeton University Press.

Prichard, Harold A. (1935), 'The Meaning of Agathon in the *Ethics* of Aristotle', *Philosophy*, Vol. X, pp. 27–39.

Prideaux, Tom (1977), 'Rich and Rugged Thracian Life', *Smithsonian*, Vol. 8, pp. 42–51.

Raaflaub, Kurt A. (1983), 'Democracy, Oligarchy, and the Concept of "Free Citizen" in Late Fifth-Century Athens', *Political Theory*, Vol. 11, pp. 517–44.

Randall, John Herman Jr (1960), *Aristotle*, New York: Columbia University Press.

Randall, John Herman Jr (1970), *Plato: Dramatist of the Life of Reason*, New York and London: Columbia University Press.

Rasmussen, Douglas B. and Den Uyl, Douglas J. (1991), *Liberty and Nature: An Aristotelian Defense of Liberal Order*, La Salle, Illinois: Open Court.

Rawls, John A. (1971), *A Theory of Justice*, Cambridge, Mass.: Belknap Press of Harvard University Press.

Reeve, Charles D.C. (1988), *Philosopher-Kings: The Argument of Plato's Republic*, Princeton, NJ: Princeton University Press.

Resnick, Seymour and Pasmantier, Jeanne (eds) (1958), *An Anthology of Spanish Literature in English Translation*, 2 vols, New York: Frederick Ungar.

Reves, Emery (1945), *The Anatomy of Peace*, New York: Harper & Brothers.

Rhodes, Peter J. (1981), *A Commentary on the Aristotelian* Athenaion Politeia, Oxford: Clarendon Press.

Rhodes, Peter J. (ed.) (1986), *The Greek City States: A Source Book*, Norman and London: University of Oklahoma Press.

Rhodes, Peter J. (1992), review of John J. Keaney, *op. cit.*, *Polis*, Vol. 11, pp. 89–94.

Riginos, Alice Swift (1976), *Platonica: The Anecdotes concerning the Life and Writings of Plato. Columbia Studies in the Classical Tradition*, Vol. III, Leiden: E.J. Brill.

Ritter, Constantin (1910), *Platon: Sein Leben, Seine Schriften, Seine Lehre*, 2 vols, Munich, C.H. Beck'sche Verlagsbuchhandlung, Oskar Back.

Ritter, Constantin (1968), *The Essence of Plato's Philosophy* (1933), tr. from the German by A. Alles, New York: Russell & Russell.

Robb, Nesca A. (1935), *Neoplatonism of the Italian Renaissance*, London: George Allen & Unwin.

Roberts, Jennifer Tolbert (1994), *Athens on Trial: The Antidemocratic Tradition in Western Thought*, Princeton: Princeton University Press.

Rose, Peter W. (1992), *Sons of the Gods, Children of Earth: Ideology and Literary Form in Ancient Greece*, Ithaca and London: Cornell University Press.

Rosen, Stanley (1995), *Plato's Statesman: The Web of Politics*, New Haven and London: Yale University Press.

Ross, William D. (1964), *Aristotle*, 5th edn, London: Methuen & Co.

Rossiter, Clinton (c. 1960), 'The Democratic Process', *The Report of the President's Commission on National Goals: Goals for Americans*, New York: The American Assembly, Columbia University, reprinted by Prentice-Hall/Spectrum.

Rowe, Christopher J. (1983), 'Plato on the Sophists as Teachers of Virtue', *History of Political Thought*, Vol. IV, pp. 409–27.

Rowe, Christopher J. (ed.) (1994), *Reading the* Statesman (Proceedings of the Third Symposium Platonicum), *International Law Studies*, Vol. 4, Sankt Augustin: Academia Verlag.

Ruderman, Richard S. (1997), 'Aristotle and the Recovery of Political Judgment', *American Political Science Review*, Vo. 91, pp. 409–20.

Russell, Bertrand (1945), *A History of Western Philosophy, and Its Connection with Political and Social Circumstances from the Earliest Times to the Present Day*, New York: Simon and Schuster.

Rutherford, Richard B. (1995), *The Art of Plato: Ten Essays in Platonic Interpretation*, London: Gerald Duckworth; Cambridge, Mass.: Harvard University Press.

Ryle, Gilbert (1966), *Plato's Progress*, London: Cambridge University Press.

Ryle, Gilbert (1967), 'Plato' in *Encyclopedia of Philosophy*, Vol. VI, ed. Paul Edwards, New York: Macmillan Co.

Sagan, Eli (1991), *The Honey and the Hemlock: Democracy and Paranoia in Ancient Athens and Modern America*, New York: Basic Books.

Ste Croix, Geoffrey E.M. de (1981), *The Class Struggle in the Ancient World: From the Archaic Age to the Arab Conquests*, London: Gerald Duckworth.

Salkever, Stephen G. (1990), *Finding the Mean: Theory and Practice in Aristotelian Political Philosophy*, Princeton, NJ: Princeton University Press.

Salkever, Stephen G. (1991), 'Women, Soldiers, Citizens: Plato and Aristotle on the Politics of Virility' in Lord and O'Connor, *op. cit.*

Santas, Gerasimos (1988), *Plato and Freud: Two Theories of Love*, Oxford and New York: Basil Blackwell.

Saunders, Trevor J. (1991), *Plato's Penal Code: Tradition, Controversy, and Reform in Greek Penology*, Oxford: Clarendon Press of Oxford University Press.

Saxonhouse, Arlene W. (1983), 'Further Reflections on Aristotle on the Peoples of Europe and Asia', *Polis*, Vol. 5, pp. 34–9.

Saxonhouse, Arlene W. (1986), 'From Tragedy to Hierarchy and Back Again', *American Political Science Review*, Vol. 80, pp. 403–18.

Saxonhouse, Arlene W. (1988), 'The Tyranny of Reason in the World of the Polis', *American Political Science Review*, Vol. 82, pp. 1261–75.

Saxonhouse, Arlene W. (1992), *Fear of Diversity: The Birth of Political Science in Ancient Greek Thought*, Chicago and London: University of Chicago Press.

Scheffel, Wolfgang (1976), *Aspekte der Platonischen Kosmologie: Untersuchungen zum Dialog 'Timaios'*, Leiden: E.J. Brill.

Schroeder, Donald N. (1982), 'Aristotle on Law', *Polis*, Vol. 4, pp. 17–31.

Scolnicov, Samuel (1976), 'Three Aspects of Plato's Philosophy of Learning and Instruction', *Paideia*, Vol. 5, pp. 50–62.

Sealey, Raphael (1987), *The Athenian Republic: Democracy or the Rule of Law?*, University Park, Pa., and London: Pennsylvania State University Press.

Seery, John Evan (1990), *Political Returns: Irony in Politics and Theory from Plato to the Antinuclear Movement*, Boulder, Co., San Francisco, and Oxford: Westview Press.

Sesonke, Alexander (ed.) (1966), *Plato's* Republic: *Interpretation and Criticism*, Belmont, Ca.: Wadsworth Publishing Co.

Sheldon, Garrett W. (1991), *The Political Philosophy of Thomas Jefferson*, Baltimore and London: Johns Hopkins University Press.

Shorey, Paul (1933), *What Plato Said*, Chicago and London: University of Chicago Press.

Sinclair, Robert K. (1988), *Democracy and Participation in Athens*, Cambridge: Cambridge University Press.

Sinclair, Thomas A. (1968), *A History of Greek Political Thought*, Cleveland: Meridian Books, World Publishing Co.

Sinclair, Thomas A. (1984), *Studies in Platonic Political Philosophy*, Cleveland: Meridian Books, World Publishing Co.

Singer, Irving (1966), *The Nature of Love: Plato to Luther*, New York: Random House.

Smith, Nicholas D. (1983), 'Plato and Aristotle on the Nature of Women', *Journal of the History of Philosophy*, Vol. 21, pp. 467–78.

Smucker, Samuel M. (1856), *The Life and Reign of Nicholas I, Emperor of Russia*, Philadelphia: J.W. Bradley.

Sorabji, Richard (1980), *Necessity, Cause, and Blame: Perspectives on Aristotle's Theory*, Ithaca, NY: Cornell University Press.

Spear, Kareb (1984), 'The *Paideia Proposal*: The Problem of Means and Ends in General Education', *Journal of General Education*, Vol. 36, pp. 79–86.

Stahl, Michael (1987), *Aristokraten und Tyrannen im archaischen Athen: Untersuchingen zur Überlieferung, zur Sozialstruktur und zur Entstehung des Staates*, Stuttgart: Franz Steiner Verlag.

Stalley, Richard F. (1983), *An Introduction to Plato's Laws*, Indianapolis, Ind.: Hackett Publishing Co.

Stalley, Richard F. (1995), 'The Unity of the State: Plato, Aristotle, and Proclus', *Polis*, Vol. 14, pp. 129–49.

Stansky, Peter (1983), *William Morris*, Oxford and New York: Oxford University Press.

Steinberger, Peter J. (1989), 'Ruling: Guardians and Philosopher-Kings', *American Political Science Review*, Vol. 83, pp. 1207–25.

Stern, Paul (1997), 'The Rule of Wisdom and the Rule of Law in Plato's *Statesman*', *American Political Science Review*, Vol. 91, pp. 264–76.

Stockton, David (1990), *The Classical Athenian Democracy*, Oxford and New York: Oxford University Press.

Stone, Isidore F. (1989), *The Trial of Socrates*, New York: Anchor Books, Doubleday.

Strauss, Barry S. (1987), *Athens after the Peloponnesian War: Class, Faction and Policy, 403–386 BC*, Ithaca, NY: Cornell University Press.

Strauss, Barry S. (1991), 'On Aristotle's Critique of Athenian Democracy' in Lord and O'Connor, *op. cit.*

Strauss, Leo (1964), *The City and Man*, Chicago: Rand McNally and Co.

Strauss, Leo (1975), *The Argument and the Action of Plato's Laws*, Chicago and London: University of Chicago Press.

Strauss, Leo (1984), *Studies in Platonic Political Philosophy*, ed. Thomas Pangle, Chicago: University of Chicago Press.

Swanson, Judith A. (1992), *The Public and the Private in Aristotle's Political Philosophy*, Ithaca and London: Cornell University Press.

Taylor, Alfred E. (1955), *Aristotle*, rev. edn, New York: Dover Publications.

Taylor, Alfred E. (1960a), *The Mind of Plato*, Ann Arbor: Ann Arbor Paperbacks, University of Michigan Press.

Taylor, Alfred E. (1960b), *Plato: the Man and His Work*, 7th edn, London: Methuen & Co.

Taylor, Alfred E. (1963), *Platonism and Its Influence*, New York: Cooper Square Publishers.

Taylor, Christopher C.W. (1986), 'Plato's Totalitarianism', *Polis*, Vol. 5, pp. 4–29.

Tessitore, Aristede (1996), *Reading Aristotle's Ethics: Virtue, Rhetoric, and Political Philosophy*, Albany, State University of New York Press.

The Encyclopedia of Judaism (1989), ed.-in-chief Geoffrey Wigador, New York: Macmillan; Jerusalem: Jerusalem Publishing House.

Thorson, Thomas L. (ed.) (1963), *Plato: Totalitarian or Democrat?*, Englewood Cliffs, NJ: Prentice-Hall.

Todd, Stephen C. (1993), *The Shape of Athenian Law*, Oxford: Clarendon Press of Oxford University Press.

Traill, John S. (1975), *The Political Organization of Attika: A Study of the Demes, Trittyes, and, Phylai and their Representation in the Athenian Council* (Supplement to Hesperia Series: No. 14), Princeton, NJ: American School of Classical Studies at Athens.

Troeltsch, Ernst (1931), *The Social Teaching of the Christian Churches*, 2 vols, tr. from the German by Olive Wyon, George Allen & Unwin; New York: Macmillan Co.

Ullmann, Walter (1949), *Medieval Papalism: The Political Theories of the Medieval Canonists*, London: Methuen & Co.

Ullmann, Walter (1961), *Principles of Government and Politics in the Middle Ages*, London: Methuen & Co.

Ullmann, Walter (1965), *A History of Political Thought: The Middle Ages*, Harmondsworth, Penguin Books.

Ullmann, Walter (1967), *The Individual and Society and the Middle Ages*, London: Methuen & Co.; Baltimore, Md: The Johns Hopkins Press.

Ullmann, Walter (1975), *Law and Politics in the Middle Ages: An Introduction to the Sources of Medieval Political Ideas*, Ithaca, NY: Cornell University Press.

Vanhoutte, Maurice (1954), *La Philosophie Politique de Platon dans les <<Lois>>*, Louvain: University of Louvain Publications.

Vaughn, Olufemi (1988), 'Les chefs traditionnels face au pouvoir politique', *Politique Africaine*, Vol. 32, *Nigeria: Le fédéralisme dans tous ses États*, pp. 44–56.

Veatch, Henry B. (1974), *Aristotle: A Contemporary Appreciation*, Bloomington and London: Indiana University Press.

Vile, Maurice J.C. (1967), *Constitutionalism and the Separation of Powers*, Oxford: Clarendon Press.

Vlastos, Gregory (1941), 'Slavery in Plato's Thought', *Philosophical Review*, Vol. 50, pp. 289–304.

Vlastos, Gregory (1975), *Plato's Universe*, Seattle: University of Washington Press.

Vlastos, Gregory (1981), Platonic Studies, 2nd edn, Princeton, NJ: Princeton University Press.

Vlastos, Gregory (1983), 'The Historical Socrates and Athenian Democracy', *Political Theory*, Vol. 11, pp. 495–516.

Vlastos, Gregory (1991), *Socrates, Ironist and Moral Philosopher*, Ithaca, NY: Cornell University Press.

Voegelin, Eric (1956–74), *Order and History*, 4 vols, Baton Rouge: Louisiana State University Press.

Wallace, Robert W. (1989), *The Areopagus Council, to 307 B.C.*, Baltimore and London: Johns Hopkins University Press.

Wallach, John R. (1989), review of C. Farrar, *The Origins of Democratic Thinking: The Invention of Politics in Classical Athens* (*op. cit.*), *American Political Science Review*, Vol. 83, pp. 1362 ff.

Welton, Willam A. (1995), 'Divine Inspiration and the Origins of the Laws in Plato's *Laws*', *Polis*, Vol. 14, pp. 53–83.

West, Jason L.A. (1994), 'Distorted Souls: The Role of Banausics in Aristotle's *Politics*', *Polis*, Vol. 13, pp. 77–95.

Wilamowitz-Moellendorff, Ulrich von (1959), *Platon: Sein Leben und Seine Werke*, ed. and with an Epilogue by Bruno Snell, 5th edn, Berlin: Weidmannsche Verlagsbuchhandlung.

Wild, John (1946), *Plato's Theory of Man: An Introduction to the Realistic Philosophy of Culture*, Cambridge, Mass.: Harvard University Press.

Wild, John (1953), *Plato's Modern Enemies and the Theory of Natural Law*, Chicago: University of Chicago Press.

Will, George F. (1992), *Restoration: Congress, Term Limits and the Recovery of Deliberative Democracy*, New York: Free Press, Macmillan.

Wiltshire, Susan F. (1992), *Greece, Rome, and the Bill of Rights*, Norman and London: University of Oklahoma Press.

Winthrop, Delba (1978), 'Aristotle and Theories of Justice', *American Political Science Review*, Vol. 72, pp. 1201–16.

Wolin, Sheldon S. (1989), *The Presence of the Past: Essays on the State and Constitution*, Baltimore and London: Johns Hopkins University Press.

Wood, Ellen Meiksins (1988), *Peasant-Citizen and Slave: The Foundations of Athenian Democracy*, London and New York: Verso Books.

Wood, Ellen Meiksins and Neal (1978), *Class Ideology and Ancient Political Theory: Socrates, Plato, and Aristotle in Social Context*, New York: Oxford University Press.

Wood, Ellen Meiksins and Neal (1986), 'Socrates and Democracy: A Reply to Gregory Vlastos', *Political Theory*, Vol. 14, pp. 55–82.

Zeller, Eduard (1962), *Aristotle and the Earlier Peripatetics*, tr. from the German of Zeller (1897), *The Philosophy of the Greeks in its Historical Development*, Part II, Division II, by Benjamin F. Costelloe and John H. Muirhead, 2 vols, London: Longmans, Green and Co.; New York: Russell & Russell.

Index

United Kingdom (*see also* Parliament, British), 5, 12, 284, 285

United Nations: International Convenants on Human Rights, 257; Universal Declaration of Human Rights, 257; hopes pinned on, 286

United States of America, 5, 261, 293

Unity, 13, 15–6, 20, 43, 50–2, 76, 88, 90, 92, 96, 104–5, 145, 147–8, 152, 186–7, 189, 200, 244, 249, 255, 264, 267, 276; Aristotle opposes Plato's excessive emphasis on, 189

Unmixed government, 7, 210, 222; never rightly constituted, 7

Unwritten laws and ancestral customs (*see also* Inherent limitations), 29, 82, 125, 254

Upper classes, 170, 290

Urban classes, distrust of by Plato, Aristotle, and Jefferson, 228

Utilitarianism and utility, pleasure and pain, and provision of, 112, 118

Values (*see also* Good), scales of, 104, 114

Vaughn, Olufemi, 12

Veatch, Henry B., 166

Victors, monopolize power, 25

Victory over self (*see also* Self-superior; Self-control), 97

Vile, Maurice, J.C., 10

Virginia, Notes on (*see* Jefferson, Thomas)

Virtue (*areté*) and virtues (*see also* Ethics): wisdom, bravery, temperateness, and justice as, 53, 74; of the state, 53; in Guardian class, 53; guarded by philosophy, 59; all parts of, friendly to one another, 87; counterbalancing nature of different qualities of, 87; path of, 88; promotion of, and of good citizenship guides legislator, 120–2; in ethical economic and legal practices, 133–7; to be promoted by Nocturnal Council, 140–2; knowledge of, from religious insight, 141–2; *paideia* efficient as education in *areté* to produce virtuous citizens, 145–6; in Athenian government, 180; of military, over-emphasized in *Laws*, 195; may vary and be common or particular, 196–7; as attribute of aristocracy, 204, 206; middle course as, 207, 209, 260; and half-virtuous

tyrant, 225; necessary to goodness, justice, and best state, 234–5; relative nature of, 245; right knowledge requisite to, 247–8; of peace and peaceful occupations, 274; as means of making citizens happiest, 263, 274; means of promoting, 269; as main subject of *Laws*, 144; related to education and constitutionalism, 291

Vlastos, Gregory, 37, 70, 75, 153

Voegelin, Eric, 19, 34, 250

Voting, non-weighted, 'one person, one vote', 296

Wallace, Robert W., 18

Wallach, John R., 20, 291

Walsh, Ellen M., 10

War, primary principle and purpose of, 98, 239, 240, 274

Wardens: of the law, 115, 118–20, 135, 141; of fish, game, and forest aided Aristotle's researches, 165

Weaker, seek justice and equality, 227

Wealth and wealthy (*see also* Property; Land; Possessions): opposition of, to virtue, 113–4; as stewards, 119; piling up riches, 114; to be limited, Plato advocates, to factor of four, 113; excessive, opposed, 114; as basis of public office and honours, 119; insatiable love of, 126; feel secure under polity, 144; sufficient, not excessive, favoured, 192; as basis of justice, 199; education and good birth go more with, 206; encroachments of, evil that ruins constitution, 209–10; inheritances and estates regulated to prevent over-concentration of, 219; how tyrant should treat, 215, 221, 225

Weaving art and 'web of government', 79, 87–9, 93

Wehrli, Fritz, 286

Wehrstand (soldier class), 51

West, Jason L.A., 266

What needs to be done, 107

White Terror, 27

Wilamowitz-Moellendorff, Ulrich von, 42

Wild, John, 29, 33, 34, 35, 36, 37, 152, 270, 274

Will, George F., 280, 290